Third Edition

THE GIA DIAMOND DICTIONARY

Third Edition

EDITOR-IN-CHIEF
Richard T. Liddicoat
Chairman, The Gemological Institute of America

EDITOR
John H. Hummel, Ph.D.
Director of Education Development
The Gemological Institute of America

ASSOCIATE EDITOR
David Avshalomov, D.M.A.
Senior Editor, Course Development
The Gemological Institute of America

CONTRIBUTING EDITORS

G. Robert Crowningshield
Vice President
GIA Gem Trade Laboratory

John I. Koivula
Chief Research Gemologist
GIA Gem Trade Laboratory

Robert C. Kammerling
Director of Identification and Research
GIA Gem Trade Laboratory

James Lucey
Special Projects Officer, Ret.
The Gemological Institute of America

Alice S. Keller
Editor, Gems & Gemology
The Gemological Institute of America

James E. Shigley, Ph.D.
Director of Research
The Gemological Institute of America

Howard J. Vaughan
Diamond Information Office
Central Selling Organisation, London

COPYRIGHT © 1993

by the

GEMOLOGICAL INSTITUTE OF AMERICA
1660 Stewart St.
Santa Monica, CA 90404

First Edition — 1960

Second Edition, Revised — 1977

Third Edition, Revised — 1993

All rights reserved. No part of this work may be copied, reproduced, transferred, or transmitted in any form or by any means whatsoever— graphic, electronic, digital, or mechanical, including photocopying, photography, video or audiotape recording or taping, image scanning, optical character recognition (OCR) software, or information and retrieval systems—or translated into any human or computer language, without the express written permission of the publisher.

ISBN 0-87311-026-9

PRINTED IN THE UNITED STATES OF AMERICA

Contents

vii	Preface
ix	Introduction
xvii	Reviewers and Subject Specialists
xix	Works Consulted
1	**THE GIA DIAMOND DICTIONARY**
	APPENDICES
253	A Other Notable Diamonds
261	B American Diamonds
265	C The Iranians
267	D Color-grading Scales
269	E Clarity-grading Scales
271	F Proprietary Names of Man-made Simulants
273	G Ages of Diamond Deposits
275	H Local Weights of Old Carats

PREFACE

The first edition of GIA's Diamond Dictionary was published in 1960. Most of the compilation was the work of the late Lawrence L. Copeland, who was then the Institute's Course Editor. Much of the material was taken from the GIA Diamonds course and other Institute publications. A number of outside experts from the diamond industry were consulted on specific topics, such as historical diamonds, mining, cutting, and terms in other languages. Final editing was the responsibility of Lester B. Benson, Jeanne G.M. Martin, G. Robert Crowningshield, and myself. The changes incorporated in the second edition, published in 1977, were compiled by Robert A. P. Gaal, Ph.D. Again, a number of industry experts were consulted, and final editing was done by GIA staff members.

This new third edition is the result of truly exhaustive efforts by many of the individuals most knowledgeable in the various aspects of the world diamond scene today. Copies of the first compilation for the third edition were sent to some forty people, each of whom has special expertise in one or more of the areas covered in previous editions, as well as historical sites, marketing, diamond simulants, treatments and treatment detection. Of those invited to participate, a good score read and contributed commentary on the entire manuscript. Each specialist had an opportunity to critique not only the entries pertaining to their own specialty, but the whole spectrum of diamond terminology. By the time their contributions had been incorporated into the second draft, a broader second circle of additional specialist reviewers had been drawn into the effort, greatly enriching the basic store of entries and the accuracy and completeness of the final text.

GIA is deeply indebted to the many people who dedicated untold hours to this huge effort over the past three years. We trust that the result will assist in resolving differences of opinion among today's professionals, and will be of real value to tomorrow's crop of new diamantaires.

Richard T. Liddicoat
Editor-in-Chief

INTRODUCTION

At the beginning of the nineteenth century, "... one man could sit in a library and master the whole of classical knowledge.... But at the end of the period no one man could possibly have known all that was to be known about Greece and Rome." So said the late Gilbert Highet, Professor Emeritus of Classical Languages and Literature at New York's Columbia University.

This intellectual watershed was not limited to the humanities. The nineteenth century saw parallel advances in the sciences. In the United States and Western Europe, the intellectual tradition in the sciences was turning away from the "natural philosophy" of the Enlightenment, and towards the pragmatic experimentation of Darwin, Agassiz, and Dana. It was during this period that we began to experience what we later came to call the "information explosion": Whole new branches of knowledge were developed, while established fields were revised and elaborated. The result was a quantum leap in the amount of recorded information available (if not always easily retrievable); it became far too large for any single person to master. With it came an unprecedented self-consciousness in the application of scientific findings to industry. The age of the specialist had arrived, in the workplace as well as in the library and the research laboratory.

The great diamond discoveries in South Africa, which mark the beginning of the modern diamond industry, came at just this time. Those discoveries, like the photographs of the men who made them, have unfortunately been tinted with the sepia tones of legend. We read accounts peopled with children playing with pebbles, with South African tribesmen stubbing their toes on wealth beyond their wildest dreams. Meanwhile, a curious crowd of mineralogists and geologists, amateur and university-trained alike, was hanging about in the background. Some of them were given to the odd practice of giving local farmers geologic field manuals—a fitting symbol of nineteenth century epistemology—and counseling them to keep an eye out for shiny stones. It is typical of the age that William Atherstone, who in 1867 authenticated the diamond we now know as the Eureka, was a surgeon by profession, and but an "amateur mineralogist."

So it is not surprising that, in 1870, neither the geologists in their libraries nor the diggers on the ground were aware that the blueground which had just been uncovered was in fact the primary source of diamonds. What is astonishing is that, just over 60 years later, Vladimir Sobolev, in a great leap of the scientific imagination, was able to extrapolate from his understanding of the geology of South Africa and postulate the presence of diamonds on Siberia's Vilyiuy River. History, of course, has demonstrated the validity of his hypothesis. What is more important, the manifold increase in the sort of information and understanding which made his deduction possible continues to resonate through virtually every aspect of the diamond industry.

While, in general, modern lexicography may be said to have begun in the eighteenth century, it was, again, in the mid-nineteenth century that specialized dictionaries dealing with the new technologies (dictionaries much like this one) began to appear. Beginning in 1856 and led by the example of the great Maison Larousse in France, dictionaries devoted to specific fields followed one upon another in rapid succession. Leviticus' *Geillustreerde*

Encyclopedie der Diamantnijverheid, the first such work devoted to the diamond industry, was published, in Dutch, in 1907, less than 40 years after diamonds were discovered at Jagersfontein. The first in English (which had long since become the lingua franca of the industry) was the 1960 edition of the GIA Diamond Dictionary.

The second edition appeared in 1977, and the sixteen years that have passed since then have seen their share of changes as well. In 1977, its editor, Dr. Robert Gaal, was perfectly justified in describing Australia as "An insignificant and sporadic producer of diamonds since 1851," and in omitting any references to Jwaneng or Venetia. Today, the De Beers Mine, which had reopened in 1961, is, after 120 years, permanently closed; Jwaneng, Venetia, and Australia's AK1 are all on line; and Canada may yet take a place among the world's important diamond producers. The Sancy is back in the Louvre, and the 273.85 ct. Centenary has forced historians to revise their lists of the world's largest diamonds. Synthetic gem-quality diamonds are an imminent reality in the marketplace, and the low-pressure deposition of diamond thin film on a variety of substrates raises possibilities, and problems, undreamed-of in 1977. The Diamond Dictionary cried out for revision. If recent history is any indication, in a very few years it will do so once again.

So, while the tradition of the subject-specific dictionary is not much older than the modern diamond industry itself, in considering the form this third edition might take, we gave serious thought to issuing it on an optical disk. (Indeed, we may yet offer this as an option in the near future.) At any rate, given the dynamic nature of the industry, and the technological changes in the accumulation, storage, and retrieval of information, it seems likely that this will be the last edition which appears as a hard-bound book.

In considering the goals we might reasonably hope to achieve with this edition, we have opted for a concept very like that of *Webster's New Collegiate Dictionary,* a work familiar to several generations of Americans, or those educated in America. It was described by its Editor-in-Chief Henry Woolf as ". . . a general dictionary edited for use in school or college, and in the home—in short, wherever information about English words is likely to be sought." We might then re-state this and say that we sought to make the GIA Diamond Dictionary: ". . . a specialized dictionary edited for use in school or college, in the mine, the shop, and the store—in short, wherever information about diamonds and the diamond industry is likely to be sought."

Our work on this edition, which has taken over three years and engaged the time and attention of a great number of people, has led us, figuratively speaking, to the South African veldt, the Brazilian rain forests, and the Australian outback, into boardrooms, bourses, and retail stores, mines and laboratories, wherever diamonds are found, wherever they are bought and sold, wherever they are studied. The undertaking has been an education in itself, an opportunity to discover how vast, complex, and diverse the study of diamonds really is.

GIA has on staff an impressive array of authorities on various aspects of diamonds and the diamond market. The Institute has also been fortunate in the willingness of others to give generously of their time and talent to help us carry out our mission of serving the industry. The result has been a display of cooperation that would be unthinkable in many other industries, a reminder of how many talented and great-spirited men and women there are in the diamond world.

In some ways the diamond world is a very private one, a world unto itself. Yet geographically it covers most of the world at large. A large number of new maps were commissioned for this new edition. The areas they depict range from the Arctic Circle to latitude 40 south and below, and circle the globe from the prime meridian and back again. In contrast to the tradition of British lexicography which began with Dr. Johnson, we have elected to include place names (and proper names) in this Dictionary. We have, moreover, included them in the body of the text rather than relegating them to a separate gazetteer (or biographical dictionary) behind the general listings.

Many of the pertinent places are familiar to travelers, even the armchair variety, so we have not provided maps to indicate well-known localities—New York, Tel Aviv, Antwerp—which are found readily in any atlas. But diamonds are often recovered in inhospitable environments that are not easy to access, and that are of little interest to anyone outside the diamond world. Many important diamond locations simply do not appear at all on maps that are available to the general public. It is on localities such as these that we have concentrated our efforts.

This has created some problems of scale. Sometimes a map that provides sufficient local detail for the area under discussion is completely uninformative in terms of any larger geographic context. A map of the several thousand square miles of Western Australia necessary to show where the Argyle complex lies relative to Ellendale and the Bow River cannot at the same time indicate where either Ellendale or the Bow River are on the continent of Australia—let alone where Australia is in relation to the rest of the world.

The scale, then, varies from map to map, according to the needs of the entry. Where necessary, we have included insets to situate a remote locality within a larger, more readily recognizable geographic entity. In all instances the maps are oriented with north at the top.

In just the hundred years or so since diamonds were discovered in southern Africa, countries, cities, and colonies have come and gone. Their names speak eloquently of the changes that time and the aspirations of their indigenous peoples have wrought: German Southwest Africa became Namibia; the Belgian Congo, Zaire. On the banks of the Rio dos Marinhos, the sleepy town of Tijero becomes Diamantina; Mirnyi rises on the Siberian permafrost.

Other names are astonishing simply because they have endured: The ancient city Golconda is with us still. Other, less venerable names remind us that diamonds often change the lives of those they touch. Cecil Rhodes's Rhodesia lasted less than a hundred years; it is now Zimbabwe. On the other hand, A.J. du Toit, a farmer whose name certainly would otherwise have been forgotten, is memorialized in Dutoitspan. Diamonds offer many towns, and many people, a chance to glitter in the sun.

We tend to think that dramatic changes in the fortunes of empires are part of the past, but this is not the case. The period during which the bulk of this dictionary was drafted coincided with a tumultuous reorganization in the former Soviet Union and its satellite nations. Nevertheless, all but the very young will, for a while at least, undoubtedly continue to think in terms of the "USSR," or "Siberia." Consequently, while such entities have been glossed under their current names, readers who look for them under their former names will be referred to the appropriate new entries.

Political change on a large scale inevitably produces change at the administrative and bureaucratic level as well. Such has also been the case in the former Soviet Union. The various government bodies and state corporations responsible for the exploitation of that country's mineral wealth have been shuffled and reshuffled in the past few years. The names of many such organizations, and their responsibilities, have altered, sometimes more than once, in the course of preparing this dictionary. We have tried to stay abreast of these changes and update our entries, knowing as we did that things would continue to change. In June, 1993, President Boris Yeltsin issued a decree putting the production and marketing of Russian diamonds under his personal control. It is very possible that some of our entries will be out of date before this book is bound.

In truth, these changes in the new Confederation of Independent States are unusual primarily because they have occurred so rapidly, in such a short period of time. Similar changes continue to take place in sub-equatorial Africa, as they have since the end of World War II. New governments form, and quickly negotiate new contracts with corporations that offer the capital and expertise to develop their rich mineral resources. Sometimes this involves the creation of a new company to mine and manage a new discovery, sometimes the reorganization of an existing organization to deal with a new situation, or simply when new capital is sought.

But like all natural resources, a diamond deposit is finite. Sometimes, when mines reach the end of their economic life, the companies that owned or managed them are disbanded. Occasionally they survive as a corporate shell, to serve another purpose, or simply to wait on the off-chance the organizational structure will be needed once again. We have tried to include in this Dictionary the names of all those companies, active and inactive, of continuing or historical importance. When we were sure a company had been liquidated, we described it as "defunct," but the absence of such an indication does not necessarily mean the company is still active. Sometimes we were simply unable to find out.

Nor is our list of the various deposits, mines, mining companies, and support organizations complete. Anywhere the earth's resources are mined, there are some deposits which remain productive for many years; others never live up to the bright hopes they engender. Some companies succeed, while others fall by the wayside.

Southern Africa, for example, is dotted with kimberlitic occurrences of one sort or another, some diamondiferous and some not, and with active and exhausted alluvial deposits—and, in all probability, others as yet undiscovered. Previous editions of the Dictionary tried to accumulate entries on as many of these as possible, in the hope that a complete and authoritative listing would ultimately emerge. We have abandoned this effort and have, in fact, deleted a good many previous entries. Only those of demonstrable historic importance have been retained, and the reason for their inclusion is evident in the entry. Similarly, in countries and regions where diamond production is relatively minor in relation to world production as a whole, we have tried to make it clear that the importance of individual deposits is largely local. When kimberlitic occurrences are listed, they are normally further designated as a pipe, a sill, a dike, or a fissure. In the absence of such a designation, the reader can assume the occurrence is a pipe.

The entries in this dictionary represent, or derive from, a dozen or more languages—Afrikaans, Arabic, Bantu, Dutch, English, Flemish, French, German, Mogul, Persian, Portuguese, Russian, Yiddish, to mention but a few. But the dictionary is not, and was not intended to be, a multi-lingual glossary. Of necessity, however, it includes a substantial number of entries representing terms which have been assimilated into English from other languages. In all such instances, we have attempted to identify the language of origin: Thus, for example, a reader who looks up "gletz" will find the entry reads "Dutch, feather in a diamond."

Sometimes names or terms which derive from languages other than English are used in the original form, and sometimes in an English translation. With these, we have attempted to decide which usage is most frequent, or most appropriate. If, as is often the case, the non-English usage seems to dominate, the English-language entry simply refers the reader to a full entry under the original form. Thus a reader who looks up the "Queen of Belgium Diamond" will be referred to the entry "Reine des Belges Diamond." Admittedly, such distinctions were based on impressionistic evidence rather than a systematic quantitative survey. Not all our readers will agree with the decisions we have made, but they will eventually find the entry they are looking for.

Most of the entries are based on accepted spellings in American English. We have listed some variant spellings which are commonly seen as well (these are usually British—e.g., gemmology). There are also a very few entries which are numeric in nature—e.g., "595 line"—which are alphabetized as if the numbers were written in English ("five-ninety-five line").

Most of the entries derive from languages which use the Roman alphabet. But some (place names especially) do not, and the problem of selecting appropriate transliterations has exercised us from the outset. Unfortunately, for languages such as Chinese, there are a number of transliteration systems, the popularity of which has waxed and waned over the years; in spite of efforts at standardization, older forms continue to appear. The Wade-Giles system dates from the mid-nineteenth century, but it is still seen from time to time. We have used the pin-yin system, although it may well be that gwoyeu-romatzyh or Yale-system spellings have crept in. The pin-yin system should lead Western readers to an acceptable approximation of the Chinese pronunciation; the only problem might be the use of the Roman letter x to represent a sound which hovers somewhere between the sh in "sheet" and the h in "huge."

There are several systems used to transliterate Russian, too, and in virtually all of them there are alternate possibilities for certain sounds. In the one we chose (simply because it seems the one most used by the Western media), the letter Я as in Yakutia, for example can be rendered as ia, ja, or ya. We chose the last option, but we recognize that some readers will be frustrated, with perfect justification, looking first for Yakutia (and other words like it) under "I" or "J".

In the case of the Altaic languages, there seem to be about as many transliteration systems as there are translators (Kuh-i-Nur? Koh-i-Nur? Koh-i-Noor?). Indeed, the amateurism which has characterized many of the translations from Mogul and Turki seriously compromises our understanding of these early diamond fanciers who controlled the Indian mines for over 200 years.

It was, among other reasons, the polyglot nature of the world of diamonds which led us to abandon, with considerable regret, an attempt to include some sort of pronunciation guide. We are aware that our readership will be as international, and as multi-cultural, as the entries themselves. Our problem was to find a system for indicating the pronunciation that was equally accessible to everyone.

The International Phonemic Alphabet is an excellent system, but it is all but unknown to anyone outside the linguistics community. The system used in *Webster's New Collegiate Dictionary* is a typographical nightmare; it takes an entire page to list the symbols and two columns—some 600 words—to explain it, at which point the "serious student" is referred to a more extensive discussion in the unabridged *Third New International Dictionary*.

We first attempted to implement a system of our own devising, based on transliterating the entries into common words, approximate spellings, and implied rhymes found in American English. We apply this system in our courses, and many GIA students have found it useful—if they are speakers of American English. But to what extent will a construction like "MURR freeze burr oh" help someone who does not speak English to approach a recognizable approximation of Murfreesboro? About as much, we decided, as "puh tee CUR" would help someone who does not speak French with "Petit Coeur," and abandoned the idea.

The question of named diamonds is also one to which we have given considerable thought. It may seem likely, particularly in an industry of such ancient origins and of such a traditional and conservative nature, that there would be a set of conventions, or at least some sort of "gentlemen's agreement" regarding the process of naming diamonds (just as there are for naming minerals, mountains, bodies of water, stars, etc.). But there seems in fact to be considerable inconsistency in the naming of diamonds, and some stones change names with every change in ownership.

We raised these issues with a number of our distinguished reviewers, especially those with particular expertise in either the marketing of important polished goods or the history of the diamond trade. They all agreed that there is nothing inherently wrong with the practice of naming diamonds, an opinion with which we heartily concur. Several of them also felt, however, that the practice has been abused. That judgement seems harsh, because in fact it seems unlikely that naming a diamond could possibly cause any harm. At the same time, the fact that someone, somewhere, had once named a stone does not automatically mean it belongs in this or any other reference volume.

With their help, then, we established a set of guidelines that we used to determine which named stones to include. The first is antiquarian status. Some diamonds have, of course, borne a specific name for a very long time. Those names, and the circumstances under which they were given, are part of the established lore of the field, and including them was never in doubt. Our basic criteria for such stones, examples of which might include the Koh-i-Nur or the Sancy, was simply one or more documented citations of the name prior to 1900.

The second guideline we used is gemological significance. Here size is obviously a consideration, albeit not the only one; color is important, too, as is the source, the presence of unusual physical properties, and the like. For stones which were of interest for reasons such as these, our decisions were based on the collective expertise of the various diamond specialists at GIA and the GIA Gem Trade Laboratory. In expressing the weight of any diamond, we have used metric carats when the stone is thought to have been weighed on a modern scale. We have not attempted to convert "old carats" to metric carats; there are too many variables of time and place for this to be accurate. (A table of old carats as they were computed in various places before the standardization of the metric carat is given in Appendix H.

The third guideline was provenance. Many stones were named, whether long ago or recently, by individuals or bodies of obvious standing in the industry who by virtue of possessing the stone in question had the right to call it whatever they chose. Examples might be the Winston Diamond, or the Centenary.

But provenance proved to be a little tricky. There are also many diamonds which are named for or by various luminaries with whom they are somehow associated; often it is someone by whom they are "said to have once been owned." Frequently, however, the association or the ownership is moot, and the individuals in question vary in their historical importance or cultural interest. In such instances, we have insisted first on certain forms of documentation—viz., published inventories, catalogs, auction records, mention in recognized journals—to document the fact that the diamond in question was indeed owned by or otherwise associated with the corresponding individual. Then we have attempted to exercise a degree of common sense as to the relative importance of the personality involved.

Finally, there are many stones that simply seem to have been named somewhere along the way for one of an astonishing variety of other reasons. The name may derive from an owner, a place, an event, some special quality of the stone itself, or some particular aspect of the circumstances under which the stone was found, sold, cut, etc. It is in this category that we begin to run across numerous stones the importance of which is, to put it politely, limited. Often it resides only in the affection or the imagination of those who named them.

So our fourth guideline was simply currency. Presumably users of this dictionary (or any other) refer to it because they have encountered a term or, in this case, a name, elsewhere. We have tried to include all the named diamonds that the typical reader is likely to find in modern books and publications, and in those older works that are still read and consulted with some frequency. Again, this called for a number of subjective judgements, for which we are happy to assume the responsibility, knowing full well that particularly assiduous readers may find us wanting.

In making these decisions we were not unmindful of the fact that there are several well-known and readily accessible reference works devoted entirely to famous and notable diamonds, some of which are noted in the list of works consulted which follows this introduction. GIA itself is the American publisher of the second edition of Ian Balfour's *Famous Diamonds,* which has become the standard reference in the field. (Lord Balfour served with distinction on our board of reviewers, and helped us clarify the guidelines discussed above, although he is in no way responsible for the way we applied them.) We assume that most users of this Dictionary are familiar with such works, and have access to them.

Stones that, for a variety of reasons, we felt worthwhile to include, but not to give a full lexical entry, are listed in the appendices. Even so, we have undoubtedly omitted diamonds for which others might well make a plausible case for inclusion. For these omissions the editor also assumes full responsibility.

A large body of folklore has grown up around the world of diamonds and around diamond people; often it coheres around large or otherwise noteworthy diamonds. Taken as a whole, it is often charming and sometimes fascinating; some sophisticated researchers have suggested ways to interpret it that illuminate otherwise inaccessible aspects of the roles diamonds have played in cultural and social history. Nevertheless, we decided that to include such material would necessitate including elaborate discussions of its validity as well, thereby producing an imbalance which would in itself be misleading. We have, then, sacrificed most of the material of this sort, knowing that, once again, there are those who will miss it. But the curious are not without resources; there are many other references to which they can turn. (Again, some of these are included in the list of works consulted.)

Finally, we have also listed in the Dictionary a number of other gem materials, both natural and man-made, which derive much or all of their prestige from their putative resemblance to diamond. Some of these entries represent misnomers, often of long standing, for other well-known materials—"Herkimer diamond," for example, a misnomer for rock crystal quartz. (The misnomers for rock crystal quartz number several hundred; we are especially indebted to Si and Ann Frazer of El Cerrito, California, US, for allowing us to draw on the exhaustive list they have compiled.) Others represent names created for various materials (often synthetics, or assembled stones) which are marketed as diamond simulants. In the case of the latter, some names have been copyrighted or registered as trademarks, while others have not. Sometimes the copyrights have been allowed to lapse, while some are, or may be, still in force. We have not attempted to determine the status of these various forms of protection, if such there be; rather we have described them all simply as "proprietary names."

As we have noted, many distinguished people have contributed to this new edition of the Diamond Dictionary. The names of those who assumed specific responsibilities are on the title page; the names of those who aided us as reviewers and subject specialists are appended to this Introduction. Neither of these lists does justice to the help and encouragement we received in the course of our work, or to the resources on which we drew.

The collegiality and the intellectual atmosphere at GIA are uniquely suited to a project like this. We are, for example, fortunate in having at our disposal the resources of the Richard T. Liddicoat Library and Information Center, including the recently acquired John and Marjorie Sinkakas Collection, which is part of the Library's holdings. The Library's staff, under the direction of Senior Research Librarian Dona Mary Dirlam, performed countless searches there and provided general assistance that was invaluable. We are indebted to them, and to our other colleagues who gave unstintingly of their expertise and their assistance when we asked, as we did continually, for help.

A number of people also took part in the tasks of production. Sharon Thomson assembled the first draft entries and integrated much of the first round of outside reviewers' comments. Robin Teraoka, in GIA's Course Development department, was graphic designer, and created many of the illustrations. Irv Dierdorff, and Lisa Joko, the Assistant Editor and Art Director, respectively, of *Gems & Gemology,* worked with us in the final editorial and production stages.

None of us really grasped the magnitude of this task until it was well under way. As it became increasingly clear that additional resources would have to be allocated, GIA executive management remained committed to the project and continued to give us their support. Indeed, it is difficult to imagine where else an effort of this sort would be supported as it has been here. With their backing, we have produced what we believe to be a greatly improved new Diamond Dictionary, a reference book for the start of a new millenium. We are confident it will be of great use to the industry which GIA serves.

John H. Hummel, Ph.D.
Editor

Reviewers and Subject Specialists

Hugh Allen, past President, Institute of Mining and Metallurgy; Director, RTZ Technical Services, Ltd., Bristol, UK

Frank Arnott, RTZ Technical Services, Ltd., Bristol, UK

Dr. Edward Asscher, Royal Asscher Diamond Company, Ltd., Amsterdam, the Netherlands

Walter Baert, Director, Public Relations, Hoge Raad voor Diamant, Antwerp, Belgium

Ian Balfour (the Lord Balfour of Inchrye), London, UK

Eric Bruton, Vice-President, Gemmological Association and Gem Testing Laboratory of Great Britain, London, UK

Moonyean Buys, D. Phil., Archivist, De Beers Consolidated Mines, Ltd., Kimberley, Republic of South Africa

Alan Campbell, De Beers Centenary AG, Moscow, Russian Federation

Tim Capon, Director, De Beers Consolidated Mines, Ltd., De Beers Centenary AG, and CSO, London, UK

Eric Chubb, Diamond Manager, CSO Valuations AG, London, UK

Peter Cooke, Manager, DTC Research Centre, Maidenhead, UK

Brian Cullingworth, Director, De Beers Industrial Diamond Division, Johannesburg, Republic of South Africa

Tony Curtis, diamond industry consultant, Cranbrook, Kent, UK

Rudolf Dröschel, Edelsteinschlieferei Rudolf Dröschel, Idar-Oberstein, Germany

Roy Edwards, Consulting Geologist, Anglo American Corporation, Johannesburg, Republic of South Africa

Tarquin de la Force, Market Controller, De Beers Consumer and Advertising division, London, UK

Michael A. Grantham, Director, Diamond Trading Company, Ltd., and CSO Valuations AG, London, UK

Dieter Hahn, President, Diamant und Edelstein Börse, Idar-Oberstein, Germany

Ronnie Hazell, Geologist, Anglo American Corporation, Johannesburg, Republic of South Africa

Dick Hazelton, RTZ Technical Services, Ltd., Bristol, UK

Ulrich Henn, Ph.D., Manager, Deutsche Gemmologische Gesellschaft e.V., Idar-Oberstein, Germany

Les Hymas, Manager, CSO Polished Diamond Division, London, UK

Martin Jennings, Press Officer, De Beers Industrial Diamond Division, Ascot, UK

George R. Kaplan, Governor Emeritus, Gemological Institute of America, Vice Chairman of the Board, Lazare Kaplan & Sons, Inc., New York, US

John M. King, Laboratory Projects Officer, GIA Gem Trade Laboratory, New York, US

Bert Krashes, member, Board of Governors, Gemological Institute of America; Lake Worth, Florida, US

Laurence Krashes, Vice President, Harry Winston, Inc., New York, US

Bertie Lincoln, Director, De Beers Consolidated Mines, Ltd., De Beers Centenary AG, Johannesburg, Republic of South Africa

Kelvin Lunt, Manager, CSO Valuations AG, Kimberley, Republic of South Africa

Bill McKechnie, Geologist, De Beers Consolidated Mines, Ltd., Kimberley, Republic of South Africa

Henry O. A. Meyer, Ph.D., Department of Geosciences, Purdue University, West Lafayette, Indiana, US

Thomas M. Moses, Director, Identification and Research, GIA Gem Trade Laboratory, New York, US

George Read, Geologist, Anglo American Corporation, Johannesburg, Republic of South Africa

Steve Read, RTZ Technical Services, Ltd., Bristol, UK

Michael Ross, Manager, Education Activities, Gemological Institute of America, Santa Monica, California, US

Johnny Roux, diamond consultant; Horsham, Sussex, UK

Edward Schwartz, Director, Grading Services, GIA Gem Trade Laboratory, New York, US

Prof. Nikolai Sobolev, Institute of Mineralogy and Petrology, Russian Academy of Sciences, Novosibirsk, Russian Federation

Robert Spratford, member, Board of Governors, Gemological Institute of America; former president, C.A. Kiger Company, Inc. (ret.), Kansas City, Missouri, US

Alan Stockill, Consulting Engineer's Department, Anglo American Corporation, Johannesburg, Republic of South Africa

Gabi Tolkowsky, Director, Diatrada, Antwerp, Belgium

Kobus Van Jaarseveld, Consulting Engineer, Anglo American Corporation, Johannesburg, Republic of South Africa

Roger Van Eeghen, Press Officer, CSO Valuations AG, London, UK

Richard Wake-Walker, Manager, De Beers Centenary AG, Moscow, Russian Federation

Robin Walker, Manager, Industry/Technical Section, Marketing Liaison Department, CSO Valuations AG, London, UK

Richard Williams, Manager, Sales Department, CSO Valuations AG, London, UK

Hans Wins, Director, European Gem Services, Antwerp, Belgium

Ronald Winston, President, Harry Winston, Inc., New York, US

Jack Young, Director, CSO Valuations AG, London, UK

WORKS CONSULTED

Producing a work like the *Diamond Dictionary* would not have been possible without ready access to the numerous works, both general and specific, written about diamonds and the diamond industry.

This list enumerates only those books and publications to which we had frequent and recurring recourse. Many others, not mentioned here, were consulted to corroborate specific points.

Balfour I. (1992) *Famous Diamonds*, 2nd American ed. Gemological Institute of America, Santa Monica, CA.

Bates R.L., Jackson J.A., Eds. (1984) *Dictionary of Geological Terms*. American Geological Institute, New York.

Blakey G.G. (1977) *The Diamond*. Paddington Press, London.

Bruton E. (1978) *Diamonds*, 2nd ed. Chilton Book Co., Radnor, PA.

Chilvers H.A. (1939) *The Story of De Beers*. Cassell, London.

Gregory T. (1962) *Ernest Oppenheimer and the Economic Development of South Africa*. Oxford University Press, Cape Town.

Krashes L.S. (1988) *Harry Winston, The Ultimate Jeweler*, 3rd ed. Harry Winston, New York, and the Gemological Institute of America, Santa Monica, CA.

Legrand J., Maillard, R., Eds. (1984) *Diamonds: Myth, Magic, and Reality*, 2nd ed. Bonanza Books, New York.

Lenzen G. (1970) *The History of Diamond Production and the Diamond Trade*. Trans. by F. Bradley, Praeger Publishers, New York.

Lenzen G. (1983) *Diamonds and Diamond Grading*. Trans. by P. B. Lapworth, Butterworths, London.

Robertson M. (1974) *Diamond Fever: South African Diamond History, 1866-69, From Primary Sources*. Oxford University Press, Cape Town.

Streeter E.W. (1882) *The Great Diamonds of the World*. George Bell and Sons, London.

Tavernier J.-B. (1977) *Travels in India*, 2nd ed., Vol. 1 and Vol. 2. Trans. by V. Ball, Oriental Books Reprint Corp., New Delhi.

Watermeyer B. (1991) *Diamond Cutting*, 4th ed. Basil Watermeyer, Johannesburg.

Webster R. (1983) *Gems: Their Sources, Descriptions and Identification*, 4th ed. Rev. by B. W. Anderson, Butterworths, London.

Wilson A. (1982) *Diamonds: From Birth to Eternity*. Gemological Institute of America, Santa Monica, CA.

The dynamic nature of the industry is reflected in the following list of periodicals and occasional publications which we also monitored at various stages in the editorial process. Without them, some areas—the reorganization of the production and polishing industries in the former Soviet Union, for example—would have been impossible to elucidate.

Diamond Intelligence Briefs

Diamond International

Diamond News and S.A. Jeweller

Diamond World Review

Financial Times

Gems & Gemology

Indiaqua

Jewelers' Circular Keystone

Mazal U'Bracha

Mining Annual Review

Mining Journal

New York Times

The GIA Diamond Dictionary

Abaeté, historic alluvial deposit discovered in Minas Gerais, Brazil, in 1785. See BRAGANZA DIAMOND, BRAZIL.

aberration, see CHROMATIC ABERRATION, SPHERICAL ABERRATION.

abraded culet, culet worn along its edges; usually caused by contact with other diamonds. See BLEMISH, PAPERWORN DIAMOND.

abrasion, (1) wearing away by friction and/or impact, as when diamonds are tumbled with gravel, rocks, and minerals in a river or in the sea. (2) minute nicks along the facet edges of a fashioned diamond which give the facet junctions a white or fuzzy appearance. Often caused by contact with other diamonds when kept in diamond papers. See ALLUVIAL DEPOSIT, ALLUVIAL GRAVEL, ALLUVIAL SORTING, DE BEERS MARINE (PTY.), LTD., PAPERWORN DIAMOND, SCRATCH.

abrasion test, method of determining a gemstone's resistance to wear by abrading it with a grinding wheel charged with diamond powder for a given period of time at a specific amount of pressure; the amount of material removed is then measured. See ABRASION, DIRECTIONAL HARDNESS, HARDNESS, INDENTATION TEST, BRINELL HARDNESS TEST, KNOOP INDENTATION HARDNESS TEST, MOHS SCALE OF HARDNESS.

abrasives, grinding materials used for smoothing or polishing. Synthetic diamond abrasives are made to size, natural abrasives by crushing or milling natural industrial diamonds; some are electroplated or bonded with resin onto a variety of cutting and grinding tools; some, in powder form, are suspended in water or oil for grinding and cutting minerals and metals. See BALLAS, BORT, CARBONADO, INDUSTRIAL DIAMOND, SHOT BORT.

absorption, selective, see SELECTIVE ABSORPTION.

absorption band, relatively wide, dark area in a gemstone's spectrum indicating those wavelengths of light which have been absorbed. The terms *absorption band* and *absorption line* are sometimes used interchangeably, but a band, properly speaking, is wider than a line. (On a spectrophotometer curve, any peak more than a few nanometers wide corresponds to a band seen in an optical spectroscope.) See ABSORPTION SPECTRUM, ELECTROMAGNETIC SPECTRUM, EMISSION SPECTRUM, LIGHT ABSORPTION, SELECTIVE ABSORPTION, SPECTROMETER, SPECTROPHOTOMETER, SPECTROSCOPE.

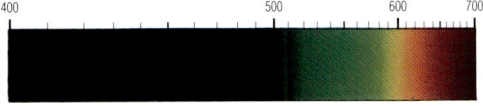

absorption band

absorption line, relatively narrow, dark line in a gemstone's spectrum (or a sharp peak on a spectrophotometer curve) indicating those wavelengths of light which have been absorbed. The terms *absorption band* and *absorption line* are sometimes used interchangeably, but a line, properly speaking, is narrower than a band. See ABSORPTION SPECTRUM, CAPE LINES, ELECTROMAGNETIC SPECTRUM, EMISSION SPECTRUM, 595 NM LINE, LIGHT ABSORPTION, SELECTIVE ABSORPTION, SPECTROMETER, SPECTROPHOTOMETER, SPECTROSCOPE.

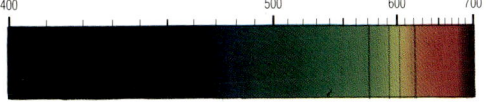

absorption line

absorption of light, see LIGHT ABSORPTION.

absorption spectrum, plural, spectra; spectrum of radiation which has been filtered through a material. When white light passes through a material, a certain portion is absorbed. In a gemstone, the amount of light absorbed determines its residual bodycolor. Seen through a spectroscope, the characteristic absorption spectrum appears as well-marked bands or fine dark lines; recorded with a spectrophotometer, the spectrum appears as distinct peaks. Absorption spectra can be used to identify gemstones and to detect some types of enhancement. See ABSORPTION BAND, ABSORPTION LINE, CAPE LINES, ELECTROMAGNETIC SPECTRUM, EMISSION SPECTRUM, 595 NM LINE, LIGHT ABSORPTION, SELECTIVE ABSORPTION, SPECTROMETER, SPECTROPHOTOMETER, SPECTRUM.

Acaeté Diamond, 161.50 ct. rough diamond found in Brazil in 1791. Current whereabouts unknown.

Accra Diamond Market (ADM), organization established in 1954 as the sole purchaser of diamonds mined by local diggers in Ghana. After 1961, all diamonds were required by law to be sold through the Accra Diamond Market. Replaced in 1963 by the Ghana Diamond Marketing Board (GDMB). Two years later, the GDMB was reincorporated as the Diamond Marketing Corporation. See GHANA CONSOLIDATED DIAMONDS, LTD.

achromatic lens, compound lens free of chromatic aberration, made by combining different optical elements to focus the various wavelengths of light at the same point. See CHROMATIC ABERRATION.

acid cleaning, use of hot acids to remove dirt or polishing residue from diamonds. Newly-mined rough diamonds are cleaned with hydrofluoric acid; newly-polished diamonds are boiled in a solution of hydrochloric and sulfuric acids to remove oil, graphite, and other debris from surface fractures and abrasions. Diamonds which have been mounted in jewelry are sometimes boiled in sulfuric acid to remove metal residue and dirt impregnated in the girdle. See HYDROCHLORIC ACID, HYDROFLUORIC ACID, SULFURIC ACID.

adamant, archaic synonym for a diamond; derived from the Greek *adamas*.

adamantine, diamond-like. See LUSTER.

adamantine luster, brilliant look of a material's surface in reflected light, seen on diamonds and other gem materials with high refractive indices, such as cassiterite and cuprite. See LUSTER.

Adamant Research Laboratory (ARL), South African laboratory established to investigate the feasibility of commercial production of synthetic diamond. ARL scientists succeeded in synthesizing minute, industrial-quality diamonds in 1959; the synthesis of larger industrial and gem-quality diamonds was achieved in the 1970s. Incorporated into the synthesis department of the De Beers Diamond Research Laboratory in Johannesburg, South Africa, in the 1960s. See DE BEERS SYNTHETIC DIAMOND, DIAMOND RESEARCH LABORATORY, SUMITOMO SYNTHETIC DIAMOND, SYNTHETIC DIAMOND.

ADEX, see AUSTRALIAN DIAMOND EXPLORATION JOINT VENTURE.

additional facets, facets added symmetrically to a standard cutting style to create variations in cut. These are not blemishes and should not be confused with extra facets. See EXTRA FACETS.

ADIA, see AMERICAN DIAMOND INDUSTRY ASSOCIATION.

adjustment factor, variable introduced into weight estimation formulas when the proportions of a polished diamond vary from standard. There are adjustment factors for thick girdles on all shapes; high shoulders and fat wings on pear shapes, hearts, or marquises; squarish corners on ovals; and bulging pavilions on emerald cuts. Adjustment factors are usually expressed as percentages, and may range from one to 25 percent. See BULGE.

ADM, see ACCRA DIAMOND MARKET, ARGYLE DIAMOND MINES (PTY.), LTD.

aeromagnetic surveying, aerial geophysical sensing technique used to measure variations in the earth's magnetic field. Anomalous magnetic readings may indicate the presence of kimberlites or lamproites.

Affenrücken, historic name for an important alluvial mining area along the Namibian coast between Oranjemund and Lüderitz; also known as Area H. Operated by CDM. See GEMSBOK, KERBEHUK, MARINE AREAS, MITTAG, UUBVLEY.

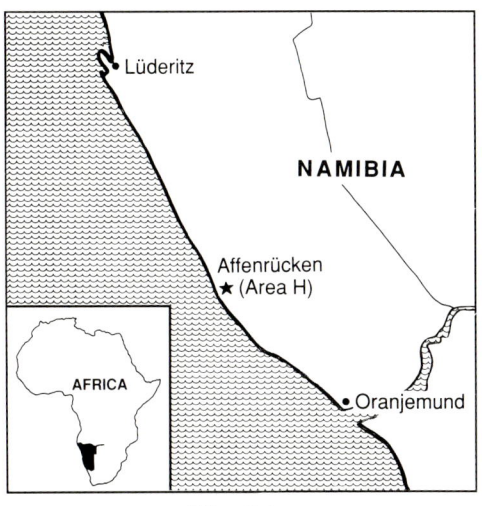

Affenrücken

African Diamond Diggers' Association, organization of independent diamond miners in Ghana, Africa; now defunct.

African Diamond Winners' Association, organization of independent diamond miners in Ghana, Africa; now defunct.

African Yellow Diamond, 112 ct. diamond, reportedly yellow, mentioned by Edwin Streeter in 1882; may be the Tennant Diamond. Current whereabouts unknown.

Afro-West Mining, Ltd., Australian diamond-mining company which operates alluvial deposits in Western Australia on Lower Smoke Creek, downstream from the Argyle Diamond Mines.

Aga Khan III Diamond, 33.13 ct. flawless, E-color pear-shape diamond recut from a 38 ct. pear shape. Named for Sultan Mohammed Shah Aga Khan III (1877-1957), 48th Imam of the Shia Imami Ismaili Muslims. Sold from the Aga Khan's collection in 1988.

age (of diamonds): mineral inclusions found in diamonds indicate that they range between 990 million and 3,300 million years in age; thus they are at least ten times older than the kimberlites and lamproites which transported them to the surface of the earth. See DIATREME, EMPLACEMENT (OF DIAMOND), HYPABYSSAL ZONE, INTERNAL CHARACTERISTIC, KIMBERLITE, LAMPROITE, ORIGIN (OF DIAMOND).

aggregate, solid made up of minute crystals, either intergrown or held together by a natural binding agent. Individual crystals may be discernible only under high magnification. Diamond aggregates include ballas, bort, carbonado, framesite, and stewartite.

Agra Diamond, 28.15 ct., light pink modified cushion-shape Indian diamond believed to have once belonged to the first Mogul Emperor, Babur (1483-1530). Named for the city of Agra, it was purchased by the Duke of Brunswick in 1844. Originally 46 ct., it was recut to 32.24 ct.; later owned by Edwin Streeter. After his retirement in 1904, it was sold by Christie, Manson & Woods of London. In 1990, the Agra was graded by GIA's Gem Trade Laboratory as Fancy Pink, VVS$_1$, and sold by Christie's to the CIBA Corporation of Hong Kong. It was then repolished to its present shape and weight.

Agra Diamond

photo courtesy of CSO

AGS, see AMERICAN GEM SOCIETY.

AGS clarity-grading scale, range of diamond clarity grades running from 0 (the highest, corresponding to the GIA grade Fl) to 10. See AMERICAN GEM SOCIETY (AGS), APPENDIX E, CLARITY, CLARITY GRADING, CLARITY-GRADING SCALE, CLARITY-GRADING SYSTEM, GIA CLARITY-GRADING SCALE.

AGS color-grading scale, range of diamond color grades used by the American Gem Society for colorless to light yellow (or light brown) stones and employing a scale from 0 (colorless) to 10. At one time, AGS master diamonds were graded using the AGS Colorimeter, but this method is no longer in use; masters are now graded against GIA master sets and then assigned an estimated Colorimeter value. See AMERICAN GEM SOCIETY (AGS), APPENDIX D, BODYCOLOR, COLOR GRADE, COLOR GRADING, COLOR-GRADING SCALE, COLOR-GRADING SYSTEM, COLORIMETER, GIA COLOR-GRADING SCALE, MASTER DIAMOND.

AGS cut-grading system, system for grading the make of polished diamonds, used by the American Gem Society. Five proportions are each assigned a grade on a scale from 0 (highest) to 10; the lowest of these sets the proportions grade. Symmetry/polish is assigned a grade from 0 to 10. The lower of the two (proportions and symmetry/polish) sets the final cut grade. See AMERICAN GEM SOCIETY (AGS), CUT, CUT GRADING, FINISH, FINISH GRADING, MAKE, PROPORTION GRADING, PROPORTIONS.

Agua Suja Mine, eighteenth century diamond mine on the Bagagem River, Minas Gerais, Brazil, near Estrela do Sul, now worked by hydraulic mining methods. Noted for gem-quality diamond cubes, a form of rough seldom encountered in gem quality until the discovery of the Jwaneng Mine in Botswana. See BAGAGEM, JWANENG MINE.

Ahmedabad Diamond, 157.25 ct. rough diamond purchased in India in the mid-seventeenth century by Jean-Baptiste Tavernier. He had the diamond cut to 94.50 ct. and sold it in Persia (Iran); current whereabouts unknown.

Aikhal, town near the Aikhal Pipe in Sakha (Yakutia), the Russian Federation, CIS, where the recovery plant for the Aikhal, Sytikanskaya, and Jubilee pipes is located.

Aikhal Pipe, one of the major diamond-bearing kimberlite pipes in Sakha (Yakutia), the Russian Federation, CIS. Discovered in 1960 and worked as an open pit mine, it is 80 kilometers (50 miles) south of the Arctic Circle and 45 kilometers (28 miles) southwest of the Udachnaya Pipe. *Aikhal* means *glory*.

Aikhal Pipe

à jour, mounting which leaves a gemstone's pavilion facets uncovered; light enters through the pavilion as well as through the crown. French, meaning *open to daylight*.

à jour

AK1 Pipe (Argyle), Argyle Kimberlite Number 1, a diamond-bearing lamproite, 1.6 kilometers (1 mile) long and 150 to 600 meters (160 to 650 yards) wide, located in Western Australia's Kimberley Mountain range. Discovered in 1979; large scale commercial production began in 1985. The world's largest producer of diamonds in terms of volume. Output includes a large percentage of industrial diamonds, and some gem rough, including stones in the pink to purple range. See ARGYLE DIAMOND MINES.

Akbar Shah Diamond, 116 ct. Indian diamond crystal acquired by Akbar Shah (1542-1619) in 1605 and later owned by his son, Jahangir

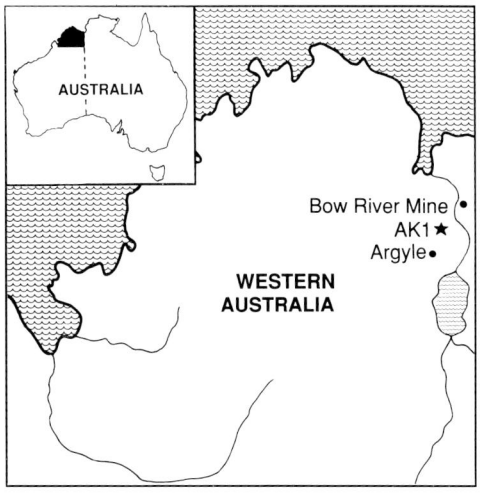
AK1 Pipe

(1569-1627). Inherited in 1628 by Shah Jahan (1592-1666), builder of the Taj Mahal, the stone was called the Akbar Shah because one of the inscriptions on the diamond was erroneously ascribed to the era in which he reigned. Believed to have been taken to Persia (Iran) in 1739 by Nadir Shah, the diamond re-appeared in Constantinople (Istanbul, Turkey) in 1866 where it was purchased and taken to London. Arabic inscriptions indicating the past ownership were destroyed when it was cut to a 73.60 ct. pear shape. Sold in 1867 to Mulhar Rao, Gaekwar of Baroda. Also called the Shepherd Stone. Current whereabouts unknown.

Akwatia, alluvial diamond-mining concession on the east bank of the Birim River in Ghana. Mined by CAST and local diggers from 1924 to 1972, the concession is now operated on a limited scale by Ghana Consolidated Diamonds. See CONSOLIDATED AFRICA SELECTION TRUST, LTD., GHANA, GHANA CONSOLIDATED DIAMONDS, LTD., GHANA DIAMOND MARKETING CORPORATION (DMC).

Alamasi, small diamond mining company in Tanzania.

Alaska black diamond, misnomer for hematite.

Alaska diamond, misnomer for rock crystal quartz from Alaska.

Alderson, William, British prospector in southern Africa, believed to have discovered the primary deposits at Dutoitspan and Bultfontein in 1869 or 1870 (although others claimed to have bought diamonds there as early as 1868). Alderson later became one of the seven founding directors of De Beers Mining Company, and was for many years its largest shareholder.

Alençon diamond, misnomer for rock crystal quartz from Alençon, a town in northeastern France. Also applied to smoky quartz.

Alenoon diamond, misnomer for rock crystal quartz.

Alexander Bay, see ALEXCOR, STATE ALLUVIAL DIGGINGS.

Alexander Bay Development Corporation, see ALEXCOR.

Alexcor, (formerly the Alexander Bay Development Corporation), company which operates the Rietfontein South diamond treatment plant 30 kilometers (18 miles) south of Alexander Bay on the west coast of South Africa. Formed in May, 1989, Alexcor replaced the government-owned state alluvial diggings which began in 1927. See RIETFONTEIN SOUTH, STATE ALLUVIAL DIGGINGS.

Alexite, proprietary name for yttrium aluminum garnet (YAG). Marketed as a diamond simulant.

Algeiba Star Diamond, 133.03 ct. cushion-shape diamond, described as yellow, from South Africa. Recut from the 139.38 Mahjal Diamond, which is said to have once been owned by the Maharajah of Kapurthala, a small princely state in the Punjab. Sold by Christie's in 1983.

alignment of facets, see FACET ALIGNMENT.

Allmana Svenska Elektriska Aktiebolaget (ASEA), Swedish electric company which reportedly achieved the first repeatable synthesis of diamonds in 1953. The process involved combining tantalum with iron carbide and graphite in a hollow soapstone sphere lined with an inner sphere of thermite. The device was subjected to pressures of 80,000 to 90,000 atmospheres at temperatures of about 2,760°C (5,000°F). ASEA did not publish the results at the time, so credit for the first successful synthesis of diamond is generally given to the General Electric Company, which announced its results in 1954.

allocation, selection of rough diamonds offered for sale to sightholders at a sight. Allocations contain a range of diamonds selected for each sightholder by the Central Selling Organisation on the basis of earlier applications and current market conditions. See APPLICATION, CENTRAL SELLING ORGANISATION (CSO).

allotrope, one of the distinct forms assumed by an allotropic element. For example, diamond and graphite are allotropes of carbon. See ALLOTROPIC.

allotropic, capable of existing in two or more forms, each of which has different properties. For example, carbon crystallizes in the cubic system as diamond and in the hexagonal system as graphite. See ALLOTROPE.

alluvial deposit, a concentration of gem materials created when rivers and streams transport sediment some distance from a primary deposit or another secondary deposit and redeposit it. See ABRASION, ALLUVIAL GRAVEL, ALLUVIAL SORTING, ELUVIAL DEPOSIT, FLUVIAL GRAVEL, OFF-SHORE MINING, RIVER DIGGINGS.

Alluvial Diamond Mining Scheme, program introduced in Sierra Leone in 1956 to reduce illicit mining. The scheme required the Sierra Leone Selection Trust, the major diamond mining company in the country, to assign some of its leases to licensed diggers. The Diamond Corporation Sierra Leone was formed as the official buying organization at the same time.

alluvial digging, see ALLUVIAL MINING.

alluvial gravel, deposit of loose material in which diamonds and/or other gemstones transported by rivers or streams are found. Also called gem gravel. See ALLUVIAL SORTING, ELUVIAL DEPOSIT, FLUVIAL GRAVEL, RIVER DIGGINGS.

alluvial mining, exploitation of mineral deposits which have been transported and concentrated by flowing water. Excavation methods range from low technology techniques such as panning to highly mechanized dredging, hydraulic, or drift mining operations. Also called alluvial digging. See ALLUVIAL DEPOSIT, ALLUVIAL GRAVEL, ELUVIAL DEPOSIT, FLUVIAL GRAVEL, OFF-SHORE MINING, RIVER DIGGINGS.

photo by Patricia Maddison

alluvial mining

alluvial sorting, natural process by which the transportation of gem minerals from their primary source serves to concentrate material that is harder or tougher (and therefore often of higher grade). Alluvial diamond deposits, such as those on the west coasts of Namibia and South Africa, frequently contain a high percentage of gem-quality rough diamonds because inferior material has been broken by the rigors of transportation. See ABRASION, ALLUVIAL DEPOSIT, ALLUVIAL GRAVEL, ELUVIAL DEPOSIT, FLUVIAL GRAVEL, OFF-SHORE MINING, RIVER DIGGINGS.

Almazexport, marketing division of Almazy Rossii-Sakha. Under a contract with De Beers, renewable in 1995, it sells 95 percent of rough material to be exported to the CSO and tenders the other five percent to Western diamantaires in Moscow. Commonly known as Almaz. See ALMAZY ROSSII-SAKHA, SAKHA, YAKUTALMAZ.

Almazjuvelirexport, state export agency of the former Soviet Union for diamonds, platinum group metals, and jewelry; subordinate to the Finance Ministry of the Russian Federation. See ALMAZEXPORT, ALMAZY ROSSII-SAKHA, RUSSAL-MAZZOLOTO.

Almazni Fund, see RUSSIAN DIAMOND FUND.

Almazy Rossii-Sakha (Diamonds of Russia and Sakha), joint stock company formed in October, 1992, owned by the Russian Federation, the Republic of Sakha, member agencies of the company, districts of Sakha, and the Fund for Soldiers. It has replaced Russalmazzoloto and Glavalmazzoloto, and reports to the Governments of both the Republic of Sakha and the Russian Federation. The company operates the diamond mines in Sakha (Yakutia) through Yakutalmaz and the marketing arrangements of its rough diamond production through its Almazexport subsidiary. See ALMAZEXPORT, KRISTALL, ROSKOMDRAGMET, RUSSALMAZZOLOTO, SAKHA, YAKUTALMAZ.

Almazzoloto, see ALMAZY ROSSII-SAKHA.

alpha particle, positively-charged nuclear particle consisting of two protons and two neutrons. Diamonds treated in radioactive salts are colored by naturally-emitted alpha particles and remain slightly radioactive; those treated in a cyclotron do not. See CYCLOTRON-TREATED DIAMOND, IRRADIATED BROWN DIAMOND, IRRADIATED DIAMOND, IRRADIATED GREEN DIAMOND, IRRADIATED ORANGE-YELLOW DIAMOND.

alpha-particle treatment, see ALPHA PARTICLE, CYCLOTRON-TREATED DIAMOND.

alpine diamond, misnomer for pyrite.

Alumag, proprietary name for colorless synthetic spinel. Marketed as a diamond simulant.

Amatite, proprietary name for yttrium aluminum garnet (YAG). Marketed as a diamond simulant.

American brilliant cut, diamond fashioned to proportions and facet angles (as determined by American manufacturers) which yield the maximum brilliance consistent with high dispersion. The proportions of the American brilliant cut approximate those confirmed mathematically by Marcel Tolkowsky in 1919. Also called the American ideal cut, ideal cut, and Tolkowsky theoretical brilliant cut. See BRILLIANT CUT; MORSE, HENRY D.; TOLKOWSKY, MARCEL.

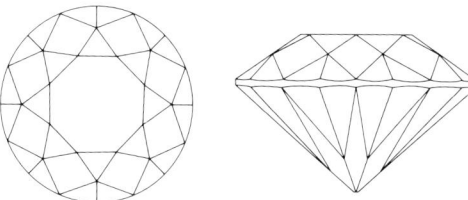

American brilliant cut

American cut, see AMERICAN BRILLIANT CUT.

American diamond, misnomer occasionally used in India for synthetic cubic zirconia (CZ).

American Diamond Industry Association (ADIA), trade organization based in New York City, US, which provides information about diamonds and the American diamond industry to government agencies, educational and financial institutions, print and broadcast media, and consumers.

American Gem Society (AGS), professional society of jewelers in the United States and Canada, founded in 1934 by Robert M. Shipley. AGS awards the titles of Registered Jeweler (RJ), Registered Supplier (RS), Certified Gemologist (CG), and Certified Gemologist Appraiser (CGA) to qualified members and member firms. See AGS CLARITY-GRADING SCALE, AGS COLOR-GRADING SCALE, AGS CUT-GRADING SYSTEM.

American ideal cut, see AMERICAN BRILLIANT CUT.

americium-241, radioactive nuclide occasionally used in its oxide form for the color enhancement of diamonds. See IRRADIATED DIAMOND, NUCLEAR REACTOR, REACTOR-TREATED DIAMOND.

AMICUT, see DIAMINIR, LTD.

amorphous, term describing materials such as glass which have no crystal structure and, therefore, no characteristic external form. See CRYSTAL, CRYSTAL SYSTEM.

Amsterdam, historically important diamond-cutting center in the Netherlands which flourished from the early 1700s until the beginning of World War I. Rising labor costs, the Great Depression in the 1930s, and the Nazi occupation during World War II accelerated its decline. Only a small manufacturing industry remains to service the city's diamond showrooms.

Amsterdam Black Diamond, 33.74 ct. pear-shape diamond with 145 facets; exhibited during Amsterdam's 700th anniversary celebration in 1975. Cut by the Amsterdam firm of D. Drukker from a 55.85 ct. opaque black rough intended originally for industrial use.

Amsterdam Diamond, see AMSTERDAM BLACK DIAMOND.

amygdaloidal diabase, dark-colored, crystalline, igneous rock of medium silica content, in which diamond has been reportedly found in Africa. It is formed by a rate of cooling rapid enough to create cavities (amygdules) yet slow enough to promote crystallization of a fine-grained structure.

Anabar River, site of an alluvial diamond deposit 900 kilometers (560 miles) north of Mirnyi, Republic of Sakha (Yakutia), CIS. Mining operations take place during the three-month summer season; severe low temperatures prevent all outdoor activity during the winter months. See MIRNYI, SAKHA.

Andrada, significant area of alluvial deposits in northeastern Angola near the Zaire border. See LUCAPA, CUANGO.

angle of incidence, the angle, measured from the normal, at which light strikes a surface. See ANGLE OF REFLECTION, ANGLE OF REFRACTION, CRITICAL ANGLE, CRITICAL ANGLE CONE, NORMAL, TOTAL INTERNAL REFLECTION.

angle of reflection, the angle between the normal and a reflected ray of light. The angle of reflection is equal to the angle of incidence. See ANGLE OF INCIDENCE, ANGLE OF REFRACTION, CRITICAL ANGLE, CRITICAL ANGLE CONE, NORMAL, TOTAL INTERNAL REFLECTION.

angle of refraction, the angle inside an optically dense medium between the normal and a light ray that has entered and been refracted. See CRITICAL ANGLE, CRITICAL ANGLE CONE, NORMAL, REFRACTION, REFRACTIVE INDEX (RI), TOTAL INTERNAL REFLECTION.

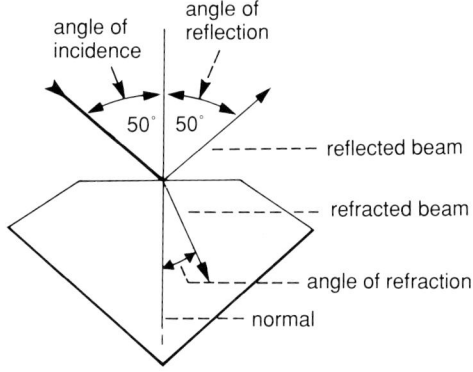

normal, angles of incidence, reflection, and refraction

Anglo American Corporation of South Africa, Ltd., the first registered South African mining finance house; established in 1917 by Ernest Oppenheimer (later Sir), with the original objective of developing the Witwatersrand gold fields. In 1920, Anglo American acquired control of the diamond mines in German South West Africa (Namibia), and ultimately an interest in De Beers. Later, the influence of Anglo American was significant in creating a new diamond marketing syndicate in 1925 and in persuading the larger producers to join De Beers in selling through a new central channel. Anglo American holds an equity interest in De Beers and in other diamond companies, and has widespread interests in agricultural, financial, and industrial concerns throughout South Africa and the rest of the world.

Angola, important diamond-producing country on the west coast of central Africa. There are many alluvial deposits and kimberlitic occurrences in the northeast, in the drainage basin of the Kasai River. The pipes are worked as open pit mines; production is of high quality, but since 1975 mining has been disrupted by civil discord. Mining rights are held by Endiama, the Angolan state diamond company, but illicit mining of alluvial deposits in the southern Cuango region of the Lunda Norte province became widespread in 1991-1992. See ANDRADA, COMPANHIA DE DIAMANTES DE ANGOLA (DIAMANG), CUANGO, EMPRESA NACIONAL DE DIAMANTES DE ANGOLA (ENDIAMA), LUCAPA, SOCIEDADE PORTUGUESA DE EMPREENDIMENTOS (SPE).

angstrom unit, unit of length equal to one ten-millionth of a millimeter, used to measure wavelengths. Abbreviated Å. See NANOMETER (NM).

anisotropic, having the property of splitting a beam of light into two rays, each traveling at different speeds, sometimes along different paths. Also called doubly refractive. Anisotropic minerals contain one or two directions of single refraction called optic axes. See ANOMALOUS DOUBLE REFRACTION (ADR), ISOTROPIC, POLARISCOPE, REFRACTION.

annealing, slow heating of a material to alter the manner in which it absorbs light. Annealing diamond requires temperatures from approximately 200°C to 800°C (392°F to 1,472°F). It changes the green color of reactor-treated or cyclotron-treated diamonds to yellow, orange, or brown. Reheating an annealed diamond with a jeweler's torch can further alter the color. See ABSORPTION SPECTRUM, IRRADIATED DIAMOND.

Annex Kleinzee, important alluvial deposit which is part of the Buffels Marine Complex in South Africa and one of three alluvial mining areas operated by De Beers Consolidated Mines

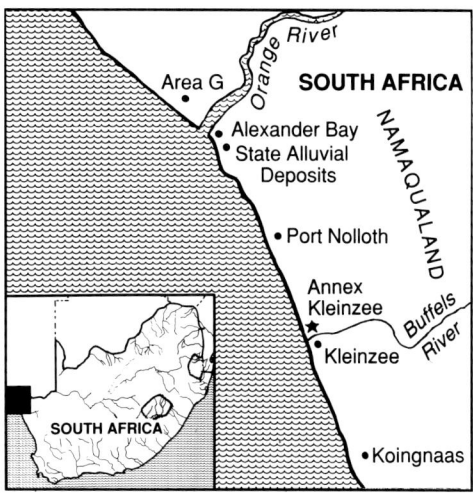

Annex Kleinzee

as part of its Namaqualand Mines Division. See BUFFELS MARINE COMPLEX, KOINGNAAS.

Anniversary Diamond, 200 ct. rough diamond found at the Jagersfontein Mine in South Africa. Cut into a 65 ct. pear shape by Baumgold Brothers of New York in 1951 to commemorate that firm's 75th anniversary. Privately owned.

anniversary ring, multi-stone diamond ring promoted as a wedding anniversary gift. Also called an eternity ring.

anniversary ring

anomalous double refraction (ADR), doubly refractive effect in a singly refractive gemstone, the result of strain caused by inclusions or structural irregularities within the stone. Also called strain double refraction or strain birefringence. ADR is seen as an irregular or patchy extinction and/or as interference colors when the stone is rotated under a polariscope in the dark position. In diamond, ADR may indicate a level of strain great enough to require special care in polishing, setting, repairing, or wearing the stone. See ANISOTROPIC, INTERNAL STRAIN, ISOTROPIC, REFRACTION.

antique cushion brilliant, traditional term for a generally rectangular or squarish stone, with slightly curved sides, rounded corners, and brilliant-cut facets. Also called cushion antique brilliant. The GIA GTL term for these cuts is cushion. See OLD MINE CUT.

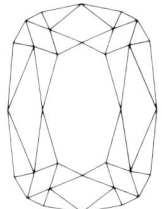 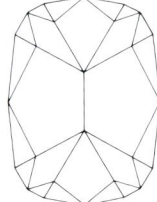

antique cushion brilliant

Anton Dunkels' Diamonds, necklace composed of large fancy-color and black diamond drops and named for the early South African diamond merchant Anton Dunkelsbühler. Current whereabouts unknown. See DUNKELSBUHLER, ANTON.

Antwerp, city in Belgium which has been a leading diamond trading and manufacturing center since the mid-fifteenth century, when trade routes from India via Venice and Lisbon were established. Currently the world's leading distributor of gem rough, polished diamonds, and natural industrial diamonds, it has four diamond bourses, including the Diamantclub van Antwerpen, which began trading in 1893. Antwerp is noted for the polishing of large diamonds and those that require particular skills, such as macles and fancy cuts. See BOMBAY, NEW YORK, TEL AVIV.

Antwerp qualities, term used to describe rough goods, such as cleavages, macles, flats, and coated crystals, the fashioning of which requires particular skills. Such goods are typical of those handled by the Belgian diamond industry. Also known as Antwerp goods.

Antwerp rose cut, rose cut developed in Antwerp around 1880, with a hexagonal girdle outline, a flat base, a pointed crown, and six trapezoidal facets outside six triangular facets. Also called Brabant rose cut.

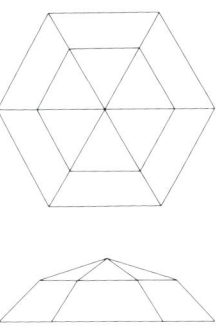

Antwerp rose cut

Antwerpsche Diamantkring C.V., Antwerp Diamond Circle. Established in 1930, it is one of four Belgian diamond bourses and a member of the World Federation of Diamond Bourses. See BOURSE, WORLD FEDERATION OF DIAMOND BOURSES (WFDB).

aplanatic lens, compound lens made up of two or more elements with different curvatures, to eliminate spherical aberration. See SPHERICAL ABERRATION.

application, request for specific quantities and categories of rough goods submitted to the Central Selling Organisation by sightholders through their CSO brokers three weeks before a sight. See ALLOCATION.

appraisal, evaluation of diamonds or other jewelry, usually for insurance or estate purposes. Appraisals normally provide a detailed description of the pieces being appraised, including the exact measurements of the important gem-

Antwerp

stones, together with their color and clarity grades, plots showing the location of inclusions or blemishes, and information on the proportions and make; they then state an estimated value.

Apukan River, river in the Danau Seran area of southeastern Kalimantan, Indonesia, which is a regional source of alluvial diamonds.

Arabian diamond, misnomer for frosted pebbles of colorless quartz found in Saudi Arabia, faceted in Thailand, and sold in Saudi Arabia. Also called Quisumah diamond, Quasuma diamond and Khasumi diamond. In early texts (e.g. Pliny), it is thought to refer to genuine diamonds.

Arabian Magic Diamond, proprietary name for colorless or yellow synthetic sapphire. Marketed as a diamond simulant.

Archduke Joseph Diamond, 78.54 ct., reportedly fine-color, slightly included, elongated cushion shape mixed-cut diamond believed to have been discovered in Golconda, India, and to have once belonged to Archduke Joseph of Austria. Offered at auction by Sotheby's in London in 1961, but withdrawn. Current whereabouts unknown.

Archduke Maximillian of Austria (1459-1519), considered the originator of the tradition of the diamond engagement ring, by having one made for his fiancée, Mary of Burgundy, daughter of Charles the Bold. A copy of the ring is in the Kunsthistorische Museum in Vienna.

Arcot Diamonds, two of five diamonds given by the Nawab Azim-ub-duala of Arcot, India, to Queen Charlotte of England (consort of King George III) in 1777. The two pear shapes (one weighing 33.70 ct., the other 23.65 ct.) were first set in earrings; after the queen's death in 1818, her son, George IV, had them set in his crown. In 1837 they were bought by the Duke of Westminster and set in a tiara with 1,421 smaller diamonds and the 32.20 ct. round brilliant King George IV Diamond. The tiara was purchased by Harry Winston in 1959, and the larger of the two Arcots was recut to 31.01 ct. (reportedly flawless), the smaller to 18.85 ct. They were sold separately in 1959 and 1960. See KING GEORGE IV DIAMOND.

Ardo Mine, narrow, almost vertical kimberlite fissure in Barkly West, South Africa. Diamonds are recovered by overhand shrinkage. See OVERHAND SHRINKAGE.

Areas C (Chameis), G (Gemsbok), H (Affenrücken), K (Kerbehuk), M (Mittag), and U (Uubvley), historic names for five important alluvial mining areas along the Namibian coast between Oranjemund and Lüderitz. Operated by CDM.

AREDOR, see ASSOCIATION POUR LA RECHERCHE ET L'EXPLOITATION DU DIAMANT ET DE L'OR.

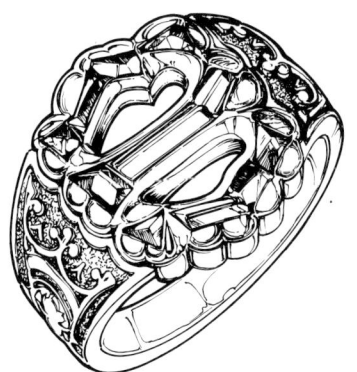

A copy of the first diamond engagement ring

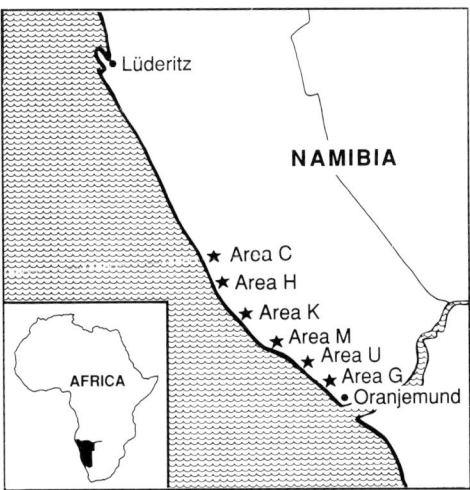

Areas C, G, H, K, M, and U

AREDOR Diamond, 181.77 ct. rough diamond found at the AREDOR Mine in 1988. Current whereabouts unknown.

AREDOR Holdings, Guinean company owned by the partners in the AREDOR Mine and Industrial Diamond Company; the company operates AREDOR Sales as a wholly-owned subsidiary.

AREDOR Mine, large alluvial diamond deposit in Guinea, near that nation's borders with Sierra Leone and Liberia. Jointly owned by Bridge Oil of Australia, Industrial Diamond Co. of London, Simonius Vischer (a Swiss commodities firm) and the Guinean government. The AREDOR mine has produced some very large stones, including the 181.77 ct. AREDOR Diamond, found in 1988, and a 255.61 ct. rough which was found in 1986 and later fashioned into the Guinea Star. A 192.9 ct. gem-quality diamond was found in May, 1991; it was the fifth gem diamond over 100 ct. produced by the mine since 1986. See AREDOR DIAMOND, GUINEA STAR.

AREDOR Mine

AREDOR Sales (Pty.), Ltd., wholly-owned subsidiary of AREDOR Holdings. The company is managed by Industrial Diamond Company, which also owns part of AREDOR Holdings.

Argyle Diamond Mines, mining complex 2,400 kilometers (1,500 miles) north of Perth and 160 kilometers (100 miles) southeast of Kununurra (the nearest town) in Western Australia's Kimberley Mountains. It includes the AK1 Pipe, a diamond-bearing lamproite, and alluvial deposits along Upper Smoke and Limestone creeks. The mines produce some gem diamonds, including some pinks, and a high percentage of brown and industrial stones. See AK1 PIPE; ARGYLE DIAMOND MINES JOINT VENTURE; ARGYLE DIAMOND MINES (PTY.), LTD.; ARGYLE DIAMOND SALES, LTD.; ASHTON EXPLORATION JOINT VENTURE; AUSTRALIA; LAMPROITE.

photo courtesy of Argyle Diamond Mines (Pty.), Ltd.

Argyle Diamond Mines

Argyle Diamond Mines Joint Venture, established in 1982 by CRA Exploration, Ashton Mining, and Northern Mining Corporation to develop and mine properties in the Argyle and Ellendale regions of Western Australia; commercial production of alluvial diamonds began in January, 1983. Managed by Argyle Diamond Mines. See ARGYLE DIAMOND MINES, ASHTON EXPLORATION JOINT VENTURE.

Argyle Diamond Mines (Pty.), Ltd. (ADM), company owned by CRA Exploration, Ashton Mining, Tanaust, and Northern Mining Company, which manages the Argyle Diamond Mines Joint Venture in Western Australia.

Argyle Diamond Sales, Ltd., organization established in 1981 which markets the production of the Argyle Diamond Mines. Owned by CRA Exploration and Ashton Mining. The company has overseas offices in Antwerp and Bombay.

Argyle Kimberlite Number 1, see AK1 PIPE (ARGYLE).

Argyle Pink Library Egg, objet d'art set with approximately 20,000 diamonds. The egg, which was manufactured in 1990, is 70 centimeters (28 inches) high and contains 15 kilograms (33 pounds) of gold and 348 carats of pink diamonds. Doors open to reveal a miniature library and portrait gallery.

Arkansas, state in the United States, and a minor source of diamonds since a lamproite pipe was discovered in 1906 near the town of Murfreesboro. A total of four pipes has been found; while commercial mining has been attempted from time to time, it has not proven profitable to date. The principal pipe is open to the public as the Crater of Diamonds State Park. See STAR OF MURFREESBORO DIAMOND, UNCLE SAM DIAMOND.

Arkansas diamond, misnomer for colorless quartz from the state of Arkansas, US.

Arkansas Herkimer diamond, misnomer for colorless quartz from upstate New York, US. See HERKIMER DIAMOND.

Arkhangelsk, northern oblast (province) on the White Sea in the Russian Federation, CIS, where numerous diamondiferous kimberlites were discovered in 1980. The area is known to contain rich diamond deposits. Also spelled Arkhangel or Arkhangel'sk.

Argyle Pink Library Egg

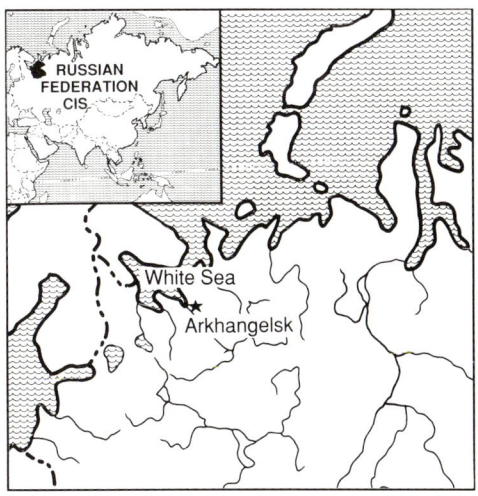

Arkhangelsk

artificial coloration, color produced in a diamond by any of several enhancement processes. See ANNEALING, COATED DIAMOND, CYCLOTRON-

TREATED DIAMOND, IRRADIATED DIAMOND, RADIUM-TREATED DIAMOND, REACTOR-TREATED DIAMOND.

artificial gem, see DIAMOND SIMULANT, SYNTHETIC DIAMOND.

ASEA, see ALLMANA SVENSKA ELEKTRISKA AKTIEBOLAGET.

Ashberg Diamond, 102.50 ct. square antique modified brilliant-cut diamond, described as fancy light yellow, and believed to have once been part of the Russian Crown Jewels. In 1934 it was sold by a Russian Trade Delegation to the Swedish banker for whom it is named. In 1959, it was offered for sale by the Swedish auction house Bukowskis, withdrawn, and later sold privately. Offered for sale by Christie's in Geneva in 1981, but again withdrawn. Current whereabouts unknown.

Ashberg Diamond

Ashton Exploration Joint Venture, consortium of CRA Exploration, Ashton Mining, and Northern Mining Corporation, formed in 1976 to prospect for diamonds in Australia. Discovered the diamond pipes at Ellendale in 1978, and alluvial deposits and a lamproite pipe south of Lake Argyle in 1979. Reorganized as Argyle Diamond Mines Joint Venture in 1982, it continues to prospect for diamonds in the Kimberley Mountains region. See ARGYLE DIAMOND MINES.

Ashton Mining, Ltd., mining company which has an interest in the Argyle Diamond Mines in Western Australia; it also conducts international prospecting efforts. See ASHTON EXPLORATION JOINT VENTURE.

Asscher, Isaac Joseph (1843-1902), master cutter and founder of the firm of I.J. Asscher in Amsterdam in 1854. The company was renamed Asscher Diamant Maatschappij (Asscher Diamond Company) in 1936; it became the Koninklijke Asscher Diamant Maatschappij (Royal Asscher Diamond Company) in 1980. See ROYAL ASSCHER DIAMOND COMPANY.

Asscher, Joseph (1871-1937), eldest son of Isaac Joseph Asscher. A noted diamond cleaver, Joseph Asscher cleaved the 3,106 ct. Cullinan Diamond in 1908. With his brother Abraham, he co-founded the Asscher Diamond Company, the successor to I.J. Asscher Company, in 1936. See ROYAL ASSCHER DIAMOND COMPANY.

Asscher cut, early emerald cut with very wide corners, a high crown, and a deep pavilion. See ROYAL ASSCHER DIAMOND COMPANY.

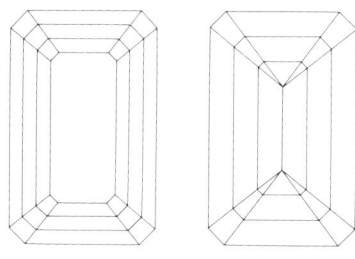

Asscher cut

Asscher Diamant Maatschappij, see ROYAL ASSCHER DIAMOND COMPANY.

Asscher Diamond Company, see ROYAL ASSCHER DIAMOND COMPANY.

assembled stone, gem made from two or more separate stones, usually to imitate other gemstones such as diamond. Stones are sometimes assembled for other reasons, such as reinforcing fragile material like opal. See DOUBLET, TRIPLET.

Association pour la Récherche et l'Exploitation du Diamant et de l'Or (AREDOR), organization established in 1981 to prospect and mine for diamonds and gold in Guinea, and the operator of the only large diamond-mining concession in that country.

Astor Sancy Diamond, see SANCY DIAMOND.

Astryl, proprietary name for synthetic rutile. Marketed as a diamond simulant.

Atherstone, William Guybon (1813-1898), South African surgeon and amateur mineralogist who authenticated the diamond now known as the Eureka in 1867. See EUREKA DIAMOND.

atomic bonding, the holding together of atoms by atomic forces. See COVALENT BONDING, IONIC BONDING.

atomic pile, see NUCLEAR REACTOR.

atomic reactor, see NUCLEAR REACTOR.

attrition milling, process of reducing diamond ores or gravels by passing them through rotating drums filled with water and pebbles or steel balls. Also called ball milling.

Auchas, small mine on the Orange River in Namibia, 50 kilometers (31 miles) upstream from Oranjemund. Developed by CDM, the mine is a modest producer of high quality gem diamonds.

Auckland Diamond, 36 ct. diamond, a model of which was displayed at the London Exhibition of 1851. Believed to have been named for Lord George Eden Auckland (1784-1849), Governor General of India from 1836 to 1842. Its weight and description are identical to the Holland Diamond, making it likely the two are the same.

audio conduction detector, testing device used to determine whether or not a diamond conducts electricity. When two probes are placed on an electrically conductive diamond (*e.g.,* Type IIb diamond, a known electrical semiconductor), the circuit is completed and, with appropriate amplification, a scratching sound is heard. When the diamond being tested is not electrically conductive, there is no audible reaction. See BLUE DIAMOND, CONDUCTOMETER, ELECTRICAL CONDUCTIVITY, IRRADIATED BLUE DIAMOND.

auger drill, industrial drill rig used to bore through overburden when exploring for alluvial diamond deposits. Auger drill bits can be as large as 1.5 meters (4.9 feet) in diameter.

Aurora collection, group of 244 colored diamonds assembled over eight years in the 1980s by diamond dealer Alan Bronstein. Named after the Aurora Borealis, the collection is on indefinite loan to the American Museum of Natural History, New York, US.

Australia, continent in the southern hemisphere, southeast of Asia; currently the world's major producer of diamonds by weight. Alluvial diamonds were discovered in New South Wales in 1851, but production was sporadic and the deposits were largely worked out by the early 1920s. Exploration by Oilmin yielded nine alluvial diamonds along the Lennard River in Western Australia between 1967-1971, but the company abandoned its efforts. In 1976, alluvial deposits were discovered along Limestone Creek and Smoke Creek near Lake Argyle in the Kimberley region of Western Australia by CRA Exploration; in 1978, diamond-bearing pipes were discovered at Ellendale. Then, in 1979, the Argyle Kimberlite Number 1 pipe (AK1) was discovered. Exploration continues in western and northern Australia and New South Wales. Most of the Australian production is industrial quality, but a small number of the gem-quality stones are fancy colors such as pinks and reddish purples. See AK1 PIPE (ARGYLE), ARGYLE DIAMOND MINES, ASHTON EXPLORATION JOINT VENTURE, BOW RIVER MINE, MOUNT ROSS, WESTERN AUSTRALIA.

Australian Diamond Exploration Joint Venture (ADEX), diamond exploration company managed by Ashton Mining, its largest shareholder; ADEX reports having found microscopic diamonds in Australia's Northern Territory and in western Queensland. See ASHTON MINING, LTD.

Austrian Diamond, see FLORENTINE DIAMOND.

Austrian Yellow Diamond, see FLORENTINE DIAMOND.

automatic blocking machine, machine used to place the table, the first four facets on the top, and four facets on the bottom of a diamond prior to polishing.

automatic bruting machine, machine used to shape the girdle outline of round brilliants to preset diameters. Some models feature a magazine in which a number of pre-centered diamonds can be loaded into dops and bruted in sequence. See BRUTING.

automatic cutting machine, see AUTOMATIC POLISHING MACHINE.

automatic dop, mechanical stone holder on a polishing machine which indexes its position semi-automatically to polish different facets of a diamond. See AUTOMATIC POLISHING MACHINE, SEMI-AUTOMATIC DOP.

automatic polishing machine, device designed to facet round brilliants automatically, in sizes from 10 points (0.1 ct.) up. The machine can block (although an automatic blocking machine is often used for this purpose), cross-work, and brilliandeer, leaving only the eight star facets and the table to be polished manually. See AUTOMATIC BLOCKING MACHINE, AUTOMATIC BRUTING MACHINE, AUTOMATIC DOP, BRUTING, FASHIONING, POLISHING.

autoradiograph, image made when a radioactive stone is placed on an unexposed sheet of photographic film. Exposure times from 30 minutes up to 24 hours are required.

autoradiography, the process of creating an autoradiograph.

average girdle diameter, value achieved by adding the largest and smallest girdle measurements of a round brilliant and dividing by two.

Ayer, N.W. and Son, see N.W. AYER AND SON.

B

Babe, Jerome L., nineteenth century American rifle salesman and one-time reporter for the *New York World* who went to South Africa as a prospector and invented a dry sifter called the "baby" (also "Yankee baby" or "baby rocker"). He also wrote *The South African Diamond Fields*, published in 1872.

baby, dry sifter used to sort diamond-bearing gravel into large, medium (called middlings), and fine sizes. Invented by Jerome L. Babe, it is still used in small, under-capitalized dry diggings. Also called the Yankee baby, baby rocker, and babe. See JIG, PANNING, TROMMEL.

Baby Rose Diamond, see PREMIER ROSE DIAMOND.

backing, application of foil, metallic paint, or other reflective material to the pavilion or back of a diamond to enhance its appearance. See ENHANCEMENT, FOILBACK.

Baden Solitaire Diamond, 30 ct. diamond set in the clasp of a necklace containing 114 pear-shape diamonds. The necklace, which once belonged to the Hapsburgs, was taken to Switzerland in 1918; it is then believed to have been stolen and taken to South America. Current whereabouts unknown.

Baffa diamond, misnomer for rock crystal quartz. Variously thought to be from Scotland or the island of Cyprus.

Bagagem, diamond-producing region southwest of Diamantina, Minas Gerais, Brazil. It produced the 261.24 ct. Star of the South and a number of other large diamonds. See STAR OF THE SOUTH DIAMOND.

Bagillion cut, proprietary name for a rectangular baguette with a brilliant-cut pavilion. Marketed by World Fancies.

Bagagem

bagshot diamond, misnomer for angular pieces of quartz crystals from Great Britain, commonly used in jewelry in the late eighteenth century.

baguette, small, usually rectangular to square step-cut diamond; sometimes tapered. French, meaning *rod*.

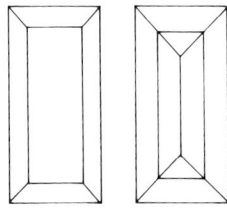

baguette

Bahia, state in Brazil; diamonds were discovered there in the mid-eighteenth century. Noted for an abundance of carbonado and for poor color gem diamonds, the region is still being prospected.

bahias, diamonds of inferior color; named for the quality of stones typically found in the Bahia region of Brazil.

Bakwanga, see MBUJI-MAYI.

balance, see CHAIN BALANCE, COUNTERWEIGHT BALANCE, DIAMOND BALANCE, ELECTRONIC BAL-

ANCE, MECHANICAL BALANCE, PORTABLE BALANCE, RIDER BALANCE, SINGLE-PAN BALANCE.

Bal de Feu, proprietary name for synthetic strontium titanate, which is sometimes marketed as a diamond simulant.

Ball, Sydney H. (1878-1949), American geologist and mining engineer. Ball was consulting engineer for Forminière and directed technical operations on the expedition that found the first diamonds in Zaire. Author of numerous papers on geology and mineralogy, and *A Roman Book on Precious Stones*, an updated version of Chapter 37 of Pliny's *Natural History*. See SOCIETE FORESTIERE ET MINIERE DU CONGO.

Ball, Valentine (1843-1895), authority on economic geology, and on the occurrence and distribution of diamonds in India. Helped translate *Les Six Voyages de Jean-Baptiste Tavernier* into English. See TAVERNIER, JEAN-BAPTISTE.

ballas, very hard, natural polycrystalline industrial diamond made up of spherical masses of minute, intergrown diamond crystals arranged concentrically. Also called round bort, spherical bort, and shot bort. See BORT, CARBONADO, CRUSHING BORT, FRAMESITE, HAILSTONE BORT, STEWARTITE.

ballerina setting, mounting in which a center stone is surrounded by baguettes set side-by-side in a pattern suggesting a ballerina's tutu.

ball milling, see ATTRITION MILLING.

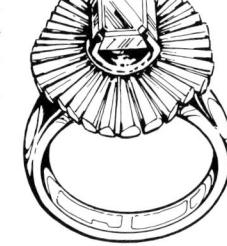

ballerina setting

Banian Diamond, 48.50 ct. diamond bought by Tavernier in India in the mid-seventeenth century and sold to an unnamed Dutch sea captain. Current whereabouts unknown.

Banjarmasin, capital city of the state of Kalimantan, Indonesia. Located near the principal diamond deposits on the island of Borneo. See BORNEO, INDONESIA.

Banjarmasin Diamond, originally a 70 ct. diamond octahedron (first thought to weigh 77 ct.). Reported to belong to the Sultan of Banjarmasin (a kingdom on the island of Borneo) in 1836, it was taken to the Netherlands when the sultanate became a Dutch colony in 1859. It was cut into a 40 ct. squarish brilliant and offered for sale after being refused by the Museum of Natural History in Leiden. There were no buyers and the stone was given to the Rijksmuseum in Amsterdam. See KALIMANTAN.

bantam, term used by prospectors in the Vaal River diggings for banded ironstone pebbles; they considered them a good indication that diamonds might be present. Also spelled bandom, bandoom.

Bantam Diamond, diamond of unknown weight and color shown to Tavernier in Java in 1648 by the Rajah of Bantam (it was set in the hilt of the Rajah's dagger). It is thought the Bantam may be the Auckland or Holland Diamond. Current whereabouts unknown. See AUCKLAND DIAMOND, HOLLAND DIAMOND.

Banya Irang, area in the Danau Seran swamp of southeastern Kalimantan, Indonesia, and a regionally important source of alluvial diamonds.

Barion cut, square mixed cut of 62 facets, with a step-cut crown and a modified brilliant-cut pavilion (the Barion emerald cut has 70 facets). Designed in 1971 by Johannesburg master cutter Basil Watermeyer to add brilliance to a step cut and to gain greater weight, or yield, from the rough stone. The name combines Watermeyer's given name with that of his wife, Marion. The cut was patented but the name was not trademarked. See YIELD.

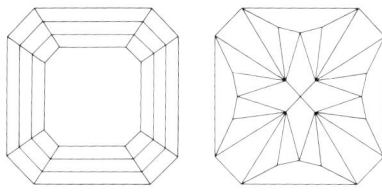

Barion cut

Barkly Mine, small, narrow, almost vertical kimberlite fissure near Barkly West, South Africa. Diamonds are recovered by overhand shrinkage. See OVERHAND SHRINKAGE.

Barkly West, town near the Vaal River, Cape Province, South Africa, the site of numerous alluvial diamond diggings. Originally called Klipdrift, renamed for Sir Henry Barkly (1815-1898), Governor of the Cape Colony (later Province) in 1870.

Barkly West

Barnato, Barney (born Barnett Isaacs, 1852-1897), English entrepreneur who went to South Africa in 1873; with his elder brother, Harry, he formed Barnato Brothers in 1875 and the Barnato Diamond Mining Company in 1880. At one time, Barnato controlled the Kimberley Central Diamond Mining Company; in 1888 he consolidated his holdings with De Beers Consolidated Mines. A life governor of De Beers, Barnato expanded his interests into gold mining in the Transvaal Republic, and formed the Johannesburg Consolidated Investment Company ('Johnnies'), an important mining finance company. See BARNATO BROTHERS; BARNATO, HARRY; BARNATO DIAMOND MINING COMPANY, LTD.; BEIT, ALFRED; COMPAGNIE FRANCAISE DES MINES DE DIAMANT DU CAP DE BONNE ESPERANCE; KIMBERLEY CENTRAL DIAMOND MINING COMPANY.

Barney Barnato

Barnato, Harry (born Henry Isaacs, 1850-1908), elder brother of Barney Barnato, and associated with him in Barnato Brothers and the Barnato Diamond Mining Company. See BARNATO, BARNEY; BARNATO BROTHERS; BARNATO DIAMOND MINING COMPANY, LTD.; COMPAGNIE FRANCAISE DES MINES DE DIAMANT DU CAP DE BONNE ESPERANCE; KIMBERLEY CENTRAL DIAMOND MINING COMPANY.

Barnato Brothers, South African firm of diamond dealers and mining property owners formed in 1875 by Barney and Harry Barnato. The company eventually expanded into gold mining, real estate, and investments, and, as a member of the first London Diamond Syndicate, bought 20 percent of the output of De Beers Consolidated Mines. In 1911 the company acquired control of the Premier Mine, which it sold to De Beers Consolidated Mines in 1917. During the 1920s, Barnato Brothers joined with Anglo American to buy the production of mines in Angola, the Congo, and what is now West Africa. See BARNATO, BARNEY; BARNATO DIAMOND MINING COMPANY, LTD.; COMPAGNIE FRANCAISE DES MINES DE DIAMANT DU CAP DE BONNE ESPERANCE; KIMBERLEY CENTRAL DIAMOND MINING COMPANY; OPPENHEIMER, SIR ERNEST; RHODES, CECIL JOHN.

Barnato Diamond Mining Company, Ltd., company founded by the Barnato brothers in 1880, which later merged with the Kimberley Central, then the largest holding in the Kimberley Mine. When the Barnato Brothers and Cecil Rhodes formed De Beers Consolidated Mines, they liquidated the Kimberley Central and bought the Kimberley Mine. See BARNATO, BARNEY; COMPAGNIE FRANCAISE DES MINES DE DIAMANT DU CAP DE BONNE ESPERANCE; KIMBERLEY CENTRAL DIAMOND MINING COMPANY; OPPENHEIMER, SIR ERNEST; RHODES, CECIL JOHN.

Baroda gem, proprietary name for a glass foilback. Marketed as a diamond simulant.

Baroness Cut, proprietary name for a 65-facet octagonal fancy shape derived from the oval; developed by the Israeli firm of Raphaeli-Stschik to make the most of flat or misshapen rough. See DUCHESS CUT, EMPRESS CUT, GRACE CUT, ROYAL CUTS.

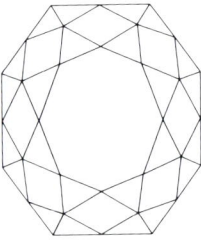
Baroness Cut

Bas-Congo-Katanga Railway Company (BCK), see COMPAGNIE DU CHEMIN DE FER DU BAS-CONGO-KATANGA (BCK).

base, see PAVILION.

bast, frosted rough diamond. Dutch, meaning *bark*.

bastard diamond, misnomer for rock crystal quartz from Great Britain; used in jewelry between 1770 and 1800.

Basutoland, see LESOTHO.

Basutoland Diamond Corporation, company which held exclusive mining rights in Lesotho (formerly Basutoland) in 1956, a forerunner to the De Beers Lesotho Mining Company.

Battershill Diamond, 65 ct. rough diamond found at the Williamson Diamond Mine, Mwadui, Tanganyika (Tanzania), in 1945. Named for William Battershill, Governor of what was then Tanganyika. Current whereabouts unknown. See WILLIAMSON DIAMOND MINE.

Baumgold Brilliant Diamond, 52 ct. round, reportedly colorless brilliant with a polished girdle. Recut from a 55 ct. round which had originally been fashioned from a South African rough weighing 167.25 ct. Privately owned.

Baumgold Pear Diamonds, two pear-shape diamonds, each weighing approximately 50 ct., cut from the Baumgold Rough Diamond. Current whereabouts unknown. See BAUMGOLD ROUGH DIAMOND.

Baumgold Rough Diamond, 609.25 ct. rough diamond, reportedly bluish, found in 1922 at the Wesselton Mine in South Africa. Cut by the New York firm of Baumgold Brothers into 14 stones, including the Baumgold Pear Diamonds. The current whereabouts of all 14 are unknown.

Bazu Diamond, rough diamond purchased by Tavernier from India's Kollur Mines in the seventeenth century. Reportedly cleaved into a number of smaller stones in the Netherlands.

BCK, abbreviation for the Bas-Congo-Katanga Railroad Company. See COMPAGNIE DU CHEMIN DE FER DU BAS-CONGO-KATANGA (BCK).

beach mining, extraction of diamonds from the section of a beach left uncovered between high and low tides. Sand is pushed seaward as much as 200 meters (656 feet) to form a seawall while diamond-bearing gravel and conglomerate is broken up and removed from behind the wall. The final cleaning of potholes in the bedrock is often done by hand. Also called foreshore mining. See DE BEERS MARINE (PTY.), LTD.; OFFSHORE MINING.

bead cut, roughly spherical double rose cut.

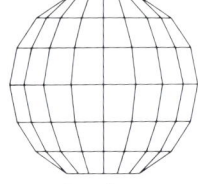
bead cut

beard, see BEARDED GIRDLE.

bearded girdle, fuzzy- or feathered-looking girdle; the effect is caused by numerous hair-like feathers extending from the girdle a short dis-

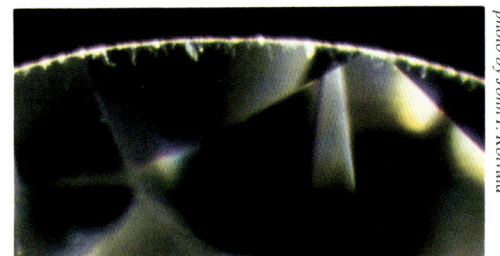
bearded girdle

tance into the stone. Usually the result of bruting too quickly, or with too much force. See BRUTING.

Beaumont Diamond, 273 ct. rough diamond found near Windsorton, South Africa. Sold to Bernard Oppenheimer, eldest brother of Ernest Oppenheimer. Current whereabouts unknown.

Beau Sancy Diamond, see LITTLE SANCY DIAMOND.

Bécéka, French transcription of BCK. See COMPAGNIE DU CHEMIN DE FER DU BAS-CONGO-KATANGA (BCK).

Bechuanaland, see BOTSWANA, REPUBLIC OF.

bedrock, solid rock underlying soil or alluvia such as sands and gravels.

Beit, Alfred (1853-1906), diamond dealer and financier; advisor and close friend to Cecil Rhodes, Beit was one of the original directors, and a life governor, of De Beers Consolidated Mines. It was through Beit's introduction to the Rothschild family of London that Rhodes obtained the capital to buy the Compagnie Française des Mines de Diamant du Cap de Bonne Espérance, thus enabling De Beers to gain control of the Kimberley Mine.

Belgian box, Central Selling Organisation allocation of rough diamonds to Belgian sightholding dealers, intended for resale in smaller quantities to local manufacturers, but part of which is often sold abroad. See ALLOCATION.

Belgian Congo, see ZAIRE.

Bellsbank, kimberlite deposit consisting of two mineable fissures (Bobbejaan and Bellsbank) near Barkly West, Cape Province, South Africa. Diamonds are recovered by overhand shrinkage; tailings from earlier operations are being treated by the Trans Hex Group.

Bellsbank Mine, narrow, almost vertical kimberlite fissure near Barkly West, Cape Province, South Africa. Diamonds are recovered by overhand shrinkage. See OVERHAND SHRINKAGE.

belly, (1) slightly curving center of the long side of a marquise, oval, or pear-shape diamond. (2) vertical section of a fancy cut when seen in profile.

bench, wide, stepped terrace in the wall of an open pit mine to prevent the sides from caving in. Benches diminish in diameter as they descend to the lower levels; a ramp for trucks spirals down through the benches to permit ore to be removed from the pit. See PIPE MINING.

bench

bench mining, see OPEN BENCH MINING.

bench placer, gravel bed on the side of a valley above a stream. These beds represent one of the stream's previous banks when the water level was higher; historically, they have often proved to be rich alluvial deposits.

Benedito Valadares Diamonds, three emerald-cut diamonds, all fashioned from a 108.25 ct. rough found in 1940 in the Corrego River, Minas Gerais, Brazil. The Benedito Valadares Diamond I is 30 ct.; II is 20 ct.; and III is 8 ct. (although some sources list it as 6 ct.). Current whereabouts of all three are unknown.

Benoto drill, proprietary coring device used to sample the mineral content of a prospective mine site. It consists of a steel caisson which is sunk to depths of as much as 30.5 meters (100 feet); the sample is pulled up through the center. Originally used for beach prospecting.

Berbice River, source of alluvial diamonds in eastern Guyana, South America.

Berquem, Louis de, see VAN BERCKEN, LODEWYK.

Berquen, Louis de, see VAN BERCKEN, LODEWYK.

Berquen, Robert de, seventeenth century Parisian jeweler who wrote *Marvels of Western and Eastern India* in 1661. Neither his claim to be descended from Lodewyk Van Bercken (whom he identified as Louis de Berquem) nor his suggestion that Van Bercken invented diamond polishing is true.

beta particle, high energy electron derived from the decay of radioactive atoms. Can be used to irradiate diamonds but, due to absorption, only the surface color is altered. See RADIUM-TREATED DIAMOND.

Beurs voor Diamanthandel NV, diamond bourse established in Antwerp in 1904; member of the World Federation of Diamond Bourses. See BOURSE, WORLD FEDERATION OF DIAMOND BOURSES (WFDB).

bevel cut, simple step cut with a large table joined to the girdle by one or two bevels; also called a table cut. The bottom may be cut like the top; in this case it is called a double bevel cut. When used to cover miniatures set in jewelry, it is called a portrait stone or lasque.

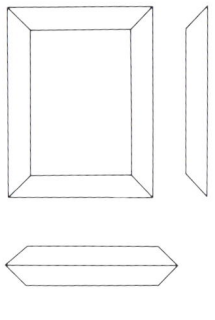
bevel cut

bezel, (1) inclined surface on the crown of a round brilliant between the table and the girdle. (2) polisher's term for the four facets between the top corner facets. (3) the setting edge, that part of the crown just above the girdle which is gripped by prongs or a bezel mounting. (4) thin strip of metal encircling a stone to secure it in a mounting; used frequently for cabochons, occasionally for faceted diamonds.

bezel-angle gauge, see DIAMOND-ANGLE GAUGE.

bezel facet, any of the eight large, four-sided, kite-shaped facets on the crown of a round brilliant-cut diamond. Modified brilliant cuts may

bezel facets

have more than eight bezel facets. Also called top main facets.

bezel-main facet, see BEZEL FACET.

Bhavnagar, Indian city 400 kilometers (249 miles) northwest of Bombay and a major diamond-manufacturing center. Originally noted for polishing small single cuts, the city now produces a range of tapered and baguette cuts. See INDIA.

Bicker-Carteen Diamond, 56 ct. reportedly colorless diamond believed to have been purchased by one of the Aga Khan's sons in 1958. Current whereabouts unknown.

bicycle tire, industry slang for a very thick girdle on a round brilliant.

Big Hole, open pit at the site of the now-closed Kimberley Mine. The Open Mine Museum is nearby. See KIMBERLEY MINE.

Big Hole

Big Rose Diamond, see PREMIER ROSE DIAMOND.

Bingara, historical diamond-producing area in the state of New South Wales, Australia; prospecting continues today.

Bin Hai Mine, large kimberlite mine in the People's Republic of China. Located near Fu Xian, Liaoning Province, the mine works a kimberlite pipe and its associated alluvials; it is reported to have produced a number of stones above 10 ct., including the 60.6 ct. Fenggu No.1 diamond. See WAFANGDIAN MINE.

binocular head loupe, see HEAD MAGNIFIER.

binocular microscope, complex magnifier equipped with two ocular elements to provide a three-dimensional image. See MICROSCOPE, MONOCULAR MICROSCOPE.

birefringence, strength of double refraction, determined by the difference between the highest and lowest refractive indices (RI). Although diamond is singly refractive, it usually shows anomalous birefringence due to strain. Specialists believe that all regular rough crystals, such as octahedrons, show birefringence in the center. See ANOMALOUS DOUBLE REFRACTION (ADR).

Birim River, site of alluvial diamond deposits in Ghana. Stretching approximately 70 kilometers (44 miles) along the river, the deposits, which have been worked for many years, include the Birim Diamond Field and the Akwatia concession. See GHANA.

Birim River

birthstone, gemstone usually associated with a particular month. Diamond is the birthstone for April. There are also birthstones for days, hours, seasons, and the signs of the zodiac.

bishop's head, either of the pieces produced when an octahedron is sawn off-center to make two stones of unequal sizes.

black diamond, (1) very dark gray, blue, brown, or green diamond, or one which appears black or opaque due to numerous submicroscopic inclusions (often graphite) which block all, or nearly all, transmission of light. Black diamonds may have transparent colorless to grayish areas alternating with opaque areas. Color can be modified by blue, brown, gray, green, olive, or purple. Such stones may show mottled strong blue fluorescence under longwave ultraviolet radiation, chalky greenish fluorescence under shortwave ultraviolet. Black diamonds typically show no absorption spectrum. When the color is caused by inclusions, the surface is often pitted and fissured and has an almost metallic appearance; they are very difficult to polish. (2) carbonado. (3) misnomer for faceted hematite or anthracite coal.

Black Diamond of Bahia, 350 ct. black diamond found in Bahia, Brazil. Shown at the Crystal Palace Exhibition in London in 1851. Current whereabouts unknown.

blackened culet, culet to which a spot of black paint or pitch has been applied. Usually seen on older cuts, it may have been done to reduce or eliminate the bright flash or read-through effect produced by the large culets characteristic of early cutting styles.

black light, popular term for ultraviolet lamps. See ULTRAVIOLET.

Black Orloff Diamond, 67.50 ct. cushion-cut diamond, described as gun-metal in color and reportedly cut from a 195 ct. rough. Set in a diamond and platinum necklace, the

Black Orloff Diamond

Black Orloff has been widely exhibited. Last sold by Sotheby's, New York, in December 1991. Also called the Eye of Brahma Diamond. Privately owned.

Black Star of Africa Diamond, 202 ct. black diamond exhibited in Tokyo in 1971.

blemish, term used in the GIA clarity-grading system for any nick, scratch, abrasion, pit, polish mark, graining, or polish line on the surface of a polished diamond. Naturals on the girdle and extra facets on, or visible through, the crown are also considered blemishes.

block caving, method of single level underground mining. Large cave-like excavations are made at intervals across the pipe until the roof falls in under the weight of the rock above; the ore is hauled out to a collection level. Block caving is less labor-intensive and more efficient than chambering. See BEACH MINING, CHAMBERING, OPEN BENCH MINING, OPEN PIT MINING.

blocker, person who places the table and the first four facets on the crown and the first four facets on the pavilion of a diamond. The process is often combined with cross-working in stone under 50 points. See BLOCKING, BRILLIANDEER, CROSS-WORKER.

blocking, process of placing the table, the first four facets on the crown, and the first four facets on the pavilion of a rough or prepared diamond. To a large extent, blocking determines the symmetry and weight of the polished diamond as well as its brilliance and dispersion. In stones under 50 points, the process is often combined with cross-working. See BRILLIANDEERING.

Bloemhof, alluvial mining area in Transvaal Province, South Africa.

blue, the, early South African diggers' term for blueground. See BLUEGROUND.

Blue Brilliant Diamond, 1.25 ct. diamond, described as a blue and once, but no longer, thought to be a fragment from the French Blue. Suggestions that stone might be the Pirie Diamond have been refuted; the Pirie reportedly weighs only one carat. Current whereabouts unknown.

blue diamond, fancy color diamond with a distinctly blue natural bodycolor, which can be modified by black, brown, gray, green, or purple. Blue diamonds are usually Type IIb, but some Type IaA diamonds from Australia are also blue, as are very rare Type IIa diamonds. When the color is due to traces of boron in the crystal structure, the stones have the properties of a semi-conductor. (Type IaA diamonds are electrical insulators.) Noted natural blue diamonds include the Hope, the Brunswick Blue, the Roberts Victor, and the Wittelsbach. See BRUNSWICK BLUE DIAMOND, FRENCH BLUE DIAMOND, HOPE DIAMOND, IRRADIATED BLUE DIAMOND, ROBERTS-VICTOR MINE, TYPE IA DIAMOND, TYPE IIA DIAMOND, TYPE IIB DIAMOND, WITTELSBACH DIAMOND.

Blue Diamond of the Crown, see FRENCH BLUE DIAMOND.

blue earth, see BLUEGROUND.

blueground, grayish blue to blue-green unoxidized kimberlite in which diamonds may be found; typically encountered under a layer of decomposed yellowground. See DIATREME, HARDEBANK, KIMBERLITE, YELLOWGROUND.

Blue Heart Diamond, 31 ct. heart-shape diamond, described as dark blue, sold by Cartier in 1911. It was set in a pendant and exhibited by Van Cleef in 1953. Sold privately in 1960.

blue jager, see JAGER.

Blue Lili Diamond, 30.06 ct. tapered cushion modified brilliant-cut diamond, described as intense medium to dark blue. Fashioned by William Goldberg of the William Goldberg Company in New York, US, and named for his wife. Current whereabouts unknown.

Blue Tavernier Diamond, see TAVERNIER BLUE DIAMOND.

blue Wesselton, see TOP WESSELTON.

blue-white, phrase traditionally used to describe colorless diamonds. Due to flagrant misuse, Federal Trade Commission rulings limit its application in the US to stones which are blue, or bluish, in color; similar restrictions apply in some other countries as well.

blue-white Wesselton, see TOP WESSELTON.

boart, see BORT.

boat-shape rose cut, rose cut with an elliptical girdle outline; a flat, unfaceted base; a pointed, dome-shaped crown; and usually 24 triangular facets (the number may vary).

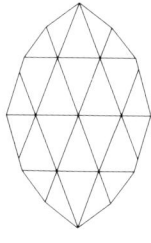

boat-shape rose cut

Boa Vista Mine, diamond mine near Diamantina, Minas Gerais, Brazil. Underground mining operations were planned in the late 1980s, but not begun; the deposit may be worked out.

Bobbejaan, see BELLSBANK.

Bob Gove Diamond, 337 ct. diamond crystal, found in 1908 on the Vaal River, Cape Province, South Africa. Current whereabouts unknown.

bodycolor, the basic color of a diamond or other gemstone seen when brilliance and dispersion (which can mask bodycolor) are ignored. Bodycolor is determined by selective absorption; the eye perceives only the color of those wavelengths of light that exit the stone unabsorbed. The amount of color seen is often influenced by the size and cut. See COLOR GRADE, COLOR GRADING, DIAMONDLITE, FACE-UP COLOR, FANCY COLOR DIAMOND, IRRADIATED DIAMOND, MASTER DIAMONDS.

Bogenfels, early diamond-producing area 80 kilometers (50 miles) south of Lüderitz, Namibia. Although largely mined-out by 1950, its tailings may have some potential in the future. See ELIZABETH BAY.

Bohemian diamond, misnomer for rock crystal quartz from western Bohemia, the Czech Republic (formerly Czechoslovakia).

Boin-Taburet Diamond, 8.75 ct. faceted diamond believed to be one of the Mazarins. Current whereabouts unknown. See MAZARIN DIAMONDS.

Boismenu, Eugene Guyot de, French scientist who unsuccessfully attempted to synthesize diamonds in 1908, by heating calcium carbide at low pressure in a carbon arc. See SYNTHETIC DIAMOND.

bombarded diamond, see IRRADIATED DIAMOND.

Bombay, city in the state of Maharastra, on the west coast of India; that country's financial capital and a major diamond marketing center. Bombay's diamond and diamond jewelry manufacturing industry involves American, Indian, Japanese, and European companies. Construction of a new Diamond Center is scheduled for completion in 1997. See BHAVNAGAR, GOLCONDA, INDIA, KRISHNA RIVER, NAVSARI, PANNA, SURAT.

bonding, atomic, see ATOMIC BONDING.

Bonsa Diamond Field, site of alluvial diamond deposits along the Bonsa River in Ghana, Africa. See GHANA.

Boot, A. Boetius de (1550-1634), Belgian gem enthusiast, personal physician to Holy Roman Emperor Rudolph II, and author of the *Gemmarum et Lapidum Historia*, published in 1604. The work describes and illustrates contemporary polishing equipment, making it a valuable source of information on the early history of diamond cutting.

Borneo, large island in the Malay Archipelago in southeast Asia. After India, Borneo is the second oldest known producer of fine diamonds; its deposits are believed to have been worked as early as the tenth century. The state of Kalimantan, Indonesia, occupies most of the island. Diamonds have historically been found in its western part, and alluvial deposits are being mined currently in the Danau Seran swamp near

Martapura in southeastern Kalimantan. See BANJARMASIN, DANAU SERAN SWAMP, MARTAPURA.

Bornholm diamond, misnomer for rock crystal quartz from Bornholm, an island in Denmark.

boron, element (atomic number 5, atomic weight 10.81) which occurs as an impurity in Type IIb diamonds. It is thought to cause their blue color and semi-conductive properties. See BLUE DIAMOND, IRRADIATED BLUE DIAMOND.

Borsa Diamanti D'Italia, Italian diamond bourse; located in Milan, it is a member of the World Federation of Diamond Bourses. See BOURSE, WORLD FEDERATION OF DIAMOND BOURSES (WFDB).

bort, natural, polycrystalline diamond which occasionally forms as single crystals; it is milled for use in industrial abrasives. Also spelled boart. See BALLAS, CARBONADO, CRUSHING BORT, FRAMESITE, HAILSTONE BORT, SHOT BORT, STEWARTITE.

Botswana, Republic of, major diamond-producing country in south-central Africa, formerly called Bechuanaland; the Orapa and Letlhakane mines in the north, and the Jwaneng mine in the south, are all operated by Debswana Diamond Company, a joint venture of De Beers Centenary AG and the Botswana government.

Botswana Diamond Valuing Company, Ltd. (BDVC), subsidiary of the Debswana Diamond Company. Located in Gaborone, capital of Botswana, the company sorts and values the rough diamonds produced by the Orapa, Letlhakane, and Jwaneng Mines for sale through the Central Selling Organisation.

bottom-break facets, see GIRDLE FACETS.

bottom-corner facets, see QUOIN FACETS.

bottom-half facets, see GIRDLE FACETS.

bottom-main facets, see PAVILION FACETS.

Boungou River, see CENTRAL AFRICAN REPUBLIC.

bourse, French, an exchange or meeting place where merchants transact business. See DIAMOND BOURSE.

bowing effect, illusion of a curve created by the straight edges of the table and the adjoining star facets on a polished diamond. The amount of bowing depends on the size of the table and the length of the star facets; thus, as the table gets larger, the curve appears to bend out toward the girdle; conversely, as table size decreases, the curve appears to bow in toward the center. See BOWING METHOD.

bowing method, means of estimating table size by observing the extent of the bowing effect. If the table and star facet edges appear to form a straight line, the table is approximately 60 percent; if the line bows out noticeably, the table is 65 to 67 percent; if it bows in noticeably, the table is 52 to 53 percent. Such estimates must be corrected for the length of the star facets. See BOWING EFFECT.

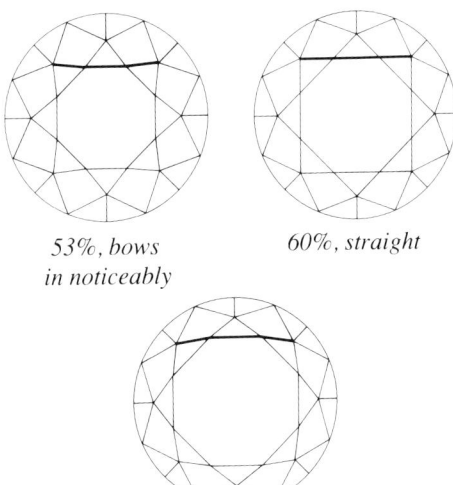

53%, bows in noticeably *60%, straight*

67%, bows out noticeably

bowing method

Bow River Mine, Australian diamond mine located 50 kilometers (31 miles) southeast of Kununurra, Western Australia, about 17 kilometers (11 miles) downstream from the Argyle Diamond Mines. Owned and operated by Nor-

bow tie ➤ Brazil

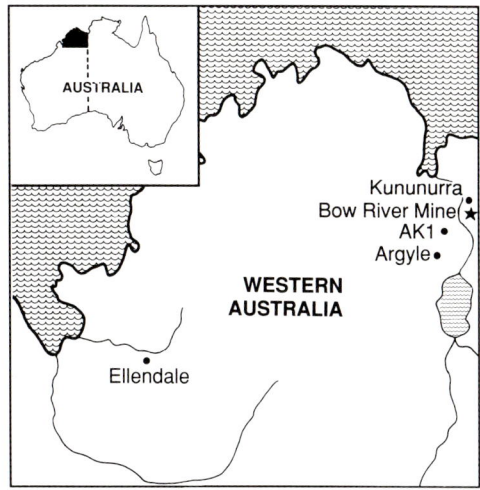
Bow River Mine

mandy Poseidon, the mine opened in 1988; its output is marketed through the Central Selling Organisation. See AK1 PIPE (ARGYLE).

bow tie, dark area resembling a bow tie, seen through the table, across the center of a marquise, oval, or pear-shape diamond and, in rare instances, in other fancy cuts, such as the kite. It occurs in shallow or very deep stones, those with long culets, or those in which the pavilion facets are incorrectly oriented. Sometimes called a butterfly.

bow tie

bow tie effect, see BOW TIE.

Boyle, Robert (1627-1691), English chemist who in 1672 first explained the process of octahedral cleaving in diamond; also the first to burn a diamond at temperatures exceeding 700°C (1,290°F).

Brabant rose cut, alternative name for the Antwerp rose cut; named for the Duchy of Brabant in Belgium, to which Antwerp once belonged. See ANTWERP ROSE CUT.

Brady, James Buchanan (1856-1917), American financier, philanthropist, and millionaire famous for his flamboyant lifestyle and his love of diamonds, which earned him the nickname "Diamond Jim."

Braganza Diamond, 144 ct. (old carats) rough diamond found in Brazil, in 1791, probably along the Abaeté River, by three convicts who exchanged it for a pardon. The Braganza's weight was long alleged to be 1680 ct., but this is apparently the result of confusing it with another stone which is now thought to have been a topaz or an aquamarine. The Braganza may be the Abaeté Brilliant Diamond. Also called the King of Portugal Diamond. Current whereabouts unknown.

Brahamani River, site of early alluvial diamond deposits northeast of Golconda, in India.

Brahamani River

Brakfontein Mine, alluvial diamond mine near Hopetown, South Africa. Diamonds are found in river gravels and recovered by mechanical excavation.

Brazil, largest country in South America and a source of diamonds since about 1725. The country's three principal diamond-producing states are Minas Gerais, Mato Grosso, and Bahia, all of which have extensive alluvial deposits. Most of the mining is done by individuals or small groups.

Brazilian cut, modification of the old mine or triple cut with an additional eight facets polished around the culet. See TRIPLE-CUT BRILLIANT.

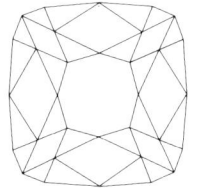
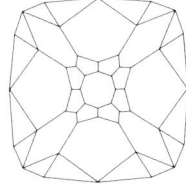

Brazilian cut

Brazilian diamond, misnomer for rock crystal quartz from Brazil.

break facets, see GIRDLE FACETS.

breaks, see GIRDLE FACETS.

breccia, coarse-grained rock composed of angular fragments held together by a mineral cement or a fine-grained matrix; the upper levels of kimberlite and lamproite pipes are generally filled with such material. See DIATREME.

Briançon diamond, misnomer for rock crystal quartz cut in Briançon, France, and originally used in chandeliers. Also called Dauphine diamond.

Bridge Oil & Gas, Australian company which operates the AREDOR Mine in Guinea. Bridge Oil's subsidiary, AREDOR Holdings, is part owner of AREDOR Guinea, the company that manages the mine.

Bridgman, Percy W. (1882-1961), American physicist who won the Nobel Prize in 1946 for his work in high pressure physics. Though Bridgman himself did not succeed in synthesizing diamond experimentally, his work contributed to General Electric Company's success in 1954. See SYNTHETIC DIAMOND.

briefca, see DIAMOND PAPER.

Briggs' scale, ranking of the comparative toughness of brittle minerals. Position on the scale is determined by pressing fragments of different minerals against each other until one breaks; the first to break is lower in toughness. Carbonado is at the top of the scale.

Brighton diamond, misnomer for rock crystal quartz from Brighton, England.

brilliance, intensity of the internal and external reflections of white light from the crown of a polished diamond or other gemstone. Hardness, refractive index, reflectivity, polish, luster, and proportions all affect a gemstone's brilliance. See CRITICAL ANGLE, DISPERSION, REFRACTION, SCINTILLATION.

brilliandeer, person who places and polishes the remaining facets (16 halves and 8 stars on the crown; 16 halves on the pavilion) on a diamond after the bezel and pavilion main facets have been put on by the blocker or cross-worker, or both. Also spelled brillianteerer. See BLOCKER, BLOCKING, CROSS-WORKER, CROSS-WORKING.

brilliandeering, act of placing and polishing the remaining facets (16 halves and 8 stars on the crown; 16 halves on the pavilion) on a diamond after the bezel and pavilion main facets have been put on. See BLOCKING, CROSS-WORKING.

brilliant, see BRILLIANT CUT.

Brilliant Circle, proprietary name for a diamond with a polished girdle.

brilliant cut, cut with a facet arrangement that radiates from the center of the stone towards the

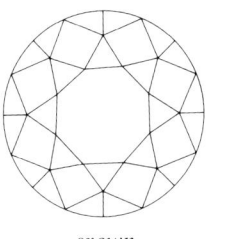
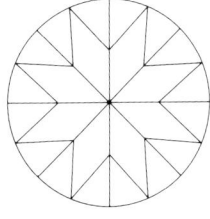

crown   *pavilion*

brilliant cut

girdle, and triangular or kite-shaped facets. The most common brilliant cut is the standard round brilliant; modifications include the marquise, half moon, pear shape, heart shape, oval, cushion, and antique cushion brilliant cuts.

Brilliante, (1) proprietary name for synthetic strontium titanate. (2) proprietary name for synthetic rutile. Both are marketed as diamond simulants.

brillianteerer, see BRILLIANDEER.

brillianteering, see BRILLIANDEERING.

brillionette, see HALF-BRILLIANT CUT.

Bril-Lite, proprietary name for colorless synthetic sapphire. Marketed as a diamond simulant.

Brinell hardness test, indentation hardness test developed by Swedish metallurgist and engineer Johan A. Brinell (1849-1925). The test consists of forcing a hardened steel or carbide ball into a surface under a known load. Results are expressed in kilograms/square millimeter. See DIRECTIONAL HARDNESS, HARDNESS, HARDNESS POINTS, INDENTATION TEST, KNOOP INDENTATION HARDNESS TEST, SCLEROMETER, SCRATCH HARDNESS, VICKERS HARDNESS TEST.

briolette, teardrop-shaped cut, circular in cross section and covered with triangular (or occasionally rectangular) facets.

Briolette of India Diamond, 90.38 ct. briolette cut diamond, fashioned in 1908-1909 and sold by Cartier in 1910; sold again in 1946 to Harry Winston, who subsequently re-sold and re-purchased it several times. In 1971 it was sold to a European family. Also called the Briolette.

Briolette of India Diamond

Bristol diamond, misnomer for rock crystal quartz from Bristol, England. Also called Bristos, Bristowes, and Bristol stones.

British Crown Jewels, large collection of gold, diamonds, and gem-set regalia (crowns, scepters, swords, etc.) owned by the British Monarchy. The collection accumulated over 500 years, beginning in the 1300s. Much of the regalia assembled by Charles I (1600-1649) was destroyed after his death, but the collection was rebuilt after the Restoration in 1660. Until the mid-twentieth century, Britain's colonies in India and South Africa provided access to the largest diamond deposits in the world, and today the British Crown Jewels include some of the world's largest and finest polished diamonds: the 530.2 ct. Cullinan I, mounted in the Cross of the Scepter; the 317.4 ct. Cullinan II, in the Imperial State Crown; and the 105.6 ct. Koh-i-Nur. The collection is on display in the Jewel House at the Tower of London.

British diamond, misnomer for quartz crystals found in limestone in Gloucester, England; sometimes used to refer to Bristol diamonds. See BRISTOL DIAMOND.

British Diamond Distributors, Ltd. (Britmond), affiliate of the Central Selling Organisation which purchases the MIBA production at Mbuji-Mayi, Zaire. See MIBA MINE.

British Guiana, see GUYANA.

Britmond, see BRITISH DIAMOND DISTRIBUTORS, LTD.

brittleness, see TOUGHNESS.

broker, (1) independent intermediary who arranges wholesale diamond transactions between suppliers and purchasers. Brokers are usually members of bourses or diamond clubs and receive a commission on the sales they arrange. (2) one of five firms known as Diamond Trading Company or Central Selling Organisation brokers, who act for sightholders in negotiations over sights, earning a commission on each purchase. They also identify potential clients in the various diamond trading centers and bring them to the attention of the CSO. The broker-sightholder relationship continues from one sight to the next. See ALLOCATION, APPLICATION, SIGHT.

Brooke Diamond, colorless rough diamond which looks red face-up. Found on the Brookeborough Estate in northern Ireland in 1816, it is one of only two diamonds discovered in the British Isles; the other, said to be of industrial quality, was found in Sutherland, Scotland. The stones were presumably deposited by glaciers. Owned by the Brooke family.

brown diamond, the most commonly occurring natural diamond color. In light tones, within the GIA D-Z color scale, brown and yellow diamonds are similar in appearance, and are color graded against the same master diamonds. In darker tones, browns are usually graded slightly lower than a comparable depth of yellow. The brown hue can be modified by black, olive, orange, pink, purple, red, or yellow. In the GIA color-grading system, stones with a deep-brown color are considered fancy diamonds. A brown diamond not dark enough to be called a fancy color may be called slightly brown, light brown, or a "brownie." Brown diamonds are often described with impressionistic terms like brandy, bronze, chocolate, cinnamon, clove, coffee, cognac, garnet, golden and honey. See C1, C2, . . . C7; COLOR GRADE, COLOR GRADING, GIA COLOR-GRADING SCALE, IRRADIATED BROWN DIAMOND.

Bruges, Belgian town, historic diamond manufacturing center, and former North Sea port which received rough diamonds from India (through Venice) throughout the fourteenth century. Diamond cutting and trading operations ended in the mid-fifteenth century when Bruges was cut off from the sea by the silting up of the Zwin River.

bruise, crumbled area on the surface of a fashioned diamond, caused by a blow; usually white and often outlined by minute cleavages or fractures. The term bruise is also used to describe marks on rough diamonds, particularly those from alluvial deposits. Also called a percussion mark.

bruise

Brunswick, Duke of, see CHARLES II.

Brunswick Blue Diamond, pear-shape diamond, described as blue and variously reported to weigh as little as 6 or as much as 13 ct. Named for the Duke of Brunswick (Charles II, ca. 1810-1873), who owned it. Once, but no longer, thought to have been cut from the French Blue Diamond. Reportedly sold with the Duke's effects in 1874; current whereabouts unknown. See HOPE DIAMOND.

Brunswick Yellow Diamond, 30 ct. Indian diamond once owned by the Duke of Brunswick (Charles II, ca. 1810-1873), and purchased from his estate in 1874 by Tiffany's. Current whereabouts unknown.

bruter, person responsible for the rounding up, or girdling, of a rough diamond, which establishes the face-up outline of a polished brilliant or curved fancy cut. See BRUTING.

bruting, shaping process performed on a rough diamond or a portion thereof, to establish the characteristic face-up outline of a round brilliant or of some mixed and fancy cuts. It is done by rotating the diamond in a lathe and shaping it with another diamond; today the process is often automated. Also called girdling, rounding up, or rondisting. See AUTOMATIC BRUTING MACHINE.

bruting dop, retainer used to hold a rough diamond, or a portion thereof, during the bruting process. See SHARP.

bruting lathe, machine that rotates the diamond during the bruting process. See AUTOMATIC BRUTING MACHINE, FASHIONING.

bubble, see GAS BUBBLE.

Buffels Inland Complex, alluvial mining area 40 kilometers (25 miles) northeast of the mouth of the Buffels River in Namaqualand, South Africa. The deposit is one of three in the area owned by De Beers Consolidated Mines and operated by the company's Namaqualand Mines Division. Diamonds are found among fluvial gravels and are recovered by overburden stripping, mechanical mining, and hand sweeping.

Buffels Marine Complex, mining area which extends north for 40 kilometers (25 miles) from the mouth of the Buffels River in Namaqualand, South Africa; it includes Annex Kleinzee and Kleinzee. Ore is treated at the AK3 and Tweepad recovery plants. Buffels Marine Complex is owned by De Beers Consolidated Mines and operated by the company's Namaqualand Mines Division. Diamonds are found in paleo-marine gravels and are recovered by overburden stripping, mechanical mining, and hand sweeping. See ANNEX KLEINZEE, KLEINZEE.

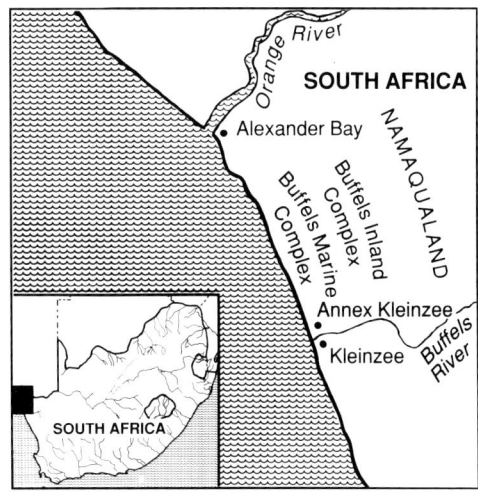

Buffels Marine Complex

bulge, bowing out of the pavilion on a step cut, as seen in cross-section, the result of enlarging the angles on the steps to increase the yield.

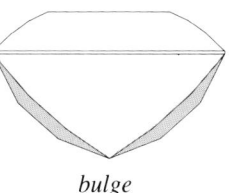

bulge

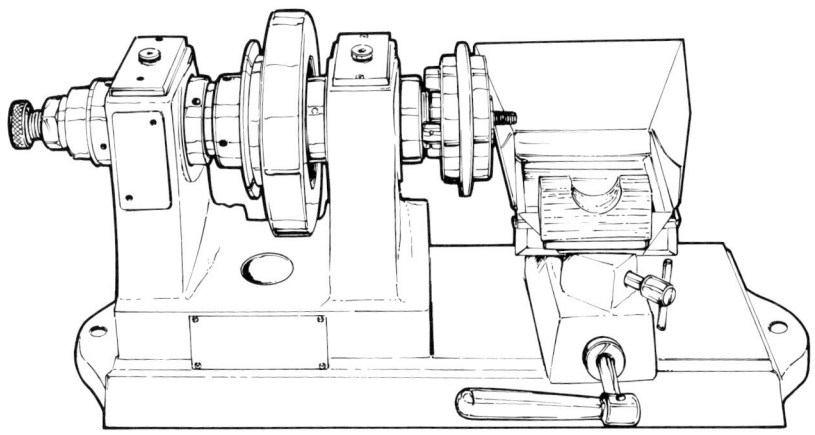

bruting lathe

bullet cut, modification of the pentagon cut resembling a bullet in outline.

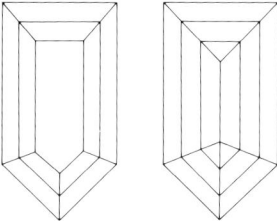

bullet cut

Bultfontein Mine, kimberlite pipe mine in Kimberley, South Africa, 1 kilometer (0.6 miles) from the Dutoitspan Mine, operated by De Beers Consolidated Mines. Diamonds were first discovered here in 1869, but the site was not recognized as a primary source until 1872. The mine shares a vertical shaft with Dutoitspan; an inclined drift has been developed near the bottom of the shaft to reach the lower levels of the mine. Diamonds are recovered by block caving and sub-level caving. See DUTOITSPAN MINE.

Bultfontein Mine

bunch ring, ring set with a tiny diamond which is sometimes only partially faceted; inexpensive and sold in bunches.

burn mark, surface clouding or irregularity caused by excessive heat generated during polishing. Also called a polishing mark.

Burton, Charles V., early investigator into diamond synthesis who, in 1905, claimed to have produced minute diamond crystals at relatively low temperatures and pressures by using an alloy of lead and metallic calcium to hold charcoal in solution. Most researchers discount his claims. See SYNTHETIC DIAMOND.

Buryatya, province in the CIS; in 1990, ten diamond sites were reported there, along the eastern slope of the Sayan mountain range.

Bushimaie River, site of important alluvial diamond deposits in Zaire. See MBUJI-MAYI.

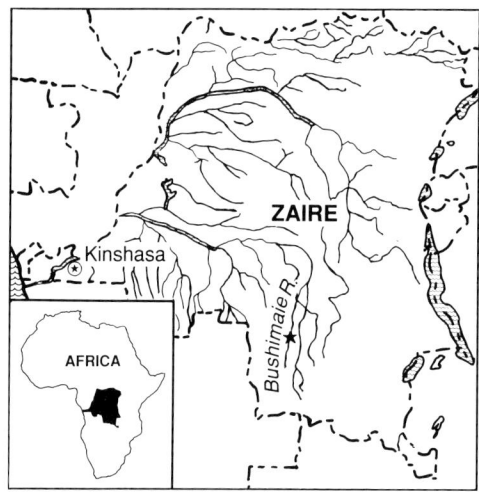

Bushimaie River

buttercup head, six-prong setting with a scalloped base resembling a flower. See CLUSTER SETTING, ILLUSION HEAD, TIFFANY HEAD.

butterfly, see BOW TIE.

Buxton diamond, misnomer for rock crystal quartz from Buxton,

buttercup head

England, usually occurring as doubly terminated crystals.

buyer's box, cardboard container holding the various packets of rough offered to a sightholder at a sight. See ALLOCATION, CENTRAL SELLING ORGANISATION (CSO), SIGHT, SIGHTHOLDER.

bye, archaic mining term for a rough diamond with a deep cape color. When cut, these stones usually fall into the cape and yellow grades. Also byewater. See CAPE.

byewater, see BYE.

Byfield Diamond, 54.74 ct. diamond once owned by Vala Byfield. Sold by Parke-Bernet Galleries in 1971; current whereabouts unknown.

bywater, see BYE.

C, chemical symbol for the element carbon.

C1, C2, . . . C7, proprietary color-grading scale created by Argyle Diamonds for grading brown diamonds. There are seven grades: C1, light champagne; C2, champagne; C3, medium champagne; C4, light cognac; C5, medium cognac; C6, cognac; and C7, fancy cognac.

CAD, acronym for the Consumer and Advertising Division of the Central Selling Organisation. Based in London, the organization is responsible for all of De Beers' international marketing and advertising campaigns.

Cagniard de la Tour, Charles (1777-1859), French chemist who unsuccessfully attempted to synthesize diamonds in 1823.

Cairo star cut, style of brilliant cut with 74 facets; developed from the briolette to retain maximum yield, or weight, from the rough, with a minimum loss of brilliance. See YIELD.

calcrete, hardened form of calcium carbonate which binds sand, diamonds, and gravel in alluvial deposits. It is often concrete-like in consistency and must be drilled or blasted out.

calf's-head cut, modification of the triangle cut, produced by varying the lengths and angles of the sides.

calibré cut, small stone, usually under 0.20 ct., fashioned to standard dimensions, generally for channel setting. Most are step cuts such as baguettes or square cuts, but some are round brilliants. Also spelled calibre.

Calonda, important kimberlite pipe, with associated alluvial deposits, in northeastern Angola. See ANGOLA, EMPRESA NACIONAL DE DIAMANTES DE ANGOLA (ENDIAMA), LUCAPA.

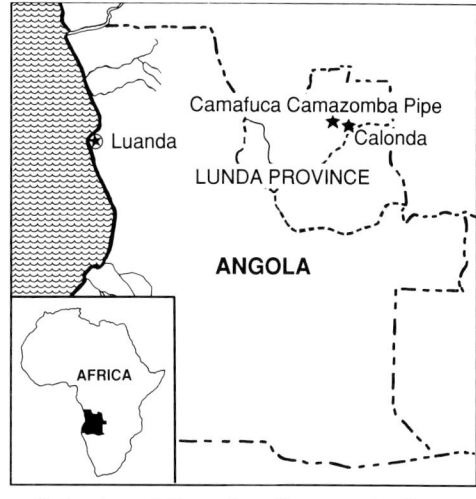

Calonda and Camafuca Camazomba Pipes

Camafuca Camazomba Pipe, diamond-bearing kimberlite pipe on the Chicapa River in northeastern Angola. See ANGOLA, EMPRESA NACIONAL DE DIAMANTES DE ANGOLA (ENDIAMA), LUCAPA.

Camagico, site of a kimberlite in northeastern Angola. See ANGOLA, EMPRESA NACIONAL DE DIAMANTES DE ANGOLA (ENDIAMA), LUCAPA.

Camatchia, kimberlite pipe in northeastern Angola, near the Chicapa River. See ANGOLA, EMPRESA NACIONAL DE DIAMANTES DE ANGOLA (ENDIAMA), LUCAPA.

Camatué Pipe, site of a kimberlite in northeastern Angola, near the Luachimo River. See ANGOLA, EMPRESA NACIONAL DE DIAMANTES DE ANGOLA (ENDIAMA), LUCAPA.

Cambridge Diamond, 20 ct. pear-shape diamond said to have belonged to Catherine the Great of Russia (1729-1796). Set in a necklace for an English owner in the 1920s; later pur-

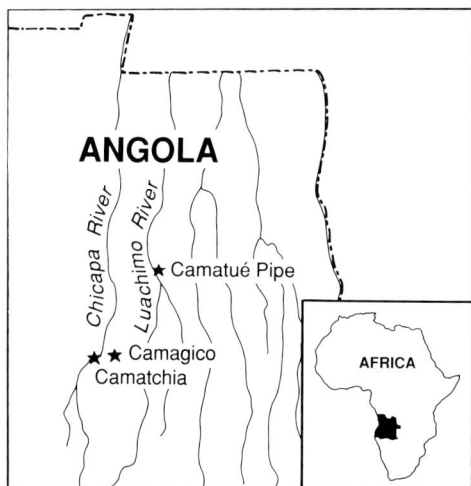

Camagico, Camatchia, and Camatué Pipes

chased by Harry Winston and sold in the 1950s. Current whereabouts unknown.

Canada, large nation occupying roughly the northern third of the North American continent. Occasional diamond finds have led to extensive prospecting; kimberlite pipes or dikes have been found in most provinces. No large-scale commercial exploitation has yet been done, although major mining companies are actively exploring large tracts, especially in Alberta and the Northwest Territories. Some diamonds found in the United States were transported from Canada by glaciers.

Canadian Gemmological Association (CGA), Toronto-based educational organization which administers gemology courses and examinations in Canada leading to the Fellow of the Canadian Gemmological Association (FCGA) title. Incorporated in 1968, the CGA is an affiliate of the Gemmological Association and Gem Testing Laboratory of Great Britain (GAGTL).

canary diamond, term used to describe an intensely-colored yellow diamond; it may be very slightly greenish or orangy. The color must be deep enough to be a fancy color. See TRUE CANARY, TYPE IIB DIAMOND.

Canyon Diablo Meteorite, one of the first meteorites in which diamonds were found. Discovered in Arizona in 1893, the diamonds were polycrystalline cubes and cubo-octahedra; they are believed to have been formed by the heat and shock generated by impact when the meteorite struck the earth. See LONSDALEITE, METEORITIC DIAMONDS.

cap cut, diamond with haphazardly placed facets.

cape, (1) rough or polished Type Ia diamond with a distinct yellow bodycolor. Named after early diamonds from Cape Province, South Africa. Stones in this category are also called capish, cape stones, or cape diamonds; they range from light to very dark in tone. Small stones in the lighter end of the range may not show their color face-up; darker colors are sometimes called low cape. (2) term in the Scan. D.N. color-grading system for diamonds over 0.47 ct. in the faint yellow to light yellow range; corresponds to M–Z on the GIA color-grading scale. See APPENDIX D, CRYSTAL, DARK CAPE, FINE CAPE, LIGHT CAPE, PREMIER DIAMOND, RIVER, SILVER CAPE, TOP CAPE, TOP CRYSTAL, TOP SILVER CAPE, TOP WESSELTON, WESSELTON.

cape and yellow spotted, obsolete term once used to designate diamond crystals similar in clarity to spotted stones, but yellow in color. See SPOTTED STONE.

cape ballas, ballas from South Africa. See BALLAS.

Cape Colony, see CAPE PROVINCE.

Cape Diamond, 297 ct. well-formed medium yellow octahedral diamond, found at the Dutoitspan Mine in South Africa. Owned by the Central Selling Organisation and displayed at its London headquarters as part of a permanent exhibit of representative rough diamonds.

cape lines, absorption lines produced in the spectrum of Type Ia diamonds with a distinct yellow bodycolor. There is often a strong band at about 415.5 nm and a fairly strong one at 478.0 nm, with four weaker lines between the two. Such

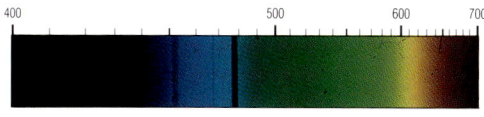

cape lines

diamonds may also fluoresce blue, yellow, or orange. There is no cape spectrum in Type Ib diamonds. See ABSORPTION LINE, ABSORPTION SPECTRUM, SELECTIVE ABSORPTION, TYPE IA DIAMOND, TYPE IB DIAMOND.

Cape May diamond, misnomer for waterworn pebbles of rock crystal quartz from New Jersey, US. The deposit is believed to have been discovered in 1790.

Cape Province, the Province of the Cape of Good Hope in South Africa, and an important diamond-producing region; the Kimberley and Finsch mines are in Cape Province. Prior to the Boer War with the British (1899-1902), the area was known as the Cape Colony; its name was changed upon the formation of the Union of South Africa in 1910.

cape series, diamonds ranging in color from near colorless to dark yellow just above the fancy-color range. See CAPE, CAPE LINES.

cape spectrum, see CAPE LINES.

cape stone, (1) any diamond found in Cape Province, South Africa. (2) any distinctly yellow diamond. See CAPE.

Cape Town, major port city in South Africa.

capish, see CAPE.

C.A.R., see CENTRAL AFRICAN REPUBLIC.

carat, metric carat, the standard unit of weight used for gemstones; adopted in the US in 1913. One carat equals .200 grams (or 200 milligrams). Usually abbreviated ct. or ¢ (especially in Europe or Great Britain). See CAROB SEED, KARAT, OLD CARAT.

carat, old, see OLD CARAT.

carat goods, parcels of diamonds each approximately one carat in weight. See GRAINER.

carat weight, weight of a diamond expressed in metric carats. See CARAT, OLD CARAT.

carbon, (1) non-metallic element (atomic number 6, atomic weight 12.01115), occurring in nature in crystalline form as diamond, graphite, and lonsdaleite. (2) misnomer for a dark inclusion in a diamond.

carbonado, polycrystalline aggregate of minute diamond crystals with a granular-to-compact structure; it may be black, brown, or dark gray. Used for industrial purposes, carbonado is the toughest form of diamond. Sometimes called black diamond. See BALLAS, BORT, CRUSHING BORT, FRAMESITE, HAILSTONE BORT, POLYCRYSTALLINE DIAMOND, STEWARTITE.

carbon pinpoint, very small carbon spot. See PINPOINT.

carbon spot, misnomer for a black-looking inclusion in a diamond. Truly black inclusions are rare; inclusions which look black to the unaided eye under ordinary lighting are, under magnification with darkfield illumination, usually seen to be transparent cleavages or included crystals.

Cardinal Mazarin, see MAZARIN, CARDINAL JULES.

Cariué Pipe, kimberlite in northeastern Angola near the Luachimo River, north of Lucapa. See ANGOLA, EMPRESA NACIONAL DE DIAMANTES DE ANGOLA (ENDIAMA).

Carlotta Diamond, 40.3 ct. pear-shape diamond, described as fancy light-pink, cut by Lazare Kaplan from a rough diamond found in Lesotho; named for his wife, Charlotte.

Carnegie Gem, proprietary name for a doublet with a synthetic spinel crown and a strontium titanate pavilion. Marketed as a diamond simulant.

Carlotta Diamond

photo courtesy of CSO

carob seed, seed from the fruit of the carob tree (*ceratonia siliqua*). Because they are relatively uniform in weight, the seeds were once used throughout the Mediterranean basin as counterweights in simple balances; thus they came to be accepted as units of measurement. The word carat is derived from *keration*, the Greek name for the tree.

Caroní River, site of several regionally important alluvial diamond discoveries in Venezuela.

Caroní River

Carrara diamond, misnomer for well-formed quartz crystals found in the white marble of Carrara, Italy. First used in 1973-74.

carré, French, meaning *square*. (1) square step-cut diamond. (2) any small square diamond.

Carrig Diamonds, diamond mining group in South Africa. Carrig is said to operate the smaller Ardo, Du Plessis, Mallin, and Southern Fissures Diamond Mines, among others.

Cartier Diamond, see TAYLOR-BURTON DIAMOND.

Cartier-Kenmore Diamond, 38.31 ct. cushion-shape diamond, described as fancy yellow; purchased in India in 1971 by Rosemarie Kenmore, wife of the then chairman of the Board of Cartier's USA. Thought to have been fashioned some 300 years ago, it still retains the original "skin" of the rough around its girdle. Current whereabouts unknown.

Cascalho Rico, alluvial diamond-mining area in Minas Gerais, Brazil.

Cassamba, site of alluvial diamond deposits in eastern Angola.

Cassanquide Mine, alluvial diamond-mining operation in Angola.

CAST, see CONSOLIDATED AFRICAN SELECTION TRUST, LTD.

castings, industrial diamonds which cannot be used for drilling. They are generally used in impregnated bits.

cathode ray, beam of electrons emitted from negatively charged electrodes (cathodes) when an electrical discharge occurs in a vacuum tube, or when a metal filament is heated. Cathode rays can be used to help determine the origin and properties of gemstones and minerals. See CATHODOLUMINESCENCE.

cathodoluminescence, visible fluorescence produced in a gemstone after being subjected to cathode rays; helps determine the origins and properties of gemstones and minerals. See CATHODE RAY, X-RAY FLUORESCENCE.

Catoca Pipe, large, diamond-bearing kimberlite near the Chicapa River in Angola, which is thought to be economic to mine. See ANGOLA, EMPRESA NACIONAL DE DIAMANTES DE ANGOLA (ENDIAMA), LUCAPA.

Catskill diamond, misnomer for colorless quartz crystals from Greene County in the Catskill Mountains, New York, US.

Catumbela River, river basin in western Angola in which alluvial diamond deposits are located. See ANGOLA, EMPRESA NACIONAL DE DIAMANTES DE ANGOLA (ENDIAMA), LUCAPA.

cavity, any opening or indentation on the surface of a polished diamond. Cavities sometimes result from a cleavage that reaches the surface, from a knot or included crystal which has been pulled out during polishing, or from a negative

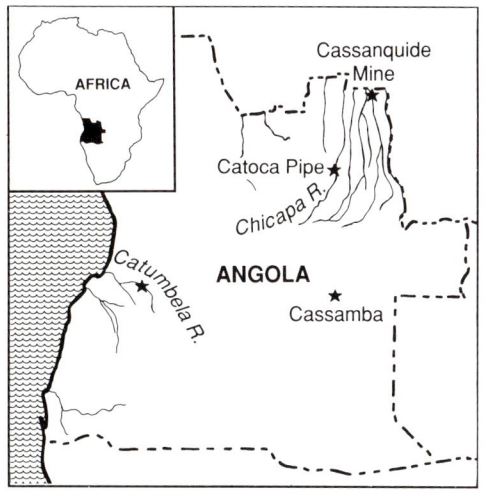

Cassamba, Cassanquide Mine, Catoca Pipe, and Catumbela River

crystal that has been polished through. See INTERNAL CHARACTERISTIC, PIT.

Cayniard, Charles, see CAGNIARD DE LA TOUR, CHARLES.

CDM (Pty.), Ltd., formerly Consolidated Diamond Mines of South West Africa, Ltd. Now incorporated in Namibia as a wholly-owned subsidiary of De Beers Centenary AG. Formed in February, 1920, when Ernest Oppenheimer, acting on behalf of Anglo American Corporation, acquired ten diamond mining companies that had been active in the region before World War I, when it was a German protectorate (German South West Africa). See ANGLO AMERICAN CORPORATION OF SOUTH AFRICA, LTD.; BEACH MINING; OFF-SHORE MINING; DE BEERS MARINE (PTY.), LTD.

Cellini, Benvenuto, (1500-1571) Italian goldsmith and sculptor whose *Treatise on Goldsmithing* (1568) describes several large diamonds. Cellini executed a number of important commissions for Pope Clement VII, King Francis I of France, and the Medicis. See CELLINI GREEN DIAMOND, CELLINI PEACH DIAMOND.

Cellini Green Diamond, diamond, reportedly pale green, described by Benvenuto Cellini in his *Treatise on Goldsmithing* (1568). Current whereabouts unknown.

Cellini Peach Diamond, diamond, reportedly peach-colored, described by Benvenuto Cellini in his *Treatise on Goldsmithing* (1568). Current whereabouts unknown.

cement, adhesive material used to hold diamonds in place during cleaving and bruting. Contents vary, but such cements often contain a mixture of shellac, resin, sand, and ground glass. Traditional cements soften when heated and harden when cooled.

Centenary Diamond, flawless 273.85 ct. diamond cut from a 599 ct. rough diamond found at the Premier Mine in South Africa in 1988. Fashioned over a period of three years (1989-1991) by a select team led by master diamond cutter Gabi Tolkowsky at the De Beers Diamond Research Laboratory in Johannesburg, South Africa, the diamond has 247 facets (164 on the crown and pavilion, 83 on the girdle). Named to commemorate the 100th anniversary of De Beers Consolidated Mines, the Centenary is believed to be the third largest high quality, high color polished diamond in the world; only the Great Star of Africa and the Lesser Star of Africa, both of which are among the British Crown Jewels, are larger. See UNNAMED BROWN DIAMOND.

Centenary Diamond

Central African Republic (C.A.R.), diamond-producing country in the center of Africa, north of Zaire. Alluvial diamond deposits are found along the Boungou, Kadei, Kotto, Lobaye, and Mambéré Rivers, among others. Mining operations were nationalized in 1969; the diamond cutting center and National Diamond Office are located in Bangui, the country's capital.

Central Selling Organisation (CSO), group of companies associated with De Beers Consolidated Mines and De Beers Centenary AG to purchase, sort, evaluate, and market rough diamonds. Gem quality diamonds are sold through the Diamond Trading Company and industrial-grade material through De Beers Industrial Diamond Division. In 1992, the CSO, which has evolved over the years from the Diamond Syndicate and the Diamond Corporation via a series of corporate reorganizations, marketed about 80 percent of the world's output of rough diamonds. This, coupled with its ability, when necessary, to stockpile large quantities of rough, enables it to maintain the stability of rough diamond prices by balancing supply and demand. See DE BEERS INDUSTRIAL DIAMOND DIVISION (DEBID); DIAMOND CORPORATION (PTY.), LTD.; DIAMOND SYNDICATE; DIAMOND TRADING COMPANY, (PTY.), LTD.; OPPENHEIMER, SIR ERNEST.

Central Sorting Office, Kimberley, company which once sorted, graded, and priced rough diamonds produced in South Africa and South-West Africa (Namibia). The stones were later sold to the Diamond Trading Company. Now defunct; not to be confused with the Central Selling Organisation.

Centre Français des Pierres Précieuses, French diamond bourse; member of the World Federation of Diamond Bourses. See BOURSE, WORLD FEDERATION OF DIAMOND BOURSES (WFDB).

Ceres Diamond Probe, proprietary name for a thermal diamond tester.

cert, slang, popular term for a GIA GTL Diamond Grading Report.

certificate, see DIAMOND GRADING REPORT.

certificated diamond, diamond accompanied by a Diamond Grading Report. Also called a certificate diamond.

Certified Gemologist (CG), title awarded to qualified applicants by the American Gem Society, upon the successful completion of a specified course of training and examinations. See AMERICAN GEM SOCIETY (AGS), CERTIFIED GEMOLOGIST APPRAISER (CGA).

Certified Gemologist Appraiser (CGA), title awarded by the American Gem Society to qualified Certified Gemologists upon the successful completion of additional training and examinations. See AMERICAN GEM SOCIETY (AGS), CERTIFIED GEMOLOGIST (CG).

Ceylon, see SRI LANKA.

Ceylon cut, (1) gemstone with a brilliant-cut crown, a step-cut pavilion, and a round, oval, or cushion-shaped girdle outline. (2) term denoting stones polished in Sri Lanka (formerly Ceylon).

Ceylon diamond, misnomer for colorless zircon.

chain balance, mechanical balance which uses loose or rider arm counterweights to measure carats (or grams), and an adjustable chain counterweight to measure points and tenths of a point. See RIDER BALANCE.

chambering, underground diamond-mining method developed by Gardner F. Williams around 1890 at the Kimberley Mine in South Africa. Chambers are excavated across the pipe with wide pillars between them; then, on the level below, chambers are excavated beneath the pillars. Weight causes the upper structure to cave in and drop into the lower chamber. The technique was used until the mid-1950s when it was replaced by block caving. See BLOCK CAVING; OPEN PIT MINING; WILLIAMS, GARDNER.

Chameis, historic diamond-producing area 100 kilometers (62 miles) north of the mouth of the Orange River in Namibia; now being re-worked by CDM.

Chameleon Diamond, 2.24 ct. polished diamond, found in 1943, which is reported to change color from bronze to green when exposed to light. The name, coined by C.A. Kiger Company, is now used generically for any diamond that changes color. Current whereabouts unknown. See CHAMELEON-TYPE DIAMOND.

chameleon-type diamond, diamond which changes color, generally from grayish green to bright yellow, when heated slightly. Such stones generally become yellower when left in darkness and have a strong yellow phosphorescence to ultraviolet light. See CHAMELEON DIAMOND, DOUBLE-COLOR DIAMOND, THERMOCHROMATIC, TRANSICHROMATIC.

champagne diamond, yellowish brown or brownish yellow diamond that is too light in color to be considered a fancy color. See BROWN DIAMOND; C1, C2, . . . C7.

Changlin Diamond, 158.79 ct. diamond, reportedly yellow, found near the Chenjiabu Mine in Shandong Province, China, in 1977. The mine is located among scattered alluvial deposits between the towns of Linyi and Tancheng.

Changma, open pit mine working two small kimberlite pipes near the town of Changma Zhuang in Shandong Province, China. Discovered in 1965, the pipes (named Shengli I and II) merge underground. In 1992, the pit was reported to be 55 meters (180 feet) deep. Production is 30 percent gem quality; stones up to 119 ct. have reportedly been found.

channel setting, setting style in which brilliant or step-cut gemstones of the same size are set girdle-to-girdle, with no metal between them, between two parallel outer metal walls. See CALIBRE CUT.

channel setting

Charlemont Diamond, 20 ct. rough diamond, described as yellow and reportedly found in Cape Province, South Africa, in 1854. The diamond is said to have been taken to Charlemont, Ireland, and given to the local Church; the monstrance in which it was set, and so presumably the diamond, was stolen in 1872. Since the Charlemont Diamond, like the Gordon and Hanger Diamonds, is not known to have been examined by a competent authority, its gemological identity is unconfirmed. For that reason, the Eureka, which was discovered in 1866, is considered the first authenticated diamond discovered in South Africa. Current whereabouts unknown. See PLATBERG, PNIEL.

Charles the Bold (1433-1477), Duke of Burgundy, whose royal regalia was among the first to emphasize the prestige of the diamond. His collection contained the Sancy Diamond; the Charles the Bold Diamond; the Order of the Garter, which was fashioned in gold and set with seventy pearls, five rubies, and four large diamonds; a dress sword set with diamonds; and a gold ring with the letter N set in diamonds, among other treasures. He wore his diamonds into battle, as talismans; when he was killed in an attack on the French city of Nancy in 1477, they were stripped from his body by Swiss mercenaries.

Charles the Bold Diamond, large, reportedly pyramid-shaped yellow diamond with its apex in the form of a four-rayed star, supposedly lost in battle by Charles the Bold (1433-1477). It may later have belonged to Henry VIII of England (1491-1547) and then to his daughter, Queen Mary Tudor; she is said to have given it to her husband, Philip II of Spain. Current whereabouts unknown.

Charles II (ca. 1810-1873), French Duke of Brunswick and ardent collector of jewels who owned a number of notable diamonds, including the Brunswick Blue and the Brunswick Yellow. An acknowledged eccentric, the Duke constructed elaborate security systems at his home in Paris to protect the collection and refused to spend a single night apart from his gems. Many of the jewels were sold as part of his estate following his death.

Châtellerault diamond, misnomer for rock crystal quartz from the town of Châtellerault in west-central France. Also spelled Châtelherault.

chemical composition, those chemical elements which make up a mineral. Gem diamond is about 99.95 percent to 99.98 percent pure carbon. Impurities, some of which may contribute to a diamond's color, include iron, silicon, calcium, magnesium, nitrogen, aluminum, and boron. See TRACE ELEMENT.

chemical vapor deposition (CVD), process of diamond synthesis in which a thin film of tetrahedrally-bonded carbon atoms is deposited on a substrate. It is done in the presence of hydrogen and methane in a low-pressure, moderate-temperature environment. Also called plasma-enhanced chemical vapor deposition. See DIAMOND-LIKE CARBON (DLC), SYNTHETIC DIAMOND THIN FILM.

Chicapa River, important source of alluvial diamonds in northeastern Angola. See ANGOLA, CHIUMBE RIVER, EMPRESA NACIONAL DE DIAMANTES DE ANGOLA (ENDIAMA), LUCAPA.

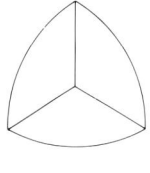

chiffre cut, shield-shaped rose cut with a flat, unfaceted base and three crown facets.

chiffre cut

China, People's Republic of (PRC), major nation occupying the eastern part of the Asian land mass. Alluvial and primary kimberlitic deposits have been found in Shandong, Hunan, and Liaoning Provinces, and more than 100 kimberlite dikes and pipes have been found in close proximity to the Tanlu fault in Liaoning Province. In 1992, about 200,000 ct. were produced from these sources. The country also produces synthetic diamonds and has a manufacturing industry. See BIN HAI MINE, CHANGMA, EVERAY JEWELLERY, LTD., FUXIAN PIPE 50, LIAONING, POLI, PUDONG, SHENGLI I MINE, TANCHENG, WAFANGDIAN MINE, XIYU, YINCHENG, YUAN RIVER.

chip, (1) shallow break on a diamond which extends from a facet junction or girdle edge and is larger or deeper than a nick. (2) irregularly shaped broken piece of diamond rough weighing less than 1.8 ct. See CLEAVAGE, INTERNAL CHARACTERISTIC, NICK.

chipped culet, culet that has been broken or otherwise damaged. See ABRADED CULET, CHIP, CULET, NICK.

Chiumbe River, important source of alluvial diamonds in northeastern Angola. See ANGOLA, EMPRESA NACIONAL DE DIAMANTES DE ANGOLA (ENDIAMA), LUCAPA.

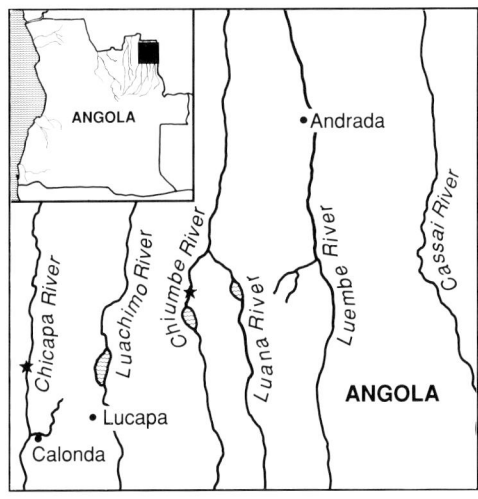

Chicapa and Chiumbe Rivers

chromatic aberration, optical effect seen when different colors of light refracted through a convex lens fail to meet at the same point: any bright objects in the field of view appear to be surrounded by a colored halo. Eliminated by combining different optical elements made of materials with different dispersions. See ACHROMATIC LENS, DISPERSION, REFRACTION, REFRACTIVE INDEX (RI), SPHERICAL ABERRATION.

chrome diopside, CrDi, bright green variety of diopside containing a small amount of chromium oxide (Cr_2O_3), found in metamorphic rock. It has a refractive index of 1.675 to 1.70, a specific gravity of 3.2, a hardness (Mohs scale) of 5 to 6, and a vitreous luster. It is an indicator mineral for kimberlite. See PYROPE GARNET.

CIBJO, see CONFEDERATION INTERNATIONALE DE LA BIJOUTERIE, JOAILLERIE, ORFEVRERIE, DES DIAMANTS, PERLES ET PIERRES.

CIBJO international clarity/purity scale, range of diamond clarity grades, running from LC (loupe clean) through two grades each of VVS (very, very slightly included), VS (very slightly included), SI (slightly included), and three grades of *piqué*, which is equal to the GIA grade I. See APPENDIX E, CONFEDERATION INTERNATIONALE DE LA BIJOUTERIE, JOAILLERIE, ORFEVRERIE DES DIAMANTS, PERLES ET PIERRES (CIBJO); CLARITY; CLARITY GRADING; CLARITY-GRADING SCALE; CLARITY-GRADING SYSTEM; GIA CLARITY-GRADING SCALE; IDC CLARITY-GRADING SCALE; SCAN. D.N. CLARITY SCALE.

CIBJO international color-grading scale, range of diamond color grades used to describe colorless to light yellow, light brown, and light gray stones. CIBJO grades are: exceptional white +, exceptional white, rare white +, rare white, white, slightly tinted white, tinted white, and tinted color. See APPENDIX D, BODYCOLOR; CONFEDERATION INTERNATIONALE DE LA BIJOUTERIE, JOAILLERIE, ORFEVRERIE DES DIAMANTS, PERLES ET PIERRES (CIBJO); COLOR GRADING; COLOR-GRADING SCALE; COLOR-GRADING SYSTEM; GIA COLOR-GRADING SCALE; IDC INTERNATIONAL COLOR-GRADING SCALE; SCAN. D.N. COLOR SCALE.

CIBJO Rules of Application for the Diamond Trade, set of guidelines for diamond clarity grading, color grading and nomenclature, cut description, and certification, established by the Conféderation Internationale de la Bijouterie, Joaillerie, Orfèvrerie des Diamants, Perles et Pierres (CIBJO). See IDC RULES FOR GRADING POLISHED DIAMONDS, SCANDINAVIAN DIAMOND NOMENCLATURE (SCAN. D.N.) AND GRADING STANDARDS.

C.I.E., see COMMISSION INTERNATIONALE DE L'ECLAIRAGE.

Cincora, historically important alluvial deposit in Bahia, Brazil; active during the mid-1850s.

Circle of Light, proprietary name for a diamond with a polished girdle.

Cirolite, proprietary name for yttrium aluminum garnet (YAG). Marketed as a diamond simulant.

CIS, see COMMONWEALTH OF INDEPENDENT STATES.

CIS Polishing Factories, located at Vinnitsa and Kiev in the Ukraine, Gomel in Belarus, Erevan in Armenia, and Chardzhou in Turkmenistan, they purchase supplies from Almazy Rossii-Sakha and are sometimes sub-contracted to polish diamonds for Western diamantaires. Their domestic output is sold through Almazjuvelirexport or to Western dealers direct. See ALMAZJUVELIREXPORT, ALMAZY ROSSII-SAKHA, KRISTALL, RUSSALMAZZOLOTO, YAKUTALMAZ.

Cissie Patterson Necklace, diamond necklace set with more than 400 carats of diamonds, including a reportedly flawless, colorless, 22 ct. cushion shape. Once owned by Eleanor Medill Patterson, former owner of the *Washington Times Herald*; current whereabouts unknown.

claim, portion of land over which an individual or group of individuals has obtained mining rights.

clarity, a gemstone's relative freedom from inclusions and blemishes. Sometimes called purity; in Europe, quality. See CLARITY GRADE.

clarity characteristic, (1) internal or external feature of a gemstone which can aid in establishing its identity and quality. The number, size, position, color, and nature of the characteristics in or on a diamond determine the stone's clarity grade in the GIA system. (2) term preferred in retail sales for inclusions and blemishes. See BLEMISH, EXTERNAL CHARACTERISTICS, INTERNAL CHARACTERISTICS.

clarity enhancement, any process, such as the filling of fractures and cavities with glass or resin, used to improve the apparent clarity of a gem. See FILLED DIAMOND, LASER DRILLING.

clarity grade, professional assessment of the clarity characteristics observable in or on a diamond or other gemstone, with reference to a systematic set of standards. Grades are usually based on how visible the clarity characteristics are, and how they affect the stone's durability; they are typically represented by a standardized nomenclature of terms (or their abbreviations), letters, numbers, or a combination thereof, which describe the extent to which a diamond varies from flawless. See AGS CLARITY-GRADING SCALE, BLEMISH, CIBJO INTERNATIONAL CLARITY/PURITY SCALE, CLARITY, CLARITY CHARACTERISTIC, CLARITY GRADING, GIA CLARITY-GRADING SCALE, IDC CLARITY-GRADING SCALE, INTERNAL CHARACTERISTIC, SCAN. D.N. CLARITY SCALE.

clarity grading, process of examining a diamond's clarity characteristics, determining their effect on its overall quality, and assigning a grade with reference to a systematic set of standards described in terms of a standardized nomenclature. See AGS CLARITY-GRADING SCALE, CIBJO INTERNATIONAL CLARITY/PURITY SCALE, CLARITY, CLARITY CHARACTERISTICS, CLARITY GRADING, GIA CLARITY-GRADING SCALE, IDC CLARITY-GRADING SCALE, SCAN. D.N. CLARITY SCALE.

clarity-grading scale, graduated series of clarity grades, usually beginning with flawless as the highest and ending with heavily included or imperfect as the lowest. See AGS CLARITY-GRADING SCALE, APPENDIX E, CIBJO INTERNATIONAL CLARITY/PURITY SCALE, CLARITY GRADE, CLARITY GRADING, CLARITY-GRADING SYSTEM, GIA CLARITY-GRADING SCALE, IDC CLARITY-GRADING SCALE, SCAN. D.N. CLARITY SCALE.

clarity-grading system, standardized set of procedures and terms for evaluating a diamond's clarity. The clarity-grading systems in use today are based on a variety of nomenclatures, ranging from letters and/or numbers to descriptive or historically derived terms. See AGS CLARITY-GRADING SCALE, CIBJO INTERNATIONAL CLARITY/PURITY SCALE, CLARITY GRADE, CLARITY GRADING, CLARITY-GRADING SCALE, GIA CLARITY-GRADING SCALE, IDC CLARITY-GRADING SCALE, SCAN. D.N. CLARITY SCALE.

clatersal, Dutch term for small fragments of industrial or gem quality diamond produced during bruting and later crushed into powder.

claw, see PRONG.

clean, term used to describe a diamond that appears to have no inclusions, or only a few inclusions, under cursory examination. Its use in sales promotion is prohibited by the Federal Trade Commission in the US, and by similar authorities elsewhere, unless the stone is flawless. See BLUE-WHITE, EYE-CLEAN, LOUPE CLEAN.

cleavage, (1) tendency of a crystalline mineral, such as diamond, to break along crystallographic planes (parallel to possible crystal faces), leaving a more or less smooth, planar surface. (2) any break in a diamond parallel to one of its four pairs of octahedral faces; it may also occur parallel to the dodecahedral faces, although less easily. Cleavage can be caused by inherent internal strain or by a sharp blow. Cleavages may extend to the surface of a diamond or surround a crystal inclusion. (3) one of the pieces of diamond resulting from a complete break along a cleavage plane. (4) CSO term for an irregularly-shaped, broken piece of diamond rough weighing more than 1.80 ct. Many of the world's largest rough diamonds, such as the Cullinan and the Centenary, were cleavages. See CLEAVAGE MASS, CLEAVAGE PLANE, CLIVAGE, CRYSTAL PLANE, FRACTURE, GRAIN.

cleavage crack, see CLEAVAGE.

cleavage grain, see GRAIN.

cleavage mass, large piece of diamond produced by cleaving. See CLEAVAGE.

cleavage plane, plane parallel to a possible crystal face, along which cleavage may occur. The primary cleavage planes in diamond parallel the possible octahedron faces. The secondary cleavage planes parallel the dodecahedron faces.

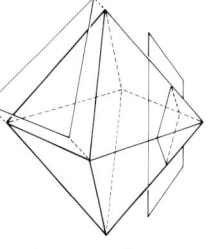

cleavage plane

cleaver, person with the skill, training and experience to cleave, or split, a diamond along a cleavage plane. The cleaver may also be responsible for planning the fashioning of a polished gem. See SPLITTER.

cleaver's blade, wedge-shaped steel blade used in cleaving diamonds.

cleaver's knife, see CLEAVER'S BLADE.

cleaver's mallet, wooden instrument used to strike the cleaver's blade in order to split the diamond.

cleaver's stick, long wooden holder, 15 to 25 centimeters (6 to 10 inches) long, one end of which is filled with cement to fix either the diamond being cleaved or the sharp used to form the kerf. See DOP, KERF, SHARP.

cleaver's wedge, see CLEAVER'S BLADE.

cleaving, act of dividing a diamond into two pieces along a cleavage plane; normally done to produce sizes or shapes which can be cut more economically or into better quality stones, thereby improving the model. See MODEL.

cleaving

cleaving box, box fitted with two pegs against which the cleaver's sticks are placed, and which catches diamond powder and fragments produced during cleaving.

cleft, V-shaped area between the lobes of a heart-shape diamond.

Clerici's solution, caustic, poisonous, heavy liquid composed of thallium formate and thallium malonate in a saturated water solution. It is sometimes calibrated with distilled water to a specific gravity of 3.52 and used to separate diamond (3.52) from spinel (3.60) and sapphire (4.00) by SG. See SPECIFIC GRAVITY (SG).

Cleveland Diamond, 50 ct. (old carats), 128-facet cushion-shape diamond, named for US President Grover Cleveland and fashioned in New York in 1884 from an estimated 100 ct. rough found in Kimberley, South Africa. At the time, it was the largest diamond ever cut in the US. Worn by Minnie Palmer, a musical-comedy star of the 1880s. Current whereabouts unknown. See OLD CARAT.

clivage, any size or shape of rough diamond which must be split into smaller pieces by cleaving, lasering, or sawing prior to polishing.

closed culet, point of the pavilion on a brilliant-cut diamond on which no culet has been polished, or on which it is too small to be seen. A knife-edged keel on an emerald cut is considered a closed culet.

closed setting, mounting, widely used during the Renaissance, which completely encloses a gemstone's pavilion; often the stone is bezel set.

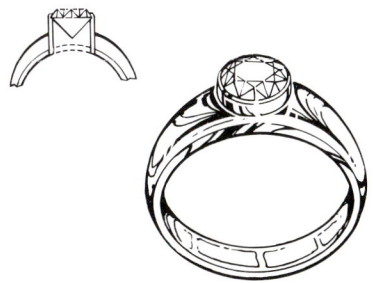

closed setting

closed table, small table diameter relative to the girdle diameter. Generally used to refer to a table diameter less than 53-57 percent. See OPEN TABLE, TABLE DIAMETER, TABLE PERCENTAGE, TOLKOWSKY THEORETICAL BRILLIANT CUT.

cloud, hazy or milky area in a diamond; a cloud may be small in area or spread throughout the stone, and may or may not possess a distinct outline.

cloud

cloverleaf effect, see UMBRELLA EFFECT.

cluster, group of closely-set stones, sometimes arranged to create the illusion of a single, large stone.

cluster setting, head in which several small diamonds are set close together, creating the illusion of one large stone. See BUTTERCUP HEAD, ILLUSION HEAD, TIFFANY HEAD.

cluster setting

CMOO, see COMPAGNIE MINIÈRE DE L'OUBANGUI ORIENTAL.

Coalinga diamond, misnomer for colorless quartz crystal from Coalinga, California, US.

coastal workings, see BEACH MINING.

coated crystal, diamond crystal with a natural opaque diamond overgrowth containing a high percentage of impurities and inclusions; usually found in alluvial deposits. The stone's surface has the granular appearance of an orange peel; the coating (which may be a secondary growth) may be several millimeters thick and require the polishing of a window to determine the natural color and/or clarity of the stone. Coated crystal colors range from light greenish gray through light yellow green, dark green, gray, or black. Coated crystals are common in Zaire and west Africa and are sometimes known as "Congo coated."

coated crystal

coated diamond, polished diamond which has been partially or wholly coated with a colored substance (usually bluish, although it can be other colors) to mask a yellowish bodycolor. Coating, which is always considered a deceptive practice, is usually done by applying the coloring agent to the pavilion or girdle, often to a single facet or in a single spot although, in some cases, the entire stone may be coated. Also called a painted diamond.

cobalt-60, unstable, radioactive nuclide of cobalt which emits gamma and beta rays as it decays. Its half-life is 5.3 years. Used to irradiate diamonds to enhance their color. Such stones are not radioactive and are safe to wear. See IRRADIATED DIAMOND.

coefficient of expansion, rate at which a material expands in relation to a given rise in temperature. Because diamond has a very low coefficient of expansion, it can be safely heated to higher temperatures than other gemstones.

cognac, see BROWN DIAMOND; C1,C2, . . . C7.

Cognac-Over-Ice Diamond, 34 ct. pear-shape diamond, described as fancy brown; reportedly owned by actress Elizabeth Taylor.

Colenso Diamond, 133.14 ct. octahedron, described as fine light yellow, believed to have been found in the De Beers Mine. It was given to the British Museum of Natural History by author John Ruskin (1819-1900) in honor of his friend, John William Colenso (1814-1883), a mathematician and the first Anglican bishop of Natal, South Africa. Stolen in 1965, its current whereabouts are unknown.

Colesberg Kopje, site of the Kimberley Mine; also called De Beers New Rush or New Rush.

collet, (1) a metal cone, slit in two or more planes and designed to be enclosed in a tapered metal sleeve to grip a diamond during polishing. See DOP. (2) culet. (3) metal portion of a finger ring in which a gemstone is set.

Collins, Samuel V., American oil man and entrepreneur who in 1961 pioneered the dangerous process of recovering diamonds from the seabed. The concession held by his Marine Diamond Corporation proved unprofitable; it is now leased to CDM. See OFF-SHORE MINING.

Collis Diamond Syndicate, group which financed prospecting for diamonds on Halifax Island, off the coast of what is now Namibia, in 1906. Shortly after the 45-man expedition landed, the government of the Cape Colony (later Province), to which the island belonged, forced them to leave.

color, see BODYCOLOR.

Colorado diamond, misnomer for transparent smoky quartz.

color blindness, inability to distinguish one or more of the colors red (red-green color blindness), blue (blue-yellow color blindness), or green. Color blindness can affect the ability to color grade diamonds. Also called color discrimination deficiency.

color center, structural defect in a mineral's atomic lattice which absorbs light and imparts color to the stone. See COLORED DIAMOND, IRRADIATED BLUE DIAMOND, IRRADIATED GREEN DIAMOND.

color discrimination deficiency, see COLOR BLINDNESS.

colored diamond, diamond which is noticeably yellow, brown, pink, red, blue, orange, purple, green, gray, or black. This does not include diamonds in the normal color range that are slightly yellowish, slightly brownish, or slightly grayish. When the color is natural, the diamonds are called fancy color diamonds, fancy diamonds, or fancies. When the color is induced by irradiation, the stones are called treated diamonds. See DISCLOSURE, IRRADIATED DIAMONDS.

color grade, relative position of a diamond's bodycolor on a colorless-to-light-yellow scale, denoted by standard nomenclature such as letters, numbers, words, or a combination thereof. Color grades are established by comparing a diamond to a set of standard master diamonds under controlled conditions. Such grades are normally assigned only to colorless, near colorless, or light yellow, light brown, and light gray diamonds; other colors are considered fancy colors and are described differently. See AGS COLOR-GRADING SCALE, BODYCOLOR, CIBJO INTERNATIONAL COLOR-GRADING SCALE, COLORED DIAMONDS, COLORIMETER, FANCY COLOR DIAMOND, GIA COLOR-GRADING SCALE, IDC INTERNATIONAL COLOR-GRADING SCALE, SCAN. D.N. COLOR SCALE.

color grading, process of evaluating the bodycolor of colorless to light yellow, light brown, or light gray diamonds by comparing them to a set of master diamonds under controlled conditions, and assigning a grade. Color grading is usually done only on natural, untreated diamonds; others can be graded, but with less accuracy. Special nomenclature is used for fancy color diamonds. See AGS COLOR-GRADING SCALE, BODYCOLOR, CIBJO INTERNATIONAL COLOR-GRAD-

ING SCALE, COLOR GRADE, COLOR-GRADING SCALE, DIAMONDLITE, GIA COLOR-GRADING SCALE, IDC INTERNATIONAL COLOR-GRADING SCALE, SCAN. D.N. COLOR SCALE, Z MASTER DIAMOND.

color-grading scale, graduated series of diamond color grades normally covering stones in the range from colorless to light yellow, light brown, or light gray. See AGS COLOR-GRADING SCALE, APPENDIX D, BODYCOLOR, CIBJO INTERNATIONAL COLOR-GRADING SCALE, COLOR GRADE, COLOR GRADING, COLOR-GRADING SYSTEM, GIA COLOR-GRADING SCALE, IDC INTERNATIONAL COLOR-GRADING SCALE, SCAN. D.N. COLOR SCALE.

color-grading system, standardized set of procedures and terms for evaluating a diamond's bodycolor by comparing it to a set of master diamonds ranging from colorless to light yellow. The color-grading systems in use today employ a variety of nomenclatures, ranging from letters and/or numbers to descriptive or historically derived terms. See AGS COLOR-GRADING SCALE, CIBJO INTERNATIONAL COLOR-GRADING SCALE, COLOR GRADE, COLOR GRADING, COLOR-GRADING SCALE, GIA COLOR-GRADING SCALE, IDC INTERNATIONAL COLOR-GRADING SCALE, MASTER DIAMONDS, SCAN. D.N. COLOR SCALE.

color-grading tray, holder used in color grading to position master diamonds and the diamond being color graded.

colorimeter, instrument used to color grade a diamond by measuring its relative transmission of yellow and blue light. Colorimeters can be used only on colorless to yellow diamonds, and are most effective on round brilliants; they cannot grade browns, grays, fancy colors, or fluorescent stones, and are less useful for fancy shapes. See AGS COLOR-GRADING SCALE.

colorless, term used to describe a transparent diamond or other gemstone completely devoid of bodycolor. Colorless materials transmit all wavelengths of light equally, without absorption. See LIGHT ABSORPTION, COLOR GRADING, SELECTIVE ABSORPTION.

color range, see NORMAL COLOR RANGE.

color temperature, a measure of the spectral characteristics and distribution of a light source. Measured on the Kelvin scale of absolute temperature, sunlight has a color temperature of approximately 6,000 K; a typical light bulb has a color temperature of approximately 2,500 K. Light with a color temperature falling between these two points is generally classified as white light.

color-treated diamond, see COATED DIAMOND, IRRADIATED DIAMOND.

color zoning, occurrence of gem color in discrete areas or bands. In diamonds, color-zoning is most common in fancy colors, which may show a different color face-up than face-down. When color is concentrated near a culet or keel line, it is an indication the stone may have been treated. Sometimes called uneven color.

color zoning

photo by John I. Koivula

Comdiam, Belgian company which manufactures and markets diamond manufacturing products designed by Wetenschappelijk en Technisch Onderzoekcentrum voor Diamant, a research facility linked to the Hoge Raad voor Diamant of Antwerp.

commercially clean, misleading term usually applied to a diamond which is reasonably free from inclusions but not flawless. The US Federal Trade Commission prohibits its use in sales promotion, as do comparable authorities elsewhere, unless the stone is flawless. See BLUE-WHITE.

commercially perfect, misleading term usually applied to a diamond which is almost flawless.

The US Federal Trade Commission prohibits its use in sales promotion, as do comparable authorities elsewhere, unless the stone is flawless. See BLUE-WHITE.

commercial white, misleading color term usually applied to a diamond which has a slight trace of color. The US Federal Trade Commission prohibits its use in sales promotion, as do comparable authorities elsewhere, unless the stone is colorless. See BLUE-WHITE, OFF-COLOR DIAMOND.

Commission Internationale de L'Éclairage (CIE), International Lighting Commission. Paris-based organization which establishes standards of illumination, color measurement, and color description.

common goods, sorting term for low-quality rough diamonds, including rejection chips and bort, not suitable for cutting.

Commonwealth of Independent States (CIS), loosely-knit federation of Republics that formerly comprised the Union of Soviet Socialist Republics (USSR).

Compagnie Diamantifère de la Haute-Sangha (Sangha Mine), small diamond-mining company that operated in the Central African Republic before that country's independence in 1960.

Compagnie du Chemin de Fer du Bas-Congo-Katanga (BCK), (the Lower Congo-Katanga Railway Company), Belgian company which built a railway from Elisabethville (now Lubumbashi) to the mouth of the Congo River in 1916. Granted prospecting rights in the region, the company discovered the diamond deposits of Bakwanga (Mbuji-Mayi) in western Kasai Province in 1918. Also called the Bas-Congo-Katanga Railway Company. See MBUJI-MAYI, SOCIETE MINIERE DE BAKWANGA (MIBA).

Compagnie Française des Mines de Diamant du Cap de Bonne Espérance, (French Diamond Mining Company of the Cape of Good Hope), known as the French Company. An important concern in the early history of the South African diamond industry; in 1887, the Paris-based French Company was, after Barney Barnato's Kimberley Central Mining Company, the leading claimholder in the Kimberley Mine. In that year, with the help of a loan from N.M. Rothschild of London, Cecil Rhodes purchased the French Company, a move which precipitated a struggle for control between Rhodes and Barnato. See BARNATO, BARNEY; BEIT, ALFRED; RHODES, CECIL JOHN.

Compagnie Minière de L'Oubangui Oriental (CMOO), diamond-mining company which first worked the alluvial deposits in the West Oubangui region of the Central African Republic in the 1930s and 1940s; now defunct.

Companhia de Pesquisas Mineras de Angola (PEMA), company formed in 1913 to prospect and mine for diamonds in Angola; the forerunner to DIAMANG. See ANGOLA, COMPANHIA DE DIAMANTES DE ANGOLA (DIAMANG), EMPRESA NACIONAL DE DIAMANTES DE ANGOLA (ENDIAMA).

Companhia de Diamantes de Angola (DIAMANG), Lisbon-based company which was given an exclusive 50-year diamond-mining concession in Angola in 1917. The terms of the concession were reduced in 1970; the Angolan government acquired a majority interest in the company in 1977. This passed to the government-established agency ENDIAMA in 1981 and, in 1986, DIAMANG was dissolved. See ANGOLA, COMPANHIA DE PESQUISAS MINERAS DE ANGOLA (PEMA), EMPRESA NACIONAL DE DIAMANTES DE ANGOLA (ENDIAMA).

comparison diamonds, see MASTER DIAMONDS.

comparison gauge, demonstration device which holds a series of mounted round brilliant diamond simulants of various carat weights; used in retail sales to provide customers with an indication of how a diamond of a given size looks when it is mounted.

comparison stones, see MASTER DIAMONDS.

compressibility, extent to which a material can be reduced in volume under pressure. Diamond is the least compressible of all minerals; its relative compressibility is represented numerically at 18 (compared to quartz at 267).

concentrate, residue of diamonds and heavy minerals which remains after ore is crushed and lighter material is removed.

conchoidal fracture, curved, shell-like fracture in a crystalline or amorphous material. Many diamond simulants show conchoidal fracture; in diamonds, the fracture is occasionally conchoidal but usually splintery.

concussion mark, see BRUISE.

Condé Diamond, see GRAND CONDE DIAMOND.

conduction, transmission of electrical or thermal energy in a material. See CONDUCTOMETER, ELECTRICAL CONDUCTIVITY, THERMAL CONDUCTIVITY.

conductivity meter, see CONDUCTOMETER.

conductometer, device used to detect a material's ability to conduct electrical current. Generally consists of a small power supply and an ohmmeter; the diamond to be tested is placed in the circuit between a positive lead and a negative ground, and its resistance is measured. The conductometer can be used to separate natural-color blue diamonds (Type IIb), which are electrically conductive, from irradiated blue diamonds, which are not. See AUDIO CONDUCTION DETECTOR.

cone crusher, machine used to reduce ore; it consists of a cone rotating on an eccentric axis inside a large funnel; large blocks of ore are fed between the cone and the funnel walls and crushed into smaller pieces.

Confédération Internationale de la Bijouterie, Joaillerie, Orfèvrerie, des Diamants, Perles et Pierres (CIBJO), international trade organization founded in 1961 for the promotion of the worldwide jewelry industry. CIBJO is composed of groups from some twenty countries and is organized into four independent sectors: Manufacturing of Jewelry and Silverware; Wholesaling of Jewelry and Silverware; Dealing and Cutting of Diamonds, Gemstones, and Pearls; and Retailing of Jewelry and Silverware. Intersectoral commissions for diamonds, pearls, and gemstones meet periodically to update the Confederation's practices in diamond clarity grading, color nomenclature, and certification. See CIBJO INTERNATIONAL CLARITY/PURITY SCALE, CIBJO INTERNATIONAL COLOR-GRADING SCALE, CIBJO RULES OF APPLICATION FOR THE DIAMOND TRADE.

conglomerate, coarse-grained sedimentary rock composed primarily of rounded fragments larger than two millimeters (0.1 inch) in diameter in a matrix of fine-grained sediment or a natural cementing material. Conglomerates are sometimes diamond-bearing.

Congo, see ZAIRE, REPUBLIC OF.

consignment, wholesale trade practice of supplying a client with diamonds on approval ("on consignment" or "on memo"). Clients pay only for the stones they want or sell and return the rest.

Consolidated African Selection Trust, Ltd. (CAST), once the principal diamond-mining company in Ghana; now defunct. CAST also mined diamond deposits in Sierra Leone through the Sierra Leone Selection Trust. In 1972, the Ghanaian government acquired 55 percent of CAST and formed Ghana Consolidated Diamonds; in 1982, the government acquired the remainder of the stock.

Consolidated Diamond Mines of South West Africa, Ltd., see CDM (PTY.), LTD.

Constantin Diamond, 46.05 ct., D-color, internally flawless emerald-cut diamond; sold by Christie's, Geneva, in 1970. Current whereabouts unknown.

contact goniometer, see GONIOMETER.

contact liquid, medium placed on the hemicylinder of a refractometer to ensure optical contact with the surface of the stone being tested. A refractometer cannot be used to test stones with a refractive index higher than that of the contact liquid. A mixture of sulfur, tetradoethylene, and methylene iodide calibrated to an RI of 1.81 is the contact liquid used with most standard refractometers. See REFRACTIVE INDEX (RI), REFRACTOMETER.

contact twin, crystal in which two or more single diamonds have joined together in a symmetrical fashion late in their formation. See CRYSTAL STRUCTURE, MACLE, TWIN CRYSTAL.

contact twin

Continental Jewels, proprietary name for synthetic strontium titanate. Marketed as a diamond simulant.

Cooperative Africaine de Récherches et d'Exploitations Diamantifères, (African Cooperative of Diamond Prospecting and Mining). Organization established in 1960 to license diggers in the Ivory Coast; now defunct.

Cooperative Bekima, cooperative society of miners created in Guinea in 1957 to eliminate illicit diamond marketing by channeling production into legal exports; now defunct.

Copenhagen Blue Diamond, 45.85 ct. emerald-cut blue diamond fashioned from rough found at the Jagersfontein Mine; named in honor of an exhibition in Copenhagen in 1960. Privately owned.

Copeton, diamond-producing area in New South Wales, Australia. See NEW SOUTH WALES.

Coral Sea mv, mining vessel belonging to De Beers Marine, equipped with a rotating drill for extraction of diamond gravels from the seabed.

core drill, hollow drill which cuts, removes, and brings to the surface a cylindrical sample of the material below. See BENOTO DRILL, CORE SAMPLING.

core sampling, prospecting technique in which a hollow drill is sunk into the ground to cut and extract a long, cylindrical stratigraphic sample for examination and analysis. See BENOTO DRILL, CORE DRILL.

Cornflower Blue Diamond, 31.92 ct. flawless, pear-shape, fancy blue diamond fashioned from a 158 ct. rough purchased by Harry Winston in 1958. Current whereabouts unknown.

Cornish diamond, misnomer for rock crystal quartz.

Coromandel, regionally important alluvial diamond-mining area in Minas Gerais, Brazil.

Coromandel

Coromandel Diamonds, four large diamonds from the Coromandel district, Minas Gerais, Brazil. The stones were numbered in the order of their discovery: the 180 ct. Coromandel I was found in 1934; the 141 ct. Coromandel II in 1935; the 226 ct. Coromandel III in 1936; and the 400.65 ct. Coromandel IV in 1940. The Coromandel IV was sold to Harry Winston, who had it fashioned into an unreported number of polished stones.

corrected loupe, see DOUBLET LOUPE, TRIPLET LOUPE.

corrected weight, hypothetical calculation of approximately what a polished diamond would have weighed had it been fashioned to the proportions of the Tolkowsky theoretical brilliant cut. See TOLKOWSKY THEORETICAL BRILLIANT CUT.

Corundolite, proprietary name for synthetic spinel. Used as a diamond simulant.

Côte d'Ivoire (Ivory Coast), African republic which has been a producer of alluvial diamonds since 1928. The deposits were originally mined by SAREMCI, formed in 1945 by a group of Paris diamond merchants, and SODIAMCI, a local company started in 1955. Mining is now undertaken by very small companies and local diggers, but SODIAMCI continues prospecting operations. SAREMCI ceased operating in 1975. See SOCIETE DE RECHERCHES ET D'EXPLOITATIONS MINIERES EN COTE D'IVOIRE (SAREMCI), SOCIETE DIAMANTIFERE DE LA COTE D'IVOIRE (SODIAMCI).

counterweight balance, any balance which uses small counterweights (usually metal) to determine the weight of a gemstone. See MECHANICAL BALANCE, PORTABLE BALANCE, RIDER BALANCE.

Countess Széchényi Diamond, 62.05 ct. pear-shape diamond given to American Gladys Moore Vanderbilt when she married Hungarian Count Laszlo Széchényi. Sold to Harry Winston in 1959 and repolished to VVS, D-color, 59.38 ct.; it was mounted in a necklace and sold in the US in 1966. Current whereabouts unknown.

country rock, common geological/mining term often used to describe the host rock immediately surrounding a kimberlite pipe; its use is not, however, limited to kimberlites.

covalent bonding, atomic bonding achieved through the sharing of electrons.

CRA, Ltd., Conzinc Riotinto-Australia, Australian mining and natural resources company which, with Ashton Mining, is part owner of, and manages, the Argyle Diamond Mines Joint Venture. See ARGYLE DIAMOND MINES; ARGYLE DIAMOND MINES JOINT VENTURE; ASHTON MINING, LTD.; AUSTRALIA.

crack, see FRACTURE.

cradle, simple wooden device once used for separating diamonds from alluvial gravels; seldom used in modern diggings. Also known as a rocker. See BABY, PAN, TROMMEL.

Crater of Diamonds, largest diamond-bearing lamproite pipe in the US, located four kilometers (2.5 miles) south of Murfreesboro, Arkansas. The site is operated as a state park where, for a fee, visitors can search for diamonds; although most stones are industrial quality, some gem diamonds have been found. Efforts to mine the deposit are made periodically but, to date, none have proved economically viable.

Crater of Diamonds

craton, large stable block of the earth's crust; typically found in the interiors of continents. Cratons are generally more than one billion years old; historically they are less subject to faulting, earthquakes, or volcanoes than other areas of the earth's land mass. They are apparently associated with diamond formation, although the precise relationship is not entirely understood.

critical angle, largest angle from the normal at which a ray of light can escape from an optically dense medium (*e.g.*, diamond) into a less dense medium, such as air. Light striking the internal surface of a diamond at an angle less than the critical angle passes out of the stone;

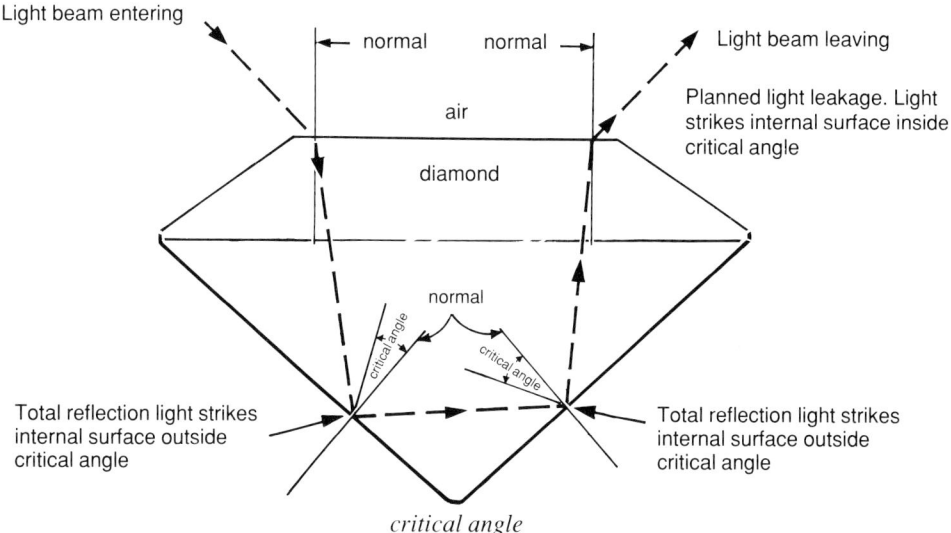

critical angle

light striking at an angle greater than the critical angle is all reflected internally. The critical angle is directly related to the refractive index (RI) of the material—the greater the RI, the smaller the critical angle. Diamond has a relatively high RI, and thus a small critical angle of 24°26", which is in part responsible for its brilliance. See BRILLIANCE, CRITICAL ANGLE CONE, NORMAL, REFRACTION, REFRACTIVE INDEX (RI), TOTAL INTERNAL REFLECTION.

critical angle cone, three-dimensional space described by rotating the critical angle around the normal, thus defining an imaginary cone. See ANGLE OF REFRACTION, NORMAL, REFRACTION, REFRACTIVE INDEX (RI), TOTAL INTERNAL REFLECTION.

croix, French, meaning *cross*. See FOUR-SQUARE STONE.

Crookes, William (1832-1919), British physicist who attempted to synthesize diamonds in 1905, first by dissolving carbon in molten iron and subjecting the solution to sudden cooling, and later by exploding gunpowder and cordite in closed steel cylinders. In 1904, he was the first to experiment with radium salts to irradiate diamonds. See SYNTHETIC DIAMOND.

cross, see FOUR-SQUARE STONE.

cross cut, see FOUR-SQUARE STONE.

cross-cutter, see CROSS-WORKER.

cross-cutting, see CROSS-WORKING.

cross facets, see GIRDLE FACETS.

cross-grained stone, irregularly shaped, intergrown diamond crystal; sometimes used incorrectly to denote any twinned diamond crystal. See MACLE, TWIN CRYSTAL.

cross naat, Dutch term for non-parallel multiple twinning. See NAAT, TWIN CRYSTAL.

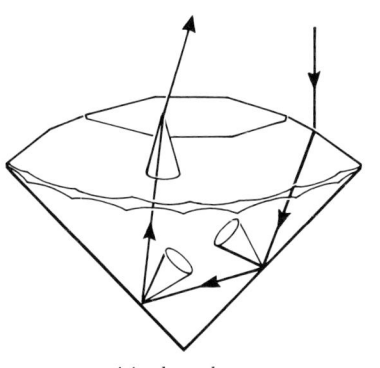

critical angle cone

cross-rose cut, rose cut with an eight-sided girdle outline; a flat, unfaceted base; and a pointed, dome-shaped crown with eight diamond-shaped facets, eight triangular facets, and eight narrow, trapazoidal facets around the girdle.

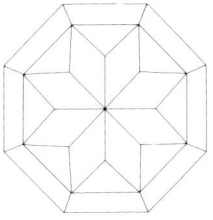
cross-rose cut

cross-worker, person who performs the cross-working operations during diamond polishing; sometimes called a cross-cutter.

cross-working, the second stage, after blocking, in polishing round and fancy shapes, when the four bezel facets are placed on the top of the stone, the four pavilion facets placed underneath, and additional work is done to the table. Sometimes combined with the blocking process, especially on smaller stones. Sometimes called cross-cutting. See BLOCKING, BRILLIANDEERING.

crown, the part of a diamond above the girdle plane. See PAVILION.

crown angle, angle measured between the girdle plane and the bezel facets. Crown angle and table size together determine the amount of dispersion a finished diamond displays. See PROPORTIONS.

Crown Diamond, 84 ct. cushion cut, described as fancy yellow, which once belonged to the Russian Imperial Family. Exhibited in the De Beers House of Jewels at the New York World's Fair in 1939-40; recut to a 52 ct. round brilliant in the 1950s. The diamond was recut again to 50 ct., when it was sold to an undisclosed buyer in 1963. Current whereabouts unknown.

crown height, distance between the girdle and table planes, usually measured in millimeters. See CROWN HEIGHT PERCENTAGE, PROPORTIONS.

crown height percentage, distance between the girdle and table planes expressed as a percentage of the average girdle diameter. See CROWN HEIGHT, PROPORTIONS.

crown jewels, (1) collection of gems and jewelry which belongs, or once belonged, to a royal house. (2) among English speakers, an elliptical reference to the British Crown Jewels. (3) proprietary name for synthetic colorless sapphire; marketed as a diamond simulant. See BRITISH CROWN JEWELS, FRENCH CROWN JEWELS, IRANIAN CROWN JEWELS, RUSSIAN DIAMOND FUND.

crown main facets, see BEZEL FACETS.

crowned rose cut, see DUTCH ROSE CUT.

crushing bort, lowest quality of industrial diamond; crushing bort is ground into diamond powder for use as an abrasive. See BALLAS, BORT, CARBONADO, FRAMESITE, HAILSTONE BORT, SHOT BORT, STEWARTITE.

crushing plant, facility in which ore is reduced to manageable size.

cryogenic cooling, cooling to temperatures below -45°C (-49°F) with dry ice or liquid nitrogen. Cooling slows molecular vibrations, thereby sharpening the absorption spectra of many colored diamonds.

crystal, (1) homogeneous solid material with a regular internal arrangement of atoms that may be outwardly expressed by plane surfaces which have a definite angular relationship to one another. (2) early color-grading term for a very slightly yellowish diamond (so-named for its resemblance to the slightly yellowish tint common in nineteenth century English glassware). (3) term on the Scan. D.N. color scale for near-colorless stones, over 0.47 ct., corresponding to the GIA color grade J. See APPENDIX D. (4) sharp-edged octahedron rough. See GLASSIE. (5) fine lead glass when used as glassware, art objects or, historically, as a diamond simulant.

Crystal, see KRISTALL.

crystal aggregate, group of crystals grown together in which individual crystals are eye-visible.

crystal face, see FACE.

crystal form, geometric shape of a well-formed crystal, such as a diamond octahedron. See CUBE, DODECAHEDRON, HABIT, HEXOCTAHEDRON, OCTAHEDRON, TETRAHEXAHEDRON, TRAPEZOHEDRON, TRISOCTAHEDRON.

crystal growth line, see GROWTH LINE.

crystal habit, see HABIT.

crystallographic axes, imaginary reference lines intersecting at specific angles in the center of a crystal; used as a reference in describing crystal structure and symmetry. One or all of the axes may coincide with axes of symmetry. See CRYSTAL SYSTEM.

crystal plane, any plane, crystal face, cleavage, or lattice plane which can be described mathematically in terms of the lengths and directions of the crystallographic axes. See CRYSTAL STRUCTURE, UNIT CELL.

Crystalprint, proprietary name for a photomicrograph taken with the Nomarski differential contrast microscope; a cast-shadow effect exposes extremely small topographic differences on polished diamond surfaces, including growth or grain patterns, which can then be photographed and classified. See GEMPRINT.

crystal structure, regular, repeating arrangement of atoms in a given mineral. Crystal structure is responsible for many of a mineral's characteristic properties, including hardness, brittleness, specific gravity, and optic character.

crystal system, one of seven classifications of crystal structure, based on the symmetry of crystal faces and the relative length and relationship of the crystallographic axes.

CSO, see CENTRAL SELLING ORGANISATION.

CSO Valuations AG, part of the Central Selling Organisation, formed in 1977 to sort and classify diamonds for sale through the Diamond Trading Company, and to act as a service company to affiliates. See CENTRAL SELLING ORGANISATION (CSO), DIAMOND TRADING COMPANY (PTY.), LTD. (DTC).

ct., abbreviation for carat. Also represented by ¢, especially in Europe and Great Britain. See CARAT.

Cuango, important area of alluvial deposits and known kimberlite pipes in northeastern Angola. Mining is undertaken by ENDIAMA, the state diamond company, and by the Brazilian group Odebrecht; production is sold through the Central Selling Organisation.

Cuanza River, river basin in Angola and an important alluvial diamond-mining area. Also spelled Kwanza.

Cuango and Cuanza River

Cuban Capitol Diamond, 23 ct. diamond, described as yellow, set in the floor of the Cuban Capitol Building in Havana, the point from which all highway distances in the country are measured. It was bought by subscription of the capitol building employees. Stolen in 1946, but recovered.

cube, (1) one of the seven crystal forms in the isometric (cubic) crystal system. Cubes have six equivalent square faces at 90° to one another; each face intersects one crystallographic axis and is

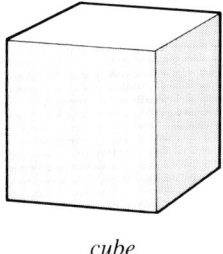

cube

parallel to the other two. Cube-shaped gem diamond crystals were once considered extremely rare; today, although the Jwaneng Mine in Botswana produces them in relatively large numbers, they are still uncommon. (2) sorting term for one of the basic shapes of large rough diamond crystals. See DODECAHEDRON, HEXOCTAHEDRON, OCTAHEDRON, TETRAHEXAHEDRON, TRAPEZOHEDRON, TRISOCTAHEDRON.

cubic crystal system, see ISOMETRIC CRYSTAL SYSTEM.

cubic form, see CUBE.

cubic planes, planes of atoms parallel to a possible cubic crystal face.

cubic zirconia, zirconium oxide (ZrO_2) crystallizing in the cubic system, the rare, naturally occurring mineral form of cubic zirconia, sometimes found as inclusions in zircon. See SYNTHETIC CUBIC ZIRCONIA (CZ).

Cuiaba Diamond, 60.75 ct. diamond, described as light rose-colored, found at Cuiaba, Minas Gerais, Brazil. Current whereabouts unknown.

culet, small facet on the point of the pavilion of a brilliant-cut diamond or on the keel of a step cut; fashioned to reduce the risk of damage. See CLOSED CULET, OPEN CULET.

culette, see CULET.

Cullinan, Thomas (1862-1936), building contractor who made a fortune in construction in South Africa and then turned to diamond prospecting. Cullinan led the syndicate which purchased the Elandsfontein Farm, 32 kilometers (20 miles) northeast of Pretoria, the site of the Premier Mine. He subsequently served as Chairman of the Premier (Transvaal) Diamond Mining

Thomas Cullinan

Company. The Premier Mine produced the 3,106 ct. Cullinan Diamond, which was named after him.

Cullinan Diamond, 3,106 ct. rough diamond, discovered in 1905 at the Premier Mine. The Cullinan is reportedly the largest gem diamond ever found. Named for Thomas Cullinan, the mine's Chairman, the great rough was purchased by the Transvaal Province government and presented to King Edward VII of Britain in 1907. When cut by the I. J. Asscher Company in Amsterdam in 1908, it produced nine major stones and 96 small brilliants. The nine large stones are in either the British Crown Jewels or the personal possession of the Royal Family. See CULLINAN I, II, . . . IX.

Cullinan I, 530.20 ct. reportedly very fine color, very fine clarity, pear-shape Type IIa diamond with 74 facets; mounted in the Imperial Sceptre and on display among the British Crown Jewels in the Tower of London. Also known as the Great Star of Africa.

Cullinan II, 317.40 ct. reportedly very fine color, very fine clarity, cushion-shape Type IIa diamond with 66 facets (33 crown, 33 pavilion); mounted in the Imperial State Crown, it is on display among the British Crown Jewels in the Tower of London. Also known as the Lesser Star of Africa.

Cullinan III, 94.40 ct. pear-shape diamond set in a crown; it can, however, also be worn with the Cullinan IV in a pendant brooch.

Cullinan IV, 63.60 ct. square brilliant-cut set in a crown; it can, however, also be worn with the Cullinan III in a pendant brooch.

Cullinan V, 18.50 ct. heart-shape diamond set in a brooch that can also be worn in the band of a crown.

Cullinan VI, 11.50 ct. marquise-cut diamond set in a diamond and emerald necklace.

Cullinan VII, 8.80 ct. marquise-cut diamond set with the Cullinan VIII as a pendant on a diamond brooch.

Cullinan VIII, 6.80 ct. oblong brilliant-cut diamond set with the Cullinan VII in a diamond brooch.

Cullinan IX, 4.39 ct. pear-shape diamond set in a ring.

Replicas of the nine major stones cut from the Cullinan, vertically from the left, I and II; center, V, IV, III; right, VII, VIII, IX, VI.

Cumberland Diamond, 32 ct. Indian diamond named for William Augustus, Duke of Cumberland, and probably bequeathed to him in 1820 by either his father, King George III of England, or his mother, Queen Caroline. Returned to Germany as part of the Hanoverian Crown Jewels in 1858, the Cumberland disappeared until 1935 when Cartier declined to buy it on account of its "banal color and shape." Current whereabouts unknown.

cushion, see ANTIQUE CUSHION BRILLIANT, CUSHION BRILLIANT, CUSHION SHAPE.

cushion brilliant, GIA GTL term for a diamond with a rectangular or squarish girdle outline,

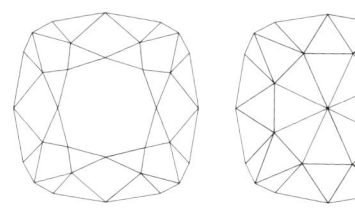

cushion brilliant

curved sides, rounded corners, and brilliant-cut facets.

cushion crystal, rough diamond crystal with a flattened shape.

cushion shape, GIA GTL term for rectangular or squarish brilliants with curved sides and rounded corners.

cushion-shape brilliant, see CUSHION BRILLIANT.

cut, (1) shape and style of a polished diamond, such as a round brilliant or an emerald cut. (2) proportions and finish of a diamond. One of the Four Cs; also called make. See FINISH, MAKE, PROPORTIONS.

cut-corner triangle cut, modification of the triangle cut on which two, or all three, corners are removed.

cut grading, process of evaluating and describing the proportions and finish of a polished diamond, principally with regard to their overall effect on brilliance and dispersion and the balance between them. See AGS CUT-GRADING SYSTEM, FINISH, FINISH GRADING, MAKE, PROPORTIONS, PROPORTION GRADING, SCAN. D.N. SCALE FOR THE QUALITY OF CUT.

cuttable, rough diamond or a portion thereof which has the shape, clarity, and color to produce a polished stone suitable for setting in jewelry. Also called cuttable rough. See GEM QUALITY.

cutter, see DIAMOND CUTTER.

cutting, see FASHIONING.

cutting machine, machine used to polish some or all of the facets on a diamond. See AUTOMATIC BRUTING MACHINE, AUTOMATIC POLISHING MACHINE.

cutting style, see CUT.

CVD, see CHEMICAL VAPOR DISPOSITION.

cyclotron, atomic particle accelerator used principally in the study of the structure of matter, occasionally to treat diamonds. See CYCLOTRON-TREATED DIAMOND, IRRADIATED DIAMOND, LINEAR ACCELERATOR, NUCLEAR REACTOR, VAN DE GRAAFF GENERATOR.

cyclotron-treated diamond, diamond colored by irradiation with alpha particles, deuterons, or protons in a cyclotron. The resulting colors typically include green, bluish green, blue-green, yellow-green, brownish green, or black. Diamonds so treated are usually heat-treated next to produce yellow-brown, yellow, greenish yellow, orangy brown, orange, reddish brown, or brownish pink stones; they are not radioactive and are safe to wear. See ALPHA PARTICLE, IRRADIATED DIAMOND, UMBRELLA EFFECT.

Cyprian diamond, misnomer for rock crystal quartz from the island of Cyprus. Also called Baffa diamond.

CZ, see SYNTHETIC CUBIC ZIRCONIA.

Czochralski pulling, technique for making synthetic crystals from a nutrient melt and a seed crystal. Some materials used as diamond simulants, including synthetic rutile, synthetic sapphire, and GGG, are among those which have been produced by this method.

D

D, highest color grade in the GIA color-grading scale, designating a colorless diamond with exceptional transparency. See AGS COLOR-GRADING SCALE, CIBJO INTERNATIONAL COLOR-GRADING SCALE, COLOR GRADING, GIA COLOR-GRADING SCALE, IDC INTERNATIONAL COLOR-GRADING SCALE, SCAN. D.N. COLOR SCALE.

Dahlia Cut, registered name of one of five "Flower" cuts designed by CSO consultant Gabi Tolkowsky in 1988. A 12-sided symmetrical oval with 67 facets, the Dahlia Cut combines brilliant and step-cut features; it is said to enhance reflection and color and produces a higher yield from elongated, lower color crystals than can be achieved with traditional fancy shapes. See FIRE-ROSE CUT, FLOWER CUTS, MARIGOLD CUT, SUNFLOWER CUT, ZINNIA CUT.

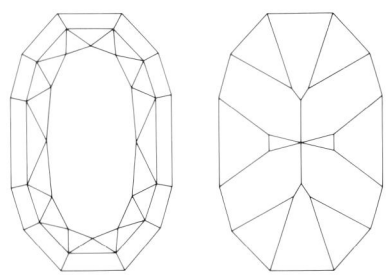

Dahlia Cut

damage report, descriptive account of the nature and extent of damage suffered by a polished diamond or other gemstone.

Danau Seran Swamp, area in southeastern Kalimantan, Indonesia, and a regionally important source of alluvial diamonds. Gem quality stones produced are near-colorless, yellow, brown, pink, and blue.

Dancarl Mine, very small, narrow, almost vertical kimberlite fissure near Barkly West, South Africa. Diamonds are recovered by overhand shrinkage.

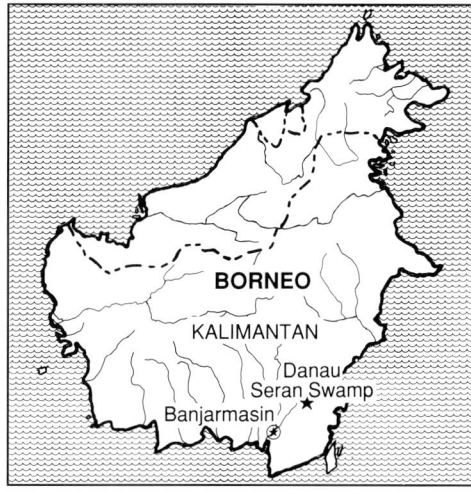

Danau Seran Swamp

Dar-Challa, Compagnie Diamantifère du Dar-Challa, subsidiary of Compagnie Minière de l'Oubangui Oriental, active in what is now the Central African Republic in the 1950s. See COMPAGNIE MINIERE DE L'OUBANGUI ORIENTAL (CMOO).

dark cape, noticeably yellow to obviously yellow color in the lower end of the cape range. Diamonds in this range are sometimes separated into very light yellow, light yellow, and yellow grades. Dark cape stones are not considered fancy colors. See CAPE.

dark center, gray or black area discernible through the table of a round brilliant-cut diamond, the result of light leakage caused by too deep a pavilion. See NAILHEAD, PAVILION DEPTH PERCENTAGE, PROPORTIONS, TABLE REFLECTION.

darkfield illumination, system for lighting a diamond from the side against a black background, to reduce surface reflections and make inclusions stand out in sharp relief.

Darya-i-Nur Diamond, light pink diamond with an estimated weight of 175 to 195 ct., alleged to have been cut, along with the Nur-ul-Ain, from the Great Table Diamond. The stone is engraved with the name Fath Ali Shah and a date equivalent to 1834, when it is thought to have been cut. Believed to have belonged to the first Mogul emperor of India, the Darya-i-Nur was taken by the Persian general Nadir Shah when he sacked Delhi in 1739. Now part of the Iranian Crown Jewels, the Darya-i-Nur was exhibited in the Central Bank of Iran in 1992. The name, which is also spelled Darya-i-Noor and Durria-i-Nur, or Noor, means *sea*, or *river, of light* in Persian. See GREAT TABLE DIAMOND, IRANIAN CROWN JEWELS, NUR-UL-AIN DIAMOND, SACK OF DELHI.

Dauphiné diamond, misnomer for rock crystal quartz from the French Alps. Also called Briançon diamond.

DCA, see DIAMOND COUNCIL OF AMERICA.

DDC, see DIAMOND DEALER'S CLUB, INC.

dealer, person acting as an intermediary between diamond suppliers and retailers. Operations vary from independent representatives who handle the work of a single manufacturer to large companies which market complete lines of diamond and colored stone jewelry. Dealers offer different types of goods, terms, and services and earn a commission on each sale. See BROKER, MANUFACTURER, SIGHTHOLDER, SUPPLIER.

De Beer, Diederik Arnoldus and Johannes Nicholaas, brothers, and owners of the Vooruitzigt farm (originally a portion of Bultfontein), South Africa, where diamonds were discovered in 1871. The farm was the site of the two large pipes which became the De Beers and Kimberley Mines. See DE BEERS CONSOLIDATED MINES, LTD.; DE BEERS MINE; RHODES, CECIL JOHN.

De Beers, term commonly used to refer to any or all of the companies owned or controlled by De Beers Consolidated Mines, De Beers Centenary AG, or their subsidiaries and affiliates.

De Beers Botswana Mining Company (Pty.), Ltd. (Debswana), see DEBSWANA DIAMOND COMPANY.

De Beers Centenary AG, sister company of De Beers Consolidated Mines, established in 1990 in Lucerne, Switzerland, to hold De Beers' non-South African assets. These include interests in the Debswana Diamond Company and CDM; De Beers Industrial Diamond Division (DEBID); and elements of the Central Selling Organisation (CSO) including research activities in England and diamond service operations in Belgium.

De Beers Consolidated Mines, Ltd., company established by Cecil Rhodes after the amalgamation of the De Beers and Kimberley mines in 1888. The company currently operates the Wesselton, Bultfontein, Dutoitspan, Finsch, Premier, Koffiefontein, and Venetia mines; alluvial deposits in Namaqualand; and off-shore deposits through De Beers Marine.

De Beers Diamond, 428.50 ct. (old carats) diamond octahedron, described as yellow, found at the De Beers Mine, South Africa, in 1888, shortly after De Beers Consolidated Mines was incorporated. The crystal was fashioned into a 234.50 ct. cushion shape and sold to an Indian maharajah in 1889. In 1925 it was set in a necklace and sold by Cartier. Last sold in 1982 to a private buyer.

De Beers Diamond

De Beers Industrial Diamond Division (DEBID), subsidiary of De Beers Consolidated Mines and De Beers Centenary AG, which markets a wide range of natural and synthetic diamond and cubic boron nitride-based products for industrial purposes. DEBID operates research and development centers, diamond synthesis factories, and technical support facilities in Europe, Asia, and South Africa (including the De Beers Diamond Research Laboratory in Johannesburg), and has sales offices throughout the world. See ADAMANT RESEARCH LABORATORY, BORT, CARBONADO, DIAMOND RESEARCH LABORATORY (DRL), INDUSTRIAL DIAMOND, SYNTHETIC DIAMOND.

De Beers Lesotho Mining Company, company formed in 1977 to operate the Letseng-la-Terai Mine in Lesotho, in southern Africa. The mine was closed in 1982 and has not been reopened. See BASUTOLAND DIAMOND CORPORATION, LESOTHO, LETSENG-LA-TERAI MINE.

De Beers Marine (Pty.), Ltd., wholly-owned subsidiary of De Beers Consolidated Mines, based in Cape Town, South Africa. De Beers Marine operates a fleet of four mining and two technical support vessels in deep water (120 meters; 394 feet) off the coasts of Namaqualand and Namibia. Crawler-based and rotary drilling systems are used to retrieve gravels from the seabed; concentrates are flown ashore for diamond recovery. With the exception of the offshore oil drilling industry, this is said to be the largest ocean mining operation in the world.

De Beers Mine, fifth kimberlite pipe discovered in South Africa; found in 1871 on the Vooruitzigt farm owned by Diederik and Johannes De Beer, in the present city of Kimberley; it was not, however, recognized as a primary source until 1872. In 1880, Cecil Rhodes and Charles Rudd formed the De Beers Mining Company and by 1887 had amalgamated most of the claims in the De Beers Mine. The mine was closed in 1908, re-opened in 1966, and closed permanently in 1990.

De Beers Mines, see DE BEERS CONSOLIDATED MINES, LTD.

De Beers Mining Company, company formed in 1880 by Cecil Rhodes, Charles Rudd, and others to buy up claims in the De Beers Mine. By 1887, it owned most of the claims and also had substantial interests in the Dutoitspan and Bultfontein Mines. See DE BEERS CONSOLIDATED MINES, LTD.; DE BEERS MINE.

De Beers New Rush, see KIMBERLEY MINE.

De Beers Prospecting (Rhodesian Areas), Ltd., company, now defunct, formed by De Beers in 1955 to undertake diamond prospecting in Rhodesia (now Zimbabwe).

De Beers synthetic diamond, industrial-to-gem-quality synthetic diamond grown by the Diamond Research Laboratory in Johannesburg,

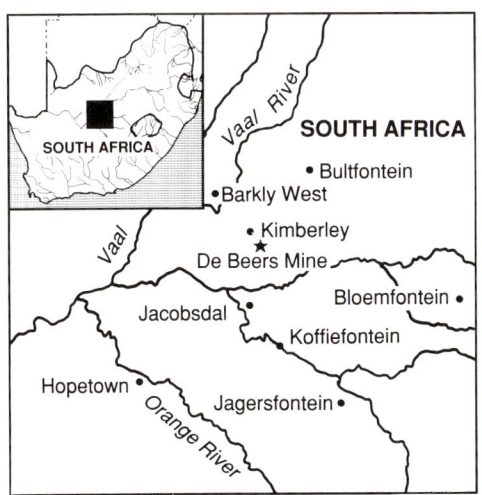

De Beers Mine

De Beers synthetic diamond

South Africa. The diamonds fall into two broad categories: grits for impregnating a wide range of diamond tools, and larger, clean, single crystals up to several carats, which are used as wire-drawing blanks or sold as cut plates for advanced diamond tooling. Generally modified octahedra grown by a high pressure, high temperature flux method, they can show geometric graining, small metallic inclusions, and uneven color; they are easily identifiable through growth sectors and cathodoluminescence.

de Berquem, Louis, see VAN BERCKEN, LODEWYK.

de Berquen, Robert, see BERQUEN, ROBERT DE.

Debswana Diamond Company, formerly De Beers Botswana Mining Company, or Debswana. Joint venture between De Beers Centenary AG and the government of Botswana, established to develop and exploit the Orapa, Letlhakane, and Jwaneng mines in Botswana. After valuation by the BDVC, the production is sold through the Central Selling Organisation. See BOTSWANA DIAMOND VALUING COMPANY, LTD. (BDVC).

deceptive practice, any misrepresentation of the color, clarity, condition, weight, value, or nature of a diamond; failure to disclose that a diamond has been enhanced in any way, or to advise that a material is a diamond simulant or synthetic; altering a diamond with the intent to defraud. See ASSEMBLED STONE, COATED DIAMOND, DIAMOND DOUBLET, FILLED DIAMOND, FOILBACK, IRRADIATED DIAMOND.

Deepdene Diamond, originally a 104.88 ct. square cushion-shape diamond, described as light yellow. The owner, Cary W. Bok, named it after her family estate and loaned it to the Philadelphia Academy of Sciences, where it was displayed for many years; it was purchased by Harry Winston in 1954 and sold, set in a necklace, to a Canadian buyer in 1955. (In 1971, a 104.52 ct. yellow diamond alleged to be the Deepdene was found to be an enhanced stone rather than a natural color diamond. Now owned by Friedrich of Frankfurt, Germany.)

deep pavilion, on a polished diamond, a pavilion of a depth which exceeds 44 percent of the average girdle diameter. A pavilion depth of 45 percent or more can lead to significant light leakage and consequent loss of brilliance. Stones with deep pavilions may show a dark center when examined through the table. See NAILHEAD, PAVILION DEPTH PERCENTAGE, PROPORTIONS, TABLE REFLECTION.

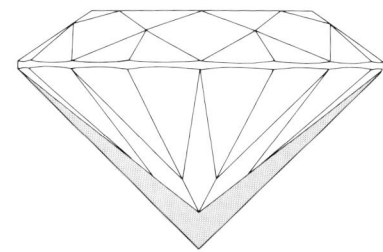

deep pavilion—the shaded area represents a pavilion depth of about 50 percent.

De Kalk farm, site near the Orange River where the first authenticated diamond was found in South Africa, in 1866. Originally owned, in part, by Schalk van Niekerk, the farm was later sold to Johannes Jacobs. See EUREKA DIAMOND; JACOBS, ERASMUS.

Delhi, Sack of, see SACK OF DELHI.

Delport's Hope, historic alluvial diamond digging on the Vaal River, Cape Colony (later Province), South Africa.

Demidoff Diamond, see SANCY DIAMOND.

density, see SPECIFIC GRAVITY (SG).

deposit, concentration of minerals occurring either in an original host rock (primary deposit), or as a result of having been transported and subsequently re-concentrated in a new location (secondary deposit). See ALLUVIAL DEPOSIT, ELUVIAL DEPOSIT, PRIMARY DEPOSIT.

deproclaimed area, term in South African mining law describing alluvial diamond claims which are thought to be exhausted and no

depth, dimension of a diamond from the table to the culet; usually recorded in millimeters. See TOTAL DEPTH PERCENTAGE.

longer require licensing. See PRECIOUS STONES ACT OF 1927, PROCLAIMED AREA.

depth, dimension of a diamond from the table to the culet; usually recorded in millimeters. See TOTAL DEPTH PERCENTAGE.

depth of color, see HUE, SATURATION, TONE.

depth percentage, see TOTAL DEPTH PERCENTAGE.

De Punt Mine, marine deposit on the Namaqualand coast; diamonds are recovered by diver-manipulated suction pumps operated from small boats and from shore. See BEACH MINING; DE BEERS MARINE (PTY.), LTD.; OFF-SHORE MINING.

Derbyshire diamond, misnomer used in the 1950s for colorless quartz crystals from England.

Derrea-i-Nur Diamond, square-cut diamond, estimated to weigh 66 ct., displayed at the Crystal Palace Exhibition in 1851 by the East India Company. Reportedly sold to the Nawab of Dacca, Bangladesh, following the exhibition; set in a gold bracelet, it was last offered for sale in 1959. Current whereabouts unknown.

desaturated colors, non-vivid colors tending towards gray or brown. Also described as low saturation colors. See HUE, SATURATION, TONE.

desert diamond, misnomer for colorless quartz crystal from Kern County, California.

deuteron, nucleus of a heavy hydrogen atom (deuterium) made up of one proton and one neutron. One of the cyclotron-accelerated particles used to irradiate diamonds. See CYCLOTRON-TREATED DIAMOND, IRRADIATED DIAMOND.

Deutsche Gemmologische Gesellschaft e.V., (German Gemological Association), technical and scientific association founded in Idar-Oberstein, Germany in 1932.

Deutsche Stiftung Edelsteinforschung (DSEF), (German Foundation for Gemstone Research), research and gem-testing laboratory in Idar-Oberstein, Germany, specializing in gem identification, pearl identification, and diamond grading.

Deutsches Edelsteinmuseum, (German Precious Stone Museum), gemological museum in Idar-Oberstein, Germany, which has an extensive collection of rough and polished gemstones.

Deutsches Gemmologisches Ausbildungszentrum/Deutsches Berufsfortbildungswerk für Edelsteinkunde, (German Gemological Training Center), educational centers of the German Gemological Association in Idar-Oberstein, Germany, which offer diplomas in gemology and diamond grading.

De Young Diamond, 2.9 ct. pear-shape brilliant diamond, described as fancy pink, found in Tanzania. Sydney De Young of Boston, US, presented the stone to the Smithsonian Institution in Washington, D.C., US.

Dia-Bud, proprietary name for yttrium aluminum garnet (YAG). Marketed as a diamond simulant.

Diagem, proprietary name for synthetic strontium titanate. Marketed as a diamond simulant.

DIALAP, see SOCIEDADE PORTUGUESA DE LAPIDACAO DE DIAMANTES.

Dialite, proprietary name for a doublet consisting of synthetic strontium titanate and synthetic spinel. Marketed as a diamond simulant.

DIAMANG, see COMPANHIA DE DIAMANTES DE ANGOLA.

Diamanite, proprietary name for yttrium aluminum garnet (YAG). Marketed as a diamond simulant.

diamantaire, (1) French term, used throughout the diamond industry for a manufacturer or dealer. (2) any knowledgeable or experienced person in the diamond industry.

diamant caillou, misnomer for rock crystal quartz.

Diamantclub van Antwerpen NV, one of Antwerp's four diamond bourses, founded in 1893; member of the World Federation of Diamond Bourses. See BOURSE, WORLD FEDERATION OF DIAMOND BOURSES (WFDB).

Diamantina, town, originally called Tijero, near the site of the first diamond discovery along the Rio dos Marinhos in Minas Gerais, Brazil. Also applied to the area around the town.

Diamantina

Diamant-Klub Wien, Austrian diamond bourse; member of the World Federation of Diamond Bourses. See BOURSE, WORLD FEDERATION OF DIAMOND BOURSES (WFDB).

diamantoid, having the nature of diamond or resembling diamond in appearance.

Diamant Prüflabor, GmbH, German diamond grading laboratory in Idar-Oberstein; part of the Diamant und Edelsteinbörse Idar-Oberstein.

Diamant und Edelsteinbörse Idar-Oberstein e.V., German diamond bourse and the first combined diamond and precious stone bourse in the world; member of the World Federation of Diamond Bourses. See BOURSE, WORLD FEDERATION OF DIAMOND BOURSES (WFDB).

Diamatic, proprietary name of a line of computerized polishing machines manufactured and marketed by Best of Israel. The company's 5000 and 6000GS systems were marketed in the 1980s; the Diamatic 7000GS, capable of handling rough (including naats) from 10 points to 27 ct., was introduced in 1990. See NAAT.

Diamdel, large sightholding company associated with the Central Selling Organisation (CSO) and De Beers Centenary AG. Established in 1965 to provide smaller Belgian manufacturers with access to adequate supplies of rough diamonds for processing in Antwerp and the nearby Kempen region. There are now similar operations in Hong Kong, Israel, and South Africa. The company purchases and sorts both CSO rough and goods obtained on the outside market to meet the specialized requirements of local manufacturing industries in these centers.

diameter, see GIRDLE DIAMETER.

Diaminir, Ltd., Israeli manufacturer of computerized polishing machines. The company first marketed the Moach 1 machine, a model discontinued when the Diaminir AMICUT system was introduced in 1991. The AMICUT is capable of handling rough weighing up to 10 ct. and can be operated either as a single workstation or as part of a multi-unit production line controlled by one computer.

Diamite, proprietary name for yttrium aluminum garnet (YAG). Marketed as a diamond simulant.

Diamogem, proprietary name for yttrium aluminum garnet (YAG). Marketed as a diamond simulant.

DiamoLite, see DIAMONDLITE.

Diamonair, proprietary name for yttrium aluminum garnet (YAG). Marketed as a diamond simulant.

Diamonaura, proprietary name for yttrium aluminum garnet (YAG). Marketed as a diamond simulant.

Diamon-Brite, proprietary name for yttrium aluminum garnet (YAG). Marketed as a diamond simulant.

diamond, mineral composed essentially of carbon crystallized at extremely high temperatures and pressures; in nature, diamonds form 150 to 200 kilometers (93 to 124 miles) or more below the earth's surface. Diamond is the hardest of all known natural substances (10 on the Mohs scale); its refractive index is 2.417, dispersion 0.044, specific gravity 3.52, and its luster is adamantine. Diamond forms in the cubic, or isometric, crystal system, has four directions of perfect octahedral cleavage, and shows a step-like fracture surface. Its color ranges from colorless to yellow, brown, gray, orange, green, blue, white, black, purple, pink, and, extremely rarely, red. Transparent and near-colorless in a desirable color, diamond is a highly valued gemstone; poorly colored or heavily included single crystals are used for a wide variety of industrial purposes; polycrystalline material is crushed and used as an abrasive powder. See AGE (OF DIAMONDS), EMPLACEMENT (OF DIAMOND), ORIGIN (OF DIAMOND).

diamond-angle gauge, measuring device used to determine the accuracy of the bezel facet angles, pavilion facet angles, and the orientation of girdles in straight-sided fancy cuts. Also called a bezel-angle gauge.

diamond anniversary, traditionally the 60th anniversary of an event; now being promoted as a 25th anniversary occasion.

diamond anniversary band, see ANNIVERSARY RING.

Diamond Area No. 1, mining area in Namibia extending from the mouth of the Orange River north for approximately 322 kilometers (200 miles) and inland about 80 kilometers (50 miles), now under lease to CDM. Once called Sperrgebiet, German for *restricted area.*

diamond balance, sensitive scale used to weigh diamonds and sometimes to determine specific gravity (by the hydrostatic weighing method). See CHAIN BALANCE, COUNTERWEIGHT BALANCE,

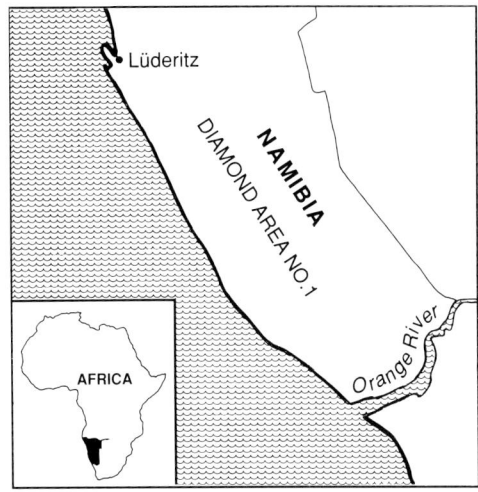

Diamond Area No. 1

ELECTRONIC BALANCE, MECHANICAL BALANCE, PORTABLE BALANCE, RIDER BALANCE, SINGLE-PAN BALANCE.

diamond bourse, (1) organization of diamond dealers, manufacturers, brokers, and wholesalers who join together to transact business and protect their mutual interests. There are diamond bourses in almost every major manufacturing center. Twenty bourses belong to the World Federation of Diamond Bourses. Some bourses call themselves diamond clubs or diamond exchanges. (2) the building or rooms housing such an organization. See INTERNATIONAL DIAMOND MANUFACTURERS' ASSOCIATION (IDMA), WORLD FEDERATION OF DIAMOND BOURSES (WFDB).

diamond cement, any of several adhesives used to hold diamonds during bruting, cleaving, sawing, and polishing. Cements differ according to their use.

diamond chain, see DIAMOND PIPELINE.

diamond club, see DIAMOND BOURSE.

Diamond Club of South Africa, South African diamond bourse; member of the World Federation of Diamond Bourses. See BOURSE, WORLD FEDERATION OF DIAMOND BOURSES (WFDB).

Diamond Club West Coast, Inc., American diamond bourse, based in Los Angeles; member of the World Federation of Diamond Bourses. See BOURSE, WORLD FEDERATION OF DIAMOND BOURSES (WFDB).

diamond coating, see COATED DIAMOND, DIAMOND THIN FILM.

Diamond Corporation Côte D'Ivoire, Ltd. (DICORCOT), African diamond-buying company incorporated in the Côte D'Ivoire (Ivory Coast), in 1961, as part of the Central Selling Organisation. In addition to its role as a buyer, DICORCOT also prospected.

Diamond Corporation (Pty.), Ltd., company established in 1930 as the successor to earlier diamond-purchasing and marketing syndicates; a part of the Central Selling Organisation, it purchases rough diamonds from producers, and markets them through the Diamond Trading Company and De Beers Industrial Diamond Division. See CENTRAL SELLING ORGANISATION (CSO).

Diamond Corporation Sierra Leone, Ltd. (DICOSIL), former subsidiary of the Diamond Corporation, licensed to buy diamonds in Sierra Leone. Now defunct.

Diamond Corporation West Africa, Ltd. (DICORWAF), subsidiary of the CSO, licensed to export diamonds from Sierra Leone and manage the Government Diamond Office. It ended its association with Sierra Leone in 1989 when laws were passed requiring all diamonds mined there to be exported through a government agency. See GOVERNMENT GOLD AND DIAMOND OFFICE (SIERRA LEONE).

Diamond Council of America (DCA), a not-for-profit educational foundation headquartered in Kansas City, Missouri, USA, representing some 2,000 retail jewelers and suppliers; founded in 1944. Completion of the Council's *Diamontology* course leads to the title of Certified Diamontologist.

diamond cut, (1) brilliant cut; used primarily in referring to the finish of gemstones other than diamond. (2) finish applied to precious metals with diamond-tipped bits.

diamond cutter, generic name for any of several technicians or entrepreneurs involved in the manufacture of polished diamonds. See BLOCKER, BRILLIANDEER, CROSS-WORKER, DIAMOND MANUFACTURER, POLISHER.

Diamond Day, prestigious European horse racing event, sponsored by De Beers and held annually in July at Ascot, England. Diamond jewelry is presented to the winner of the "Ladies Race," an event which is named after a different diamond each year, and to the winning owner, trainer, and jockey of the "King George VI and Queen Elizabeth Diamond Stakes," the main event on the card.

Diamond Dealers' Club, Inc. (DDC), trading association founded in 1931 and composed of over 2,000 diamond importers, wholesalers, and manufacturers. Located in New York City, US, the DDC is a member of the World Federation of Diamond Bourses. See BOURSE, WORLD FEDERATION OF DIAMOND BOURSES (WFDB).

Diamond Development Company of Ghana, one of nine licensed diamond-buying companies in Ghana. Established in the 1950s.

diamond doublet, assembled stone consisting of a diamond crown cemented to a pavilion fashioned from another colorless material. The term is also used to describe a diamond crown and pavilion cemented together. Usually set in a mounting with a closed back. See ASSEMBLED STONE, DOUBLET, PIGGY-BACK DIAMOND, TRIPLET.

diamond dressing tool, device containing a single diamond crystal, a shaped diamond, or multiple rows of diamonds, used to dress grinding wheels. Also called a dresser or a truer.

diamond drill, drill in which either a natural single crystal or a synthetic polycrystalline diamond has been set, or to which natural or synthetic industrial diamond has been bonded; used for full hole boring or core drilling a variety of hard materials (rock, concrete, etc.).

Diamond drills are as large as a meter (3.3 feet) in diameter.

diamond dust, see DIAMOND POWDER.

diamond, emplacement of, see EMPLACEMENT OF DIAMOND.

diamond exchange, see DIAMOND BOURSE.

Diamond Exchange of Singapore, diamond bourse established in 1976, originally under the name Diamond Importers Association of Singapore; member of the World Federation of Diamond Bourses. See BOURSE, WORLD FEDERATION OF DIAMOND BOURSES (WFDB).

Diamond Eye, proprietary name for a reflectivity meter developed by W.W. Hanneman.

diamond file, file, usually made of copper, to which diamond powder has been bonded.

diamond grader, person trained in and responsible for weighing, measuring, and examining polished diamonds, for noting any evidence of enhancement, treatment, or alteration, and for assigning color, clarity and sometimes cut grades according to a pre-determined set of standards.

diamond grading, process of weighing, measuring, examining, and assigning color, clarity and sometimes cut grades to polished diamonds, according to a pre-determined set of standards. It includes looking for evidence of alteration, treatment, or enhancement.

Diamond Grading Report, report written by the GIA Gem Trade Laboratory or one of its licensees, describing a diamond's weight, proportions, finish, color grade, and clarity grade. No valuation is stated. Informally called a certificate.

diamond grading system, comprehensive set of methods, terms, and standards for determining and describing the relative quality of a polished diamond's clarity, color, and cut. See AGS CLARITY-GRADING SCALE, AGS COLOR-GRADING SCALE, AGS CUT-GRADING SYSTEM, CIBJO INTERNATIONAL CLARITY/PURITY SCALE, CIBJO INTERNATIONAL COLOR-GRADING SCALE, CIBJO RULES OF APPLICATION FOR THE DIAMOND TRADE, CLARITY, CLARITY CHARACTERISTICS, CLARITY GRADING, COLOR GRADING, COLORIMETER, FANCY COLOR DIAMOND, GIA CLARITY-GRADING SCALE, GIA COLOR-GRADING SCALE, IDC CLARITY-GRADING SCALE, IDC INTERNATIONAL COLOR-GRADING SCALE, IDC RULES FOR GRADING POLISHED DIAMONDS, SCANDINAVIAN DIAMOND NOMENCLATURE (SCAN. D.N.) AND GRADING STANDARDS, SCAN. D.N. CLARITY SCALE, SCAN. D.N. COLOR SCALE, SCAN. D.N. SCALE FOR THE QUALITY OF CUT.

diamond grit, see DIAMOND POWDER.

Diamond High Council, Belgium, see HOGE RAAD VOOR DIAMANT VZW (HRD).

diamond hone, tool used to sharpen metal cutting tools; the honing agent is diamond powder, which is usually bonded to a substrate.

diamondiferous, diamond-bearing.

Diamond Importers Association of Singapore, see DIAMOND EXCHANGE OF SINGAPORE.

diamond industry, inclusive term for all the various enterprises involved in any aspect of the mining, manufacture, and marketing of diamonds.

Diamond Industry Steering Committee (DISC), trade association established in 1990 to attract new buyers and expand the diamond manufacturing industry in New York City, US. DISC acts as an umbrella organization for the combined efforts of the Diamond Trade and Precious Stones Association, the Diamond Dealer's Club, the Diamond Manufacturers and Importers of America, and the Indian Diamond and Colored Stone Association.

Diamond Information Center (DIC), public relations service which supports the advertising and promotional campaigns mounted by De Beers in major consumer markets, on behalf of the international diamond jewelry industry. The DIC disseminates publicity and information on all aspects of diamonds and diamond jewelry to the public media and the diamond industry, and oversees the biennial Diamonds-International Awards competition. See N. W. AYER AND SON.

Diamondite, proprietary name for synthetic sapphire. Marketed as a diamond simulant.

Diamond Jim Brady, see BRADY, JAMES BUCHANAN.

diamond jubilee, see DIAMOND ANNIVERSARY.

diamond lamp, any type of lighting specifically designed to help grade, sell, or display diamonds. See DIAMONDLITE, DIAMONDLUX.

diamond lap, see SCAIFE.

diamond-like carbon (DLC), synthetic, polycrystalline thin film produced by the chemical-vapor deposition process, in which the carbon atoms are bonded like the atoms in graphite. DLC has many of diamond's properties, but is easier to produce than synthetic diamond. See CHEMICAL VAPOR DEPOSITION (CVD), DIAMOND THIN FILM.

DiamondLite, proprietary name for an instrument that provides a constant source of daylight-equivalent artificial light for color grading diamonds; it includes a longwave ultraviolet light source for detecting fluorescence. Manufactured by GIA Gem Instruments. Formerly called DiamoLite. See DIAMONDLUX.

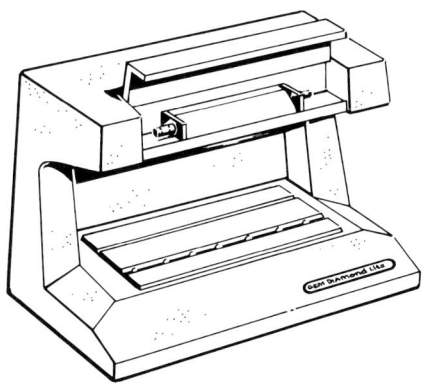

DiamondLite

Diamondlux, proprietary name for an overhead light fixture with special baffles, designed to produce daylight-equivalent illumination; often used in jewelry stores to illuminate diamond displays. Without the baffles, the fixture is known as the Verilux. Manufactured by GIA Gem Instruments. See DIAMONDLITE.

diamond manufacturer, owner or manager of a concern which fashions polished diamonds from rough for resale on a wholesale basis. Also applied loosely to indicate the concern itself.

Diamond Manufacturers' and Importers' Association of America, Inc. (DMIAA), American trade association of diamond manufacturers and importers of rough and polished diamonds. The association represents the industry before the United States Tariff Commission and other government agencies, cooperates with the US Federal Trade Commission (FTC) to discourage misrepresentation in diamond advertising and sales, and represents its members in labor negotiations.

Diamond Marketing Corporation (DMC), organization established by the Ghanaian government in 1965 to buy and sell all the diamonds recovered by indigenous miners in Ghana. See ACCRA DIAMOND MARKET (ADM).

diamond mortar, small steel container in which industrial diamond is pulverized manually for small-scale or occasional use. It consists of a cylindrical steel block with a hollow insert of hardened steel, and a pestle; a rubber seal prevents the diamond powder from escaping.

diamond, origin of, see ORIGIN (OF DIAMOND).

diamond paper, one or more sheets of paper folded to form a packet in which diamonds are stored. Information about the stones is usually written on the outer flap. Also called a briefca.

diamond-paper weight, small folding metal frame used to hold diamond papers open while examining their contents.

diamond paste, mixture of diamond grit and other substances such as oil or water, used as an abrasive. Modern pastes often contain wetting and dispersing agents, carriers for holding the diamond particles in uniform suspension, plasticizers to provide the desired consistency, and/or dyes to aid in distinguishing between different grit sizes.

diamond pencil, diamond-tipped tool used to inscribe or mark such materials as metal, glass, and plastic.

diamond photometer, instrument used to detect the strength of a diamond's absorption of light at a wavelength of 415.5 nanometers, in order to establish a color grade. Photometers can be used only for colorless to yellow diamonds in the cape series, and are most effective with round brilliants; browns, grays, fluorescent stones, and fancy cuts give misleading readings. See COLORIMETER.

diamond pipe, see PIPE.

diamond pipeline, metaphor describing the various stages through which diamonds pass, from mining to marketing, before they are sold to the consumer. Also known as the diamond chain.

diamond plow, diamond-tipped tool used for engraving glass.

diamond point, diamond-tipped stylus. See POINT CUT.

diamond powder, small particles of diamond used in industrial grinding, and for polishing diamonds and colored stones. Commonly bonded to the surface of grinding, drilling, and machining tools. Also called diamond grit or diamond dust.

Diamond Preserve of the United States, Inc., see CRATER OF DIAMONDS STATE PARK.

diamond probe, see THERMAL INERTIA METER.

Diamond Producers' Association (DPA), South African organization formed in 1934 to monitor the sale of diamonds produced by its members, which included the government of South Africa, the Diamond Board for South West Africa, De Beers Consolidated Mines, the Premier Mine, and the Diamond Corporation. The DPA was dissolved in 1987.

Diamond Promotion Service (DPS), service provided by De Beers to support diamond jewelry manufacturers, wholesalers, and retailers in major consumer markets around the world. The DPS is responsible for De Beers' training programs, retail promotional activities, and the supply of point-of-sale materials in support of De Beers' advertising campaigns. See DIAMOND INFORMATION CENTER (DIC), N. W. AYER AND SON.

Diamond Proportion Analyzer, eyepiece for the Gemolite microscope, with a graticule designed to aid in examining the proportions of round brilliant-cut and some fancy-shape diamonds. Can be used on stones ranging from 0.10 ct. to 5.75 ct. Manufactured by GIA Gem Instruments. See GRATICULE, PROPORTIONSCOPE.

Diamond Research Laboratory (DRL), research organization in Johannesburg, South Africa, operated by De Beers Industrial Diamond Division (DEBID). Established in 1947 to help mining companies improve extraction processes, increase output, and reduce costs. Also conducts advanced research into industrial and synthetic diamonds. See ADAMANT RESEARCH LABORATORY.

diamond room, small private area in a retail jewelry store reserved for the sale of diamonds; usually painted in neutral tones and equipped with good lighting, a microscope, and a mirror.

diamond rush, sudden influx of large numbers of people into areas where diamonds have been discovered. Rushes are sometimes organized and controlled; often they are completely spontaneous.

diamond saw, (1) rotary sawing device for dividing diamonds and colored stones. Cutting is

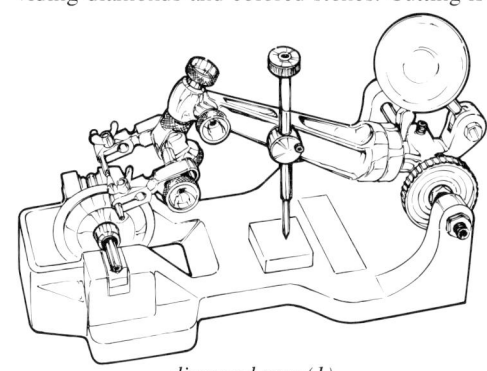

diamond saw (1)

done by a thin metal disk, usually phosphor-bronze, coated with a mixture of oil and diamond powder. Introduced about 1900. (2) any saw blade to which natural or synthetic industrial diamond has been bonded; used for cutting through hard materials such as rock, steel, or concrete. See DIAMOND DRILL.

diamond scoop, see DIAMOND SHOVEL.

diamond setter, (1) person trained and skilled in setting polished diamonds in jewelry. (2) person who fixes a diamond in a dop for sawing or polishing.

diamond shovel, open-ended, stainless-steel pan used to handle diamonds in bulk. Also called a diamond scoop.

diamond sieve, plate, usually made of stainless steel, perforated with a number of holes of a specified diameter; used as a screen to separate round brilliants according to size (the carat weight of a round brilliant is closely related to its diameter). Sieves are usually numbered 1 to 23, with half sizes in between, indicating the diameters of the holes. Number 1 sieves have holes 1.09 millimeters (0.043 inches) in diameter; number 23 sieves have holes 10.2 millimeters (0.402 inches) in diameter.

diamond simulant, any material which is not diamond or synthetic diamond, but which simulates a diamond's appearance and is used in its place. Common diamond simulants include synthetic cubic zirconia, gadolinium gallium garnet (GGG), synthetic spinel, and yttrium aluminum garnet (YAG). Also called diamond substitute. See APPENDIX F.

Diamonds-International Awards competition, bi-annual international jewelry design competition, sponsored by De Beers to encourage new design talent and promote the use of diamonds in jewelry. Initial judging takes place in the US, Europe, and Japan.

Diamonds of Russia and Sakha, see ALMAZY ROSSII-SAKHA.

diamond sorter, (1) person trained to separate rough or polished diamonds according to shape, size, clarity, and color. (2) computer-controlled device which uses a system of filters to separate lighter from darker colored rough; it can sort up to 75,000 stones per hour.

diamond substitute, see DIAMOND SIMULANT.

Diamond Syndicate, group of ten firms dealing in rough diamonds, headquartered in London, which combined in 1890 to buy and market the output of De Beers Consolidated Mines in Kimberley, South Africa. Subsequently replaced, in 1924, by a group informally known as the Oppenheimer Syndicate. This in turn was supplanted, in 1930, by the Diamond Corporation and four years later, by the Diamond Trading Company. The term "Syndicate" is still used loosely to designate the Central Selling Organisation. See DIAMOND CORPORATION (PTY.), LTD.; DIAMOND TRADING COMPANY, (PTY.), LTD.; CENTRAL SELLING ORGANISATION (CSO); OPPENHEIMER, SIR ERNEST.

diamond thin film, thin coating of synthetic diamond produced by the chemical vapor deposition process. Coatings can be applied to various materials in which the spacing between the atoms in the substrate is similar to that in diamond. Although single-crystal films have been grown on diamonds, most thin films are polycrystalline. See CHEMICAL VAPOR DEPOSITION (CVD), DIAMOND-LIKE CARBON (DLC).

Diamond Throne, throne described in Buddhist legends, imagined to have been made from a single diamond 30 meters (100 feet) in circumference. According to tradition, it stood near the Bhodi tree under which Buddha received enlightenment and is said to have remained in place despite violent storms and earthquakes.

Diamond Trade Act, law passed in 1882 in South Africa which established severe penalties for illicit diamond buying, and gave police broad investigative and enforcement powers. Other diamond producing countries have similar laws. See ILLICIT DIAMOND BUYING ACT.

Diamond Trade and Precious Stones Association, originally the Diamond Trade Association (DTA), established in New York City in 1941 by refugee Antwerp polishers as a bourse specializing in rough diamonds. Membership was expanded in the 1980s to include dealers who trade in both diamonds and colored stones; the organization officially amended its name to reflect the change, but retains the DTA initials. A member of the World Federation of Diamond Bourses. See DIAMOND INDUSTRY STEERING COMMITTEE (DISC), WORLD FEDERATION OF DIAMOND BOURSES (WFDB).

Diamond Trading Company (Pty.), Ltd. (DTC), gem-diamond marketing arm of the Central Selling Organisation (CSO). Formed in 1934, it was originally responsible for sorting, valuing, and marketing diamonds on behalf of producers. In a 1977 reorganization, the newly-formed CSO Valuations AG undertook the sorting and preparing of gem diamonds for sale; the Diamond Trading Company manages the distribution and sale of rough diamonds to CSO sightholders. See CENTRAL SELLING ORGANISATION (CSO).

diamond truer, see DIAMOND DRESSING TOOL.

diamond turning tool, machine tool set with a precisely shaped diamond, used to machine metals and other hard materials in turning operations. Diamond turning tools produce a higher grade finish and are more economical to use than similar tools of steel or tungsten carbide.

diamond type, classification of a diamond according to the types and amounts of atomic impurities it contains. See TYPE IA DIAMOND, TYPE IB DIAMOND, TYPE IIA DIAMOND, TYPE IIB DIAMOND.

diamond-washing cup, diamond cleaning device consisting of a perforated cup suspended inside a covered glass or plastic jar.

diamond wire-drawing die, high quality, near-gem natural or synthetic diamond with a tapered hole drilled through it; metal wire is pulled through the hole to reduce its diameter. In large-scale manufacturing operations, a series of dies is mounted in multi-stage wire-drawing machines capable of drawing miles of wire. In small operations, dies are often mounted in a plate which can be placed in a vise, and the wire is drawn manually.

diamond yardstick, see MASTER DIAMONDS.

diamond-yardstick holder, see COLOR-GRADING TRAY.

Diamone, proprietary name for yttrium aluminum garnet (YAG). Marketed as a diamond simulant.

Diamonette, proprietary name for synthetic sapphire. Marketed as a diamond simulant.

Diamonflame, proprietary name for synthetic sapphire. Marketed as a diamond simulant.

Diamonique, proprietary name for yttrium aluminum garnet (YAG). Marketed as a diamond simulant.

Diamonique I, proprietary name for yttrium aluminum garnet (YAG). Marketed as a diamond simulant.

Diamonique II, proprietary name for gadolinium gallium garnet (GGG). Marketed as a diamond simulant.

Diamonique III, proprietary name for synthetic cubic zirconia. Marketed as a diamond simulant.

Diamonite, proprietary name for synthetic rutile. Marketed as a diamond simulant.

Diamonte, proprietary name for yttrium aluminum garnet (YAG). Marketed as a diamond simulant.

Diamontina, proprietary name for synthetic strontium titanate. Marketed as a diamond simulant.

Diamothyst, proprietary name for synthetic rutile. Marketed as a diamond simulant.

diatreme, the upper level of a breccia-filled volcanic pipe formed by a gaseous explosion; when the breccia is kimberlite or lamproite, the diatreme may be diamond-bearing. In kimberlite pipes, the diatreme is located beneath the surface crater and above the hypabyssal zone. See HYPABYSSAL ZONE, KIMBERLITE, LAMPROITE, PIPE.

DICORWAF, see DIAMOND CORPORATION WEST AFRICA, LTD.

DICOSIL, see DIAMOND CORPORATION SIERRA LEONE, LTD.

diffraction grating, polished glass inscribed with fine parallel grooves, used to disperse light into a spectrum. See SPECTROSCOPE.

dike, tabular body of igneous rock which has intruded across the planes of earlier rocks. Diamonds are sometimes found in kimberlite dikes. Also spelled dyke.

DIMINCO, see NATIONAL DIAMOND MINING COMPANY (SIERRA LEONE), LTD.

dimorphism, type of polymorphism; the ability of a substance to crystallize in two different crystal systems. Carbon crystallizes in the cubic crystal system as diamond and in the hexagonal crystal system as graphite.

directional hardness, tendency for the hardness of a mineral to vary with crystallographic direction. Hardness depends on the number and strength of atomic bonds, which are usually greater within a crystal plane than between planes. Diamond's hardest polishing direction is parallel to octahedral planes; the easiest is on the dodecahedral face. A direction of intermediate hardness, which is also used in polishing, is parallel to a cubic face. See ATOMIC BONDING, POLISHING, SCRATCH HARDNESS.

direct measurement, measuring the dimensions of a diamond or other gemstone with any of several measuring instruments, as distinct from estimating them.

DISC, see DIAMOND INDUSTRY STEERING COMMITTEE.

disclosure, practice of fully advising a customer of the weight, quality (clarity, color, cut), nature (natural or synthetic), and condition (treated or untreated; damage) of a diamond.

dispersion, separation of white light into spectral colors, each of which vibrates at a different frequency. As light passes through an optically dense material, such as diamond, different wavelengths are refracted to different degrees and have slightly different refractive indices (RI). Dispersion is usually expressed as the difference between the RIs of the red and violet rays. Diamond's dispersion is 0.044. Also called fire.

distorted crystal, irregularly shaped rough diamond, the shape of which results from conditions present during its formation. Distorted crystals are often free from strain.

Di'Yag, proprietary name for yttrium aluminum garnet (YAG). Marketed as a diamond simulant.

Djevalite, proprietary name for cubic zirconia (CZ). Marketed as a diamond simulant.

DLC, see DIAMOND-LIKE CARBON.

DMIA, see DIAMOND MANUFACTURERS' AND IMPORTERS' ASSOCIATION OF AMERICA, INC.

dodecahedral cleavage, secondary, poorly developed cleavage plane in diamond parallel to any of the six opposing pairs of possible dodecahedral faces. See CLEAVAGE PLANE.

dodecahedral face, one of the flat surfaces on a dodecahedron-shaped crystal. See FACE.

dodecahedral plane, crystal plane parallel to a possible dodecahedral face.

dodecahedron, one of the seven basic forms of the cubic, or isometric, crystal system. A dodecahedron has 12 rhomb-shaped faces, each of which intersects two of the crystallographic axes and is parallel to the third. Also called a rhombic-dodecahedron. See CRYSTALLOGRAPHIC AXES.

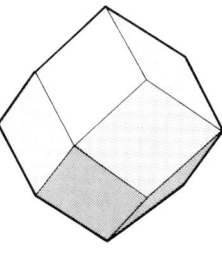

dodecahedron

dominant eye, the eye which has better vision (most people have one eye which is stronger than the other). A dominant eye can affect color grading. See MASTER-EYE EFFECT.

Doornkloof, small diamond-bearing fissure mined near Barkly West, Cape Province, South Africa.

dop, general term for the device used to hold a diamond during sawing, bruting, or polishing. See BRUTING DOP, MECHANICAL DOP, PRESS POT, SAWING DOP, SEMI-AUTOMATIC DOP, SOLDER DOP.

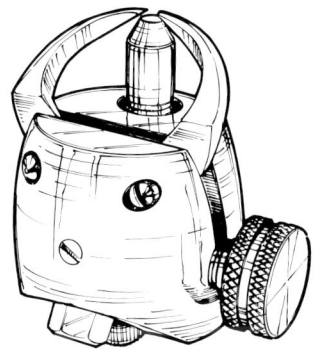

polishing dop

dop marks, see BURN MARK.

double bevel cut, see BEVEL CUT.

double-color diamond, diamond which appears one color under incandescent light and another in natural sunlight. The difference in appearance is due to strong fluorescence. See CHAMELEON-TYPE DIAMOND, TRANSICHROMATIC.

double cut, cut believed to have been developed around 1615, at the request of Cardinal Mazarin (it is often referred to as the "Mazarin cut"). It has a cushion-shaped girdle and a total of 34 facets: 16 on the crown, 16 on the pavilion, a table, and a culet.

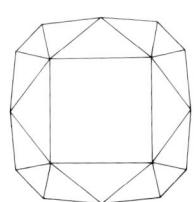

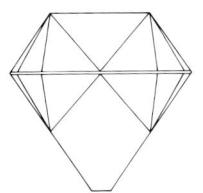

double cut

double-cut brilliant, brilliant cut with 34 facets: four bezel and pavilion main facets, 12 upper and lower girdle facets, a table, and a culet.

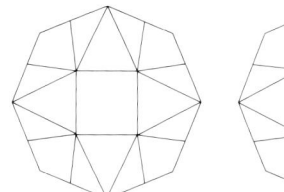 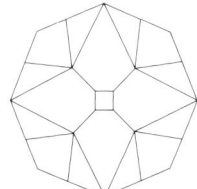

double-cut brilliant

double-Dutch rose cut, rose cut with a circular girdle outline, a flat, unfaceted base, a pointed, dome-shaped crown, and 36 triangular facets. Also called rose recoupée.

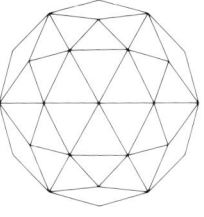

double-Dutch rose cut (crown view)

double-Holland rose cut, see DOUBLE-DUTCH ROSE CUT.

double refraction, see ANISOTROPIC.

double rose cut, rose cut that is essentially two Dutch rose cuts, base to base, with a circular girdle, no table or culet, and 48 triangular facets. See DUTCH ROSE CUT.

doublet, assembled stone made up of a crown and pavilion cemented or fused together. Doublets designed to imitate diamond may be composed of colorless synthetic or natural sapphire, synthetic or natural spinel, quartz, or glass. See ASSEMBLED STONE, DIAMOND DOUBLET.

doublet lens, see DOUBLET LOUPE.

doublet loupe, compound, aplanatic magnifier corrected for spherical aberration. See CHROMATIC ABERRATION, SPHERICAL ABERRATION, LOUPE, TRIPLET LOUPE.

doubly refractive, see ANISOTROPIC.

Douglas Bay mv, mining vessel belonging to De Beers Marine. The ship is equipped with a small-scale recovery plant and is used for sampling and exploration of off-shore deposits.

DPA, see DIAMOND PRODUCERS' ASSOCIATION.

drag line, (1) scratch caused during polishing when minute fragments of diamond, which frequently derive from surface-reaching inclusions, are inadvertently dragged across the surface by the scaife. Drag lines are seen only on one side of the inclusion. (2) excavating equipment used to remove overburden.

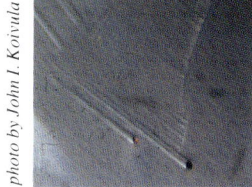

drag line

draw color, tendency of a diamond to take on the color of whatever metal, or other gemstone, is nearby; thus a colorless diamond may appear yellowish when it is mounted in yellow metal (gold), or next to a deeper yellow stone.

Dresden Diamond, see ENGLISH DRESDEN DIAMOND.

Dresden Drop Diamond, see ENGLISH DRESDEN DIAMOND.

Dresden Green Diamond, 40.70 ct., green, Type IIa, pear-shape diamond. The largest known diamond of this color, it was originally purchased by Frederick Augustus of Saxony in 1741. It is mounted in a hat ornament with several smaller diamonds and is on display in the Green Vaults at the Dresden Palace in Germany.

Dresden White Diamond, 49.71 ct. antique-cut diamond, reportedly near-colorless, originally purchased by Augustus the Strong of Saxony. It is mounted in an elaborate shoulder knot with 19 other large diamonds and 216 smaller rose-cut stones, and is on display in the Green Vaults at the Dresden Palace in Germany. Also called the Saxon White Diamond.

Dresden Green Diamond

Dresden Yellow Diamond, 38 ct. yellow, brilliant-cut diamond on display in the Green Vaults at the Dresden Palace in Germany.

dresser, see DIAMOND DRESSING TOOL.

drift, term used in underground mining to describe tunnels excavated horizontally through a kimberlite pipe. In block caving, the drifts are used for collecting the collapsed ore.

drill, diamond, see DIAMOND DRILL.

DRL, see DIAMOND RESEARCH LABORATORY.

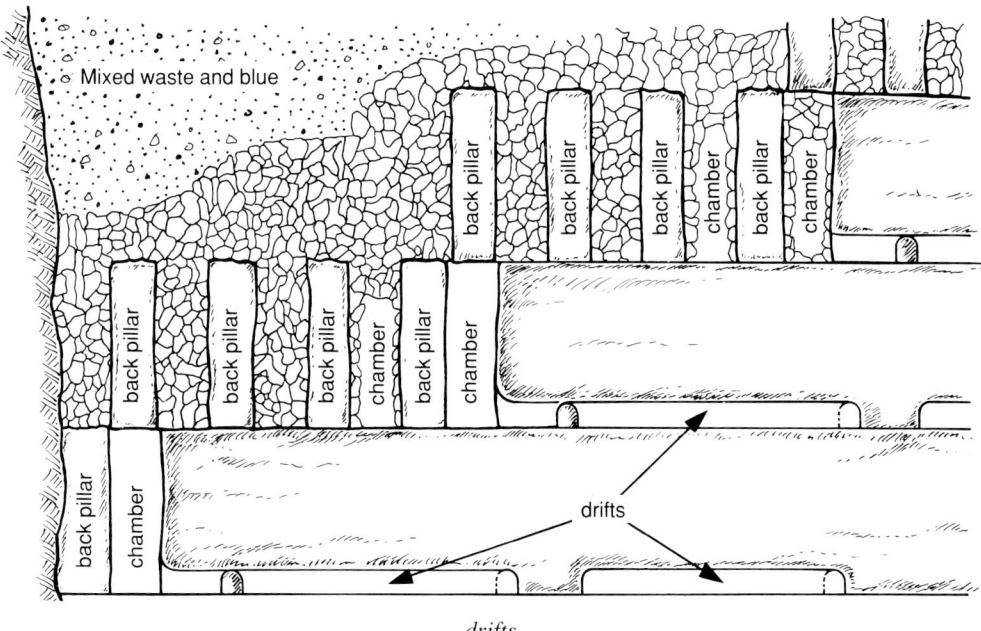

drifts

Droogeveld Channel, narrow, shallow, gravel-filled fissure, 3.2 kilometers (2 miles) long, in Droogeveld, South Africa, discovered in 1912. Once a prolific producer, it is now worked out. Also called Droogeveld Sluit.

drop cut, any cut such as the briolette or pear shape suitable for use in pendants or earrings.

dry diggings, prospector's term for alluvial operations which are not on or near a watercourse; used in the early South African diamond fields to refer to the first alluvial diggings away from the banks of the Orange River. See RIVER DIGGINGS.

DTC, see DIAMOND TRADING COMPANY (PTY.), LTD. (DTC).

ducat, a small, distorted octahedron on which only a table has been polished. Corruption of duke cut; also called ducut or duke.

Duchess Cut, proprietary name for a 63-facet, straight-edged fancy-cut diamond derived from the marquise shape; developed by the Israeli firm of Raphaeli-Stschik to make the most of flat or misshapen rough. See BARONESS CUT, EMPRESS CUT, GRACE CUT, ROYAL CUTS.

ducut, see DUCAT.

Dudley Diamond, see STAR OF SOUTH AFRICA DIAMOND.

duke, see DUCAT.

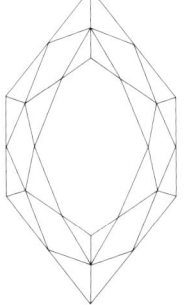

Duchess cut

Dunkelsbühler, Anton, uncle of Sir Ernest Oppenheimer, prominent diamond dealer, and a member of the original Diamond Syndicate; later known as Anton Dunkels. See ANTON DUNKELS' DIAMONDS.

Du Plessis Diamante, kimberlite fissure near Barkly West, South Africa. Diamonds are recovered by overhead shrinkage.

durability, resistance to wear and damage. In gemstones, durability depends on hardness,

Dutch bort, misnomer for zircon.

Dutch rose cut, rose cut with 24 triangular facets arranged over a flat base; it is more pointed than other rose cuts (the height is usually half the diameter of the stone). Also called full-Dutch rose cut, full-Holland rose cut, Holland rose cut, or crowned rose cut.

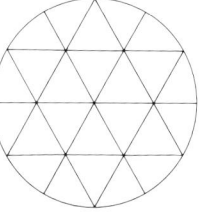

Dutch rose cut

Dutoitspan Mine, fourth kimberlite pipe discovered in South Africa; found on the Dorstfontein farm, one kilometer (0.6 miles) from the Bultfontein Mine, near the present city of Kimberley, in 1870 (but not recognized as a primary source until 1872). Named for the pan, or natural land basin, in which it is located, the mine is operated by De Beers Consolidated Mines; diamonds are recovered by block caving and sublevel caving. It shares a vertical shaft with the Bultfontein Mine; a decline has been developed

Dutoitspan Mine

near the bottom of the shaft to reach the lower levels. Dutoitspan is noted for its large yellow or cape diamonds. See BLOCK CAVING, PAN, SUBLEVEL CAVING.

dyke, see DIKE.

Dynagem, proprietary name for synthetic strontium titanate. Marketed as a diamond simulant.

toughness, and stability; diamond is extremely durable.

E

Earth Star Diamond, 111.59 ct. pear-shape brilliant diamond, described as naturally colored fancy brown, fashioned from a 248.90 ct. rough found at the Jagersfontein Mine, South Africa, in 1967. Sold privately in Florida, US, in 1983.

Ebelyakh River, tributary of the Anabar River in northern Sakha (Yakutia), the Russian Federation, CIS, along which a large alluvial diamond deposit has been found.

eccentric culet, see OFF-CENTER CULET.

eccentric table, see OFF-CENTER TABLE.

eclogite, one of two rocks in which diamonds crystallize. See KIMBERLITE, LAMPROITE, PERIDOTITE.

economy stone, diamond of inferior cut, color, or clarity which sells for a modest price.

edge up, position of a gemstone which allows it to be examined parallel to the girdle plane. Diamonds are commonly positioned edge up during color grading. See FACE-UP, TABLE DOWN.

Edna Star Diamond, 115 ct. emerald-cut diamond purchased by Harry Winston in 1956. The diamond was set in a combination pendant and clip and sold to a Middle Eastern buyer in 1957.

eight-by-eight, see SINGLE CUT.

eight cut, see SINGLE CUT.

eighth, diamond weighing one eighth of a carat (0.125 ct.).

eights, common expression describing diamonds which weigh 0.125 ct., or one-eighth of a carat. See EIGHT-SQUARE STONE.

eight-square stone, diamond on which the first eight crown mains, or bezel facets, and the first eight pavilion main facets have been polished. See BLOCKING, CROSS-WORKING, FOUR-SQUARE STONE.

EKL, see ENTRE-KASAI-LUEBO GROUP.

Elandsfontein, farm, 39 kilometers (24 miles) east of Pretoria, South Africa, on which the pipe later developed as the Premier Mine was discovered. See CULLINAN DIAMOND; CULLINAN, THOMAS; JONKER DIAMOND.

Elandsputte, alluvial diamond digging near Lichtenburg, Transvaal Province, South Africa; site of a famous diamond rush in 1926 in which thousands of people took part.

Elandsputte

electrical conductivity, relative ease with which electrical current passes through a material. Materials are classed as conductors, semi-conductors, or insulators (non-conductors). Most diamonds are non-conductors; the rare Type IIb diamonds are semi-conductors. See AUDIO CONDUCTION DETECTOR, CONDUCTOMETER, IRRADIATED BLUE DIAMOND.

electromagnetic mapping, see ELECTROMAGNETIC SURVEYING.

electromagnetic separation, technique used to separate diamonds from concentrates which contain large amounts of magnetic and paramagnetic materials (called ironstone). The concentrate is exposed to a strong electromagnetic field which attracts the ironstone and allows the diamonds to pass through. See ELECTROSTATIC SEPARATION, SEPARATION (2).

electromagnetic spectrum, entire continuous range of radiant energy, from very long radio waves to very short gamma and X-rays. Visible-light wavelengths occupy a narrow range from 360 nm to 700 nm near the center of the electromagnetic spectrum. See SPECTRUM.

electromagnetic surveying, surface or aerial geophysical technique which measures the electrical conductivity of the terrain. Kimberlites and lamproites cause anomalies in the conductive patterns.

electron-bombarded diamond, see IRRADIATED BLUE DIAMOND, LINEAR ACCELERATOR, VAN DE GRAAFF GENERATOR.

electronic balance, instrument for weighing diamonds which uses a piezoelectric transducer instead of counterweights and generates a digital read-out of the measurement. See CHAIN BALANCE, COUNTERWEIGHT BALANCE, DIAMOND BALANCE, MECHANICAL BALANCE, PORTABLE BALANCE, RIDER BALANCE, SINGLE-PAN BALANCE.

electronic micrometer, see MICROMETER.

electron treatment, see IRRADIATED BLUE DIAMOND, LINEAR ACCELERATOR, VAN DE GRAAFF GENERATOR.

electrostatic separation, recovery method which employs a charged electrical field to remove small diamonds (less than 1.65 mm/.007 in. in diameter) from alluvial gravels and certain kimberlite concentrates. Concentrate is dropped between a series of charged rollers, half of which are negatively grounded and half positively charged, creating an electrical field. Diamonds (usually poor conductors) drop through;

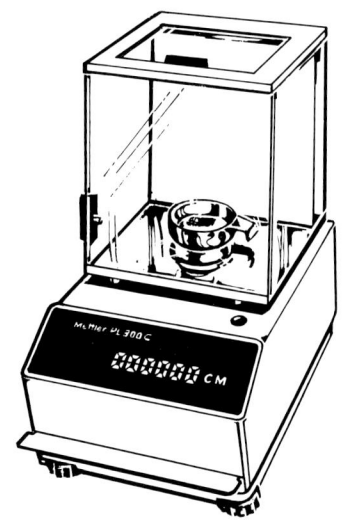

electronic balance

associated heavy minerals (relatively good conductors) are attracted to the positively-charged electrodes. The process is less expensive and more accurate than hand sorting. See ELECTROMAGNETIC SEPARATION, SEPARATION (2).

Elizabeth Bay, historic area of alluvial diamond mining 25 kilometers (16 miles) south of Lüderitz, Namibia; site of a new mine opened by CDM in 1991, but with a limited life expectancy.

Ellendale, area of numerous diamond-bearing lamproite pipes in Western Australia, discovered by the Ashton Joint Venture in 1976. Prospecting indicates the presence of diamonds but the mine grade is low. See AK1 PIPE (ARGYLE), ARGYLE DIAMOND MINES.

Ellure Group, see GOLCONDA.

eluvial deposit, secondary mineral deposit resulting from the disintegration or decomposition of the original host rock, with minimal transportation of the material; thus eluvial deposits remain relatively close to the primary deposit from which they are derived. See ALLUVIAL DEPOSIT.

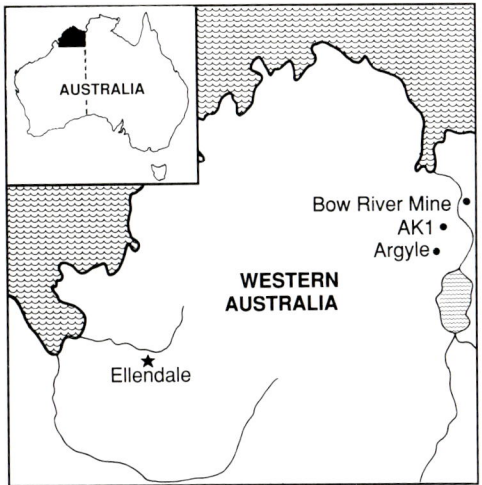

Ellendale

emerald cut, rectangular or square step cut with diagonally cut corners and two, three, or four rows of facets parallel to the girdle on the crown and pavilion. If the shape is square, it is called a square emerald cut. It is frequently used to fashion emeralds; hence the name.

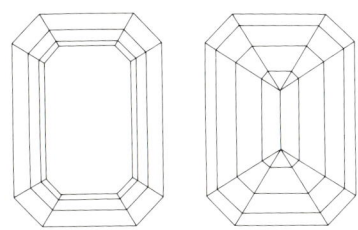

emerald cut

emission spectrum (plural, spectra), spectrum generated by fluorescence produced as the result of excitation by X-rays, ultraviolet rays, cathode rays, or visible light. Emission spectra are sometimes continuous, but they usually appear as a series of bright lines in the spectroscope (or as distinct peaks under the spectrophotometer). Characteristic spectra can be used in gem identification. See ABSORPTION SPECTRUM.

Emperor-lite, proprietary name for colorless synthetic sapphire. Marketed as a diamond simulant.

Emperor Maximilian Diamond, 41.94 ct., VS_1, I-color cushion-shape diamond with very strong blue fluorescence. Discovered and reportedly fashioned in Brazil; it was purchased in 1860 by Austrian Archduke Maximilian, (Ferdinand Maximilian Joseph, 1832-1867), later Emperor of Mexico. He was wearing the diamond when he was executed at Querétaro, Mexico, on June 19, 1867. The diamond was returned to his widow, the Empress Carlotta (1840-1927), who sold it to pay medical expenses. The Emperor Maximilian Diamond was displayed in Chicago in 1934 and last sold in 1983, together with the Idol's Eye and a 70.54 fancy yellow diamond called the Sultan Abdul-Hamid II, in one of the biggest single transactions in the history of diamond sales. Current whereabouts unknown. See IDOL'S EYE DIAMOND, MAXIMILIAN DIAMOND.

Emperor Maximillian Diamond

photo courtesy of CSO

emplacement (of diamond): diamonds, formed up to 3,300 million years ago at depths of 150-200 km (93-124 miles), were transported to the surface as xenocrysts in kimberlitic and lamproitic magmas. These magmas traveled to the surface in the form of volcanic pipes, dikes, or sills. Kimberlite pipes tend to be carrot-shaped; lamproite pipes are stem-like, but curve out into a bell shape at the top. Most diamonds are emplaced in the middle section of the pipes, known as the diatreme zone. See CRATON, DIAMOND, DIATREME, HYPABYSSAL ZONE, KIMBERLITE, LAMPROITE, MAGMA, ORIGIN (OF DIAMOND), SILL, XENOCRYST.

Empresa Nacional de Diamantes de Angola (ENDIAMA), agency established in 1981 by the Angolan government to assume the government's interests in DIAMANG (Companhia de Diamantes de Angola). DIAMANG was dissolved in 1986, with all rights passing to ENDIAMA.

Empress Cut, proprietary name for a 64-facet fancy-cut diamond developed from the pear shape by the Israeli firm of Raphaeli-Stschik to make the most of flat or misshapen rough. See BARONESS CUT, DUCHESS CUT, GRACE CUT, ROYAL CUTS.

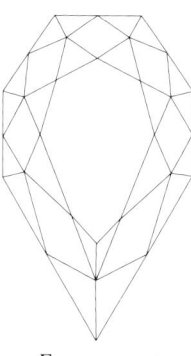

Empress cut

Empress Rose Diamond, 72.79 ct. diamond, reportedly flawless and described as pink, from South America. It is the largest pink diamond reported, but its whereabouts are unknown.

ENDIAMA, see EMPRESA NACIONAL DE DIAMANTES DE ANGOLA.

engagement ring, ring, usually set with one or more diamonds, traditionally given by a man to a woman in token of betrothal. See ARCHDUKE MAXIMILLIAN OF AUSTRIA, MARY OF BURGUNDY.

English double-cut brilliant, see ENGLISH SQUARE-CUT BRILLIANT.

English Dresden Diamond, 78.53 ct., reportedly colorless, flawless pear shape cut from a 119.50 ct. diamond found in 1857 in the Bagagem diggings in Minas Gerais, Brazil. Purchased by Edward Z. Dresden of London and fashioned in Amsterdam. Purchased in 1864 by a British merchant living in Bombay and later sold to the Gaekwar of Baroda. Now privately owned in India. Also called the Dresden Drop or the Star of Dresden.

English round-cut brilliant, cutting style, considered the first round-girdle cut; fashionable in England in the mid-nineteenth century. The facet arrangement on the crown resembles a modern brilliant, but the total depth is almost equal to the girdle diameter. Weight retention from the octahedron is very high, but the make is unattractive by modern standards.

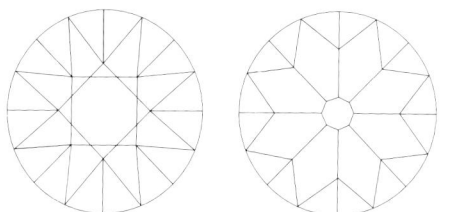

English round-cut brilliant

English square cut, one of two alternate forms of the double cut (the other is the English square-cut brilliant), with an octagonal table and girdle.

English square-cut brilliant, early form of the double cut, with a cushion-shaped crown. Also called an English double-cut brilliant.

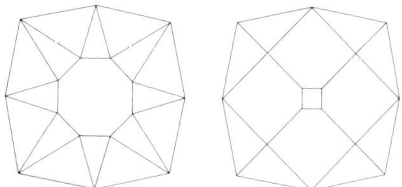

English square-cut brilliant

English star cut, early variation of the double cut, with a distinctive angular crown and altered pavilion facets. See ENGLISH SQUARE CUT, OLD MINE CUT.

enhancement, any post-recovery process which alters the appearance, especially the color or clarity, of a natural diamond or other gem material. Coating, fracture filling, irradiation, heating (annealing), and lasering are all forms of enhancement. Also called treatment. See ANNEALING, BACKING, COATED DIAMOND, DISCLOSURE, IRRADIATED DIAMOND, KOSS TREATMENT, LASER DRILLING, YEHUDA TREATMENT.

Entre-Kasai-Luebo Group (EKL), consortium of the Société Minière du Kasai, Société Minière du Luebo, and Société Minière de la Lueta which jointly worked concessions in the Luebo Valley, in what is now Zaire.

Entreprise Guinéene d'Exploitation de Diamants, government organization established in Guinea after the nationalization of the gold and diamond industries in 1961, to regulate all mining and commercial activities involving those materials.

epaulet, modified pentagon cut produced by varying the length and angles of the sides. Also spelled epaulette.

epigenetic inclusion, inclusion which develops after the formation of the crystal in which it is contained. See PROTOGENETIC INCLUSION, SYNGENETIC INCLUSION.

Eppler fine cut, see PRACTICAL FINE CUT.

eroded crystal, see ETCHED CRYSTAL.

Estrêla de Minas Diamond, see STAR OF THE SOUTH DIAMOND.

Estrêla do Sul, one of a number of small alluvial diamond mining areas in Minas Gerais, Brazil. See STAR OF THE SOUTH DIAMOND.

Estrêla do Sul Diamond, see STAR OF THE SOUTH DIAMOND.

etched crystal, diamond crystal that was partially dissolved while in the earth. The shape of the pits left on the surface by the process reflect the diamond's crystal structure. See ETCH PIT.

etch figure, see ETCH PIT.

etch pit, indentation on the face of a diamond crystal that was partially dissolved during growth. Etch pits are triangular on octahedral faces, boat-shaped on dodecahedral faces, and square on cube faces. Also called etch figures. See ETCHED CRYSTAL, TRIGON.

eternity ring, see ANNIVERSARY RING.

Étoile du Désert, 50.67 ct., D-color, pear-shape diamond set in a necklace with more than 250 other diamonds. Sold in 1977 by Harry Winston to a buyer in Saudi Arabia. Current whereabouts unknown.

Étoile du Désert

Eugénie Blue Diamond, see UNZUE HEART DIAMOND.

Eugénie Diamond, 52.35 ct. oval, brilliant-cut diamond, believed to have been fashioned from a rough crystal of approximately 100 ct. found in Minas Gerais, Brazil, in 1760. First owned by Russian Empress Catherine II (Catherine the Great, 1729-1796) and set in a hair ornament; in 1787, she gave it to Prince Grigory Aleksan-

etch pit

drovich Potemkin (1739-1791), her lover and chief counselor. The diamond (then known as the Potemkin) was inherited by the Prince's grandniece, who sold it to Emperor Napoleon III (1808-1873) of France in 1853. He presented it to his bride, Eugenia Maria de Montijo (1826-1920) as a wedding gift. After the fall of the French Empire in 1870, the Empress took the Eugénie with her to England; it was eventually sold to the Gaekwar of Baroda, India. The diamond disappeared when the Gaekwar was deposed; it eventually reappeared in the possession of Mrs. N.J. Dady of Bombay, India. Now privately owned in Antwerp.

Eureka Diamond, 21.25 ct. yellow diamond, the first authenticated diamond found in South Africa. Discovered in late 1866 on the De Kalk farm, near the Orange River, by 15-year old Erasmus Jacobs. It was identified as a diamond by W. G. Atherstone of Grahamstown, an amateur mineralogist. Originally purchased by Sir Philip Wodehouse, Governor of the Cape Colony, and fashioned into a 10.73 ct. oval brilliant, the stone passed through the hands of several owners until 1967, when it was acquired by De Beers Consolidated Mines and presented to the Parliament of South Africa in Cape Town. It is now on display at the Open Mine Museum in Kimberley, South Africa. See ATHERSTONE, WILLIAM GUYBON; JACOBS, ERASMUS; VAN NIEKERK, SCHALK.

photo courtesy of CSO

Eureka Diamond

European fine cut, see PRACTICAL FINE CUT.

Everay Jewellery, Ltd., Hong Kong-based company which operates six diamond manufacturing factories in the People's Republic of China; five are located in Guangdong Province, the sixth in Guangzhou Province. Production from Everay's Chinese factories is approximately 70 percent makeables and 30 percent sawables.

Excelsior Diamond, 995.20 ct. diamond, G color, containing several inclusions, found in the Jagersfontein Mine, Orange Free State, South Africa, on June 30, 1893. Cleaved by the I. J. Asscher Company in Amsterdam in 1903 and fashioned into eight pear shapes weighing 69.68 ct., 47.03 ct., 46.90 ct., 34.91 ct., 24.31 ct., 16.78 ct., 13.86 ct., and 9.82 ct.; three marquise cuts weighing 40.23 ct., 28.61 ct., and 26.30 ct.; and ten round brilliants with a combined weight of 20.33 ct. The largest stone, Excelsior I, was last sold in 1984; it was offered at auction in 1991, but withdrawn. The current whereabouts of the others are unknown.

exceptional white, term, together with the qualifier exceptional white +, on the CIBJO and IDC color-grading scales; exceptional white + is equivalent to D, and exceptional white to E, on the GIA color-grading scale. See APPENDIX D, CIBJO INTERNATIONAL COLOR-GRADING SCALE, GIA COLOR-GRADING SCALE, IDC INTERNATIONAL COLOR-GRADING SCALE.

external characteristic, any of several types of marks found on the surface of a gemstone but which do not penetrate it significantly. See BLEMISH, INCLUSION.

extra facets, facets in excess of those normally required to complete the faceting pattern of a given cutting style. Usually found near the girdle, extra facets are the result of smoothing out nicks, chips, naturals, abrasions, and other blemishes or, in some instances, of errors in polishing. Not to be confused with additional facets. See ADDITIONAL FACETS, SYMMETRY.

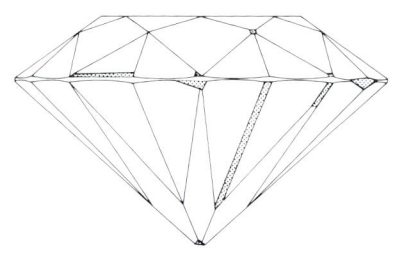

extra facets

eye-clean, clarity-grading term for a diamond in which no inclusions are visible to the unaided eye. In the US, use of the term for sales promotion is prohibited by the Federal Trade Commission if the stone does not meet this criterion. Comparable authorities elsewhere enforce similar regulations.

eye diamond, see FISHEYE.

eye loupe, magnifying lens which can be held in the eye socket or attached to eyeglasses. Eye loupes usually offer a magnification range from two to three power (2X to 3X). See LOUPE.

Eye of Brahma Diamond, see BLACK ORLOFF DIAMOND.

Eye of Shiva Diamond, see NASSAK DIAMOND.

eye perfect, see EYE-CLEAN.

eye loupe

eye-visible, visible to the unaided eye (without magnification but allowing for the use of eyeglasses or contact lenses that correct towards normal visual acuity); used to describe the visual prominence of clarity characteristics.

F

Fabulite, proprietary name for synthetic strontium titanate. Used as a diamond simulant.

face, (1) natural, flat surface on a crystal, normally corresponding to an internal crystal plane. (2) in brilliandeering, that group of facets which can be placed on a diamond without repositioning the stone in the dop, *e.g.,* the two star facets and four upper-girdle facets. See BRILLIANDEERING, SET.

face-down, position of a gemstone which orients the pavilion or culet toward the viewer. Diamonds are usually positioned face-down during color grading. See EDGE UP, FACE-UP.

facet, flat, polished surface on a finished diamond.

facet alignment, placement of the crown and pavilion facets such that the bottom points of the bezel facets are directly above the top points of the pavilion mains. In this position, the junctions of the upper girdle facets should be just above those of the lower girdle facets. In diamond grading, facet alignment is evaluated as an aspect of symmetry. See POINTING, SYMMETRY.

facet angle, angle between the plane of a facet and the girdle plane.

facet design, shape and arrangement of the facets on a diamond.

facet diagram, drawing of a diamond's facet design (crown or pavilion). When inclusions and blemishes are recorded on a facet diagram, it is called a plot. See PLOT, PLOTTING, PLOTTING SYMBOLS.

faceted girdle, girdle which has been polished with a series of flat facets. See POLISHED GIRDLE.

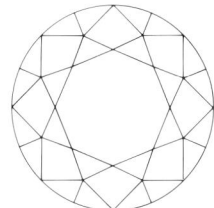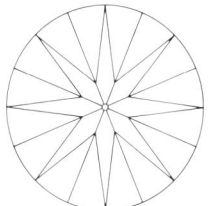

facet diagram of a round brilliant

faceting, process of grinding and polishing facets on a diamond or other gem. See BLOCKING, BRILLIANDEERING, CROSS-WORKING, POLISHING.

facet junction, ridge on a polished stone where two adjoining facets meet; also called a rib line.

face-up, position of a gemstone which orients the table toward the viewer. Diamonds are clarity graded and mounted in jewelry in the face-up position. See FACE-DOWN, FACE UP WELL.

face-up appearance, the apparent condition, brilliance, color, and clarity of a diamond when examined face-up. See FACE-UP COLOR, FACE UP WELL.

face-up color, apparent color of a diamond when examined face-up. Brilliance, surface reflections, and dispersion can mask bodycolor in the face-up position, particularly on stones with high color grades (F, G, H, and I in the GIA scale). Bodycolor becomes noticeable in the face-up position at about J or K. See COLORED DIAMOND, COLOR GRADING, FACE UP WELL, FANCY COLOR DIAMONDS.

face up well, term applied to a diamond which, when it is examined face-up, appears to have a higher color grade than it actually has. Fancy color diamonds that "face up well" look more saturated in color face-up than they do face-down. Well cut fancy shapes which do not show a bow tie are also said to face up well. See FACE-UP COLOR.

Fachmitglied der Deutschen Gemmologischen Gesellschaft (F.G.G.), (Fellow of the German Gemological Association), title awarded to individuals who complete a prescribed course of study and pass a series of examinations administered by the German Gemological Association in Idar-Oberstein, Germany. See DEUTSCHE GEMMOLOGISCHE GESELLSCHAFT E.V.

faisel, see FEZEL.

faizel, see FEZEL.

false-colored diamond, slightly yellow diamond which fluoresces blue in daylight, making the color grade appear higher than it is. See PREMIER DIAMOND.

false diamond, misnomer for rock crystal quartz; sometimes used for colorless minerals which resemble diamond, such as sapphire, zircon, topaz, or quartz. See SIMULANT.

false facet, see EXTRA FACETS.

Falun Brilliant, proprietary name for a lead glass diamond simulant.

fanciful cut, see FANCY CUT.

fan cut, see FAN-SHAPE CUT.

fancy color diamond, any naturally colored diamond with a noticeable depth of bodycolor considered to be rare or attractive. Red and green are the rarest fancy colors, followed by purple, violet, orange, blue, and pink. Yellow (sometimes called canary diamonds) and greenish yellow diamonds are more common. While white, black, and gray are strictly speaking not spectral colors, they are also considered fancies. Light, or low-saturation colored diamonds other than yellow or brown may be classed as fancies but, in the GIA color-grading system, yellows and browns must be darker than the Z master diamond to merit a fancy grade. Fancy color grades are described as faint, very light, light, fancy light, fancy, fancy intense, and fancy dark in the GIA system; treated diamonds are not considered fancy diamonds, but are sometimes referred to as "treated fancy diamonds" in the trade. See COLORED DIAMOND.

fancy cut, any cut other than a round brilliant or single cut. Traditional fancy cuts include the marquise, emerald cut, heart shape, oval shape, pear shape, keystone, half moon, kite, triangle, and various modified brilliant cuts. See BARION CUT, BRILLIANT CUT, FLOWER CUTS, NOVELTY CUTS, ROYAL CUTS, STEP CUT.

fancy diamond, see COLORED DIAMOND, FANCY COLOR DIAMOND.

fancy light yellow, GIA color-grading term for yellow diamonds the color of which matches or slightly exceeds the color of the Z master diamond.

fancy shape, see FANCY CUT.

fan-shape cut, cut which resembles a partly opened fan.

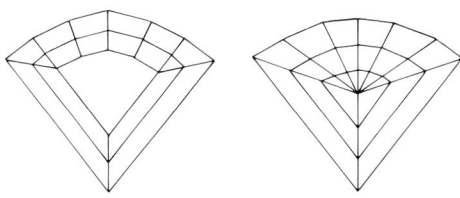

fan-shape cut

fantasy cuts, free-form shapes which alternate curved and flat surfaces; derived from the Dutch "fantasie."

fashioning, (1) general term used to describe the entire process of manufacturing a polished diamond from the rough, including design, cleaving, sawing, bruting, and polishing; also called cutting. (2) industry term for bruting. See BRILLIANDEERING, BRUTING, CLEAVING, POLISHING, SAWING.

fault, see BLEMISH, INTERNAL CHARACTERISTIC.

faultless, see FLAWLESS.

fancy color diamonds

faulty structure, see CLEAVAGE, GRAIN LINES, TWIN CRYSTAL.

feather, cleavage or fracture; may be transparent, but usually has a whitish appearance when seen at right angles to the break. Also called a gletz. See HAIRLINE FEATHER.

feather

photo by John I. Koivula

feathered girdle, see BEARDED GIRDLE.

Federal Trade Commission (FTC), regulatory body of the United States government responsible for deterring unfair or deceptive trade practices and preventing restraint of trade. The FTC works with the industries it regulates to develop and promote American trade practice rules, such as the *Guides for the Jewelry Industry*.

Fellow of the Gemmological Association of Australia (FGAA), title awarded to individuals who complete a prescribed course of study and pass a series of examinations administered by the Gemmological Association of Australia (GAA); graduates may use the suffix FGAA. The GAA is affiliated with the Gemmological Association and Gem Testing Laboratory of Great Britain.

Fellow of the Gemmological Association of Great Britain (FGA), title awarded to individuals who complete a prescribed course of study and pass a series of examinations administered by the Gemmological Association and Gem Testing Laboratory of Great Britain. The GAGB was founded in 1908, making the FGA one of the oldest gemological titles in the world.

Ferouba, important alluvial diamond digging in Guinea, now part of the AREDOR concession area. See ASSOCIATION POUR LA RECHERCHE L'EXPLOITATION DU DIAMANT ET DE L'OR.

Fersman, Alexander E., Russian mineralogist and geologist, researcher into the crystal morphology of diamond, and an authority on the Romanoff Crown Jewels; co-author, with V. Goldschmidt, of *Der Diamant* in 1911.

fezel, jagged, streamer-like inclusion seen in diamonds. Fezels typically appear along the twinning planes of macles; usually white, but may be gray or black. Also spelled faisel, faizel, vezel.

FGA, see FELLOW OF THE GEMMOLOGICAL ASSOCIATION OF GREAT BRITAIN.

FGAA, see FELLOW OF THE GEMMOLOGICAL ASSOCIATION OF AUSTRALIA.

F.G.G., see FACHMITGLIED DER DEUTSCHEN GEMMOLOGISCHEN GESELLSCHAFT.

Field, Charles M., nineteenth-century American diamond cutter from Boston, Massachusetts who, while working for Henry Morse, developed a steam-driven machine to improve the quality of bruting.

Fiery Astrolite, proprietary name for lithium meta-niobate. Marketed as a diamond simulant.

fifth, gem weighing approximately one fifth of a carat (0.20 ct.).

Fifty Years of Aeroflot Diamond, 232 ct. diamond said to have been found near Mirnyi, Sakha (Yakutia), the Russian Federation, CIS, in 1973; named in commemoration of Russian Aviation Day. It may have been renamed the Star of Yakutia, the discovery of which in the same area was announced a few months later, and which is also reported to weigh 232 ct.

file test, use of a jeweler's file to separate glass from diamonds. With a Mohs hardness rating of 6½, the file, which is steel, will not scratch diamond, but it will scratch glass; however, some diamond simulants and many natural gems are also harder than 6½. Improperly used, a file may chip a diamond.

filled diamond, diamond in which surface-reaching cleavages, fractures, or laser drillholes have been filled with glass or epoxy to make them less visible; similar to the process used to enhance rough and polished emeralds. Fillings can be identified by flow lines, flattened gas bubbles, or web-like patterns in the filling material; they may appear greasy or oily, and sometimes show an interference flash effect when rotated under darkfield illumination. They can be damaged or displaced by high temperatures or sulfuric acid cleaning, and may lower the apparent color grade of the stone. GIA's Gem Trade Laboratory, among others, does not grade filled diamonds. See ENHANCEMENT, KOSS TREATMENT, YEHUDA TREATMENT.

fine cape, see SILVER CAPE.

fine silver cape, see SILVER CAPE.

finest water, see WATER.

fine working, see FINISH.

finish, quality of a diamond's polish, the condition of its girdle, and the precision of the cut. See MINOR SYMMETRY.

finisher, see BRILLIANDEER.

finish grading, process of evaluating and describing the finish details of a polished diamond. See FINISH.

Finsch Mine, large kimberlite pipe near Postmasburg, Cape Province, South Africa, worked by De Beers Consolidated Mines since 1965. The mine operated first as an open pit until 1990; underground mining began in 1991.

fire, see DISPERSION.

fire damage, whitish, irregularly granulated surface which occurs as a consequence of exposing a diamond to high temperatures. It is usually the result of failing to protect a stone with firecoat when it is heated with a jeweler's torch, but it can be caused by any fire, such as a

Finsch Mine

house fire. It can be removed only by repolishing.

Fire Rose Cut, registered name for one of five "Flower" cuts designed by CSO consultant Gabi Tolkowsky in 1988. Especially effective with heavy, misshapen crystals, it can be executed as a hexagon with 61 facets, a pear or heart shape with 67 facets, a square or octagon with 81, or a marquise with 105. See DAHLIA CUT, FLOWER CUTS, MARIGOLD CUT, SUNFLOWER CUT, ZINNIA CUT.

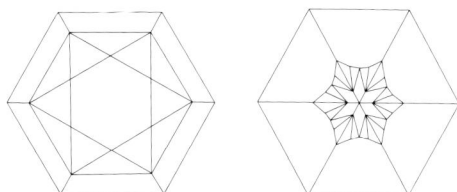

Fire Rose Cut

first water, see WATER.

fisheye, diamond with a pavilion depth of less than 40 percent, in which a circular gray reflection of all or part of the girdle appears through the table when the stone is examined face-up.

fisheye

flash effect

fissure, (1) elongated cavity in a diamond's surface. (2) geological term for a narrow opening or crack in the earth's surface.

595 nm line ("five ninety-five line"), sharp absorption line seen in the spectra of many yellow or brown diamonds which have been artificially colored by radiation treatment and subsequent annealing. In rare instances, a weak line is present in naturally colored green, yellow, and brown stones. See ABSORPTION SPECTRUM, CYCLOTRON-TREATED DIAMOND, IRRADIATED DIAMOND, SPECTROSCOPE.

Fl, abbreviation for flawless.

Flame of Gold Diamond, 29 ct. pear-shape diamond, described as fancy yellow, and set in a necklace that won the 1957 Diamonds-International Awards competition. Bought for American screen actress Greer Garson by her husband, Buddy Fogelson, in 1963.

flash effect, easily recognized visual feature of glass-filled cracks in diamonds: When a filled diamond is examined under darkfield illumination nearly parallel to the plane of the crack, a single interference color is visible; if the stone is then tilted very slightly until the background becomes bright (through secondary reflection), the interference color changes to a second color.

The two pairs of flash effect colors thus far observed are yellowish orange (darkfield) and blue (bright), and pinkish purple (darkfield) and yellowish green (bright). See DARKFIELD ILLUMINATION.

flat, flat rough diamond crystal, or a flat piece of a diamond crystal; often associated with macles.

flat stone, polished diamond with a very shallow crown and/or a very shallow pavilion.

flaw, see BLEMISH, INTERNAL CHARACTERISTIC.

flawless, GIA clarity grade applied to a polished diamond which shows no blemishes or inclusions when examined by a trained grader with a fully corrected 10x loupe or microscope. The Scan. D.N. clarity scale has a corresponding FL grade. See APPENDIX E, PERFECT.

Fleischman Star Diamond, 74.44 ct. emerald-cut diamond, described as fancy yellow. Purchased by Harry Winston in 1956, it was recut to 71.07 ct. and set in a combination pendant and clip with 32 brilliants. Sold to a private buyer in 1957; current whereabouts unknown.

Fleurus diamond, misnomer for rock crystal quartz from southwestern Belgium.

Flinders diamond, misnomer for colorless topaz from Tasmania.

flint glass, see LEAD GLASS.

floating reef, country rock caught up within the kimberlite intrusion and left in the pipe.

floor, see WEATHERING FLOOR.

Florentine Diamond, 137.27 ct. irregular, nine-sided, 126-facet, double rose cut Indian diamond, described as greenish yellow. First documented by Tavernier, who saw it in 1657 amid the treasures of Ferdinando II, Grand Duke of Tuscany, the Florentine became part of the Austrian Crown Jewels in 1736. It is believed to have been stolen in 1918, along with the Frankfurt Solitaire, and sold in South America; its current whereabouts are unknown. Also called the Tuscan, the Grand Duke of Tuscany, the Austrian Diamond, and the Austrian Yellow.

Flower Cuts, registered name for five diamond cuts designed by CSO consultant Gabi Tolkowsky to heighten the appeal of polished diamonds in the lower color ranges, and to increase the yield from the rough. The collection was introduced at the World Diamond Congress in Singapore in 1988. Their use is not restricted and the cuts have not been patented. See DAHLIA CUT, FIRE ROSE CUT, MARIGOLD CUT, SUNFLOWER CUT, ZINNIA CUT.

fluorescence, emission of visible light by a material such as diamond when it is stimulated by higher energy X-rays, ultraviolet radiation, or other forms of radiation. Fluorescence continues only as long as the material is exposed to the radiation. See FLUOROCHROMATIC, JAGER, PHOSPHORESCENCE, PREMIER DIAMOND.

fluorescence

fluorescent color, color of visible light emitted by a gemstone when subjected to X-rays, ultraviolet radiation, or other radiation. Gem quality diamonds usually fluoresce blue. See FLUORESCENCE.

fluoride coating, coating used to alter the color of diamonds. The coating is extremely thin and is usually applied near the girdle of a stone by vacuum sputtering. (Coating takes place in a vacuum; the coating substance is introduced into the vacuum chamber as a vapor.) It may appear as iridescence on the pavilion surface. Fluoride coatings can be damaged or removed by some ordinary jewelry cleaning methods.

fluorochromatic, term applied to a diamond which, because of fluorescence, shows an apparent color change under different kinds of visible light, such as incandescent light and daylight.

flute, thin, translucent liner inside a diamond paper; usually light blue, white, off-white, or yellow. See DIAMOND PAPER.

fluvial gravel, sand or gravel deposits in a stream or river; alluvial diamonds are often found in fluvial gravel. See ALLUVIAL DEPOSIT, ALLUVIAL MINING, RIVER DIGGINGS.

foilback, diamond or other gemstone, or simulant, which has been enhanced by the application of a thin, metallic foil (either silvery or colored) to its pavilion, to increase its brilliance or to give it color. See BACKING, DIAMOND SIMULANT, RHINESTONE.

footwall, rocks which underlie a horizontal or inclined fault, dyke, orebody, mine workings, or chamber. See HANGING WALL.

foreshore mining, see BEACH MINING.

form grinding truing tool, diamond dressing tool used to dress special radial and step form abrasive wheels. Truing tools usually contain either an uncut diamond crystal or a shaped diamond. There are three main types: chisel truers, cone truers, and roller truers. See DRESSER.

FORMINIÈRE, see SOCIETE FORESTIERE ET MINIERE DU CONGO.

Forty-Seventh Street (47th), street in New York City, US, between Fifth Avenue and the Avenue of the Americas, the center of the city's diamond manufacturing and trading activity.

foss, irregular furrow or groove in the surface of a diamond, characteristic of diamond crystals in the gray color range.

Four Cs, the four factors—color, clarity, cut, and carat weight—which determine the value of a diamond.

four grainer, one-carat diamond. See GRAINER.

four-point diamond, diamond with the table parallel to a possible cube face.

four-square diamond, see FOUR-SQUARE STONE.

four-square stone, diamond on which the first four crown mains (which later become bezel facets) and the first four pavilion mains have been ground by the cross-worker. Also called a cross, or croix. See BLOCKING, CROSS-WORKING, EIGHT-SQUARE STONE.

fracture, chip or break on a diamond along a direction other than a cleavage plane. Fractures in diamond usually occur as irregular step-like or splintery breaks.

framesite, polycrystalline diamond similar to carbonado, found in many mines. Named after Ross Frames, a former chairman of the Premier Mine. See BALLAS, BORT, CARBONADO, CRUSHING BORT, HAILSTONE BORT, STEWARTITE.

Frankfurt Solitaire Diamond, 44.62 ct. (old carats) brilliant-cut diamond purchased in 1764 by Francis I, Grand Duke of Tuscany. The stone was originally set in a hat ornament; following Francis' death, it was remounted in a tiara. It is thought to have been stolen, along with the Florentine, in 1918, by a Hapsburg family retainer and sold in South America. Current whereabouts unknown.

Frank Smith Mine, kimberlite pipe mine near Barkly West, South Africa. Diamonds are recovered by chambering.

Fraunhofer lines, group of absorption lines across the visible spectrum resulting from the absorption of light by elements in the sun's chromosphere (the lower part of its atmosphere, composed of hydrogen gas). Discovered by Joseph Fraunhofer in the nineteenth century, the lines are designated by letters of the alphabet. The dispersion of gem materials is measured between the B (687 nm) and G (430.8 nm) lines.

French Blue Diamond, 67.5 ct. (old carats) heart-shape diamond, described as natural blue, and fashioned from the 112.5 ct. (old carats) Tavernier Blue. Once the center stone in the Flame of the Golden Fleece, the badge of a chivalric order, it was among the jewels stolen from the French Royal Treasury in 1792. Believed to have been recut into the 45.52 ct. Hope Diamond. Also called the Blue Diamond of the Crown. See BRUNSWICK BLUE DIAMOND, HOPE DIAMOND.

French Company, see COMPAGNIE FRANÇAISE DES MINES DE DIAMANT DU CAP DE BONNE ESPERANCE.

French Crown Jewels, collection of jewelry and gem-set regalia owned by the French Monarchies. The collection was begun in 1530 by Francis I (1494-1547); it was greatly expanded by Louis XIV (1638-1715), in particular via purchases of important Indian diamonds from Jean-Baptiste Tavernier. The collection was severely reduced by the robbery of the Garde Meuble in 1792, then to some extent rebuilt by Napoleon I (1769-1821). Many important items were sold in 1887, during the Third Republic; some have since been repurchased by the French Government. Most of the remaining items are now in the Louvre; some are in the École des Mines and in other regional museums. See CHARLES THE BOLD, COTE DE BRETAGNE DIAMOND, FRENCH BLUE DIAMOND, GRAND MAZARIN DIAMOND, GUISE DIAMOND, HORTENSIA DIAMOND, MAZARIN DIAMONDS, MIRROR OF PORTUGAL DIAMOND, PEACH BLOSSOM DIAMOND, REGENT DIAMOND, RICHELIEU DIAMOND, SANCY DIAMOND, TAVERNIER A DIAMOND, TAVERNIER B DIAMOND, TAVERNIER BLUE DIAMOND, TAVERNIER C DIAMOND.

French cut, square cut with a square table, the sides of which are oriented at $45°$ to those of the girdle.

French tip, faceting variation used on marquise, pear-shape, and heart-shape cuts, in which the large bezel facet at the point is replaced with several smaller facets.

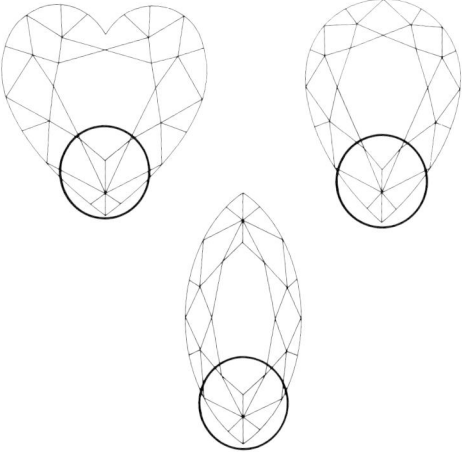

French tip

friability, term for a material's relative susceptibility to decomposition by abrasion. In diamond grits and powders, the more friable a powder is, the faster it breaks down and decreases in performance (although some degree of friability is required to generate fresh cutting edges).

fringed girdle, see BEARDED GIRDLE.

frosted crystal, diamond crystal with a translucent or frosted appearance. While frosted crystals are not always alluvial in origin, the phenomenon is often caused by water transportation and river tumbling. See ABRASION.

frosted girdle, normal appearance of a well-bruted, unpolished, unfaceted girdle. See BRUTING, POLISHED GIRDLE.

FTC, see FEDERAL TRADE COMMISSION.

full cut, brilliant cut fashioned with at least 57 facets; 58 if there is a culet.

full-cut brilliant, brilliant-cut diamond with the complete set of 32 crown facets, 24 pavilion facets, a table, and (usually) a culet. The term is usually applied to melee. See MELEE, SINGLE CUT.

full-Dutch rose cut, see DUTCH ROSE CUT.

full gauge, polished diamond which approaches the proportions of the Tolkowsky theoretical brilliant cut. See TOLKOWSKY THEORETICAL BRILLIANT CUT.

full-Holland rose cut, see DUTCH ROSE CUT.

fully-corrected lens, see ACHROMATIC LENS.

furrow, see FOSS.

furrowed stone, see FOSS.

Fuxian Pipe 50, reportedly the richest kimberlite pipe in the Fuxian district of Liaoning Province, Peoples' Republic of China; full-scale production began in 1990, 15 years after the pipe was discovered.

fuzzy girdle, see BEARDED GIRDLE.

G

Gabon, country in equatorial West Africa, bordered by Guinea, Cameroon, and the Congo Republic, in which scattered alluvial deposits of diamonds have been located. None are known to be worked commercially.

gabbro, a common coarse-grained basic igneous rock, sometimes found in kimberlite pipes. See BASIC IGNEOUS ROCK, OPEN PIT MINING, PREMIER MINE, UNDERGROUND MINING.

gadolinium gallium garnet (GGG), diamond simulant manufactured by the Czochralski pulling process. Not a true garnet because it contains no silica; chemically, it is a galliate belonging to the cubic crystal system. It is singly refractive; its specific gravity is 7.05; dispersion, 0.038; refractive index, 2.03; and hardness (Mohs scale), 6.75.

GAGTL, see GEMMOLOGICAL ASSOCIATION AND GEM TESTING LABORATORY OF GREAT BRITAIN.

Galliant, proprietary name for gadolinium gallium garnet (GGG). Marketed as a diamond simulant. See GADOLINIUM GALLIUM GARNET.

gamma ray, high-energy electromagnetic radiation emitted from the nucleus of an atom during its radioactive decay. See COLORED DIAMOND, ENHANCEMENT, FANCY COLOR DIAMOND, GAMMA RAY TREATMENT, IRRADIATED DIAMOND.

gamma ray treatment, early method of altering the color of a diamond to blue or bluish green by exposing it to gamma rays from the radioactive isotope Cobalt-60. The process is slow (often taking several months), but the irradiated color penetrates throughout the stone. Rarely used today. Subsequent heat treatment alters the color of the irradiated stones to green or yellow. See GAMMA RAY.

Garde Meuble, government building on the Place de la Concorde in Paris, which served as a storehouse for French Crown property in the eighteenth century. In 1791-1792, shortly after the French Revolution, the public was allowed for the first time to visit the collections (each Monday). In 1792, the Garde Meuble was robbed and the French Crown Jewels stolen. The building later housed the Naval Ministry. See FRENCH CROWN JEWELS.

garimpeiro, Brazilian Portuguese, an unlicensed prospector or miner.

garnet-and-glass doublet, assembled stone made from a slice of almandite garnet fused to a glass body. The garnet slice, which prevents excessive wear, usually covers the table and part of the star facets. Despite the reddish color of the garnet, when the imitation is seen face-up, it takes on the color of the glass, even when the glass is colorless. Garnet and glass doublets are sometimes used as diamond simulants.

garniture de diamants, French, a setting with diamonds.

gas bubble, void, usually spherical but sometimes elongated, found in glass, in flame-fusion and Czochralski-pulled synthetic sapphire and synthetic spinel, and in garnet-and-glass doublets (all of which are sometimes used as diamond simulants), and in the filling material in

gas bubble

glass-filled diamonds. Rarely seen in other simulants such as CZ, YAG, or GGG and never in diamond. Sometimes used incorrectly to describe a transparent included crystal in diamond. Also called a bubble. See NEGATIVE CRYSTAL.

gauge, see MICROMETER.

GE, see GENERAL ELECTRIC COMPANY.

Geiger counter, instrument used to detect residual radioactivity; sometimes used to confirm whether diamonds have been irradiated, but not all irradiated diamonds register. See RADIUM-TREATED DIAMOND.

gem, (1) polished gemstone. (2) rough gem material which has the weight, shape, clarity, and color to produce a polished stone suitable for use in jewelry. (3) an especially fine gemstone. See GEMSTONE, GEM QUALITY.

gem color, trade term for colorless; often misapplied to diamonds of average to good color.

Gemeter, proprietary name for a reflectivity meter. See REFLECTIVITY METER.

Gemette, proprietary name for synthetic sapphire. Marketed as a diamond simulant.

gem gravel, see ALLUVIAL GRAVEL.

Geminair, proprietary name for yttrium aluminum garnet (YAG). Marketed as a diamond simulant.

Gem Instruments, see GIA GEM INSTRUMENTS.

Gemmological Association and Gem Testing Laboratory of Great Britain (GAGTL), London-based organization which operates a gem testing laboratory, administers an educational program leading to the FGA title, and publishes the quarterly *Journal of Gemmology*. Founded in 1908 as the educational committee of the National Association of Goldsmiths (NAG), it became a branch of the NAG in 1931, and was then incorporated as a separate entity in 1944. In 1991, the GA merged with the Gem Testing Laboratory of Great Britain, the oldest gem testing laboratory in the world, which is associated with both GIA and CIBJO. The Gemmological Association of Australia and the Canadian Gemmological Association are affiliates. See FELLOW OF THE GEMMOLOGICAL ASSOCIATION OF GREAT BRITAIN (FGA), GEM TESTING LABORATORY OF GREAT BRITAIN (GTLGB).

gemmologist, British (UK) spelling of gemologist.

gemmology, British (UK) spelling of gemology.

GemoLite, proprietary name for a series of binocular gemological microscopes with zoom magnification and variable lighting. Manufactured by GIA Gem Instruments.

Gemological Institute of America (GIA), nonprofit educational institution established in 1931 to serve the jewelry industry and the public. Headquartered in Santa Monica, California, US, GIA offers training in a variety of fields related to the jewelry industry, such as gemology, jewelry arts, and business. The Institute awards a number of diplomas and certificates, including the Graduate Gemologist diploma, and publishes the quarterly journal *Gems & Gemology*. It has affiliates in Great Britain, Korea, Japan, and Taiwan; a subsidiary in Italy; and, through its US subsidiary, GIA Enterprises, owns the GIA Gem Trade Laboratory and GIA Gem Instruments. See GIA CLARITY-GRADING SCALE, GIA COLOR-GRADING SCALE, GIA GEM INSTRUMENTS, GIA GEM TRADE LABORATORY (GTL).

gemological microscope, binocular microscope specifically designed to examine gemstones. Gemological microscopes may have a combination of darkfield and brightfield illumination, and zoom magnification starting at 10x or below. Some models are fitted with a stoneholder.

gemologist, (1) specialist in gem materials who has successfully completed a recognized course of study in gemology including gem identification and grading. Spelled gemmologist in the UK and elsewhere. (2) when capitalized (Gemologist), title awarded to an individual who completes a specific program of study and passes a series of examinations administered by

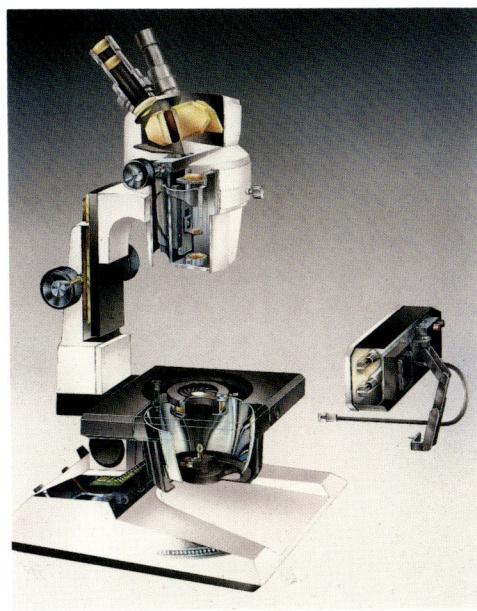

gemological microscope

the Gemological Institute of America. See GEM-OLOGIST, GRADUATE GEMOLOGIST (GG).

gemology, the study of gemstones, including their sources, descriptions, formation, identification, and grading. Spelled gemmology in the UK and elsewhere.

Gemopolis, a 105 hectare (260 acre) complex of 80 gem manufacturers, jewelry producers, trading offices, a loose stone bourse, Customs office, hotels, and worker's quarters in Bangkok, Thailand. The Thai government has declared Gemopolis, which opened in 1993, a tax-free zone to encourage investment in the country's diamond and colored stone industry. See THAILAND.

gem placer, see PLACER.

Gemprint, instrument which produces reflections of the polished surface of a faceted diamond with a laser beam and photographs them. Gemprints of diamonds are distinct from those of other materials, and the reflections of individual diamonds are said to be distinguishable from each other. Based on research conducted by the Weizmann Institute of Science in Israel, the Gemprint is designed and manufactured by Kulso. See CRYSTALPRINT.

gem quality, term describing rough gem material which has the weight, shape, clarity, and color to produce a polished stone suitable for use in jewelry. Sometimes used to describe fine diamonds. See CLARITY GRADING, COLOR GRADING, GEMSTONE, INDUSTRIAL DIAMOND.

Gemsbok, historic name for one of the important alluvial mining areas along the Namibian coast between Oranjemund and Lüderitz; also known as Area G. Operated by CDM. See AFFENRUCKEN, KERBEHUK, MITTAG, MARINE AREAS, UUBVLEY.

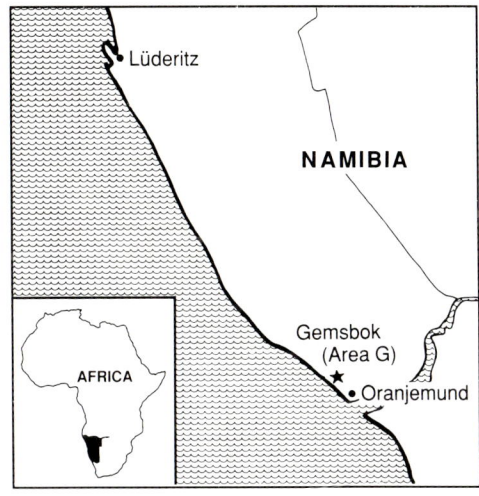

Gemsbok

gemstone, mineral or organic material (such as amber, ivory, shell, pearl) with sufficient beauty, rarity, and durability to be set into jewelry.

Gem Testing Laboratory of Great Britain (GTLGB), the oldest gemological trade laboratory in the world, founded in 1924 by Basil Anderson (1901-1984) to test and identify gem materials, particularly pearls. The GTLGB, which is associated with the Gemological Institute of America, the Gemmological Association of Great Britain, and CIBJO, also grades diamonds and identifies colored stones. See GEM-

MOLOGICAL ASSOCIATION AND GEM TESTING LABORATORY OF GREAT BRITAIN (GAGTL).

General Electric Company (GE), diversified American manufacturing company and one of the world's major producers of synthetic industrial diamonds. GE was the first to publish the results of its experimental synthetic diamond production in 1954. The company announced the experimental production of gem-quality diamond crystals colored by the addition of trace amounts of elements such as nitrogen and boron in 1970. See ADAMANT RESEARCH LABORATORY, ALLMANA SVENSKA ELEKTRISKA AKTIEBOLAGET (ASEA), DE BEERS SYNTHETIC DIAMOND, SUMITOMO SYNTHETIC DIAMOND.

geology, study of the earth, including its structure, origin, history; its constituent materials such as rocks and minerals; and the processes which act on it.

German diamond, misnomer for rock crystal quartz.

German Foundation for Gemstone Research, see DEUTSCHE STIFTUNG EDELSTEINFORSCHUNG (DSEF).

German Gemmological Association, see DEUTSCHE GEMMOLOGISCHE GESELLSCHAFT E.V.

German Gemmological Training Center, see DEUTSCHES GEMMOLOGISCHES AUSBILDUNGSZENTRUM/DEUTSCHES BERUFSFORTBILDUNGSWERK FUR EDELSTEINKUNDE.

German Gem Museum, see DEUTSCHES EDELSTEINMUSEUM.

German South-West Africa, see NAMIBIA.

GG, see GRADUATE GEMOLOGIST.

GGDO, see GOVERNMENT GOLD AND DIAMOND OFFICE (SIERRA LEONE).

GGG, see GADOLINIUM GALLIUM GARNET.

Ghana, country on the west coast of equatorial Africa, formerly called the Gold Coast, and an important source of alluvial diamonds since their discovery there in 1919. The principal deposits are along the Birim River in the Akwatia and Birim concession areas, and in the Oda district; the two concessions were mined by CAST from 1924 until 1972. Extensive exploration of the Birim River Valley was assisted by the United Nations Development Program in 1980. The region's diamonds are said to be small and primarily of industrial quality; they are sold through the state-owned Precious Minerals Marketing Corporation. See ACCRA DIAMOND MARKET (ADM); AFRICAN DIAMOND DIGGERS' ASSOCIATION; CONSOLIDATED AFRICA SELECTION TRUST, LTD. (CAST); GHANA CONSOLIDATED DIAMONDS, LTD. (GCD); HOLLAND SYNDICATE.

Ghana Consolidated Diamonds, Ltd. (GCD), government-owned company which manages mining operations in Ghana's Akwatia/Birim River Valley alluvial deposits. Established in 1972, when the government of Ghana acquired a 55 percent share in CAST (it acquired the remaining 45 percent in 1982). Production is marketed through the government-owned Precious Minerals Marketing Corporation. See CONSOLIDATED AFRICAN SELECTION TRUST, LTD. (CAST).

Ghana Diamond Marketing Corporation, company incorporated in Ghana in 1965 and licensed by the government as the sole legal purchaser of diamonds mined in the country. Originally called the Ghana Diamond Marketing Board, and now the Precious Minerals Marketing Corporation.

GIA, see GEMOLOGICAL INSTITUTE OF AMERICA.

GIA clarity-grading scale, range of diamond clarity grades established by the Gemological Institute of America. The scale runs from FL (flawless) and IF (internally flawless) through two grades each of VVS (very, very slightly included), VS (very slightly included), and SI (slightly included), and three grades of I (included). See APPENDIX E, CLARITY, CLARITY GRADING, CLARITY-GRADING SCALE, CLARITY-GRADING SYSTEM.

GIA color-grading scale, range of color grades established by the Gemological Institute of America for diamonds in the normal colorless to light yellow, light brown, or light gray range. D represents colorless diamonds, Z the last in the normal range. Yellow and brown diamonds must be darker than the Z master diamond to be considered fancy colors. See APPENDIX D, BODY-COLOR, COLOR GRADING, COLOR-GRADING SCALE, COLOR-GRADING SYSTEM.

GIA *Diamonds* course, training offered by the Gemological Institute of America to provide product knowledge and information about the diamond and diamond jewelry industry. It is a prerequisite for the GIA *Diamond Grading* course.

GIA *Diamond Grading* Certificate, see GIA DIAMOND GRADING DIPLOMA.

GIA *Diamond Grading* course, training offered by the Gemological Institute of America in the theory and techniques of grading loose and mounted diamonds for color, clarity, and cut.

GIA *Diamond Grading* Diploma, document awarded by the Gemological Institute of America upon successful completion of the GIA *Diamonds* and *Diamond Grading* courses.

GIA Gem Instruments, a division of GIA Enterprises which designs and manufactures a range of professional equipment for grading, identifying, and selling gemstones.

GIA Gem Trade Laboratory (GTL), a division of GIA Enterprises which provides professional grading and identification services for the diamond and colored stone industries.

gipsy setting, see GYPSY SETTING.

girandole, earring decorated with several pendants, often diamonds.

girdle, narrow band which circumscribes the edge of the plane separating the crown and pavilion of a polished diamond. On step cuts and most fancy-cut brilliants, the girdle is polished; on round brilliants it is not. See BEARDED GIRDLE, FACETED GIRDLE, GIRDLE PLANE, GIRDLE THICKNESS, KNIFE-EDGED GIRDLE, POLISHED GIRDLE, THICK GIRDLE, WAVY GIRDLE.

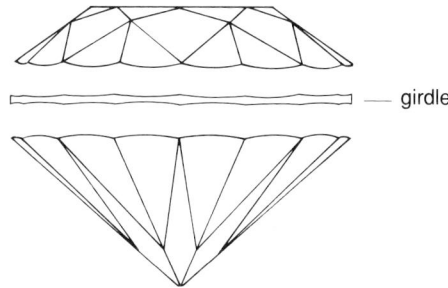

girdle, bearded, see BEARDED GIRDLE.

girdle diameter, distance from one edge of the girdle on a polished round diamond to a point directly opposite on the other side. All the proportions used to evaluate the make of a diamond are expressed in relation to the average girdle diameter. See AVERAGE GIRDLE DIAMETER, MAKE, PROPORTIONS.

girdle facets, (1) small facets placed on the girdle. Girdle facets are often called break facets, skew facets, skill facets, or cross facets, and sometimes referred to as "halfes" or little halves. (2) the triangular facets adjoining the girdle of a brilliant-cut diamond. Those on the crown may also be called upper-girdle, upper-break, top-break, or top-half facets; those on the pavilion, lower-girdle, lower-break, bottom-break, or bottom-half facets.

girdle outline, form delineated by the girdle edge of a gemstone; rounds, ovals, squares, rectangulars, pears, and marquises are the most common outlines.

girdle plane, imaginary plane passing through the girdle of a diamond, theoretically parallel to the table and the culet, and separating the crown from the pavilion.

girdle reflection, image of the girdle reflected in the pavilion facets of a brilliant-cut diamond. In well-made stones, the girdle reflection can be seen through the table only when the diamond is tilted. When the pavilion depth is less than 40 percent, however, the reflection is readily apparent. See FISHEYE, SHALLOW DIAMOND.

girdle thickness, dimension of the outer edge of a fashioned diamond (or other gem) measured between the upper and lower girdle facets; an important factor in grading proportions. Most diamonds have medium girdles which range between 0.7 and 1.7 percent of the average girdle diameter. See ADJUSTMENT FACTOR, KNIFE-EDGE GIRDLE.

glass, (1) essentially amorphous material, typically translucent or transparent, usually made by fusing silica, soda, and lime. By adding other materials, glass can be manufactured with a wide range of properties: In flint or lead glass, a common diamond simulant, lead oxide is added in place of lime to increase dispersion and brilliance. (2) term sometimes applied indiscriminately to diamond simulants, regardless of the material. See PASTE.

glass-filled diamond, see FILLED DIAMOND.

glassie, (1) common term for a well-shaped diamond octahedron with sharp, square edges. (2) adjective, sometimes applied to a fashioned diamond which lacks brilliance. Also spelled glassy.

glassy, see GLASSIE.

glassie

Glavalmazzoloto, Federal Directorate for Precious Metals and Diamonds of the former USSR from 1988 to 1991. It was replaced by Russalmazzoloto, part of which later became Almazy Rossii-Sakha. See ALMAZY ROSSII-SAKHA, RUSSALMAZZOLOTO.

glazier's diamond, industrial diamond crystal used to cut glass.

gletz, Dutch, feather in a diamond. Also spelled glatts, glatze, gles, and glets. See FEATHER.

glide plane, plane parallel to a crystal face along which gliding of the crystal lattice takes place. See GLIDING.

gliding, crystal distortion caused during growth when one part of the crystal lattice is offset in relation to the rest.

Goa, coastal state in India, formerly a Portuguese colony; in the early eighteenth century, when Brazilian diamonds were rumored to be inferior to Indian diamonds, Portuguese traders are alleged to have used Goa as a transit point for the importation of Brazilian diamonds into Europe, thereby suggesting they came from India.

Godavari River, river in the Andhra Pradesh, India; once a source of alluvial diamonds.

Goiás, state in Brazil, location of minor diamond deposits.

Goiás Diamond, deformed diamond, said to have weighed 600 ct., which was discovered along the Verissimo River, Goiás, Brazil in 1906. Allegedly shattered with a hammer to authenticate it; two fragments were later identified as diamond, and one of them was fashioned into an 8 ct. stone. Current whereabouts unknown.

Gokhran, the state depository of the Russian Federation. See ROSKOMDRAGMET.

Golconda, (1) ancient alluvial diamond diggings, once known as the Elure Group, south and east

Golconda

of the city of Golconda, in India. Alluvial deposits are located between the Godavari and Krishna Rivers. See KRISHNA RIVER. (2) Indian city, with an ancient fortress, which is thought to have been the world's first diamond-trading center; active as such during the seventeenth century. (3) archaic color term still occasionally used to describe a highly transparent diamond, either without bodycolor, or with a faint bluish tint.

Golconda Diamond, 30 ct. emerald-cut diamond from India, reportedly of high quality, which was displayed for many years in the Collection of Registered Historic Gems of Trabert & Hoefer. Purchased in 1960 by American tobacco millionaire R.J. Reynolds.

Gold Coast, see GHANA.

Golden Maharaja Diamond, 65.60 ct. pear-shape diamond, described as yellow-brown and exhibited at the 1937 World's Fair in Paris. Later loaned to the American Museum of Natural History for 15 years by its owner, Ella Friedus. Last sold in New York in 1991.

Golden Pelican Diamond, 64 ct. emerald-cut diamond, described as yellow-brown, fashioned in Antwerp and named for Pelikaanstraat, an historic street in the city's diamond trading district. Exhibited at the 1958 Brussels World's Fair by its Belgian owners; current whereabouts unknown. See PELIKAANSTRAAT.

Golden Triolette Diamond, see INCOMPARABLE DIAMOND.

Gong Gong, early alluvial diamond diggings on the Vaal River, Cape Province, South Africa; still operated by licensed prospectors.

goniometer, instrument consisting of a straight-edged, movable arm pivoting on a protractor; used to measure the angles between crystal faces.

Good Hope Diamond, see STAR OF PERSIA DIAMOND.

goods, generic term for any loose rough or polished diamonds; used, in part, for security reasons. See COMMON GOODS, GRADED GOODS, LOOSE GOODS, MOUNTED GOODS, OUTSIDE GOODS, POLISHED GOODS.

Gordon Diamond, 30 ct. rough diamond crystal, described as slightly yellow, and reported to have been found in South Africa between 1862 and 1866 by land surveyor Hugh Gordon. Like the Charlemont and Hanger Diamonds, the Gordon was never authenticated by a competent authority; hence the Eureka (discovered in 1866) is still considered the first authenticated diamond found in South Africa. Disposition and current whereabouts unknown. See CHARLEMONT DIAMOND, EUREKA DIAMOND, HANGER DIAMOND, PLATBERG, PNIEL.

Gornyak Diamond, 44 ct. rough diamond found in Sakha (Yakutia), the Russian Federation, CIS; now in the Russian Diamond Fund, Moscow.

Governador Valadares Diamond, see BENEDITO VALADARES DIAMONDS.

Government Gold and Diamond Office (Sierra Leone), regulatory branch of the Sierra Leone government which was once responsible for issuing licenses, purchasing and exporting diamonds, and enforcing the laws and regulations governing their mining and sale. Established in 1959, the organization was originally known as the Government Diamond Office (GDO). See DIAMOND CORPORATION WEST AFRICA, LTD. (DICORWAF).

Goyaz Diamond, see GOIAS DIAMOND.

Grace cut, proprietary name for a 62-facet, straight-edged fancy-cut diamond derived from the heart shape; developed by the Israeli firm of Raphaeli-Stschik to make the most of flat or misshapen rough. See BARONESS CUT, DUCHESS CUT, EMPRESS CUT, ROYAL CUTS.

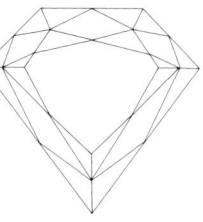

Grace cut

grade, mining term used to describe the ratio of diamonds recovered from a given weight of broken kimberlite or alluvial material. It is usually expressed in terms of carats recovered per 100 tons of material treated. See LOAD.

graded goods, polished diamonds which have been weighed and sorted for the quality of their color, clarity, and cut before they are sold. See MELANGE.

grader, see DIAMOND GRADER.

grade setting characteristic, any inclusion or blemish which establishes the clarity grade of a diamond. Other clarity characteristics may also be present which do not affect the grade. See CLARITY CHARACTERISTIC.

grading, see CLARITY GRADING, COLOR GRADING, CUT GRADING, FINISH GRADING, PROPORTION GRADING.

Graduate Gemologist (GG), title awarded by the Gemological Institute of America (GIA), upon successful completion of the GIA *Diamonds, Diamond Grading, Colored Stones, Colored Stone Grading,* and *Gem Identification* courses, and the passing of a comprehensive examination.

Graff Imperial Blue Diamond, 39.81 ct. pear-shape diamond, reportedly flawless and fancy light blue, fashioned from a 101.50 ct. rough, found in Guinea. Current whereabouts unknown.

grain, (1) unit of weight which equals one-quarter of a metric carat (0.25 ct.). (2) cleavage, sawing, or polishing plane in a diamond (cleavage grain, sawing grain, etc.). When used alone in this sense, it usually refers to a polishing direction. Not to be confused with grain lines.

grain center, small area of concentrated crystal structure distortion in a diamond; usually associated with pinpoint inclusions.

grainer, term used to describe the weights of diamonds in multiples of 0.25 ct. (one grain). Thus a one carat stone is a four-grainer.

graining, see GRAIN LINES.

grain lines, visible, shadow-like lines on the surface of, or inside, a diamond, caused by irregularities in the crystal structure. Often a result of twinning or growth defects, grain lines frequently look like polishing lines, except that they can cross facet junctions, while polishing lines cannot; they usually cannot be removed by recutting or polishing. Also called graining, knot lines, and twinning lines. See TWIN CRYSTAL.

grain lines

Grand Banks, M.V., mining vessel belonging to De Beers Marine. The Grand Banks is equipped with a rotary drill system and is used in deep-water recovery operations off the Atlantic coast of Namibia and South Africa.

Grand Coeur d'Afrique Diamond, 70.03 ct., internally flawless, G color, heart-shape diamond, one of three fashioned in New York by

Grand Coeur d'Afrique Diamond

Laurence Graff of London from a 278 ct. rough found in Guinea in 1982. The smaller stones were a 14.25 ct. marquise and a 25.22 ct. heart shape, Le Petit Coeur. The Grand Coeur d'Afrique was sold by Graff Diamonds in London in 1983.

Grand Condé Diamond, Le, 9.01 ct. pear-shape diamond, described as light pink, purchased by Louis XIII of France (1601-1643). Given in 1643 to "Le Grand Condé," Louis de Bourbon (1621-1686), Prince de Condé and Commander of the French Army during the Thirty Years War. In 1886, the diamond was bequeathed to the French Government by one of the prince's descendents; it is on permanent exhibit at the Musée de Condé at Chantilly. It was stolen in 1926, but recovered a few days later. Also called simply the Condé.

Le Grand Condé Diamond

Grand Duke of Tuscany Diamond, see FLORENTINE DIAMOND.

Grand Mazarin, square-cut diamond, estimated to weigh 19.10 ct. and described as yellowish, which was among the Mazarin Diamonds recovered after the robbery of the Garde Meuble in 1792. The only authentic Mazarin remaining from the original collection of the French Crown Jewels (which were sold in 1887), it is currently on exhibit at the Louvre in Paris.

Granny's chips, familiar term used primarily by the British Royal Family to refer to Cullinans III and IV. Originally set in a crown made for Queen Mary on the occasion of the Coronation of King George V in 1911, they are now mounted in a brooch. Queen Elizabeth II inherited them from her grandmother. See BRITISH CROWN JEWELS, CULLINAN DIAMOND, CULLINAN III, CULLINAN IV.

Gran Sabana, regionally important area of alluvial diamond deposits on the upper Caroni River in Venezuela.

Grão Mogol, historic diamond-producing region in Minas Gerais, Brazil.

graphite, allotrope of the element carbon which forms in the hexagonal crystal system. Sometimes occurs in diamond as an inclusion, or as lines inside cleavages and fractures in black diamonds. See ALLOTROPE, DIAMOND, LONSDALEITE.

Grasfontein, historically important alluvial diamond diggings near Lichtenburg, the Transvaal Province, South Africa and the site of a major diamond rush in 1927.

Grasfontein

graticule, a scale or grid etched or scribed on a transparent material and integrated into an optical instrument; used to locate or measure objects in the field of view.

gravity concentration, see ROTARY WASHING PAN.

gray diamond, fancy color diamond with a pronounced natural gray appearance (gray is strictly speaking not a spectral color). See COLOR-GRADING SCALE, FANCY COLOR DIAMOND.

grease belt, continuous grease-coated belt sometimes used in the diamond recovery pro-

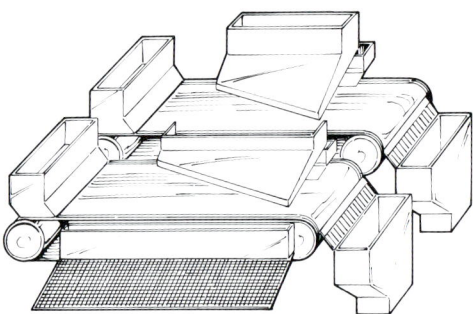

grease belt

cess; it works on the same principle as the grease table. See GREASE TABLE, SEPARATION (2).

grease table, large, sloping, oscillating table with several grease-coated steps, used to separate diamonds from other heavy minerals. A slurry of water and crushed ore flows over the table; since water does not adhere to the surface of a diamond, the diamonds stick to the grease while minerals with wettable surfaces are washed away. See GREASE BELT, SEPARATION (2).

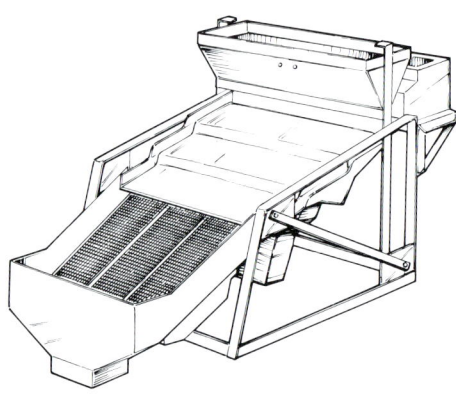

grease table

greasy luster, see LUSTER.

Great Beginning Diamond, 135.12 ct. rough diamond found in the Mir Pipe in Sakha (Yakutia), the Russian Federation, CIS; now in the Russian Diamond Fund in Moscow.

Great Blue Diamond, see WITTELSBACH DIAMOND.

Great Chrysanthemum Diamond, 198.28 ct. diamond, described as fancy brown; found in South Africa in 1963. The stone was fashioned in New York into a 104.15 ct. pear shape with 189 facets and set in a necklace with 410 oval and marquise-shape diamonds.

Great Chrysanthemum Diamond

photo courtesy of CSO

Greater Bear Diamond, 114.37 ct. rough diamond found in the Mir Pipe in Sakha (Yakutia), the Russian Federation, CIS; now in the Russian Diamond Fund in Moscow.

Greater Namaqualand, see NAMAQUALAND.

Great Harry Diamond, large, lozenge-shaped diamond originally owned by King Henry II of France (1519-1559), who had it set in an H-shaped pendant. Inherited by his son Francis II, who gave it to his wife, Mary, Queen of Scots (1542-1587); thus it became part of the Scottish Crown Jewels. Mary is believed to have named it in memory of her late father-in-law. Thought to have been acquired by Cardinal Mazarin and listed in his collection as the 15.27 ct. Mazarin IX.

Great Mogul Diamond, rough diamond said to weigh 787.25 ct. (old carats), allegedly the largest ever found in India. Believed to have been discovered in the Kollur Mines near Golconda around 1650, the diamond was owned by Shah Jahan and later by his son, Aurangzeb, who showed it to Tavernier. The latter said it resembled "half of an egg cut through the middle," and estimated its polished weight at 279.5 ct. (old carats). The description closely matches that of the Orloff Diamond (189.60 ct.), leading many historians to believe the two are one and the same, despite the apparent discrepancy in weight. Unless it is the Orloff, its current whereabouts are unknown.

Great Star of Africa Diamond, see CULLINAN I.

Great Table Diamond, 242.31 ct. (old carats) flat, oblong diamond, described as light pink with a broken corner, and seen by Jean Baptiste Tavernier in India in 1642. The weight recorded by Tavernier is thought to be incorrect; historians now estimate the stone may have weighed as much as 300 ct. At some point in its history, probably in the nineteenth century, the Great Table is said to have been damaged and recut; some historians think the Darya-i-Nur and the Nur-ul-Ain are the products of this recutting.

Great White Diamond, see VICTORIA DIAMOND.

green diamond, natural green, yellowish green, bluish green, or greenish yellow diamond of noticeable color. The Jwaneng Mine in Botswana produces many such diamonds. Since the color is usually confined to the skin of the rough, the color of a natural green diamond is often removed during fashioning. Natural color green to blue diamonds may have been exposed to radiation in nature. Yellowish diamonds can be artificially altered to green by treatment in radioactive compounds, an atomic particle accelerator (cyclotron), or an atomic reactor. See COLORED DIAMOND, DRESDEN GREEN DIAMOND, FANCY COLOR DIAMOND, IRRADIATED DIAMOND, IRRADIATED GREEN DIAMOND, RADIUM-TREATED DIAMOND.

Green Dresden Diamond, see DRESDEN GREEN DIAMOND.

grinding, process of shaping and/or polishing the initial facets on a rough diamond. See BLOCKING, BRILLIANDEERING, BRUTING, CROSSWORKING.

Griqualand West, district surrounding Kimberley, South Africa, where both primary and alluvial diamond deposits are located.

grit, see DIAMOND POWDER.

grizzly, industrial grid or screen which sizes the run of mine kimberlite or lamproite before being processed at a diamond mine's recovery plant. Also spelled grizzley. See RUN OF MINE.

Grodzinski, Paul (1901-1957), former head of the Industrial Diamond Information Bureau, editor and co-founder of the *Industrial Diamond Review*, editor-in-chief of the *Bibliography of Industrial Diamond Applications*, and authority on the industrial applications of diamond and other hard materials. Author of *Diamond Tools* (New York, 1944) and *Diamond Technology* (London, 1953).

Grosvenor, Hugh R. (1879-1959), second Duke of Westminster of Great Britain and owner of the 32.20 ct. Hastings Diamond, the 43 ct. Nassak Diamond, the 33.70 ct. and 23.65 ct. Arcot Diamonds, and a number of smaller diamonds. The original collection was acquired at the final sale of London jewelers Rundell & Bridge by the first Marquess of Westminster in 1837, and remained in the Grosvenor family for over a century. In 1930, the Paris firm of Lacloche mounted the two Arcots, the Hastings, and 1,421 smaller diamonds in the Westminster Tiara. To pay for the death duties on the Duke's estate, the Tiara was sold to Harry Winston by Sotheby's London in 1959. The three principal stones were removed and recut to improve their brilliance, and then sold in solitaire rings; the Tiara was auctioned by Sotheby's New York in October 1988.

growth line, see GRAIN LINES.

growth markings, surface features on a diamond crystal characteristic of a particular crystal form. Trigons on octahedron faces, grooves and ridges parallel to the long direction of the dodecahedron face, or square or rectangular depressions at $45°$ to the face edge on cube faces are all growth markings.

growth zoning, visible internal evidence of the crystal growth sequence of a diamond, such as growth lines or twinning; may be straight, irregular, or angular in appearance.

Grupiara, regionally important alluvial diamond-mining area in Minas Gerais, Brazil.

GTL, see GEM TRADE LABORATORY.

Guaniamo, regionally important group of alluvial deposits and small kimberlites located in the Quebrada Grande region of Venezuela.

Many of the alluvial deposits are exhausted; although the recent discovery of several kimberlites has helped maintain production levels, current reserves are limited. The area is said to be the source of 85 percent of Venezuela's diamond production.

Guinea, West African country, a diamond producer since 1934. Diamonds were mined by the Société Minière de Beyla and SOGUINEX, as well as by individual diggers, until independence in 1957. Although the country's mines were nationalized in 1961, foreign companies were re-admitted a few years later; in 1981, the mining and exploration group AREDOR was formed. Mining is centered in the southeastern region bordered by Sierra Leone, Liberia, and the Côte d'Ivoire (Ivory Coast). See AREDOR MINE, ASSOCIATION POUR LA RECHERCHE ET L'EXPLOITATION DU DIAMANT ET DE L'OR (AREDOR), SOCIETE GUINEENE DE RECHERCHES ET D'EXPLOITATIONS MINIERES (SOGUINEX).

Guinea Star, 89.01 ct. D color, internally flawless, modified shield-cut diamond, one of three fashioned by the William Goldberg Company of New York from a 255.1 ct. rough found at the AREDOR Mine in 1986, the largest rough diamond found in Guinea. The other two diamonds are an 8.23 ct. pear shape and a 5.03 ct. heart shape.

Guise Diamond, 33.25 ct. rectangular-cut diamond, described as "faultless," "white," and "fiery." Named for Henri, Duke de Guise, who once owned it; purchased by Louis XIV of France from his cousin, Marie of Lorraine, in 1665 and recut to 29.10 ct. in 1786. Stolen from the French Royal Treasury in 1792, but recovered. The Guise was reportedly sold in 1887, but was not among the original collection of the French Crown Jewels offered for sale, nor is it among those which were excluded and are exhibited in the Louvre. Current whereabouts unknown.

Guyana, country on the north coast of South America which began producing alluvial diamonds in 1890. The primary source was the Mazaruni River; smaller production occurred on the Cuyuni, Puruni, Potaro and Berbice Rivers. Guyana was known for large, high-quality stones, but the deposits are now largely worked out.

gypsy setting, style of setting in which metal from the piece of jewelry is worked into a lip around a hole or cavity sized to accommodate the entire pavilion; the lip is then forced over the edge of the girdle to hold the stone in place. Popular since the nineteenth century, it provides extra protection and is also used for setting lower-quality diamonds, diamond simulants, and doublets. Also spelled gipsy. See BEZEL.

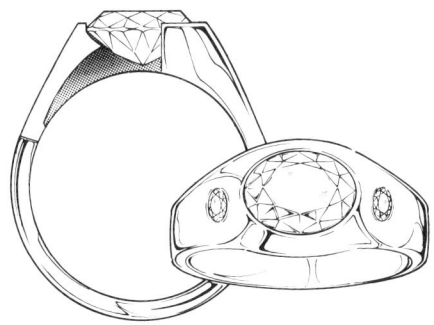

gypsy setting

H

habit, the characteristic shapes which crystals of a specific mineral assume as a result of their internal atomic structure and the environment in which they have grown. Diamond habits include the octahedron, cube, dodecahedron, hexoctahedron, and tetrahexahedron. See CRYSTAL STRUCTURE, CUBE.

hailstone bort, rounded bort composed of layers of tiny, gray to transparent, poorly- to well-crystallized diamond crystals. See BALLAS, CARBONADO, CRUSHING BORT, FRAMESITE, STEWARTITE.

hairline feather, shallow feather, which often looks like a scratch. Hairline feathers frequently extend into the stone from the girdle and are often the result of bruting. See BEARDED GIRDLE, FEATHER.

half, trade term for a half carat (0.50 ct.), a general category for stones ranging in weight from 0.47 ct. to 0.56 ct.

half-brilliant cut, cutting style with a circular girdle outline, a flat, unfaceted base, and a standard brilliant-cut crown. Often deceptively set in a closed-back gypsy setting lined with foil to simulate the pavilion. Also called a brillionette. See FOILBACK, GYPSY SETTING.

half-Dutch rose cut, rose cut with a six-sided girdle outline, a flat, unfaceted base, and a pointed, dome-shape crown with 18 triangular facets. Also called a half-Holland rose cut.

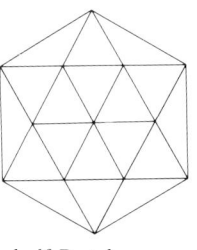

half-Dutch rose cut

half facet, see GIRDLE FACETS.

half-Holland rose cut, see HALF-DUTCH ROSE CUT.

half-moon cut, see HALF-MOON BRILLIANT CUT.

half-moon brilliant cut, modified brilliant cut resembling a round brilliant which has been divided in half vertically from table to culet; occasionally used when recutting broken rounds.

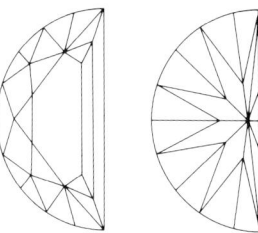

half-moon brilliant cut

Halo Cut, proprietary name for a diamond with a polished girdle.

Halphen Diamond, 1.00 ct. diamond, described as red, also called the Halphen Red Diamond. Current whereabouts unknown.

Halphen Red Diamond, see HALPHEN DIAMOND.

Hancock Red Diamond, 0.95 ct. purplish red diamond, thought to be of Brazilian origin, which set a world auction price record of $880,000 ($926,000 per carat) when it was sold at Christie's New York in April, 1987. The seller is reported to have been the owner of an American oil exploration company; the buyer a Swiss diamond dealer.

hand lens, see LOUPE.

hand loupe, see LOUPE.

hand spectroscope, see SPECTROSCOPE.

Hanger Diamond, rough diamond, described as light yellow, reportedly found in South Africa in 1858 and purchased by Captain E. S.

Hanger of the Bloemfontein Rangers. Said to have been fashioned into a brilliant rose cut in Amsterdam and purchased in 1870 by the Countess of Charlemont, County Tyrone, Ireland. As with the Charlemont and Gordon Diamonds, there is no record that the Hanger was ever properly identified as a diamond. Hence, although its discovery is purported to pre-date that of the Eureka Diamond (1866), the latter is considered the first authenticated diamond discovered in South Africa. Current whereabouts unknown. See CHARLEMONT DIAMOND, EUREKA DIAMOND, GORDON DIAMOND, PLATBERG.

hanging wall, body of rock which overlays a horizontal or inclined fault, dike, orebody, fault, mine workings, or chamber. See FOOTWALL.

Hannay, James Ballantyne (1855-1931), Scottish chemist who claimed to have produced minute synthetic diamonds in 1880, by heating amorphous carbon with bone oil and metallic lithium under great pressure. Attempts to repeat his experiments failed. See HANNAY'S DIAMONDS; LONSDALE, KATHLEEN.

Hannay's diamonds, several extremely small diamonds discovered in a bottle in the British Museum of Natural History in 1942 and originally thought to be the result of chemist James Hannay's efforts to produce synthetic diamonds. X-ray and cathodoluminescence tests performed by Kathleen Lonsdale indicated that the diamonds were probably natural, not synthetic; current whereabouts unknown. See HANNAY, JAMES BALLANTYNE; LONSDALE, KATHLEEN.

hardebank, very hard, unweathered blueground found in diamond pipes. See BLUEGROUND, DIATREME, HYPABYSSAL ZONE, KIMBERLITE, YELLOWGROUND.

hardness, resistance to scratching, abrasion, and indentation. Hardness depends on the strength of a material's atomic bonds and can vary with direction. The hardness of minerals is usually expressed in terms of the Mohs hardness scale, on which diamond's hardness is 10. Along with stability and toughness, hardness is one of the properties which constitute a gem's durability. See ABRASION TEST, ATOMIC BONDING, BRINELL HARDNESS TEST, DIRECTIONAL HARDNESS, INDENTATION TEST, KNOOP INDENTATION HARDNESS TEST, MOHS SCALE, SCLEROMETER, SCRATCH HARDNESS, TOUGHNESS, VICKERS HARDNESS TEST.

hardness points, small, pointed pieces of minerals of different hardnesses (usually 6 to 10 on the Mohs scale) used to test the relative hardness of materials; a given point will scratch a material of equal or lower hardness. Diamond hardness points are often used to prove other colorless material is not diamond but, since diamond can scratch diamond, the results can be misleading. The test is destructive and should be used only on rough. See ABRASION TEST, ATOMIC BONDING, BRINELL HARDNESS TEST, DIRECTIONAL HARDNESS, HARDNESS POINTS, INDENTATION TEST, KNOOP INDENTATION HARDNESS TEST, MOHS SCALE, SCLEROMETER, SCRATCH HARDNESS, VICKERS HARDNESS TEST.

hardness scale, see BRINELL HARDNESS TEST, HARDNESS POINTS, INDENTATION TEST, KNOOP INDENTATION HARDNESS TEST, MOHS SCALE, SCLEROMETER, VICKERS HARDNESS TEST.

hardness tester, any apparatus used to test the hardness of a mineral. See BRINELL HARDNESS TEST, HARDNESS POINTS, INDENTATION TEST, KNOOP INDENTATION HARDNESS TEST, MOHS SCALE, SCLEROMETER, VICKERS HARDNESS TEST.

Harrogate diamond, misnomer for rock crystal quartz from West Yorkshire, England.

Harvard Diamond, 82 ct. diamond octahedron, described as yellow, once part of the James A. Garland collection in the Peabody Museum of Harvard University, Cambridge, Massachusetts, US. Stolen in 1962; current whereabouts unknown.

Hastings Diamond, 101 ct. diamond presented to King George III of England by Secretary of State Lord Sydney on behalf of Nizam Ali Cawn of Hyderabad, India, in 1786. Present at the event was Warren Hastings (1732-1818), first Governor General of India; his political enemies charged that the gift was a bribe on behalf of Hastings' interests on the subcontinent, leading to his later impeachment. Current whereabouts unknown.

Hatton Garden, street in London, the traditional center of Britain's diamond trade.

Hawaiian diamond, misnomer for rock crystal quartz.

head, (1) that part of a mounting, usually consisting of four to six prongs, into which a gemstone is set. (2) rounded end of a pear-shape diamond.

head loupe, see HEAD MAGNIFIER.

head magnifier, binocular magnifying device attached to a band that is worn on the head. Used extensively by bench jewelers, sometimes worn for grading or sorting diamonds. Also called a binocular head loupe.

heart brilliant cut, modified brilliant cut in the shape of a heart, with a table, 32 crown facets, 24 pavilion facets, and a shield-shaped culet. See BRILLIANT CUT.

heart brilliant cut

heat conduction, see THERMAL CONDUCTIVITY.

heat treatment, see ANNEALING.

heavy liquids, high-density liquids used to determine the specific gravity (SG) of gemstones, based on the principle that objects float in liquids of higher SG, remain suspended in liquids of similar SG, and sink in those of lower SG. Liquids commonly used to test the SG of gems are pure methylene iodide (3.32) and mixtures of methylene iodide and benzyl benzoate, normally calibrated to SGs of 3.05, 2.67, 2.62, and 2.57. Saturated salt solution (1.13) is also used. Also called specific gravity liquids. See CLERICI'S SOLUTION, SPECIFIC GRAVITY.

heavy media separation, diamond recovery method which uses a solution of ferrosilicon particles suspended in water to act as a heavy liquid (SG 2.95). Crushed ore is fed into the liquid, which allows diamonds and other heavy minerals to be drawn off while lighter materials remain suspended. See HEAVY LIQUIDS, HYDROCYCLONE SEPARATION, JIG, SEPARATION (2), SPECIFIC GRAVITY (SG), STATIC CONE.

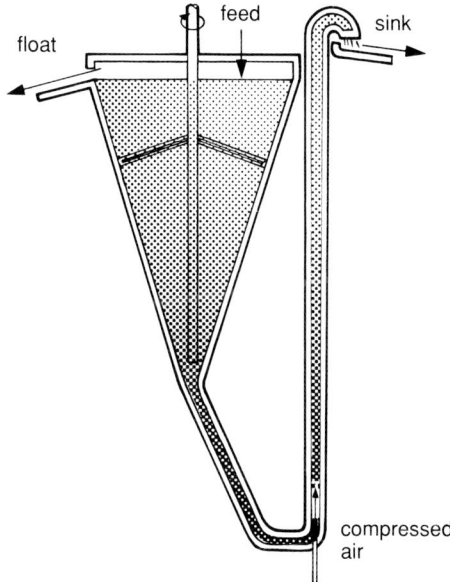

heavy media separation

heavy minerals, minerals with a high specific gravity (SG). Diamond has a relatively high SG of 3.52. See HEAVY MEDIA SEPARATION, INDICATOR MINERAL, SPECIFIC GRAVITY (SG).

heft, comparative weight (density) of a material as approximated by holding it in the hand. Minerals of higher specific gravity, such as diamond (3.52), have a greater heft than those of a lower SG, such as quartz.

Helam Mine, narrow, almost vertical kimberlite fissure at Swartruggens, South Africa. Diamonds are recovered by overhand shrinkage. See OVERHAND SHRINKAGE.

Herkimer diamond, misnomer for rock crystal quartz from Herkimer County, New York, US.

Herscheimer diamond, misnomer for rock crystal quartz; apparently a corruption of Herkimer. See HERKIMER DIAMOND.

Hershey, J. W., American investigator who in 1938 tried unsuccessfully to produce synthetic diamond using a variation of Crookes' and Moissan's earlier molten-iron process. He discussed his method in *The Book of Diamonds,* published in 1940.

hexagon cut, six-sided step cut with all sides of equal length.

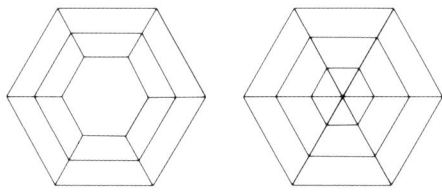

hexagon cut

hexoctahedron, one of the seven basic forms of the isometric, or cubic, crystal system, with 48 equal triangular faces, each of which intersects all three crystallographic axes at different distances. It resembles an octahedron on which each face is replaced by six triangular faces.

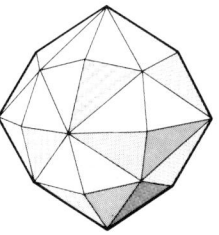

hexoctahedron

hextetrahedron, crystal form in the cubic (isometric) crystal system with 24 faces.

Hickory Hill diamond, misnomer for rock crystal quartz from Hickory Hill, New York, US; alternative name for Herkimer diamond. See HERKIMER DIAMOND.

high clarity, term describing the clarity of a diamond which falls within the flawless (Fl) to very slightly included (VS) range on the GIA clarity-grading scale.

high color, (1) term describing a colorless or near-colorless diamond. (2) trade term describing a diamond which appears colorless when set in jewelry.

high shoulders, widened head on a pear-shape diamond, which makes it look squarish rather than rounded.

Hoffman, M. K., German scientist who in 1931 repeated Moissan's experiments in an unsuccessful attempt to produce synthetic diamonds.

Hoge Raad voor Diamant vzw (HRD), Diamond High Council, non-profit organization of the Belgian diamond industry founded in 1973; today it represents all four Belgian diamond bourses, seven trade organizations, and two trade unions; provides grading services through the HRD Diamond Certification Laboratory in Antwerp; and offers gemological training. A division of HRD develops and markets automated equipment. See INTERNATIONAL DIAMOND COUNCIL (IDC).

hole gauge, perforated sheet of metal or plastic with holes corresponding to various girdle diameters; used to estimate the size and weight of unmounted diamonds. See DIAMOND SIEVE.

Holland Diamond, 36 ct. cone-shaped diamond said to be in the possession of the King of the Netherlands in 1851. There is conjecture the Holland Diamond may be the Cone, the Auckland, or the Bantam Diamond.

Holland rose cut, see DUTCH ROSE CUT.

Holland Syndicate, Dutch company which mined alluvial diamond deposits in Ghana until the country's mineral reserves were nationalized in 1961.

Hollebak Mine, marine deposit in the Admiralty strip along the Namaqualand coast of South Africa. Diamonds are recovered by mechanical excavation and diver-manipulated suction pumps operated from shore. See BEACH MINING, OFF-SHORE MINING.

hollow dop, cup-shaped copper retainer used to hold the culet of a diamond during bruting; also used for setting the stone for sawing.

Hondeklip Bay, coastal mining area in Namaqualand, South Africa. Diamonds are recovered by mechanical stripping, mechanical mining, and hand sweeping. See BEACH MINING, OFF-SHORE MINING.

Hong Kong Diamond Bourse, Ltd., Asian diamond bourse; member of the World Federation of Diamond Bourses. See BOURSE, WORLD FEDERATION OF DIAMOND BOURSES (WFDB).

Hope Diamond, 45.52 ct., VS₁, fancy dark grayish blue, cushion-shape Indian diamond, believed to have been fashioned from the 67.5 ct. (old carats) French Blue Diamond. (The latter, in turn, is thought to have been cut from the 112.5 ct. (old carats) Mogul-cut Tavernier Blue Diamond.) Named for Henry Philip Hope, who purchased it in 1830. His nephew, Henry Thomas Hope, inherited the stone in 1839; in 1908 the diamond was sold to the Sultan of Turkey. Cartier's of Paris subsequently acquired the Hope and in 1911 sold it to Evalyn Walsh McLean, heiress to an American gold-mining fortune and wife of the owner of the *Washington Post*. Despite legends which associated the diamond with a "curse" that allegedly caused a dozen violent deaths and the fall of two royal houses, McLean never considered it unlucky. Harry Winston purchased the diamond from McLean's estate in 1949, and in 1958 presented it to the Smithsonian Institution, in Washington, D.C., US, where it is on permanent display. See FRENCH BLUE DIAMOND, TAVERNIER BLUE DIAMOND.

Hope Diamond

Hopetown, small town in Cape Province, South Africa, close to where the Eureka, the first au-

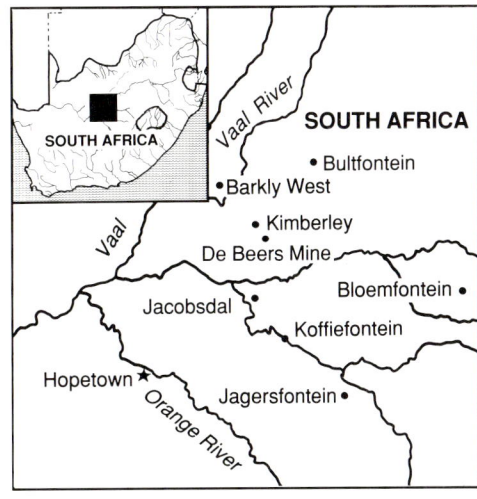
Hopetown

thenticated South African diamond, was found in 1866. See EUREKA DIAMOND.

Horatio diamond, misnomer for rock crystal quartz from Arkansas.

Hornby Diamond, 36 ct. diamond thought to have been brought to England in 1775 by William Hornby, Governor of Bombay, India. It is possible that a 38.18 ct. trapezoid-shape diamond in the Crown Jewels of Iran is the Hornby. See APPENDIX C.

Hortensia Diamond, 20.53 ct. pale pink diamond, purchased by Louis XIV of France. Stolen from the French Royal Treasury in 1792, but recovered; later worn by Napoleon I; by Hortense de Beauharnais, daughter of the Empress Josephine and Queen of Holland; and by Empress Eugénie. Stolen in 1830, and again recovered; it is now on display in the Galérie d'Apollon at the Louvre in Paris, together with the Regent, the Sancy, and other items which were excluded from the 1887 sale of French Crown Jewels because of their historic interest.

Hortensia Diamond

host crystal, crystal in which a smaller crystal or other substance is included. See INCLUSION.

Hot Springs diamond, misnomer for rock crystal quartz from Arkansas, US.

HRD, see HOGE RAAD VOOR DIAMANT VZW.

hue, basic color of a material, described in terms of the pure spectral colors (red, orange, yellow, green, blue, purple, and violet) or combinations and modifications thereof. Along with tone and saturation, hue is one of the three dimensions used to describe color. See SATURATION, TONE.

Hyderabad, state in India in which Golconda, the ancient diamond trading center and source of some of the world's most famous diamonds, is located. See GOLCONDA.

hydraulic mining, use of high-pressure water jets to remove overburden and break down alluvial gem deposits.

hydrochloric acid (HCl), acid used to clean polished diamonds. See ACID CLEANING.

hydrocyclone separation, diamond recovery process utilizing a hydrocyclone, a centrifugal device in which materials with relatively high specific gravities, such as diamond, are suspended in a ferrosilicon solution and separated from lighter materials. See HEAVY MEDIA SEPARATION, ROTARY WASHING PAN, SEPARATION (2), SPECIFIC GRAVITY (SG), STATIC CONE.

hydrofluoric acid (HF), acid sometimes used to improve a diamond's appearance by bleaching dark inclusions. See LASER DRILLING.

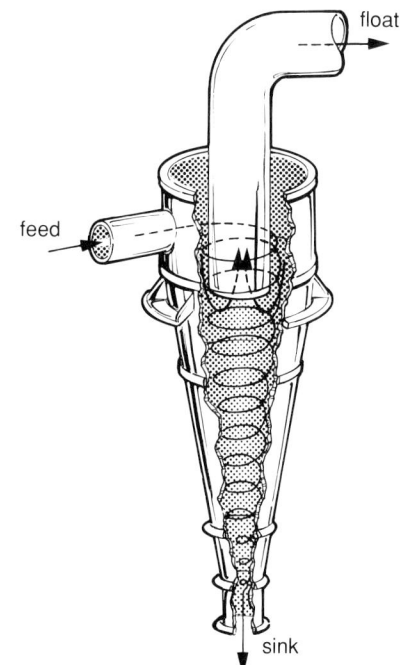

hydrocyclone

hydrostatic weighing method, method of determining a gem's specific gravity by weighing it first in air, then in water, and dividing the weight in air by the weight in water. See DIAMOND BALANCE, HEAVY LIQUIDS, SPECIFIC GRAVITY (SG).

hypabyssal zone, irregularly tapered section of volatile-rich igneous rock located near the base, or root, of a kimberlite pipe; sill complexes, dike swarms, and embedded xenoliths of country rock are commonly found in the hypabyssal zone. See KIMBERLITE, DIATREME, XENOLITH.

I, abbreviation for the included grade category on the GIA clarity-grading scale. There are three grades: I_1, I_2, and I_3. See GIA CLARITY-GRADING SCALE.

Ice Queen Diamond, see NIARCHOS DIAMOND.

Idar-Oberstein, German manufacturing and trading center for colored stones and diamonds.

IDB, see ILLICIT DIAMOND BUYING.

IDC, see INTERNATIONAL DIAMOND COUNCIL.

IDC clarity-grading scale, range of diamond clarity grades from loupe clean through *piqué*, corresponding essentially to the grades and terms in the CIBJO scale (with the exception that IDC does not split the SI grade). See APPENDIX E, CIBJO INTERNATIONAL CLARITY/PURITY SCALE, CLARITY, CLARITY GRADING, CLARITY-GRADING SCALE, CLARITY-GRADING SYSTEM, GIA CLARITY-GRADING SCALE, INTERNATIONAL DIAMOND COUNCIL (IDC), SCAN. D.N. CLARITY SCALE.

IDC international color-grading scale, range of diamond color grades used to describe colorless to light yellow, light brown, and light gray stones. Grades range from exceptional white through tinted color, corresponding essentially to the grades and terms in the CIBJO scale. See APPENDIX D, BODYCOLOR, CIBJO INTERNATIONAL COLOR-GRADING SCALE, COLOR GRADING, COLOR-GRADING SCALE, COLOR-GRADING SYSTEM, GIA COLOR-GRADING SCALE, INTERNATIONAL DIAMOND COUNCIL (IDC), SCAN. D.N. COLOR SCALE.

IDC Rules for grading polished diamonds, set of guidelines and standards for diamond clarity grading, color grading and nomenclature, cut description, and certification, established by the International Diamond Council. See CIBJO RULES OF APPLICATION FOR THE DIAMOND TRADE, SCANDINAVIAN DIAMOND NOMENCLATURE (SCAN. D.N.) AND GRADING STANDARDS.

ideal brilliant, see AMERICAN BRILLIANT CUT, PRACTICAL FINE CUT, TOLKOWSKY THEORETICAL BRILLIANT CUT.

ideal cut, see AMERICAN BRILLIANT CUT, PRACTICAL FINE CUT, TOLKOWSKY THEORETICAL BRILLIANT CUT.

identifying characteristic, (1) in gem identification, any inclusion or other internal characteristic which confirms or indicates a gem's species and variety. (2) any inclusion or blemish which is unique to a particular gemstone.

Idol's Eye Diamond, 70.21 ct. light blue, VVS_1 antique triangle modified brilliant-cut diamond, believed to have been found in Golconda, India. There are many unauthenticated legends about the diamond, but its first verifiable appearance was at auction at Christie's in 1865, when it was said to have been owned by Abdul-Hamid II (1842-1918), who became the 34th Ottoman Sultan. Eventually purchased by Harry Winston; sold in 1946 to May Bonfils Stanton, daughter of the publisher and co-founder of the Denver Post. Last sold in 1983, together with the Emperor Maximilian Diamond and a 70.54 fancy yellow diamond called the Sultan Abdul-Hamid II, in one of the biggest single transactions in the history of diamond sales. See EMPEROR MAXIMILIAN DIAMOND.

Idol's Eye Diamond

IF, abbreviation for internally flawless on the GIA clarity-grading scale. See GIA CLARITY-GRADING SCALE.

igneous rock, rock which has cooled and solidified from a molten state. Kimberlite and lamproite are igneous rocks.

I.J. Asscher Company, Dutch diamond firm founded by master diamond cutter Isaac Joseph Asscher in Amsterdam in 1854. The company cleaved and polished the Excelsior Diamond in 1903 and the Cullinan Diamond in 1908. It was succeeded by the Asscher Diamond Company in 1936. See ASSCHER, ISAAC JOSEPH; ROYAL ASSCHER DIAMOND COMPANY.

illicit diamond buyer, individual who buys rough diamonds which have been obtained illegally, probably stolen.

illicit diamond buying (IDB), practice of buying rough diamonds which have been obtained illegally, frequently from unlicensed persons working on concessions previously granted to companies or other individuals.

Illicit Diamond Buying Act, South African law passed in 1885 which made buying diamonds from unlicensed individuals a criminal offense. Other diamond producing countries have similar laws. See DIAMOND TRADE ACT.

illusion head, mounting with a scalloped metal border designed to make a diamond (or other colorless stone) look larger. Also called an illusion setting, miracle top, miracle crown, or miracle head.

illusion head

ilmenite, one of the major indicator minerals associated with kimberlite occurrences.

imitation, see DIAMOND SIMULANT.

immersion cell, small, flat, glass-bottomed container filled with liquid in which a gemstone is immersed to eliminate surface reflections and distortion while it is being examined.

immersion liquid, (1) liquid used to reduce or eliminate surface reflections while a gemstone is being examined. (2) a liquid of known refractive index, used to estimate the RI of an unknown stone. Common immersion liquids include water (1.33), clove oil (1.54), bromoform (1.59), monobromonaphthalene (1.66), methylene iodide (1.74), and glycerine (1.47). See IMMERSION CELL.

imperfect, see INCLUDED.

imperfection, see BLEMISH, INTERNAL CHARACTERISTIC.

imperfection grade, see CLARITY GRADE.

Imperial Diamond, see VICTORIA DIAMOND.

impregnated diamond dressing tool, diamond wheel or tool in which small diamond particles are embedded, or to which they have been bonded or electroplated. Used to true grinding wheels. See DIAMOND DRESSING TOOL.

impurity atoms, see IMPURITY ELEMENTS.

impurity elements, elements other than carbon present in a diamond, and thus not part of its essential chemical composition. Boron and nitrogen are common impurity elements in diamonds, and can impart color to the stone.

incandescent light, light produced by heating an object to a temperature high enough for it to glow.

included, term used to describe a diamond (or other gem) which has noticeable inclusions. Called *piqué* in Europe.

Included (I), grade category at the low end of the GIA clarity scale; assigned to diamonds with prominent eye-visible inclusions, or those which may affect the stone's durability. There are three grades in this category, abbreviated: I_1, I_2, and I_3. Diamonds in the I_3 grade are generally considered just above industrial quality. See APPENDIX E.

included crystal, crystal of diamond or other mineral enclosed in a diamond (or other gemstone) during growth. Included crystals may be transparent or dark and usually have an angular outline. Often incorrectly described as a bubble. See KNOT.

included crystals

inclusion, see INTERNAL CHARACTERISTIC.

inclusion pointer, needle either mounted on the stage of a microscope, or etched or scribed on one of the optical elements; used to indicate the location of any observable features.

Incomparable Diamond, 407.48 ct. fancy brown-yellow, internally flawless (IF) triolette-cut diamond ("triolette" is a proprietary cut from the Premier Gem Corporation). Fashioned from an 890 ct. rough by Marvin Samuels of Premier in New York, US, in 1984. The rough, which produced 14 other diamonds, is believed to have come from a West African alluvial digging. Said to be the third largest polished diamond in the world, it was offered at auction by Christie's New York in October 1988, but withdrawn. Also known as the Golden Triolette.

indentation test, hardness test in which a steel or diamond point is pressed into the surface of the material to be tested under a known amount of pressure for a specified length of time; an index of hardness is then determined from a measurement of the resulting indentation. See BRINELL HARDNESS TEST, DIRECTIONAL HARDNESS, KNOOP INDENTATION HARDNESS TEST, MOHS SCALE, VICKERS HARDNESS TEST.

indented natural, area lower than the surrounding surface of a polished diamond, in which a segment of the original surface of the rough remains. See NATURAL.

index of refraction, see REFRACTIVE INDEX (RI).

India, Asian country occupying the majority of the sub-continent between the Himalayas, the Bay of Bengal, and the Arabian Sea; the world's leading source of diamonds from about 1000 A.D. until the first Brazilian discoveries in 1725. Now a minor producer, with most of its diamonds coming from the Panna district, but the country has become a major manufacturing center for small, low-quality diamonds; as many as 600,000 to 800,000 people have been employed in the industry. Manufacturers buy their rough at Central Selling Organisation (CSO) sights; locally, from sight-holding dealers; and on the market in Antwerp. See BHAVNAGAR, BOMBAY, GOLCONDA, NATIONAL MINERAL DEVELOPMENT CORPORATION OF INDIA (NMDC), NAVSARI, SURAT.

Indian cut, lumpy form of single cut caused by attempting to retain maximum weight from rough. See MELEE, YIELD.

Indian Diamond, 250 ct. pear-shape diamond listed as "L'Indien" and illustrated in the Duke of Brunswick's 1860 catalog of celebrated diamonds known at the time. Believed to be the Nizam Diamond; current whereabouts unknown.

indicator mineral, mineral which sometimes suggests the presence of kimberlite; the most common are pyrope garnet, ilmenite, zircon, and chrome diopside.

Indonesia, Republic of, see BORNEO, KALIMANTAN.

Indore Pears, two reportedly high color pear-shape diamonds, originally 46.95 ct. and 46.70 ct., worn by the former Maharaja of Indore, India and his wife, the Maharanee (American Nancy Ann Miller). Harry Winston purchased

Indore Pears

photo courtesy of Harry Winston, Inc.

them in 1946 and had them recut to 46.39 and 44.14 ct. before selling them to a private buyer. Winston sold and repurchased the diamonds three more times between 1953 and 1976. They have since been auctioned twice by Christie's, most recently in 1987.

industrial diamond, type of diamond most suitable for use in tools, abrasives, drills, or other industrial applications. Most are polycrystalline; single gem crystals (monocrystals) are used in industry only when the application requires material free of internal strain and inclusions, or when diamond's special optical or chemical properties are needed. See BORT, CARBONADO, MONOCRYSTAL, POLYCRYSTALLINE DIAMOND, SYNTHETIC DIAMOND.

Industrial Diamond Association of America, Inc., New York-based organization of American diamond-tool manufacturers and firms involved in the industrial diamond industry. The association encourages ethical trade practices, and disseminates technical and public relations information.

inert, (1) term describing materials which do not interact chemically with other substances. (2) term describing materials which show no detectable reaction to such stimuli as X-rays, ultraviolet radiation, or cathode rays.

infra-red, band of electromagnetic energy, invisible to the unaided eye, with a wavelength between 750 nm and 1,000,000 nm. All commercial diamond manufacturing lasers produce infra-red radiation.

inherent vice, weakness in a diamond which may result in damage to the stone during fashioning or later, when it is worn. Severe internal strain or a large feather are considered common inherent vices. See ANOMALOUS DOUBLE REFRACTION (ADR).

inshore mining, see BEACH MINING.

in situ, Latin, meaning *in place*; used to describe diamonds which have been found in a primary deposit rather than in a secondary eluvial or alluvial deposit. See ALLUVIAL DEPOSIT, ELUVIAL DEPOSIT, PRIMARY DEPOSIT.

intaglio, shallow design engraved on the surface of a diamond or other gemstone.

internal characteristic, any of several types of clarity features which are enclosed within a host gemstone; they may, however, reach the surface. See CLEAVAGE, FEATHER, FRACTURE, GRAIN LINES, INCLUDED CRYSTAL, KNOT.

internal graining, grain lines or planes inside a diamond. See GRAIN, GRAIN LINES.

Internally Flawless (IF), upper grade in the GIA clarity-grading scale, assigned to diamonds which show no inclusions and only minor blemishes under 10x magnification. The Scan. D.N. clarity scale has a corresponding IF grade. See APPENDIX E, POTENTIALLY FLAWLESS.

internal reflection, reflection of light from an internal "surface" (the gem/air interface) in a diamond or other gemstone.

internal strain, stress inside a diamond, the result of structural irregularities such as twinning or distortion, or an inclusion. See ANOMALOUS DOUBLE REFRACTION (ADR), POLARISCOPE.

International Diamond Council (IDC), international organization founded by the World Federation of Diamond Bourses and the International Diamond Manufacturers' Association in 1975 to establish uniform rules for diamond grading and nomenclature. In 1978, the organization established the IDC Rules for grading polished diamonds, a system used by the Hoge Raad voor Diamant of Antwerp, the Swedish National Testing Institute, the Jewellery Council of South Africa, the Diamant Prüflabor of Idar-Oberstein, Germany, and the Central Gem Laboratory of Japan. See IDC CLARITY-GRADING SCALE, IDC INTERNATIONAL COLOR-GRADING SCALE, IDC RULES FOR GRADING POLISHED DIAMONDS.

International Diamond Manufacturers' Association (IDMA), international trade association founded in 1946 by members of the diamond industry in Belgium, England, and the Netherlands; membership now includes representative associations from France, Germany, India, Israel, South Africa, Thailand, and the United States as well. The IDMA promotes cooperation and coordination between diamond manufacturers and suppliers, monitors legislation, lobbies for advantageous international trade policies, and encourages good working conditions and fair wages for diamond workers. See WORLD FEDERATION OF DIAMOND BOURSES (WFDB).

International Pipe, kimberlite pipe mine in the Republic of Sakha (Yakutia), the Russian Federation, CIS, 11 kilometers (7 miles) south of Mirnyi. Discovered in 1969; reportedly the pipe with the highest ore grade (carats per ton) in Siberia and the producer of a high percentage of gem quality diamonds. Preparations for underground mining were underway in 1993.

International Standards Organisation (ISO), worldwide body which establishes manufacturing and trading standards for products in international commerce.

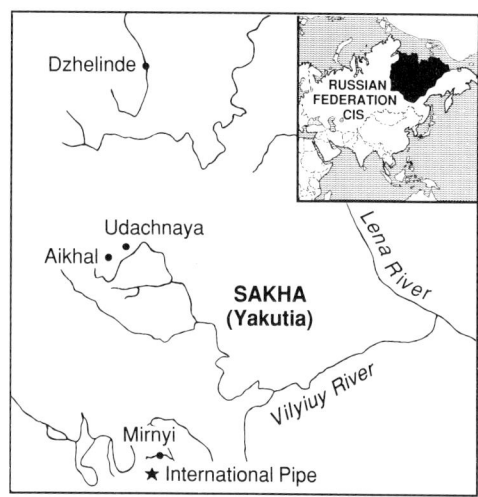

International Pipe

inter-particle crusher, sophisticated type of roller crusher used to increase the recovery of small diamonds from both primary and alluvial sources.

interpenetration twin, crystal in which two diamonds appear to have grown into one another. The degree of hardness changes across the twin plane, making separation by sawing impossible. See CRYSTAL STRUCTURE, MACLE, TWIN CRYSTAL.

intrusive rock, igneous rock which penetrates pre-existing rock, usually of a different type. See GABBRO.

ionic bond, bond formed between two ions (positively or negatively charged atomic particles) with opposite charges.

Iranian Crown Jewels, collection of gems which was once known to include such famous diamonds as the Nur-ul-Ain, the Darya-i-Nur, the Taj-e-mah, and possibly the Hornby, along with the collection known as the "Iranians." The Iranian Crown Jewels were originally housed in the Iranian Treasury in Tehran; Shah Reza Pahlevi allegedly took some items with him into exile after he was deposed in 1979, and others have reportedly been sold. A number of major pieces were placed on exhibit in the Central Bank of Iran in 1992, but the overall status of the collection remains uncertain.

Iranians, a collection of 23 large diamonds, formerly part of the Crown Jewels of Iran. Their current whereabouts are uncertain; their weights, shapes, and color descriptions are listed in Appendix C.

iris diamond, European term for a diamond coated to impart iridescence, thereby creating the appearance of higher dispersion. See COATED DIAMOND.

Irish diamond, misnomer for rock crystal quartz from Ireland.

irradiated black diamond, very dark green irradiated diamond which appears black; its dark green bodycolor may be visible only when light is passed through a thin edge, such as a girdle or culet. Such diamonds may remain radioactive. Good trade practice dictates that irradiation of any kind be disclosed to a potential buyer.

irradiated blue diamond, originally light brown, light yellowish, or colorless diamond the color of which has been artificially altered to blue to blue-green through exposure to high energy electrons from a linear accelerator. (Gamma rays have also been used to induce blue color.) Testing for electrical conductivity separates treated diamonds, which do not conduct electricity, from naturally-colored blue (Type IIb) diamonds, which are usually conductive. Good trade practice dictates that irradiation of any kind be disclosed to a potential buyer. See AUDIO CONDUCTION DETECTOR, BLUE DIAMOND, COLORED DIAMOND, CONDUCTOMETER, FANCY COLOR DIAMOND, IRRADIATED DIAMOND.

irradiated brown diamond, diamond the color of which has been artificially altered first by irradiation, which changes the color to green, and then by annealing, which changes the green to the brown to orange-yellow range. Good trade practice dictates that irradiation of any kind be disclosed to a potential buyer. See BROWN DIAMOND, COLORED DIAMOND, CYCLOTRON-TREATED DIAMOND, FANCY COLOR DIAMOND, IRRADIATED DIAMOND, LINEAR ACCELERATOR, REACTOR-TREATED DIAMOND.

irradiated diamond, diamond the color of which has been artificially altered or improved by exposure to radiation in a linear accelerator, nuclear reactor, or cyclotron (no longer in use). Such diamonds are described as "treated color" or "color enhanced." If the 595 nm treatment line is removed by annealing, diagnostic lines usually develop at 1,936 nm and 2,026 nm in the infra-red spectrum; these, however, can be detected only in a gemological laboratory. Natural yellow hues can be intensified by irradiation, followed by annealing; the stone then shows the 595 nm absorption line as well as a cape spectrum. Green, yellow, orange, and brown diamonds may also have been treated in radium bromide or with americium oxide, both of which can leave the stones radioactive. Radioactive isotopes such as cobalt-60 that are sources of gamma rays are also used to irradiate diamonds. Good trade practice dictates that irradiation of any kind be disclosed to a potential buyer. See ALPHA PARTICLE, CYCLOTRON-TREATED DIAMOND, IRRADIATED BLACK DIAMOND, IRRADIATED BLUE DIAMOND, IRRADIATED BROWN DIAMOND, IRRADIATED GREEN DIAMOND, IRRADIATED ORANGE-YELLOW DIAMOND, IRRADIATED PINK DIAMOND, IRRADIATED YELLOW DIAMOND, NUCLEAR REACTOR, RADIUM-TREATED DIAMOND, TREATED DIAMOND, VAN DE GRAAFF GENERATOR.

irradiated green diamond, diamond the color of which has been artificially altered to green by irradiation. (Subsequent annealing may convert that color to the brown to orange-yellow range.) Good trade practice dictates that irradiation of any kind be disclosed to a potential buyer. See COLORED DIAMOND, CYCLOTRON-TREATED DIAMOND, FANCY COLOR DIAMOND, GREEN DIAMOND, IRRADIATED DIAMOND, LINEAR ACCELERATOR, RADIUM-TREATED DIAMOND, REACTOR-TREATED DIAMOND.

irradiated orange-yellow diamond, diamond the color of which has been artificially altered first by irradiation (which changes the color to green) and then by annealing, which changes the green to the brown to orange-yellow range.

Good trade practice dictates that irradiation of any kind be disclosed to a potential buyer. See COLORED DIAMOND, CYCLOTRON-TREATED DIAMOND, FANCY COLOR DIAMOND, IRRADIATED DIAMOND, LINEAR ACCELERATOR, REACTOR-TREATED DIAMOND.

irradiated pink diamond, diamond the color of which has been artificially altered first by irradiation (which changes the color to green) and then by annealing, which changes the green to pink. Treated pink diamonds are rare; they sometimes occur accidentally in an attempt to produce yellow stones and may be color-zoned yellow and pink. They may show absorption lines at 594, 619, and 637 nm, as well as a 575 nm fluorescent line, and often fluoresce orange under longwave ultraviolet radiation. Good trade practice dictates that irradiation of any kind be disclosed to a potential buyer. See COLORED DIAMOND, CYCLOTRON-TREATED DIAMOND, FANCY COLOR DIAMOND, IRRADIATED DIAMOND, LINEAR ACCELERATOR, REACTOR-TREATED DIAMOND.

irradiated yellow diamond, diamond the color of which has been artificially altered first by irradiation (which changes the color to green) and then by annealing, which changes the green to the brown to orange-yellow range. Good trade practice dictates that irradiation of any kind be disclosed to a potential buyer. See COLORED DIAMOND, CYCLOTRON-TREATED DIAMOND, FANCY COLOR DIAMOND, IRRADIATED DIAMOND, LINEAR ACCELERATOR, REACTOR-TREATED DIAMOND.

irradiation stain, naturally occurring brown or green discoloration on the surface, or skin, of a rough diamond which has been exposed to radiation during formation or in nature. Often located in or near naturals, the discoloration rarely penetrates deep into the diamond. Irradiation spots on radium-treated diamonds differ in appearance and may be found on polished facets.

irregulars, rough sorting term for distorted diamond crystals which, because of their shape, usually produce lower-than-normal weight yields when polished. See YIELD.

Isaacs, Barnett, see BARNATO, BARNEY.

Isle of Wight diamond, misnomer for rock crystal quartz from the United Kingdom.

isogeometric, term used to describe similarly shaped particles in diamond polishing powders.

isometric crystal system, system in which crystals are described by three crystallographic axes of equal length, intersecting at 90°. Diamond and spinel crystallize in the isometric system. Also called the cubic crystal system.

isotropic, (1) possessing the same physical or optical properties in all directions. (2) singly refractive, permitting light rays to pass through unpolarized. Gemstones formed in the cubic crystal system, such as diamond, and amorphous materials, such as amber and glass, are isotropic. See ANISOTROPIC, ANOMALOUS DOUBLE REFRACTION (ADR), REFRACTION.

Israel, country which lies at the eastern end of the Mediterranean Sea, shares borders with Egypt, Syria, Jordan, and Lebanon, and is a major diamond manufacturing and trading center. The nation's diamond industry developed considerably after World War II, with the help of the Israeli government and an increasing number of skilled immigrants. See ISRAEL DIAMOND EXCHANGE, LTD.; ISRAEL EXPORT & TRUST CORPORATION, ISRAEL PRECIOUS STONES AND DIAMOND EXCHANGE, LTD.; ISRAELI DIAMOND INSTITUTE (IDI); ISRAELI DIAMOND MANUFACTURERS' ASSOCIATION (IDMA); KIDUM, NETANYA, RAMAT GAN, TEL AVIV.

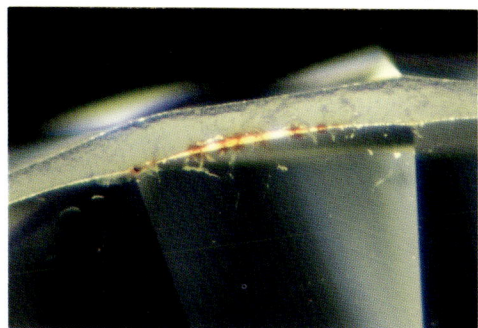

irradiation stain

Israel Diamond Exchange, Ltd., one of three diamond bourses in Israel; member of the World Federation of Diamond Bourses. See BOURSE, WORLD FEDERATION OF DIAMOND BOURSES (WFDB).

Israel Export & Trust Corporation, organization formed in 1961 by a bilateral commercial agreement between the Côte D'Ivoire (formerly Ivory Coast) and Israel, providing for an exchange of rough diamonds in return for industrial products from Israel.

Israeli Diamond Institute (IDI), trade association which provides information and technology to the Israeli diamond industry, promotes the industry abroad, and serves as a liaison between Israeli manufacturers and the research and development departments of the Central Selling Organisation in England and the Hoge Raad voor Diamant in Belgium.

Israeli Diamond Manufacturers' Association (IsDMA), national trade group established in 1946 to coordinate industry and government involvement in the promotion of the Israeli diamond manufacturing industry. Based in Ramat Gan, IsDMA consists of 2,500 merchants and manufacturers. See KIDUM.

Israel Precious Stones and Diamond Exchange, Ltd., one of three diamond bourses in Israel and the only one which trades in colored gemstones; member of the World Federation of Diamond Bourses. See BOURSE, WORLD FEDERATION OF DIAMOND BOURSES (WFDB).

Ituiutaba Diamond, 105 ct. diamond found in the Ituiutaba Mine, Minas Gerais, Brazil, in 1940. Current whereabouts unknown.

Ivory Coast, see COTE D'IVOIRE.

J

JA, see JEWELERS OF AMERICA.

Jacob Diamond, see VICTORIA DIAMOND.

Jacobs, Erasmus, Boer farmer traditionally credited with having discovered the Eureka diamond in South Africa in 1866, when he was 15 (although it may actually have been found by one of his brothers or his sister). In later life, finding himself in difficult circumstances, Jacobs swore to a detailed affidavit recounting the circumstances of the discovery; his memory, and the veracity of this document, have been questioned. See EUREKA DIAMOND.

jager, historic term used to describe colorless diamonds with strong blue ultraviolet fluorescence. The name was often applied to diamonds with a very light blue bodycolor; jagers sometimes looked slightly bluish in daylight. Occasionally the word "blue" was added ("blue jager") to imply a higher quality. Also spelled jaeger. The name was derived from that of the Jagersfontein Mine, which produced a high percentage of such stones.

Jagersfontein Mine, the third diamond-bearing kimberlite discovered in South Africa. Found on the Jagersfontein farm in the Orange Free State in 1870, it was not recognized as a primary source of diamonds until 1872. The output was characterized by a significant proportion of fine color stones, including those which appear slightly blue in daylight, a phenomenon usually attributed to strong ultraviolet fluorescence. The mine also produced a large proportion of cleavage fragments and heavily spotted diamonds. In 1971, the Jagersfontein was closed and the nearby Koffiefontein Mine was reopened. See EXCELSIOR DIAMOND, FLUORESCENCE, REITZ DIAMOND.

Jahangir Diamond, 83 ct. diamond which first belonged to Shah Jahangir (1569-1627) of the

Jagersfontein Mine

Mogul dynasty; it bears a Persian inscription: "Shah Jahangir [son] of Akbar Shah 1021" (the date corresponds to AD 1612). A second inscription, partly obscured by a drillhole, reads "Shah Jahan [son] of Jahangir Shah 1042," suggesting the stone was inherited by Jahangir's son, Jahan (1592-1666) in 1632. The Jahangir Diamond was sold in 1954 by the Maharajah of Burdwan to Greek shipping magnate Stavros Niarchos, and again in 1957 by Sotheby's of London to an Indian businessman.

jargon, see JARGOON.

jargoon, name for pale yellow to colorless zircon from Sri Lanka, often used as a diamond simulant. Possibly derived from the word *zargoon*, Arabic for *vermillion*; Persian for *gold-colored*.

Jarra Gem, proprietary name for synthetic rutile. Marketed as a diamond simulant.

Java Gem, proprietary name for synthetic rutile. Marketed as a diamond simulant.

jaw crusher, device used to crush mineral ore; large blocks of ore are dropped into a tapered sleeve containing large, ribbed plates which are then forced together. The resulting particles drop to the bottom.

Jeffries, David, eighteenth-century English jeweler, author of *A Treatise On Diamonds and Pearls* (1750), which includes rules for evaluating diamonds and a discourse on their fashioning.

Jewelers of America (JA), national organization formed in 1957 by the merger of the American National Retail Jewelers' Association and the National Jewelers' Association, to promote the interests of the US retail jewelry industry. Originally called Retail Jewelers of America.

Jewelers' Security Alliance of the United States (JSA), non-profit association of retail jewelers, formed in 1883 to improve security and crime protection throughout the industry. JSA cooperates with law enforcement agencies, provides crime prevention training, supplies members with detective services and warning signs, and encourages the use of burglar alarms and other protective devices.

Jewelers' Vigilance Committee (JVC), non-profit association formed in 1912 to promote ethical practices throughout the US jewelry industry. JVC develops and proposes the use of standard nomenclature and quality markings, and informs its members of pertinent legislative and regulatory requirements.

Jewelite, proprietary name for strontium titanate. Marketed as a diamond simulant.

Jewellery Council of South Africa, non-profit organization of the South Africa watch and jewelry industry founded in 1972; today it represents all trade and industry associations, provides short courses and laboratory services in Johannesburg, and represents industry interests in trade negotiations and through lobbying.

Jewelry Industry Council (JIC), nationwide promotional organization made up of American jewelry retailers and suppliers. It supports retail jewelry sales in the US by creating and furnishing promotional materials to its members, and by distributing press releases to the media.

JIC, see JEWELRY INDUSTRY COUNCIL.

jig, mechanical sieve, composed of two concentric water-filled compartments, used to separate diamonds from lighter materials. The water is agitated, causing lighter material to float over the edge while diamonds and other heavy minerals work down through a screen. Also called a pulsator jig or pulsator, it has been largely replaced by heavy media separation. See BABY, HEAVY MEDIA SEPARATION, ROTARY WASHING PAN, SCRUBBER, SEPARATION (2), STATIC CONE, TROMMEL.

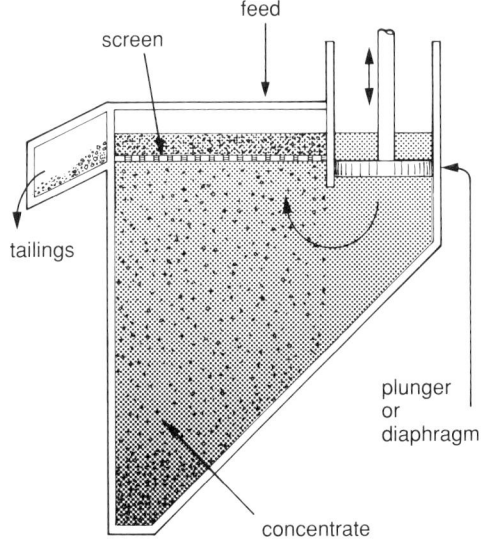

jig

jobber, independent salesperson who represents smaller diamond dealers and jewelry manufacturers in transactions with retailers. Jobbers usually represent several principals and are paid on a commission basis.

Johannesburg, major city in Transvaal Province, South Africa, closely associated with the gold-mining industry, and the country's main diamond manufacturing center.

Johannes Gem, proprietary name for synthetic rutile. Marketed as a diamond simulant.

Jonker, Johannes Jacobus, diamond digger on whose claim the Jonker Diamond was discovered by Johannes Makahi, one of his workers, in 1934.

Jonker Diamond, 726 ct. alluvial diamond found on a claim held by Johannes Jacobus Jonker at Elandsfontein, South Africa, near the Premier Mine, in 1934. Purchased by Harry Winston in 1935, it was the first large diamond to be marketed through the new Central Selling Organisation. Fashioned by master diamond cutter Lazare Kaplan, the rough yielded one marquise and 11 emerald cuts; the largest, also called the Jonker Diamond, emerged as a 142.90 ct., 66-facet emerald cut. After it was repolished in 1937 to give it a more oblong outline and greater brilliance, it was considered one of the most perfectly cut gems in existence. The resulting 125.35 ct., D, VVS$_1$ 58-facet emerald cut was sold to King Farouk of Egypt in 1951 and later acquired by Queen Ratna of Nepal. Last sold privately in Hong Kong in 1977; current whereabouts unknown. See CENTRAL SELLING ORGANISATION (CSO); KAPLAN, LAZARE.

Jonker Diamond

JSA, see JEWELERS' SECURITY ALLIANCE OF THE UNITED STATES.

jubilee cut, modification of the brilliant cut, with 88 facets. Named in honor of the Diamond Jubilee of Britain's Queen Victoria in 1897, an event celebrating the 60th year of her reign. The cut is rarely seen today.

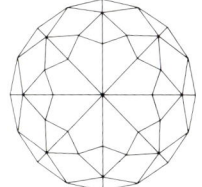 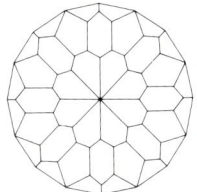

jubilee cut

Jubilee Diamond, see REITZ DIAMOND.

Jubilee Mine, diamond-bearing kimberlite discovered under 70 meters (230 feet) of sedimentary rock in the Republic of Sakha (Yakutia), the Russian Federation, CIS, 19 kilometers (12 miles) from Aikhal. Development began in 1991, and is scheduled for completion in 1993-94. Diamonds are currently being recovered from concentrates at the Aikhal plant.

JVC, see JEWELERS' VIGILANCE COMMITTEE.

Jwaneng Mine, three-lobed, diamond-bearing kimberlite discovered in 1973, 113 kilometers (70 miles) west of Gaborone, the capital of Botswana. Mining began in 1982; today Jwaneng is believed to be the world's largest producer of gem quality diamonds over two carats. The pipe was buried under some 46 meters (150 feet) of Kalahari Desert sand, sandstone, and calcrete. Reported to produce 60 percent gem quality diamonds, Jwaneng is noted for its high proportion of cube-shaped crystals, and its green diamonds which have a surface coating caused by natural irradiation. See DEBSWANA DIAMOND COMPANY, LETLHAKANE, ORAPA MINE.

K

K, abbreviation for karat.

Kaalvallei Mine, see SAMADA MINE.

Kaapse Tijd, Dutch, meaning the Cape Period, the era in the late nineteenth century when the South African diamond discoveries stimulated the growth of Amsterdam and Antwerp as diamond manufacturing centers.

Kaapvaal, central South African craton in which numerous kimberlitic occurrences have been located. Its estimated geologic age is 3.3 billion years. See CRATON.

Kadei River, see CENTRAL AFRICAN REPUBLIC (C.A.R.).

Kahama pipes, small diamond-bearing kimberlites approximately 121 kilometers (75 miles) west of the Williamson Diamond Mine, near Mwadui, in Tanzania. See WILLIAMSON DIAMOND MINE.

Kalahari Desert, desert region covering approximately 583,000 square kilometers (225,000 square miles) straddling Botswana, South Africa, and Namibia. In 1973, De Beers prospecting teams located a large three-lobed kimberlite pipe buried beneath 46 meters (150 feet) of the desert's overburden; it became Botswana's Jwaneng Mine. See DEBSWANA DIAMOND COMPANY, JWANENG MINE.

Kalimantan, state in Indonesia covering most of the southern part of the island of Borneo. Kalimantan has been a source of diamonds for over a thousand years (the name means *river of diamonds*). Alluvial diamonds have historically been found in the western part along the Landak River. Recent mining activity has been concentrated in the southeast, where ancient alluvial gravels are mined in rivers draining the Meratus Mountains and in the associated Danau Seran and Cempaka swamps. See BANJARMASIN.

Kalahari Desert

Kalimantan

Kamfersdam Mine, diamond mine north of Kimberley, Cape Province, South Africa, which was worked from 1899 to 1907 and again from 1913 to 1914. Owned by De Beers Consolidated Mines.

Kansas diamond, misnomer for clear and smoky rock crystal quartz from the Smoky Hill River, Kansas.

Kao Valley, mountainous area in northern Lesotho in which numerous small diamond-bearing kimberlite pipes have been located; some have been worked by independent diggers for several years. See LESOTHO, LETSENG-LA-TERAI MINE.

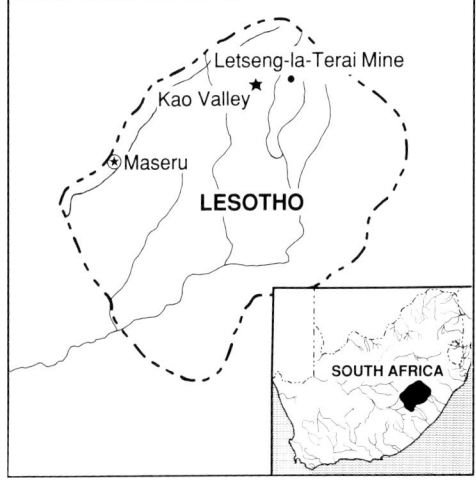

Kao Valley

Kapiolani Diamond, see STAR OF DENMARK DIAMOND.

Kaplan, Lazare (1883-1986), American master diamond cutter who planned, designed, and fashioned the 726 ct. Jonker Diamond. He also introduced the use of India ink to mark diamonds prior to cleaving, developed and introduced the oval brilliant cut, and promoted the concept of ideal proportions as a means of maximizing brilliance. See AMERICAN BRILLIANT CUT, JONKER DIAMOND, TOLKOWSKY THEORETICAL BRILLIANT CUT.

kaps, Dutch, a diamond which has been cleaved, split, or sawn, but not yet fashioned.

karat, proportion of pure gold in a gold alloy, expressed in terms of 24 parts. Pure gold is 24 karat, or 24 out of 24; 18 karat gold contains 18 parts (18/24) pure gold and 6 parts alloy. (In Europe and some other areas, the proportion is expressed as parts per thousand; thus 24 karat gold is 1000, 18 karat gold 750.) This spelling is often used for carat in Europe. See CARAT.

Kasai, province in southern Zaire, near the border with Angola, in which the Miba Mine at Mbuji-Mayi and substantial alluvial deposits are located. See MBUJI-MAYI.

Kasikci Diamond, 84 ct. pear-shape, rose-cut diamond set in a frame with 49 other diamonds. Once owned by the Grand Sultan of Turkey, it is on display at the Topkapi Museum in Istanbul. Also called the Turkey II Diamond or Spoonmaker's Diamond.

keel line, facet junction on the pavilion of a fancy-cut brilliant which forms, in effect, an extended culet running parallel to the length of the stone.

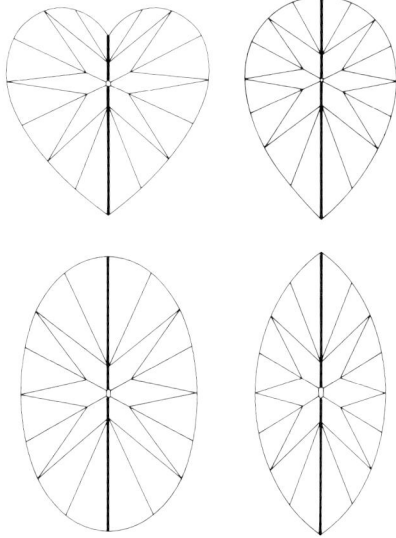

keel line

Kempen, historic diamond-manufacturing area centered around the towns of Herentals, Nijen, and Grobbendonck in what was once (ca. 1900) a depressed agricultural region northeast of Antwerp, Belgium. It became the center of a cottage industry made up of small, family-oriented, independent manufacturers who specialized in polishing small goods. The Kempen's production has declined in recent years as other countries have begun to specialize in such small diamonds. There is a diamond museum in Grobbendonck.

Kenema, town in Sierra Leone; a rough diamond trading center near numerous alluvial diamond diggings.

Kenneth Lane Jewel, proprietary name for synthetic strontium titanate. Marketed as a diamond simulant.

Kentucky diamond, misnomer for rock crystal quartz from Kentucky.

Kenya Gem, proprietary name for synthetic rutile. Marketed as a diamond simulant.

Kerbehuk, historic name for an important alluvial mining area along the Namibian coast between Oranjemund and Lüderitz; also known as Area K. Operated by CDM. See AFFENRUCKEN, GEMSBOK, MARINE AREAS, MITTAG, UUBVLEY.

kerf, (1) groove scratched in a rough diamond prior to cleaving or splitting. Traditionally done with a diamond fragment; today, it is often made with a laser. (2) as a verb, to prepare such a groove. See CLEAVER'S BLADE, CLEAVING, SHARP, SPLITTING.

key color, primary bodycolor seen when looking at a diamond or other gemstone face-up.

key cut, man-made channel excavated to divert the natural course of a river so alluvial mining can take place. See ALLUVIAL MINING.

key diamonds, see MASTER DIAMONDS.

keystone, short tapered baguette.

Khasumi diamond, see ARABIAN DIAMOND.

Khedive Diamond, 36.61 ct. emerald-cut diamond, reportedly light yellow and flawless, recut from a 43 ct. stone. Said to have been presented to France's Empress Eugénie in 1869 by Ismail Pasha, Khedive of Egypt, to commemorate the opening of the Suez Canal. French archives show no record of such a gift. Known to have been owned at one time by Miami jeweler Jack M. Werst, and exhibited at the Museum of Natural History in New York in 1976. It was last sold to a private buyer in 1986.

Kidum, independent trade organization established in 1979 for small Israeli diamond manufacturers, as an alternative to the Israeli Diamond Manufacturers' Association. See ISRAEL.

Kiev Synthetic Diamond Research Institute, Russian group in the former Soviet Union reported to have produced synthetic diamond crystals in 1967.

Killicranke diamond, misnomer for colorless topaz from Tasmania.

Kima Gem, proprietary name for synthetic rutile. Marketed as a diamond simulant.

Kimberley, center of diamond mining operations in Cape Province, South Africa. Named for the first Earl of Kimberley, John Wodehouse, then British Secretary of State for the Colonies, the city began in 1873 as a mining camp called New Rush on the Vooruitzigt farm where the De Beers and Kimberley Mines were discovered. Since 1888, the head office of De Beers Consolidated Mines has been in Kim-

Kimberley

berley. Also called the "Diamond City." See DE BEERS MINE; KIMBERLEY MINE; WODEHOUSE, JOHN.

Kimberley, Lord, see WODEHOUSE, JOHN.

Kimberley Central Diamond Mining Company, one of the principal diamond-mining companies which worked the Kimberley Mine in South Africa. Cecil Rhodes acquired control of the company in 1888 and liquidated its assets, which were bought up by De Beers Consolidated Mines for a record sum. This gave De Beers control of the mine, along with a majority of other diamond mining operations in South Africa at the time.

Kimberley Diamond

Kimberley Diamond, 490 ct. rough diamond, described as champagne-colored and believed to have come from either the De Beers or the Dutoitspan Mine. First fashioned into a reportedly flawless 70 ct. emerald cut in 1921, the diamond was recut to 55.09 ct. in 1958 to improve upon its proportions and brilliance. Privately owned.

Kimberley District, see WESTERN AUSTRALIA.

Kimberley Mine, said to be the sixth diamond-bearing kimberlite discovered in South Africa; found in 1871, but not recognized as a primary source until 1872. Located near Colesberg Kopje, Cape Colony, the mine spawned a tent-town known as De Beers New Rush which grew into a city later named after Lord Kimberley, British Secretary of State for the Colonies. The mine was named after the town but is often referred to as the "Big Hole." The massive excavation created by open pit mining operations is 1,097 meters (3,600 feet) deep, 457 meters (1,500 feet) in diameter, and covers a total of 15.4 hectares (38 acres). Before the mine closed at the outbreak of World War I in 1914, 22.6 million tons of ore had been removed, producing 15.5 million carats of diamonds. See BARNATO, BARNEY; BIG HOLE; KIMBERLEY CENTRAL DIAMOND MINING COMPANY; RHODES, CECIL JOHN; WODEHOUSE, JOHN.

Kimberley Mines, group of five well-known diamond mines near Kimberley, South Africa: the Bultfontein, De Beers, Dutoitspan, Kimberley, and Wesselton. Also called the "De Beers Mines" or the "Big Five."

Kimberley Plateau, see WESTERN AUSTRALIA.

Kimberley Pool, general term for diamonds produced by the three original De Beers mines (the Bultfontein, Dutoitspan, and Wesselton) which were still operating in 1992. (The Kimberley Mine was closed in 1914, the De Beers Mine in 1990.) See BULTFONTEIN MINE, DE BEERS MINE, DUTOITSPAN MINE, KIMBERLEY MINE, WESSELTON MINE.

kimberlite, rare type of igneous rock which is one of only two rocks known to host diamonds in primary deposits (the other is lamproite). Kimberlite formed at great depth and was forced to the surface by volcanic action; it occurs there as pipes, dikes, and sills. [Technically, it is a hybrid, volatile-rich, potassic ultramafic igneous rock, with a distinctive granular texture due to the presence of megacrysts in a fine-grained matrix of olivine and minerals such as phlogopite, carbonate (commonly calcite), clinopyroxene (commonly chrome diop-

kimberlite

side), garnet, monticellite, apatite, spinel, and ilmenite. Olivine is abundant relative to the other megacrysts, not all of which are necessarily present; the matrix is commonly altered by the processes of serpentinization and carbonatization.] On the surface kimberlite appears as oxidized yellowground; unoxidized blueground is found beneath. See BLUEGROUND, DIKE, EMPLACEMENT (OF DIAMOND), HARDEBANK, LAMPROITE, ORIGIN (OF DIAMOND), PIPE, SILL, YELLOWGROUND.

Kimberlite Gem, proprietary name for synthetic rutile. Marketed as a diamond simulant.

King Charles I Seal Diamond, diamond of unknown weight inscribed with the Royal Coat of Arms of England. Unsubstantiated accounts suggest that Charles I gave it to his son, Charles II; he, in turn, is believed to have sold it to Jean Baptiste Tavernier. Current whereabouts unknown.

King Cut, proprietary name for an 86-facet modification of the standard round brilliant cut.

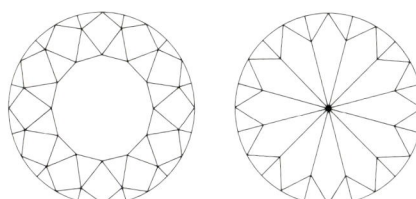

King Cut

King George IV Diamond, originally a 32.23 ct. colorless round diamond set in a coronation crown for King George IV in 1821 by Crown Jewelers Rundell Bridge & Co. of London. In 1831, it was reset with the Arcot Diamonds in a crown for Queen Adelaide for the coronation of her husband, King William IV. Purchased by the Duke of Westminster in 1837. One of the Duke's descendants had it reset, with the Arcots, in a tiara; this was acquired by Harry Winston in 1959. The King George Diamond was repolished to a modern 26.77 ct. round brilliant and sold separately; it was last sold at auction in New York in 1970.

King of Portugal Diamond, see BRAGANZA DIAMOND.

Kirsten, F. B. (active ca. 1890), De Beers employee who determined that diamonds, being nonwettable, would stick to grease while other, wettable minerals in the concentrate were washed away. This discovery led to the development of the grease table. See LABRAM, GEORGE F.

Kirti-Nur Diamond, 15 ct. pink pear-shape diamond from Golconda, India, which was cut and polished in the early eighteenth century. Later set in a diamond necklace and held among the vast collection of jewels of a prominent Indian family, its existence was virtually unknown outside India, until it was acquired by a Western diamond dealer in the early 1990s.

Kistna River, see KRISHNA RIVER.

kite cut, four-sided, roughly diamond-shaped step cut.

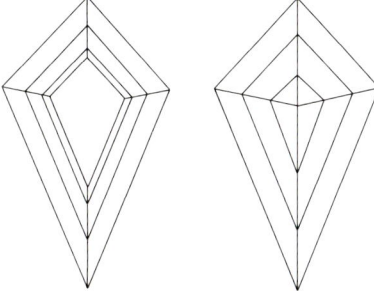

kite cut

kite facet, see BEZEL FACET.

Kleinzee, coastal alluvial diamond mining area in Namaqualand, South Africa, which was worked until 1957. Operations were transferred to Annex Kleinzee in 1958 and continue today. See ANNEX KLEINZEE, BUFFELS MARINE COMPLEX, KOINGNAAS.

Klipdrift, see BARKLY WEST.

knife-edge girdle, extremely thin girdle; such a girdle is highly susceptible to damage.

knife-edge girdle

Knoop indentation hardness test, method of measuring the hardness of metals and minerals by pressing a pyramid-shaped diamond into their surface and assessing the resulting indentation in relation to the load placed on it. When used with a pentagonal point to offset diamond's directional hardness, it can be used on diamond itself. See BRINELL HARDNESS TEST, DIRECTIONAL HARDNESS, HARDNESS, HARDNESS POINTS, INDENTATION TEST, MOHS SCALE, SCLEROMETER, SCRATCH HARDNESS, VICKERS HARDNESS TEST.

knot, (1) included diamond crystal oriented differently from the larger diamond crystal which is its host. When such diamonds are sawn, the knot may cause problems and slow the sawing process because it often presents a harder cutting direction. After polishing, a knot may stand slightly higher than the surrounding surface. (2) that section of a twinned crystal where the grain differs from that of the main mass. Also called a naat.

knot lines, see GRAIN LINES.

Koffiefontein Mine, said to have been the second diamond-bearing kimberlite discovered in South Africa; found in 1870, but not recognized as a primary source until 1872. Owned and operated by De Beers Consolidated Mines, the Koffiefontein was closed in the 1930s; it was reopened in 1970 following the close of the Jagersfontein Mine. Diamonds were originally recovered by open pit mining, but underground mining operations began in the early 1980s. Poor market conditions led to its closing in 1982; the mine reopened in 1987 when diesel-powered tracking equipment was introduced.

Koh-i-Nur Diamond, historically important Indian diamond, originally 186 ct., said to have been owned by a number of Indian rajahs, Mogul emperors, and Persian shahs before the British East India Company acquired it. It was

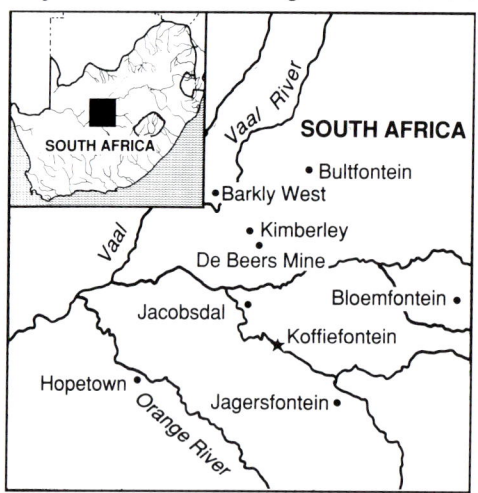

Koffiefontein Mine

photo courtesy of Her Majesty's Stationery Office

Koh-i-Nur Diamond

presented to Queen Victoria in 1850 and recut two years later to 105.60 ct. It has been variously set in a circlet for Queen Victoria, in the crown worn by Queen Mary at the coronation of George V in 1911, and in a crown made for the Queen Mother (mother of Queen Elizabeth II) in 1937 for the coronation of her husband, King George VI. It now forms part of the British Crown Jewels on permanent display in the

Jewel House at the Tower of London. *Koh-i-Nur* means *Mountain of Light* in Persian. Also spelled Kuh-i-noor or Koh-i-noor.

Koingnaas, coastal alluvial deposit in Namaqualand, South Africa, owned by De Beers Consolidated Mines and operated by the company's Namaqualand Mines Division. Diamonds are found among paleo-marine and fluvial gravels and are recovered by overburden stripping, mechanical mining, and hand sweeping. See BEACH MINING.

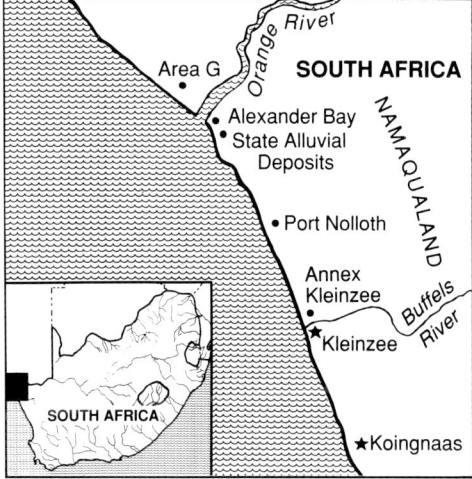

Kleinzee and Koingnaas

Kollur Diamond, 63 ct. diamond reportedly bought in 1653 by Jean Baptiste Tavernier at India's Kollur Mines. Shape, quality, and current whereabouts unknown.

Kollur Mines, ancient group of diamond mines in the Golconda region of India, one of which is believed to have produced the Orloff Diamond.

Komdragmet, the state Committee on Precious Metals and Gemstones, created in 1992 to purchase, sort, value, and store rough diamonds mined in Sakha (Yakutia). Some rough material was distributed to domestic manufacturers for polishing and sale abroad, while rough to be exported was sold to the CSO. See ALMAZY ROSSII-SAKHA, ROSKOMDRAGMET, SAKHA KOMDRAGMET.

Koninklijke Asscher Diamant Maatschappij, see ROYAL ASSCHER DIAMOND COMPANY.

Kono District, alluvial diamond-producing region in Sierra Leone.

kopje, Afrikaans, meaning *hillock*. A small, flat, roughly circular hill several feet (a few meters) in height; often covered with vegetation.

kopje walloper, slang, a buyer of rough diamonds in remote areas in the early days of the South African discoveries.

Koss treatment, diamond clarity enhancement method which uses a stable, transparent material to fill surface-reaching inclusions. Developed by the Koss Group of Ramat Gan, Israel. See FILLED DIAMOND, LASER DRILLING, YEHUDA TREATMENT.

Kott-Dar-El-Kouti, area of alluvial diamond deposits located along the Kotto River in the Central African Republic. See CENTRAL AFRICAN REPUBLIC (C.A.R.).

Kotto River, see CENTRAL AFRICAN REPUBLIC.

Kramleegte, coastal deposit in Namaqualand, South Africa. Diamonds are recovered by overburden stripping, mechanical mining, and hand sweeping. See BEACH MINING.

Krishna River, source of alluvial diamonds in central India near the ancient diamond trading

Krishna River

city of Golconda. Formerly spelled Kistna. See GOLCONDA.

Kristall, the former Russian state diamond manufacturing concern, with factories in Moscow, Smolensk, Barnaul, and Kusinski. Supplies are currently purchased from Almazy Rossii-Sakha, and most of the production is sold direct to the West. Kristall, Smolensk, has recently opened offices in Antwerp, Beverly Hills (Los Angeles, California, US), and Bangkok. Also spelled Crystal or Krystall. See ROSKOMDRAGMET, RUSSALMAZZOLOTO.

Kruger Diamond, 200 ct. alluvial diamond named for South African statesman Stephanus Johannes Paulus (Paul) Kruger (1825-1904). Reported to have belonged to an African chieftain whom Kruger took captive, and who sent Kruger the diamond as a token of gratitude after his release. Current whereabouts unknown.

Krupp Diamond, 33.19 ct. VS$_1$ emerald-cut diamond once owned by Vera Krupp, former wife of the German armaments manufacturer. Purchased in 1968 by actor Richard Burton for his wife, screen actress Elizabeth Taylor.

Krystall, see KRISTALL.

Kt., abbreviation for karat. See CARAT, KARAT.

Kwango, see CUANGO.

Kwanza River, see CUANZA RIVER.

L

Labram, George F., (active ca. 1895) chief engineer for De Beers Consolidated Mines and developer of the grease table. An American, Labram also built the "Long Cecil," an improvised cannon used during the Siege of Kimberley in the Boer War. He was killed in the hostilities. See GREASE TABLE, KIRSTEN, F.B.

Lake George diamond, misnomer for rock crystal quartz from New York state, US.

Lal Qila Diamond, 72.76 ct. round color-enhanced green diamond purchased by Harry Winston in 1949 and repolished to 70.10 ct. Sent on approval to King Farouk of Egypt in 1951, the diamond disappeared in 1952 when he was overthrown and went into exile. Current whereabouts unknown.

lamproite, rare type of igneous rock which is one of only two rocks known to host diamonds in primary deposits (the other is kimberlite). Lamproite formed at great depth and was forced to the surface; it occurs there as volcanic pipes, dikes, and sills. Technically, it is an ultrapotassic, magnesium-rich, igneous rock containing variable amounts of leucite and/or glass and usually one or more of the following primary minerals: clinopyroxene (commonly diopside), olivine, sanidine, spinel, apatite, and phlogopite, among others. See AK1 PIPE (ARGYLE), ARGYLE DIAMOND MINES, EMPLACEMENT (OF DIAMOND), KIMBERLITE, ORIGIN (OF DIAMOND).

Landak River, historical source of alluvial diamonds in Kalimantan, Indonesia, on the island of Borneo. Its deposits are believed to have been worked as early as the Sung Dynasty in China (960-1279). See BORNEO, KALIMANTAN.

Langhoogte, farm on the Buffels River in Namaqualand, South Africa, in an area known as the Buffels Inland Complex; mined for alluvial diamonds by the Namaqualand Mines Division of De Beers Consolidated Mines. See BUFFELS MARINE COMPLEX.

lapidary, polisher of colored stones; also called a lapidist.

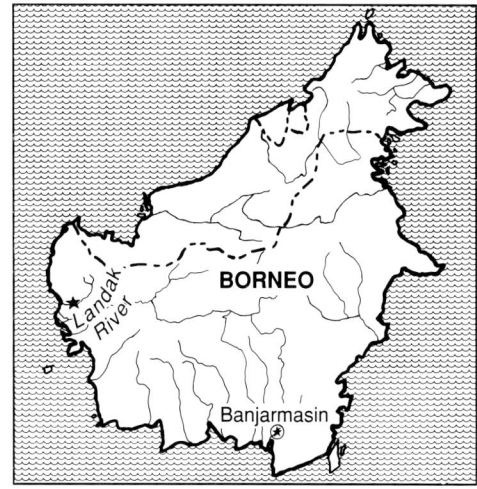

Landak River

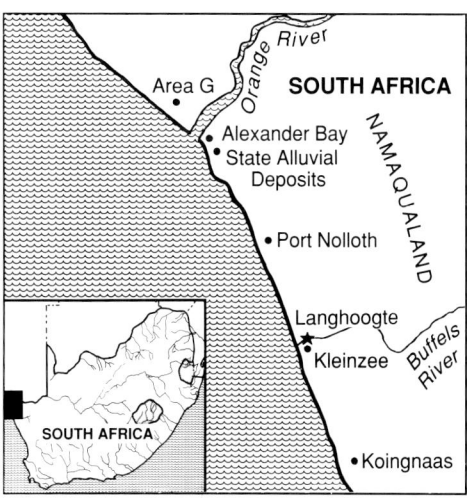

Langhoogte

La Reine des Belges Diamond, see REINE DES BELGES DIAMOND.

larger goods, sorting term for diamonds over one carat.

Larkin's Flat, historical alluvial diamond digging on the Vaal River, South Africa.

Lasarev Diamond, also spelled Lazarev. See ORLOFF DIAMOND.

laser, acronym for Light Amplification by Stimulated Emission of Radiation; a device which produces a very narrow, intense beam of coherent, monochromatic light of a single wavelength. Laser beams are capable of burning or cutting very hard materials, such as diamond, and are used in various manufacturing operations. See LASER CUTTING, LASER DRILLING, YAG LASER.

laser cutting, use of a laser to assist in kerfing a diamond, and in profiling its eventual shape. Once a diamond is kerfed with a laser, cleaving is relatively simple and is now known as splitting. Lasers allow diamonds to be shaped in any direction, permitting the fashioning of exotic fancy cuts such as stars, letters, and flowers.

laser drillhole, hole in a diamond produced by a laser. See LASER DRILLING.

laser drilling, enhancement process used to improve the appearance of a diamond which contains dark inclusions. A hole is drilled into the diamond with a laser until it reaches the inclusion; if the included material is not vaporized by the laser itself, it is dissolved or bleached with acid. See FILLED DIAMOND.

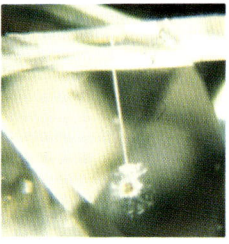

laser drilled diamond

Laser Gem, proprietary name for a doublet with a synthetic spinel crown and a strontium titanate pavilion. Marketed as a diamond simulant.

lasering, see LASER CUTTING, LASER DRILLING, LASER SAWING.

laser inscription, identifying numbers or messages engraved on a diamond (usually on the girdle) with a laser. Lazare Kaplan, Inc. holds a patent on the process; GIA, HRD, and Argyle are licensees.

laser inscription

laser kerfing, use of a laser to form the kerf in a rough diamond prior to splitting. See CLEAVING, LASER CUTTING, SPLITTER, SPLITTING.

laser photography, see GEMPRINT.

laser sawing, use of a laser to divide a diamond crystal. Laser sawing often entails greater weight loss than conventional methods, but it

laser cut diamond

can safely and easily saw intergrown crystals or those containing naats; thus such diamonds can be divided successfully, regardless of crystal orientation. It also permits rough diamonds to be polished in their optimum grain directions. See GRAIN.

laser sawn diamond

lasque, see BEVEL CUT.

Last Hope, historic alluvial diamond digging near Barkly West, Cape Province, South Africa.

lax diamond, obsolete trade term for a diamond with little dispersion and brilliance.

laxey diamonds, very shallow, brilliant-cut diamonds.

Lazare Diamond, proprietary name for round brilliants chosen for fine color and clarity and manufactured to American ideal proportions by Lazare Kaplan, Inc. Each carries a six-digit laser-inscribed identification number on the girdle, visible under 10x magnification. See AMERICAN BRILLIANT CUT, LASER INSCRIPTION.

Lazarev Diamond, also spelled Lasarev. See ORLOFF DIAMOND.

LC, abbreviation for Loupe Clean.

lead dop, retainer filled with lead solder, used to hold a diamond during polishing. Largely replaced by mechanical dops, but still used for large diamonds. See SOLDER DOP.

lead glass, glass to which lead has been added to increase its refractive index, luster, and dispersion; it also reduces its hardness. Lead glass is often used as a diamond simulant. Also called paste, crystal, flint glass, or strass glass.

leakage, term describing the behavior of light which enters a polished diamond, refracts, reflects internally, and exits. Planned leakage occurs when light leaves from the crown, unplanned leakage when it escapes from the pavilion. See BRILLIANCE, CRITICAL ANGLE, CRITICAL ANGLE CONE, LIGHT RETURN, NORMAL, REFRACTION, TOTAL INTERNAL REFLECTION.

lean pipes, kimberlite pipes which cannot be mined profitably.

Ledo Frozen Fire, proprietary name for colorless synthetic sapphire. Marketed as a diamond simulant.

Le Grand Condé Diamond, see GRAND CONDE DIAMOND, LE.

Le Grand Sancy Diamond, see SANCY DIAMOND.

Legziel and Sons, Israeli diamond company which also produces robotic bruting machines, including a fully-automated bruting system, developed in cooperation with Orpak Industries. See ORPAK INDUSTRIES.

Leister Mine, small kimberlite pipe mine near Barkly West, Cape Province, South Africa.

Lena Mine, kimberlite near Cullinan, the Transvaal Province, South Africa. Also known as the Schüller Mine.

length-to-width ratio, comparison of the length and width of the girdle outline on marquise, emerald, pear-shape, and oval cuts, determined by dividing the length by the width. (The width is expressed as 1.) Some length-to-width ratios are considered more pleasing than others; these include: marquise, 1.75-2.25:1; oval, 1.33-1.66:1; emerald cut and pear shape, 1.50-1.75:1.

lead dop

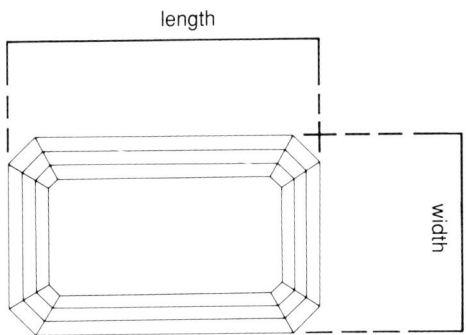

Length-to-width ratio is determined by dividing the length by the width

lens, piece of glass or other transparent material shaped to focus light passing through it into an image. Gemological loupes and microscopes have magnifying lenses. See LOUPE, MICROSCOPE.

Le Petit Coeur Diamond, see PETIT COEUR DIAMOND.

Lesotho, formerly Basutoland, a small, mountainous enclave nation in southern Africa which contains numerous kimberlite pipes, most of which are not diamond-bearing. Those which are, normally produce few stones, but spectacularly large diamonds, such as the 601.25 ct. Lesotho Diamond, are occasionally found. The best-known pipe is Letseng-la-Terai in the Maluti Mountains. Other important finds have been made at the head of the Kao Valley, elsewhere in the Maluti Mountains, northeast of Maseru. See KAO VALLEY, LETSENG-LA-TERAI MINE.

Lesotho Brown Diamond, see LESOTHO DIAMOND.

Lesotho Diamond, 601.25 ct. brown rough diamond, found at Letseng-la-Terai by Ernestine Ramaboa in 1967. Eventually acquired by Harry Winston, it was fashioned in 1968 into 18 polished diamonds totalling 242.50 ct. The largest was a 71.73 ct. emerald cut. All are now privately owned.

Lesser Botuobiya, see MALAYA BOTUOBOYA.

Lesser Star of Africa Diamond, see CULLINAN II.

Lestergem, proprietary name for synthetic spinel. Marketed as a diamond simulant.

Letlhakane Mine, kimberlite in central Botswana; one of several such occurrences in the Orapa area. Operations began in 1976; the mine is said to produce a high proportion of gem-quality diamonds. See DEBSWANA DIAMOND COMPANY, JWANENG MINE, ORAPA MINE.

Letlhakane Mine

Letseng-la-Terai Mine, highest diamond mine in the world, at 3,111 meters (10,200 feet), in the Maluti Mountains in northeastern Lesotho.

Letseng-la-Terai Mine

De Beers Lesotho Mining Company began operations in 1977 and closed in 1982: the mine grade was low and the mine unprofitable, although some large, gem-quality diamonds are known to have been found. Sometimes spelled Letseng-la-Draai; the name means *the turn by the swamp*. See LESOTHO DIAMOND.

Leveridge gauge, device used to measure the dimensions of both mounted and unmounted gems. Measurements, which are accurate to 0.1 mm, are shown on a dial. See MICROMETER, MOE GAUGE, STOPPANI GAUGE.

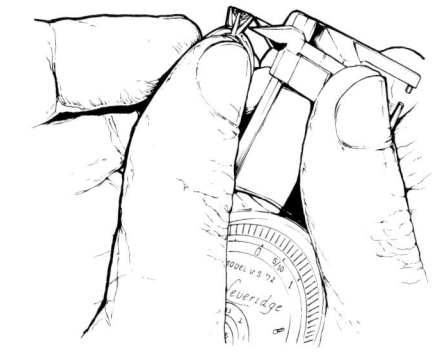

Measuring mounted diamonds with a Leveridge gauge.

Lewis, Henry Carvill (1853-1888), American professor and geologist who identified the magma associated with diamond and named it kimberlite in 1880.

Liaoning, province in northeastern China where numerous kimberlitic occurrences have been found. See CHINA, BINHAI MINE, WAFANGDIAN MINE.

Liberator Diamond, 155 ct. diamond, reportedly of high quality, found in 1942 in Gran Sabana, Venezuela. Named in honor of nineteenth

Liaoning

century political leader Simon Bolivar. Harry Winston purchased the rough in 1943 and fashioned it into three emerald cuts weighing 39.80 ct., 18.12 ct., and 8.93 ct., and a 1.44 ct. marquise. The largest emerald cut, Liberator I, is privately owned; the whereabouts of the others are unknown.

Liberia, minor diamond-producing country in western Africa. Diamonds were discovered along the Joblong River in 1910 and on the Moro and Loffa Rivers, near the Sierra Leone border, in 1955. Diamonds have also been found in the northeast, near the border with the Côte d'Ivoire (formerly the Ivory Coast). The deposits are not very rich, but the country has been a major exporter of rough smuggled in from other West African countries.

Lichtenburg, once a major alluvial diamond-producing area in the Transvaal Province, South Africa; the site of several large diamond rushes between 1925 and 1929.

Liçitacão, Brazilian agency through which local diamond production is offered for sale to the industry on a tender basis, prior to export.

life, combined effect of brilliance, dispersion, and scintillation in a diamond.

Lichtenburg

light absorption, the absorption of certain of the wavelengths making up the white light spectrum when it passes through a material such as a gemstone; those wavelengths which are transmitted together determine the perceived color of the stone. See ABSORPTION BAND, ABSORPTION LINE, CAPE LINES, ELECTROMAGNETIC SPECTRUM, EMISSION SPECTRUM, 595 NM LINE, SELECTIVE ABSORPTION, SPECTROMETER, SPECTROPHOTOMETER, SPECTRUM.

light cape, historic color grade for faint yellow diamonds in the upper middle of the Cape series, roughly equivalent to L on the GIA color-grading scale.

light carat, diamond weighing slightly less than one full (1.00) ct., usually 0.95-0.99 ct.

light half, diamond weighing slightly less than 0.50 ct., usually 0.45-0.49 ct.

light off-color, historic sorting term for rough diamonds. Obsolete.

Light of Peace Diamond, 130.27 ct. pear-shape diamond, one of 13 obtained from a 434.60 ct. rough diamond believed to have been found in Sierra Leone in the late 1960s. The other 12 were of various shapes, the largest a 9.11 ct. marquise, the smallest a 0.37 ct. pear shape. All are privately owned.

light one-carat, see LIGHT CARAT.

light return, light, including dispersed wavelengths, reflected from the internal surfaces of a diamond and returned to the eye through the crown. See DISPERSION.

light yellow, Scan. D.N. color scale term sometimes used for diamonds (over 0.47 ct.) with a noticeable (very light) yellow bodycolor, equivalent to O-R on the GIA color-grading scale.

Limestone Creek, site of alluvial diamond deposits in Western Australia, mined by Argyle Diamond Mines in the early 1980s. Closed after the AK1 Mine began production, but reopened in 1990. See SMOKE CREEK.

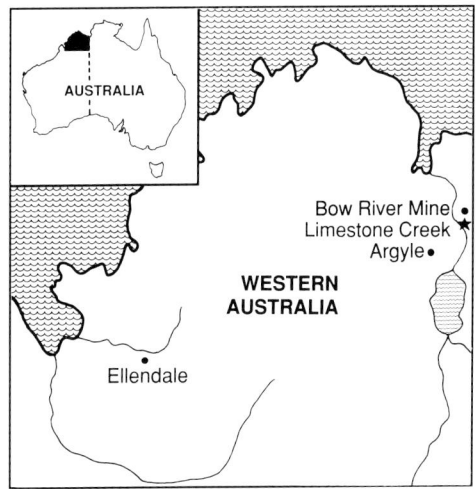
Limestone Creek

Linde Simulated Diamonds, proprietary name for yttrium aluminum garnet (YAG). Marketed as a diamond simulant.

linear accelerator, device used to accelerate electrons to high energies; used principally in studying the structure of matter, occasionally to treat diamonds. Sometimes referred to as a linac. See CYCLOTRON-TREATED DIAMOND, IRRADIATED DIAMOND, VAN DE GRAAFF GENERATOR.

Linobate, proprietary name for lithium niobate. Marketed as a diamond simulant. See LITHIUM NIOBATE.

liquid nitrogen, substance sometimes used in laboratories to cool diamonds to low temperatures (-195.8°C) to improve the resolution of the absorption spectrum. See ABSORPTION SPECTRUM, CRYOGENIC COOLING, SPECTROSCOPE.

Lisa Blue Diamond, originally a 37.21 ct. reportedly flawless, light blue round brilliant diamond. Harry Winston had it repolished to 37.05 ct. in 1961; last sold in 1967 in Europe.

Lisbon, capital city of Portugal and, in the sixteenth century, a major diamond trading center. In 1498, Portuguese explorer Vasco da Gama established a sea route between Lisbon and India. After 1725, a route was established between Lisbon and Brazil. Rough diamonds from Lisbon (and Goa) provided raw material to the emerging diamond industry in Bruges and, later, Antwerp. See GOA.

Lisbon cut, modification of the old mine or triple cut in which the main facets of the crown and pavilion are split parallel to the girdle.

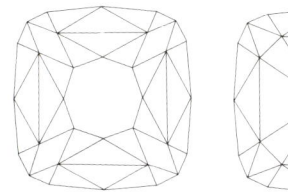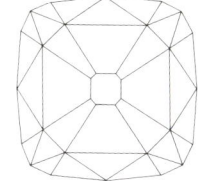

Lisbon cut

lithium niobate, relatively rare man-made gem material which, when colorless, is sometimes used as a diamond simulant. Its hardness on the Mohs scale is 6, specific gravity 4.64, refractive index 2.21-2.30, and dispersion 0.120. Manufactured from a melt by the Czochralski pulling method; marketed as Linobate.

Little Rose Diamond, see PREMIER ROSE DIAMOND.

Little Sancy Diamond, 34 ct. pear-shape diamond once owned by Nicolas Harlay, Seigneur de Sancy, a seventeenth century French nobleman. After his death in 1627, it was sold to Prince Frederick Henry (1584-1647) of Orange and inherited by his grandson, Frederick I of Prussia; the diamond was part of the Prussian Treasury for many years. The Little Sancy is now mounted as a pendant and kept in the Royal Prussian House in Bremen, Germany. Also called the Beau Sancy.

lizard-skin polish, poor polish, seen as a wavy or bumpy area, on the surface of a finished diamond.

lizard-skin polish

load, historic mining term for the volume of broken kimberlite, approximately 727 kilograms (1,600 pounds), which could be contained in a hand-pushed cart. The standard unit of measurement used to report mine yield was 100 loads (e.g., 20 carats per 100 loads). The term, now obsolete, continued to be used long after larger forms of transport were introduced. Modern mine yields are based on 100 metric tons. See YIELD.

Lobaye River, see CENTRAL AFRICAN REPUBLIC.

lobe, (1) one of the two rounded ends of a heart-shape diamond. (2) geological term describing the shape of a kimberlite or lamproite pipe.

lobe

local digger, individual who works alluvial or primary deposits in his country of origin, often by primitive means. Some local diggers are officially sanctioned by license or birthright; others operate illegally. See GARIMPEIRO.

L'Office Forestière et Minière du Congo (FORMINIÈRE), see SOCIETE FORESTIERE ET MINIERE DU CONGO (FORMINIERE).

London Diamond Bourse, one of two British diamond bourses; member of the World Federation of Diamond Bourses. Located in Hatton Garden. See BOURSE, WORLD FEDERATION OF DIAMOND BOURSES.

London Diamond Club, one of two British diamond bourses; member of the World Federation of Diamond Bourses. Located in Hatton Garden. See BOURSE, WORLD FEDERATION OF DIAMOND BOURSES (WFDB).

London Diamond Syndicate, see DIAMOND SYNDICATE.

London Syndicate, see DIAMOND SYNDICATE.

long hexagon cut, modification of the hexagon cut, created by increasing the length of one pair of sides. It resembles a baguette with two pointed ends.

long tom, archaic device consisting of a long wooden trough with battens across the bottom, used for washing and sorting alluvial gravels. Light material floats over the battens; diamonds and other heavier materials are trapped between them. See BABY, PANNING, SEPARATION.

Lonsdale, Kathleen (1903-1971), British crystallographer who developed X-ray techniques which made it possible to measure the distance between carbon atoms in diamond; using this method, she tested the rediscovered "Hannay diamonds" and suggested that they were probably natural rather than synthetic. In 1956, she was named a Dame of the British Empire in recognition of her service to science. Lonsdaleite was named in her honor. See HANNAY, JAMES BALLANTYNE.

lonsdaleite, form of carbon found in meteorites; it has the structure of graphite, but properties similar to those of diamond. A hexagonal allotrope of carbon, it has also been synthesized

Kathleen Lonsdale

from graphite by shock conversion, on an experimental basis. Named for Dame Kathleen Lonsdale. See LONSDALE, KATHLEEN.

loose goods, polished unmounted diamonds. Also called loose diamonds. See GOODS.

lot, selection of rough or polished loose diamonds, sometimes similar in sizes and qualities, sometimes mixed. See MELANGE.

lot price, per-carat price for a selection, or lot, of diamonds, contingent on the purchaser buying the entire parcel. See PICK PRICE.

Lottery Diamond, see PIGOT DIAMOND.

Louis Cartier Diamond, 107.07 ct. pear-shape diamond, reportedly flawless and colorless; one of three fashioned from a 400 ct. South African rough found in 1974. Named for the third-generation descendant of the founder of Cartier's. Current whereabouts unknown.

Louis G. Murray mv, specialized mining vessel owned by De Beers Marine, equipped with a crawler-based recovery system for use on seabeds; named in honor of the late Louis G. Murray. See MURRAY, LOUIS G.

Louis XIV Diamond, 62.05 ct. pear-shape diamond believed to have once belonged to Louis XIV of France. It was purchased by Harry Winston in 1958 and repolished into a D-flawless 58.60 ct. pear shape. Exhibited at the Louvre in 1962; sold, together with the 61.80 ct. Winston Diamond, in 1963. Last sold in Europe in 1981.

Louis XIV Diamond

loupe, (1) noun, small magnifying lens. Eye loupes, head loupes, and small folding hand loupes, or pocket lenses, are popular in the diamond and jewelry industries. Some, such as jewelers' eye loupes or watchmakers' loupes, consist of a single, uncorrected lens; some employ multiple lenses to correct for chromatic and spherical aberration. Loupes characteristically range in magnification from 2 to 20 power; 10x magnification is the standard for examining diamonds. (2) verb, to examine a diamond with a loupe. See APLANATIC LENS, CHROMATIC ABERRATION, DOUBLET LOUPE, SPHERICAL ABERRATION, TRIPLET LOUPE.

Loupe Clean, (1) term used in the CIBJO and IDC clarity-grading scales (and as a discretionary term in the Scan. D.N. System) for high clarity diamonds, corresponding to IF (internally flawless) on the GIA clarity-grading scale. (2) in the US, a term with no formal status, not capitalized when written, and used to imply that a diamond has no imperfections under 10x magnification; its use is prohibited by the Federal Trade Commission (FTC) unless the diamond is flawless. See APPENDIX E.

Lóvua, alluvial diamond deposit on the Chicapa River downstream from the Catoca kimberlite pipe in northern Angola. It is largely worked out, but small amounts of weathered kimberlite are found and treated in a nearby gravel plant.

lower-break facets, see GIRDLE FACETS.

Lower Congo-Katanga Railway Company, see COMPAGNIE CHEMIN DE FER DU BAS-CONGO-KATANGA (BCK).

lower-girdle facets, see GIRDLE FACETS.

low pressure sawing, technique of sawing strained or brittle diamonds using slower-than-normal speeds to generate less heat.

Loxton Mine, kimberlite pipe in Cape Province, South Africa; diamonds are recovered by chambering and sub-level stoping.

lozenge cut, four-sided, diamond-shaped step cut.

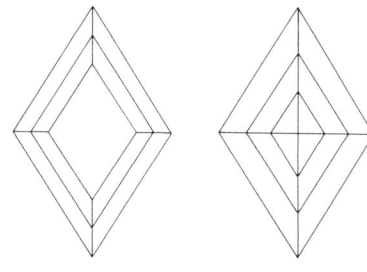

lozenge cut

lozenge facet, see QUOIN FACETS.

Luachimo River, river basin in Angola, and a significant source of diamonds; close to the Camatué and Cariué kimberlite pipes.

Lubilash, valley in Kasai Province in Zaire through which the Lubilash River flows; a source primarily of industrial diamonds.

Lucapa, region in northeastern Angola between the Luembe and Chicapa rivers (from which its name is derived). Diamonds are found where seismic faults running south/southwest cross the Chicapa, Luachimo, Chiumbe, and Calonda River valleys.

Lüderitz, town in Namibia north of the CDM concession area (Diamond Area No. 1); originally part of what was then German South West Africa. Diamonds were discovered near Lüderitz in 1908. See CDM (PTY.), LTD.; ELIZABETH BAY.

Luebo, once a major diamond-producing area in Zaire between the Lulua and Luebo Rivers; no longer active.

Lubilash and Luebo

Luembe River, river basin in Angola, in the Andrada area; a major source of alluvial diamonds. See ANDRADA, ANGOLA, LUCAPA.

luminescence, emission of visible light from a material when excited by higher energy radiation, electrical discharge, heat, or friction. See CATHODOLUMINESCENCE, EMISSION SPECTRUM, FLUORESCENCE, PHOSPHORESCENCE, PHOTOLUMINESCENCE, ULTRAVIOLET.

lumps, historical term for large pieces of kimberlite which were left in open fields, called "floors," to disintegrate. Later, steam rollers were used to expedite the process. Today, such material is passed through a crusher.

lumpy diamond, unusually deep polished diamond, often with a high crown in addition to a deep pavilion. Such diamonds were common before 1900. See DEEP PAVILION.

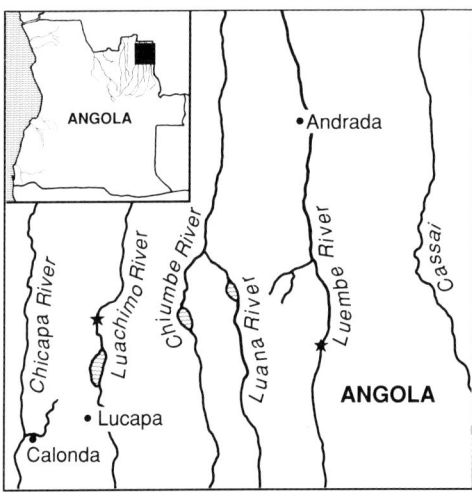

Luachimo River and Luembe River

lumpy girdle, see THICK GIRDLE.

Lunda, province in northeastern Angola, divided in 1978; Lunda Norte contains the N'Gazi (Andrada), Lucapa, and Cuango deposits. See ANDRADA, CUANGO, LUCAPA.

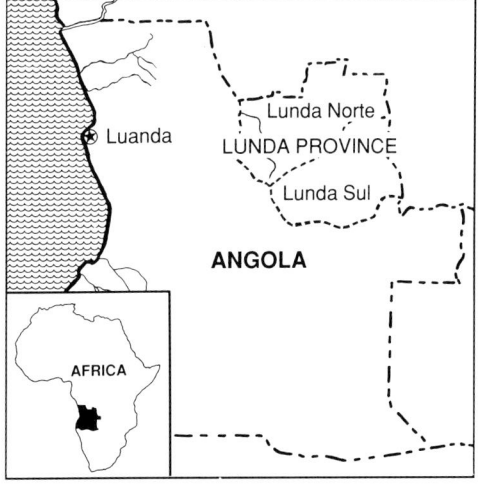

Lunda Province

luster, appearance of the surface of a polished gem in reflected light. Luster depends on refractive index (the higher the RI, the higher the luster), the reflectivity of the material, and the quality of the polish (the smoother the surface, the higher the luster—generally, the harder the material, the better the polish). Luster is described as metallic (the highest luster), adamantine, subadamantine, vitreous, subvitreous, resinous, waxy, dull, silky, or pearly; diamond's luster is adamantine.

Lusterite, proprietary name for synthetic rutile. Marketed as a diamond simulant.

Lustermeter, proprietary name for a reflectivity meter.

Lustigem, proprietary name for synthetic strontium titanate. Marketed as a diamond simulant.

M

maakbaar, Dutch, *makeable*. See MAKEABLE.

Mabel Bolls Diamond, 44.76 ct. emerald-cut diamond named for Mabel Bolls, who was known as the "Queen of Diamonds" in the 1920s; she reportedly owned more than $1,000,000 worth of diamond jewelry, at 1920s prices. Harry Winston purchased the diamond from her estate in 1950; it was last sold in Europe in 1966.

maccle, alternative spelling of macle, often used outside the US. See MACLE.

machine cutting, see AUTOMATIC BLOCKING MACHINE, AUTOMATIC POLISHING MACHINE.

macle, flat, triangular, contact-twinned diamond crystal in which the two crystals have grown together with a 180° rotation in the orientation of their internal crystal structure. Often characterized by a feathery seam on the edge, such diamonds are difficult to saw because of the different grain directions caused by the twinning. Due to their irregular, flat structure, they are often fashioned into fancy shapes. Also spelled maacle or maccle. See CONTACT TWIN, GRAIN, TWIN CRYSTAL.

Macquarie River, area in New South Wales, Australia, where diamonds were found between 1949 and 1958; the discoveries were made during gold mining operations.

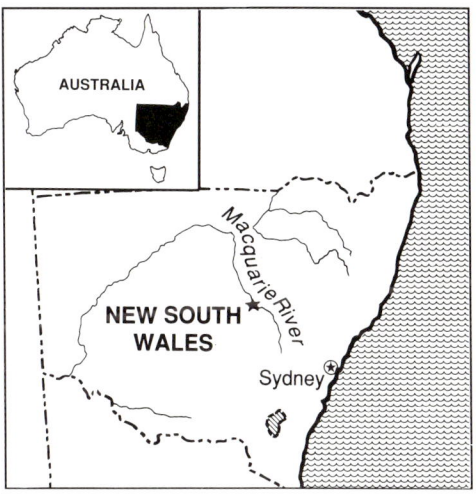

Macquarie River

macrocryst, crystals that are distinctly visible to the unaided eye.

Magalux, proprietary name for synthetic spinel. Marketed as a diamond simulant.

magic carat, diamond weighing exactly one carat or slightly more. Considered more desirable and easier to sell than a light carat. See LIGHT CARAT, MAGIC SIZE.

magic size, any of several diamond weights particularly popular with consumers: 0.25 ct., 0.33 ct., 0.50 ct., 0.75 ct., and 1.00 ct. They are called "magic" because they tend to sell more easily than diamonds weighing only a point or two less. Also called magic weight. See MAGIC CARAT.

macle

magic weight, see MAGIC SIZE.

magma, naturally occurring molten rock, generated within the earth, and capable of being intruded in existing structures or extruded onto the surface. Igneous rocks are derived from magmas through solidification.

Magna Cut, proprietary name for a modification of the standard brilliant cut, characterized by its ten-fold symmetry. It has 10 star facets, 20 bezel facets, 30 upper-girdle facets and a table on the crown; and 30 lower-girdle facets, 10 pavilion facets, and a culet on the pavilion. Seldom seen.

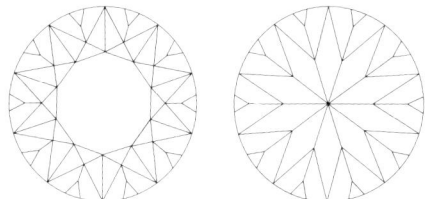

Magna Cut

Mahanadi River, watercourse approximately 375 kilometers (233 miles) northeast of Golconda, India; site of what may have been some of the richest of India's ancient alluvial diamond deposits. See GOLCONDA, SAMBALPUR GROUP.

Mahjal Diamond, see ALGEIBA STAR DIAMOND.

Maiden Lane, once the center of the diamond and jewelry industry in New York City, US; now surpassed in importance by 47th Street.

main facets, general term for the large crown and pavilion facets of a brilliant-cut diamond. See BEZEL FACET, PAVILION FACETS.

Majhgawan, site of a pipe mine and nearby alluvial diamond diggings at Ramkharia, India. Operated by the National Mineral Development Corporation (NMDC), it is now the only known primary source of diamonds in India. Majhgawan had been known since the 1800s, but was not recognized as a primary deposit until 1827. Mined on a small scale from 1937 to 1964, it was taken over by the NMDC in the 1960s and

Mahanadi River and Majhgawan

is currently reported to be a small producer of industrial and low-quality gem diamonds. See NATIONAL MINERAL DEVELOPMENT CORPORATION (NMDC), PANNA, PANNA GROUP.

major symmetry, variations in symmetry which affect a diamond's appearance, or which represent excessive weight retention; it includes such variations as perceptibly off-center tables or culets, out-of-round girdles, tables that are not parallel to the girdle, and wavy girdles. See FINISH, MINOR SYMMETRY, SYMMETRY.

make, term used to describe the relative quality of the proportions and finish of a polished diamond. See CUT.

makeable, diamond crystal, macle, cleavage, or chip which must be polished without preparation by sawing, cleaving, or splitting. The rough form often approximates the final shape after polishing, but makeables usually require more work than sawables and yield less from the rough. Also called a whole stone. Also called a maakbaar. See SAWABLE, WHOLE STONE.

Malaya Botuoboya, tributary of the Vilyiuy River in Sakha (Yakutia), the Russian Federation, CIS, said to be the site where the first diamond from the region was discovered in 1953. Also called the Lesser Botuoboya.

Malaya Botuoboya

Mallin Diamond Mines, Ltd., company which mines a dike one meter (roughly three feet) wide and 2,743 meters (9,000 feet) long near Zwar-truggens in Transvaal Province, South Africa. See HELAM MINE.

Mambéré River, see CENTRAL AFRICAN REPUBLIC.

mangelin, Indian measure of weight, equal to 1.40 ct.

man-made diamond, see SYNTHETIC DIAMOND.

mantle, the zone of the earth below the crust and above the core. Kimberlites and lamproites

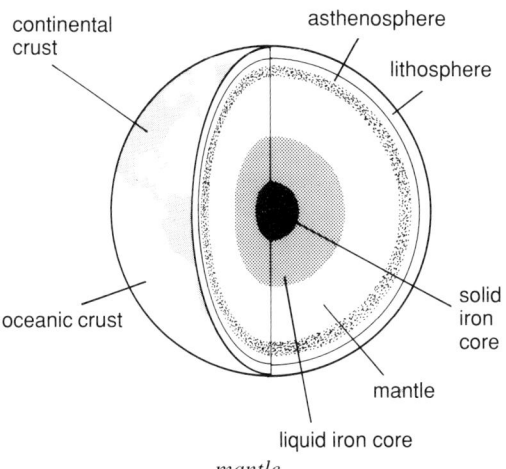

mantle

are believed to have originated in the upper part of the mantle, 150-200 kilometers (93-124 miles) below the earth's surface. See ORIGIN (OF DIAMOND).

manufacturer, individual or corporate entity responsible for planning, organizing, and administering the process of fashioning rough diamonds into polished goods for setting in jewelry. A manufacturer may execute all phases of the process, or specialize in one area, such as sawing, and may contract out one or all of the operations to others.

manufacturing, the five-stage process (design, cleaving, splitting or sawing, bruting, and polishing) of transforming a rough diamond into a polished stone. See MANUFACTURER.

Maramures diamond, misnomer for rock crystal quartz from Hungary.

Marek, Jan Ivo, British scientist who joined with Frederick B. Salt in an unsuccessful attempt to produce synthetic diamonds; they used the Moissan method, with lignite coal in place of carbon. See MOISSAN, FERDINAND FREDERIC HENRI.

Mari diamond, misnomer for rock crystal quartz from India.

Maria Diamond, 106 ct. rough diamond found in Sakha (Yakutia), the Russian Federation, CIS, by Maria Komemkima in 1966. Now in the Russian Diamond Fund in Moscow.

Marie Antoinette Blue Diamond, 5.46 ct. heart-shape diamond, described as grayish blue, set in a ring said to have belonged to Marie Antoinette. Last offered for sale in 1983, but not sold. Privately owned.

Marie Antoinette Diamond Earrings, earrings said to have been given to Marie Antoinette by Louis XVI (1754-1793) of France. The center stones are two pear-shape diamonds, reportedly colorless and weighing approximately 19 ct. and 13 ct. Now on display at the Smithsonian Institution in Washington, D.C., US.

Marie Antoinette Diamond Necklace, necklace set with 647 brilliant-cut diamonds (total weight 2,840 ct.) given to Marie Antoinette by Cardinal de Rohan in 1784. Made in two sections, the necklace was divided and sold in England in 1785. The largest diamonds were reset in another necklace, now owned by the Duke of Sutherland; other diamonds allegedly from the necklace appear from time to time.

Marigold Cut, registered name for one of five "Flower" cuts designed in 1988 by CSO consultant Gabi Tolkowsky for flat crystals which would otherwise have to be sawn, cleaved or split. A step cut with a large table, the Marigold can be polished as a hexagon with 73 facets, or a pear or heart shape with 43 facets. See DAHLIA, FIRE-ROSE, FLOWER CUTS, SUNFLOWER, ZINNIA.

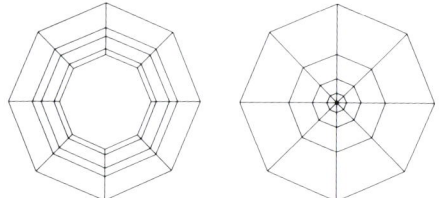

Marigold Cut

Marine areas, any of several shallow, mid-, and deep water concessions off the Namaqualand coast of South Africa and the coast of Namibia. Diamonds are recovered from the ocean bed by a variety of methods ranging from diver-operated suction devices near-shore to crawler equipment at depths of over 100 meters (328 feet); major concessionaires include Benguela Concessions, De Beers Consolidated Mines, Rand Mines, RTZ, and Trans-Hex. See BEACH MINING, DE BEERS MARINE (PTY.), LTD.; MARINE DEPOSIT, OFF-SHORE MINING.

marine deposit, coastal alluvial deposit along the shore of an ocean, and extending out to the edge of the continental shelf. Marine deposits are the result of the transportation of minerals from the interior to an ocean, usually by rivers. See ALLUVIAL DEPOSIT, MARINE TERRACE.

Marine Diamond Corporation (Pty.), Ltd., company formed in 1961 by Samuel Collins to mine off-shore diamond deposits along the coast of Namibia. The company was taken over by De Beers in 1965; it now leases its mining rights to CDM. See COLLINS, SAMUEL V.; DE BEERS MARINE (PTY.), LTD.

marine terrace, narrow, gently sloping strip of land along a coast, usually exposed by an uplifting of the foreshore or a drop in the level of the sea; subsequently eroded by the action of the waves and covered with sand, silt, or fine gravel. Diamonds are found in marine terraces north and south of the mouth of the Orange River in southern Africa. See MERENSKY, HANS; OYSTER LINE.

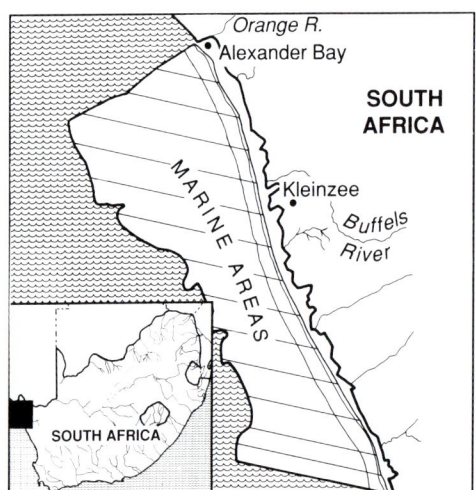

Marine areas

marine terrace

marking, task of indicating the cleaving and sawing instructions (or any special directions) on a rough diamond with India ink.

marking

markings, see GROWTH MARKINGS.

Marmarosch diamond, misnomer for rock crystal quartz from Poland, Hungary, Romania, and the Ukraine. Also spelled Marmora, Marmos, Marmoros, and Marmarozen.

marquise cut, elongated, boat-shaped brilliant cut with curving sides and pointed ends, developed in France in the 1740s. Believed to have been named after the Marquise de Pompadour, a mistress of King Louis XV. Also called navette.

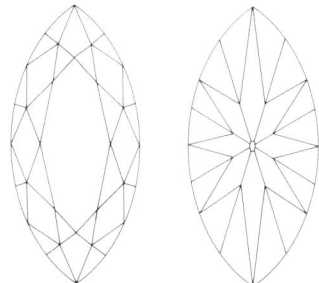

marquise cut

Martapura, diamond manufacturing and trading center in southeastern Kalimantan, Indonesia. The city is 39 kilometers (24 miles) southeast of the capital, Banjarmasin, near some of the island's historic alluvial diggings. See BORNEO, KALIMANTAN.

Martapura

Marvelite, proprietary name for synthetic strontium titanate. Marketed as a diamond simulant.

Mary of Burgundy (1457-1482), daughter of Charles the Bold of France (1433-1477), traditionally identified as the first recipient of a diamond engagement ring upon her betrothal to Archduke (later Emperor) Maximillian of Austria. The ring was set with an arrangement of "hogback" diamonds (the forerunner of today's baguette) in the shape of the Gothic letter M, an allusion either to the Virgin Mary, to Maximillian, or to Mary herself. A copy of the ring is on display in the Kunsthistorisches Museum in Vienna, Austria. See ARCHDUKE MAXIMILLIAN OF AUSTRIA, CHARLES THE BOLD.

Mascarenhas I and II Diamonds, two diamonds of 57 ct. and 67.50 ct. reportedly owned by the Portuguese Viceroy, Dom Philip Mascarenhas, and seen by Tavernier in Goa in 1648. Current whereabouts unknown.

massive, aggregate, used to describe a rock or mineral composed of closely knit groups of small crystals of one or more species. See CARBONADO.

master diamonds, sets of rough or polished diamonds of known bodycolor to which other diamonds are compared to judge their color grade. Master diamonds typically range from colorless through gradually deepening tints of yellow and brown. Also called color sample or master color set (UK), key diamonds, master set, or masterstones. See AGS COLOR-GRADING SCALE, CIBJO INTERNATIONAL COLOR-GRADING SCALE, DIAMOND GRADING, GIA COLOR-GRADING SCALE, IDC INTERNATIONAL COLOR-GRADING SCALE, NORTH DAYLIGHT, SCAN. D.N. COLOR SCALE.

master diamond cutter, term of respect given to those who have successfully planned, designed, cleaved, and supervised the polishing of large diamonds. See ASSCHER, ISAAC JOSEPH; KAPLAN, LAZARE.

master-eye effect, visual phenomenon in which the relationship between a diamond of ungraded color and an adjacent master diamond of the same color appears to change with their relative positions; the ungraded stone appears darker on one side of the master and lighter on the other. Caused by differences in color perception between the right and left eyes. See COLOR GRADING, DOMINANT EYE.

master set, see MASTER DIAMONDS.

masterstones, see MASTER DIAMONDS.

Matan Diamond, 367 ct. diamond, described as blue and variously reported to be pear-shaped, or shaped like an "indented" egg. Found on the island of Borneo in the early nineteenth century and owned by the Sultan of Matan. Some historians believe it was actually quartz. Also spelled Mattam, Matam, and Mattan. Current whereabouts unknown.

Matara diamond, misnomer for colorless-to-faintly smoky Sri Lankan zircons; they may be naturally colored or heat treated. Also spelled Matura.

Mato Grosso, state in Brazil which has been a diamond producer since the early 1700s.

Mattan Diamond, see MATAN DIAMOND.

Maui diamond, misnomer for rock crystal quartz from Hawaii, US.

Mawe, John, English author of *Treatise on Diamond and Precious Stones*, published in 1823. The book contains important information on eighteenth and nineteenth century diamond-cutting techniques.

Maxicut, proprietary name for a line of automated laser bruting machines invented by Alec Liebowitz, which use graphic image control to determine the maximum diameter and depth in relation to the optimum position of the culet. Manufactured by Diatronic Equipment of South Africa and marketed internationally by the Sure Group of Belgium. The Maxicut can be used to brute both sawn goods and makeables from 0.01 ct. up.

Maximilian Diamond, 50 ct. rough diamond, described as greenish yellow and purchased in Brazil by Maximilian, future emperor of Mexico, in 1850. Fashioned into a 33 ct. cushion shape for his wife, Princess Carlotta of Belgium, it disappeared after he was executed in Mexico in 1867. Confiscated by the US government in 1901, after an attempt to smuggle it across the border, it was sold at auction. In 1946, the diamond was acquired by Morris Nelkin, a New York jeweler. During a suspected robbery in 1961, the diamond, set in a pendant, was hidden in a garbage can and lost when the trash was collected. Current whereabouts unknown.

Maximillian, Archduke, see ARCHDUKE MAXIMILLIAN OF AUSTRIA.

Mazarin, Cardinal Jules (1602-1661), French cardinal and minister of King Louis XIV, credited with popularizing the early brilliant cut.

Mazarin cut, see DOUBLE CUT, SINGLE CUT.

Mazarin Diamonds, eighteen diamonds bequeathed to the French Crown by Cardinal Jules Mazarin. In 1691 the collection included the Sancy, the Mirror of Portugal, the Boin-Taburet, and the Grand Mazarin. A century later, another inventory of the French Crown Jewels listed different weights for the Mazarin Diamonds, suggesting that some had been exchanged, and some repolished. Only six of the Mazarins were recovered after the robbery at the Garde Mueble in 1792: the 55.23 ct. Sancy, the 19.10 ct. Grand Mazarin (Mazarin VII), the 13.97 ct. Mazarin IV, the 15.14 ct. Mazarin VIII, the 10.52 ct. Mazarin XIII, the 6.16 ct. Mazarin XVI, and two unnamed stones each weighing 18.25 ct. When the Crown Jewels were sold in 1887, the only authentic Mazarin among them was the Grand Mazarin; it was purchased by the Banque de France and the Musées de France in 1978, and is now displayed in the Galérie d'Apollon at the Louvre Museum in Paris. The current whereabouts of the rest are unknown.

mazel u'bracha, Yiddish, *luck and a blessing*; the phrase, accompanied by a handshake, is traditionally used in the diamond trade to conclude and seal business arrangements or contracts. Also spelled *mazel und broche*.

MB, abbreviation for makeable(s). See MAKEABLE.

Mbuji-Mayi, large town in southern Zaire, in the center of the Kasai diamond-producing province. The nearby mine is operated by MIBA, and there are numerous alluvial diggings in the area. The town has a population estimated at over 800,000.

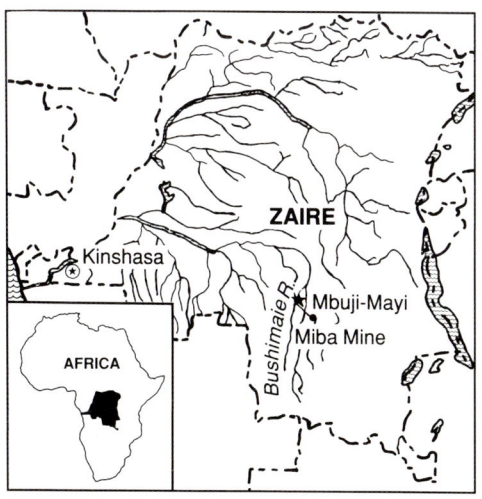

Mbuji-Mayi

McKee, R. H., American researcher who unsuccessfully attempted diamond synthesis at Columbia University in New York, US, in the 1930s by melting iron, ferro-silicon, ferro-phosphorus, and carbon and pouring the mixture into a hollow steel ball.

McLean Diamond, 31.26 ct. cushion shape, D color, VS_2 diamond named for socialite Evalyn Walsh McLean (1886-1947), who also owned the Hope, the Star of the East, and the Star of the South. When she died, the McLean was purchased by Harry Winston; it was sold to the Duchess of Windsor in 1950. In 1987, after her death, her jewelry was auctioned at Sotheby's in Geneva, and the McLean was sold to a Japanese buyer.

McLean Diamond

courtesy of Harry Winston, Inc.

mechanical balance, instrument of ancient origin, used to determine the weight of gemstones; it consists of a fulcrum on which a beam with two suspended pans is balanced. The gem is placed in one pan; counterweights are added to the other until the balance is in equilibrium. General term for all balances which work on this principle. See ELECTRONIC BALANCE, PORTABLE BALANCE, RIDER BALANCE, SINGLE-PAN BALANCE.

mechanical dop, adjustable clamp which holds a diamond at the correct facet angle on the scaife. Developed in the mid-1890s, mechanical dops are easier to use and often more accurate than solder dops. See BRUTING DOP, POLISHING DOP.

Megadiamond, proprietary name for synthetic industrial diamond developed by H. Tracy Hall in 1971.

Meister Diamond, 118.05 ct. cushion-shape brilliant diamond, described as fancy intense yellow and believed to have been found in the early days of Kimberley. Named for its owner, the late Walter Meister of Zurich, Switzerland.

mélange, assortment of diamonds of mixed weights and/or qualities, usually (but not always) in sizes larger than mêlée. French for *mixture*.

mêlée, (1) polished eight-cut, single-cut, rose-cut, or full-cut brilliants ranging from 0.05 to 0.20 ct. (2) rough sorting term for regular, sawable stones weighing up to 1 ct. from which polished mêlée can be manufactured. French, meaning *mixed*. Also spelled melée, melee. See SERIE, SIZES.

memo, see CONSIGNMENT.

Merensky, Hans (1871-1952), German geologist who discovered the "oyster line" deposits in Namaqualand, South Africa, in 1926. After he recognized the relationship between known marine diamond deposits and the fossilized oysters found in a line along the marine terraces parallel to the sea, Merensky's H.M. Association purchased claims at Alexander Bay and elsewhere along the coast. See OYSTER LINE.

Merthyr diamond, misnomer for rock crystal quartz from southern Wales, UK.

Messina Mine, narrow, vertical kimberlite fissure mined as part of the Bellsbank/Bobbejaan operations near Barkly West, South Africa. Diamonds are recovered by overhand shrinkage. See BELLSBANK, FISSURE, OVERHAND SHRINKAGE.

meteoritic diamonds, minute diamonds found in craters created by meteorites, either carried by the meteor from extra-terrestrial sources, or formed by the heat and shock of impact. Meteors are a natural source of lonsdaleite. See LONSDALEITE.

metric carat, see CARAT.

metric grain, one-quarter of a metric carat. See GRAIN.

Mexican black diamond, misnomer for faceted hematite.

Mexican diamond, misnomer for rock crystal quartz.

MIBA, see SOCIETE MINIERE DE BAKWANGA.

Miba Mine, large diamond mine in Mbuji-Mayi, Kasai Province, Zaire, 80 percent of which is owned by the government agency Société Minière de Bakwanga and 20 percent by SIBEKA, which manages the mine. Production is sold through Britmond to the CSO. See SOCIETE D'ENTREPRISE ET D'INVESTISSEMENTS S.A. (SIBEKA), SOCIETE MINIERE DE BAKWANGA (MIBA).

micrometer, instrument for making precise linear measurements such as diameter, depth, and length on a gemstone. The millimeter screw micrometer is commonly used to measure diamonds; modern micrometers often display measurements digitally. See LEVERIDGE GAUGE, MOE GAUGE, STOPPANI GAUGE.

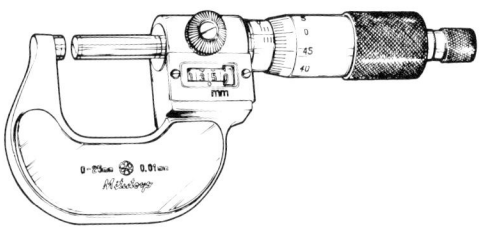

micrometer

microscope, optical instrument with a lens or combination of lenses to magnify features that may be indistinct or invisible to the unaided eye. See BINOCULAR MICROSCOPE, GEMOLOGICAL MICROSCOPE, LOUPE, MONOCULAR MICROSCOPE, OBJECTIVE LENS, OCULAR LENS.

Middleville diamond, local misnomer for rock crystal quartz from Herkimer County, New York, US. See HERKIMER DIAMOND.

Milano Industries, Ltd., Israeli manufacturer of computerized bruting and centering machines. The company's SHANY-1 system is capable of bruting two diamonds from 0.01 ct. to 5 ct. simultaneously. Other products include a Faceted Girdle Machine (FGM) and an angle setting device compatible with automated polishing machines developed by other manufacturers.

milky diamond, diamond with a hazy appearance caused by groups of minute inclusions, excessive fluorescence, graining, coating, or abrasion.

mill, alternative term for scaife.

millimeter micrometer, any micrometer that is calibrated in millimeters and fractions thereof. See LEVERIDGE GAUGE, MICROMETER, MOE GAUGE, STOPPANI GAUGE.

Minas Gerais, historic and contemporary diamond-producing state in Brazil; there are alluvial deposits at Tiros, Estrela do Sul, Coromandel, Romaria, Abaeté, Grão Mogol, and Diamantina, among other places.

mine, excavation for the extraction of metals and/or other minerals from surface or underground deposits. See ALLUVIAL MINING, BEACH MINING, OFF-SHORE MINING, OPEN BENCH MINING, OPEN PIT MINING, UNDERGROUND MINING.

mine cut, see OLD MINE CUT.

miner, person who extracts metals and/or other minerals from surface or underground deposits. See MINE.

mineral, naturally-occurring crystalline material with a characteristic chemical composition and crystal structure.

Miner Diamond, 44.62 ct. well-formed rough diamond crystal found in the Mir Pipe, Sakha (Yakutia), the Russian Federation, CIS, in the 1960s. Believed to be in the Russian Diamond Fund in Moscow.

mining, process of extracting metals and/or other minerals from surface or underground deposits. See ALLUVIAL MINING, BEACH MINING, OFF-SHORE MINING, OPEN PIT MINING, UNDERGROUND MINING.

Mining Triangle, area of historic and contemporary alluvial diamond deposits in southwestern Minas Gerais, Brazil, between the Paranaíba and Grande Rivers. In Portuguese, *Triângulo Mineiro*. See MINAS GERAIS.

Mining Triangle

minor symmetry, variations in facet shape and placement which are so slight as to have little or no effect on a diamond's beauty or value; it includes such variations as a slightly off-center table or culet, pointing, or alignment. See FINISH, MAJOR SYMMETRY, PROPORTIONS.

Mirabeau diamond, misnomer for rock crystal quartz from Ramuzat, France.

miracle crown, miracle head, miracle top, see ILLUSION HEAD.

Miridis, proprietary name for synthetic rutile. Marketed as a diamond simulant.

Mirnyi, diamond-mining town in the center of the Republic of Sakha (Yakutia), Russian Federation, CIS, where the headquarters of Yakutalmaz are located. Also spelled Mirny. See YAKUTALMAZ.

Mir Pipe, small but rich diamond-bearing kimberlite pipe (6.9 surface hectares; 17 acres) in the Vilyiuy River basin in The Republic of Sakha (Yakutia), the Russian Federation, CIS, 480 kilometers (300 miles) south of the Arctic Circle. The pipe was discovered in 1955; open pit mining began in 1960, but serious flooding in 1990-1991 caused operations to be suspended. Mir means *peace* in Russian.

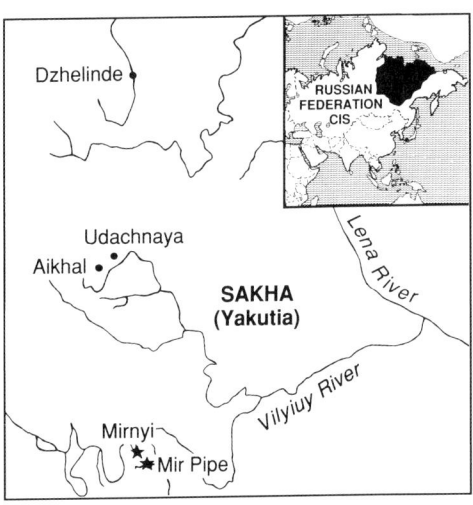

Mirnyi and Mir Pipe

Mirror of Portugal Diamond, rectangular table-cut diamond estimated to weigh 20.30 ct.; once part of the Portuguese Crown Jewels, later owned by King James I of England (1566-1625) and then by his son, Charles I (1600-1649). Used as collateral for an unpaid loan during England's Civil War, it was forfeited, sold, and came into the possession of Cardinal Mazarin of France. When he died in 1661, he bequeathed it to the French Crown; it was later stolen in the robbery of the French Treasury in 1792. Current whereabouts unknown. See MAZARIN DIAMONDS.

misgrading, incorrectly grading a diamond for color, clarity, or proportions, or misstating its size or weight.

misrepresentation, giving customers incorrect or incomplete information. In selling diamonds or other gems, this applies to color or clarity grades, weight, proportions, the nature of the material, and whether or not it has been treated or enhanced in any way. In most jurisdictions, misrepresentation is actionable under civil and, sometimes, criminal law, whether done through ignorance, omission, or intent to defraud.

Mitchell's Bay, see KOINGNAAS.

Mittag, historic name for one of the important alluvial mining areas along the Namibian coast between Oranjemund and Lüderitz; also known as Area M. Operated by CDM. See AFFENRUCKEN, BEACH MINING, GEMSBOK, KERBEHUK, UUBVLEY.

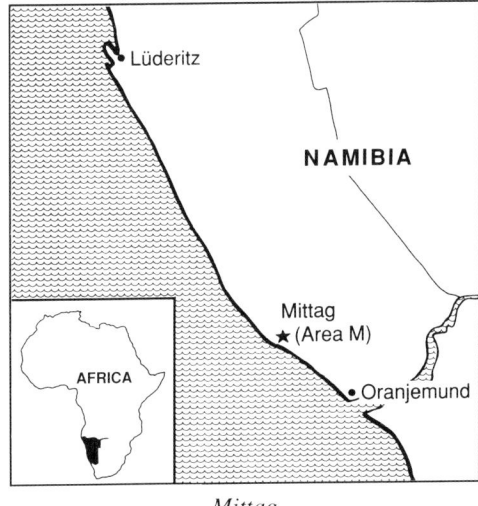

Mittag

mixed cut, stone with a brilliant-cut crown and a step-cut pavilion, or vice versa. See BARION CUT, FLOWER CUTS, ROYAL CUTS.

Moach 1, early automatic bruting machine manufactured and marketed by Diaminir Ltd. of Israel. See DIAMINIR, LTD.

Modder River, tributary of the Vaal River, between Kimberley and Bloemfontein in South Africa, once a source of alluvial diamonds.

model, (1) the shape of a rough diamond prior to polishing. (2) three-dimensional, full-size version of the proposed final shape of a diamond. Often made of transparent material; usually done when a large diamond is about to be fashioned.

mode rose cut, hexagonal rose cut with a flat base and six facets on the crown.

modified brilliant cut, cut based on the round brilliant, but with either more or fewer facets than the standard 58 (or 57).

Moe gauge, measuring device calibrated in Moes, units of measure unique to the instrument (3.2 Moes equal one millimeter). The weight of mounted or unmounted round brilliant-cut diamonds can be estimated by cross-referencing Moes measurements for diameter and depth to a set of tables supplied with the instrument. See LEVERIDGE GAUGE, MILLIMETER MICROMETER, STOPPANI GAUGE.

Moe gauge

Mogok diamond, misnomer for colorless topaz from Mogok, Burma.

Mogul cut, historic cut which usually has a broad, often asymmetrical base, a crown with either four shallow facets or a table, and two or more rows of facets angling down to the base. The Taj-i-Mah Diamond is Mogul cut.

Mogul Diamond, see GREAT MOGUL DIAMOND.

Mohs scale, commonly used imprecise scale of the comparative hardness of minerals, developed in 1822 by German mineralogist Frederich Mohs. Based on ten well-known, readily available minerals ranked in simple order of descending hardness: diamond (10), corundum (9), topaz (8), quartz (7), feldspar (6), apatite (5), fluorite (4), calcite (3), gypsum (2), and talc (1), each of which can scratch a mineral of equal or lesser hardness. The divisions are not equal or proportional, *e.g.*, the difference in hardness between diamond (10) and corundum (9) is far greater than that between corundum and topaz (8). See BRINELL HARDNESS TEST, DIRECTIONAL HARDNESS, HARDNESS, HARDNESS POINTS, INDENTATION TEST, KNOOP INDENTATION HARDNESS TEST, SCLEROMETER, SCRATCH HARDNESS, VICKERS HARDNESS TEST.

Moissan, Ferdinand Frédéric Henri (1852-1907), French chemist who unsuccessfully attempted to produce synthetic diamonds in 1893, by fusing iron and carbon in an electric furnace and plunging the molten mass into both water and molten lead.

monochromatic light, light consisting of only one color. See WHITE LIGHT.

monocrystal, single crystal, often manufactured synthetically.

monocular microscope, microscope with only one ocular lens unit. See GEMOLOGICAL MICROSCOPE, OBJECTIVE LENS, OCULAR LENS.

Montana diamond, misnomer for rock crystal quartz from Montana, US.

Moon Diamond, 183 ct., round brilliant-cut diamond, described as slightly yellow, and sold at auction in London in 1942. Current whereabouts unknown.

Moon of Baroda Diamond, 24 ct. pear-shape Indian diamond, described as light yellow, said to have been sold by an Indian prince who was in financial difficulty at the end of World War II. Worn by screen actress Marilyn Monroe in the film "Gentlemen Prefer Blondes," it was auctioned by Christie's, New York, in 1991.

Mora diamond, misnomer for rock crystal quartz from New Mexico, US.

Morro do Chapéu, site of historic alluvial diamond deposits in Bahia Province, Brazil.

Morse, Henry D. (1826-1888), American diamond manufacturer who modified the design of lumpy, European-cut diamonds to create maximum brilliance and dispersion. His Dutch-trained employees resisted these changes, so American men and women were trained instead; their repolishing skills made his Boston,

Massachusetts factory famous. Morse's efforts between 1860 and 1880 led to the development of the American brilliant cut. He also cut the Dewey Diamond in 1869. See FIELD, CHARLES M.; TOLKOWSKY THEORETICAL BRILLIANT CUT.

mount, (1) to place or arrange a gemstone in jewelry. (2) sometimes used as a noun, as a synonym for mounting. See MOUNTING.

Mountain of Light Diamond, see KOH-I-NUR DIAMOND.

Mountain of Splendor Diamond, 135 ct. diamond, reported to have once been part of the Persian Regalia, although it was not recorded as being among the Crown Jewels of Iran listed in 1966. Current whereabouts unknown.

mounted goods, diamonds set in jewelry.

mounting, metal framework in which gemstones are set to make various articles of jewelry. Usually refers to rings.

Mount Ross, site of numerous lamproite pipes in New South Wales, Australia. Early bulk sampling exploration efforts by the Cluff Copeton-Bingara Project yielded 80 cts. of diamonds from four pipes; 16 discrete pipes have been discovered in the area. Drilling projects were carried out over the pipe structures of Mount Ross, Collas Hill, and Ryders; operations were reduced to a maintenance level in 1992. Alluvial diamonds have been mined at nearby Copeton since the early 1900s.

Mr. Diamond, proprietary name for colorless synthetic sapphire. Marketed as a diamond simulant.

Multifacet Diamond, proprietary name for a brilliant cut with a polished faceted girdle.

multiple-layer diamond dressing tool, tool used to straighten and smooth grinding wheels.

Murfreesboro, town in the state of Arkansas, US, near the Crater of Diamonds State Park, site of a diamond-bearing lamproite pipe where occasional diamond discoveries are made. See CRATER OF DIAMONDS STATE PARK.

Murray, Louis G. (1924-1984), De Beers Director and Chief Geologist; killed in a helicopter accident in South America. A mining vessel belonging to De Beers Marine is named in his honor. See LOUIS G. MURRAY MV.

Mutzschen diamond, misnomer for rock crystal quartz from Germany.

Mwadui Mine, see WILLIAMSON DIAMOND MINE.

N

naat, Dutch, for *seam*. (1) twinned diamond, usually flat in its regular form, of any size. (2) seam where the twinned stones join. If a naat is encountered during sawing, problems frequently arise. (3) knot, or harder cutting direction, encountered when sawing a diamond. See CROSS NAAT, KNOT, MACLE, TWIN CRYSTAL.

NAG, see NATIONAL ASSOCIATION OF GOLDSMITHS OF GREAT BRITAIN AND IRELAND.

naif, (1) natural, unpolished surface or skin of a rough diamond. Small pieces of naif are sometimes left on polished stones, usually on the girdle, to indicate that maximum yield has been obtained. (2) well-formed, undistorted diamond crystal with bright faces. (3) diamond which is pointed rather than flat. Also spelled naife, naive, or nyf. See NATURAL, POINT NAIF.

naife, see NAIF.

nailhead, round brilliant diamond with a dark center which resembles the head of a nail; caused by a pavilion depth greater than 48 percent.

nailhead

naive, see NAIF.

Namaqualand, region south of the Orange River on the Atlantic coast of South Africa that contains extensive alluvial diamond deposits; the majority are in uplifted marine terraces where diamonds were deposited by long-shore currents. Major deposits are worked by the Namaqualand Mines Division of De Beers Consolidated Mines. To the north of the Orange River is Namibia. See BEACH MINING; MERENSKY, HANS; OFF-SHORE MINING; OYSTER LINE; STATE ALLUVIAL DIGGINGS.

Namaqualand State Mines, see ALEXCOR, STATE ALLUVIAL DIGGINGS.

Namibia, country, formerly German South-West Africa, which has been an important diamond producer since alluvial and beach terrace deposits were discovered in 1908. They are located along a 500 kilometer (310 mile) coastline which runs north along the Atlantic Ocean from the mouth of the Orange River to Conception Bay. The area is mined principally by CDM. Inland deposits are mined along the northern banks of the Orange River, while small concessions have been evaluated in the Kao-koveld. Over 90 percent of the country's production is of gem quality. See AUCHAS; CDM (PTY.), LTD.; CHAMEIS; ELIZABETH BAY; LUDERITZ; ORANJEMUND.

Nandyal Group, historical group of alluvial diamond diggings located between the Palar and Krishna Rivers in India.

nanometer (nm), unit of length equal to one billionth of a meter; used to measure electromagnetic wavelengths, such as those in the spectrum of visible light. See ANGSTROM UNIT.

Napoleon Diamond Necklace, necklace made of 47 diamonds (total weight 275 ct.) presented by the Emperor Napoleon I (1769-1821) to his wife, Empress Marie-Louise, when she gave birth to their son. Sold to a French collector in 1948, and later to Harry Winston; purchased by Marjorie Merriweather Post, who donated it to the Smithsonian Institution in Washington, D.C.

Nassak Diamond, originally an 89.59 ct. colorless, triangle-shaped Indian diamond said to have been set as an eye in a statue of the Goddess Shiva in a Hindu temple near Nasik, India, 180 kilometers (110 miles) northeast of Bombay. It was seized and presented to the British East India Company in 1818, repolished to 80.50 ct. in London, and bought at auction in

Napoleon Diamond Necklace

1837 by the Marquess of Westminster, who mounted it in the hilt of his dress sword. Sold by the second Duke of Westminster in 1926, and later purchased by Harry Winston, who had it repolished into a D-flawless 43.38 ct. emerald cut. Acquired by the King of Saudi Arabia in 1977. Sometimes called the Eye of Shiva Diamond.

National Association of Goldsmiths of Great Britain and Ireland (NAG), organization of jewelers founded in 1894. The parent company of the Gemmological Association and Gem Testing Laboratory of Great Britain; the two are no longer associated.

National Diamond Mining Company (Sierra Leone), Ltd. (DIMINCO), state-controlled mining agency in Sierra Leone. Production is obtained from alluvial diggings, although some kimberlitic occurrences are known.

National Mineral Development Corporation of India (NMDC), government agency responsible for the exploration and development of mineral resources in India. It also operates the Panna Diamond Mine some 320 kilometers (200 miles) southeast of Agra. See PANNA MINE.

natural, portion of the original surface, or skin, of a rough diamond which is sometimes left on a fashioned stone, usually on the girdle, to indicate that maximum yield has been obtained. See GROWTH MARKINGS, NAIF, TRIGON.

natural color, bodycolor of a diamond which has not been artificially altered by coating, filling, irradiation, heat, or any other means.

natural diamond, diamond formed by nature; one which is not synthetic. The color and clarity of natural diamonds may be altered by a variety of methods. See COATED DIAMOND, ENHANCEMENT, FILLED DIAMOND, IRRADIATED DIAMOND, LASER DRILLING, NATURAL COLOR, SYNTHETIC DIAMOND.

natural grit, diamond powder made by crushing natural diamonds; used as an abrasive. See SYNTHETIC DIAMOND GRIT.

natural point, elongated diamond crystal, particularly one with sharp points.

navet, see NAVETTE.

navette, French, meaning *little boat*; an alternate term for marquise, used primarily for colored stones. Also spelled navet. See MARQUISE CUT.

Navsari, major Indian diamond-manufacturing center 230 kilometers (143 miles) north of Bombay, where both medium quality brilliants and better quality fancy shapes are polished. Navsari emerged as a cutting center in the mid-1950s; by 1992, an estimated 25,000 workers were employed there.

Nd-YAG, neodymium-doped yttrium aluminum garnet (YAG). Man-made gem material also used extensively as a laser rod in automated diamond manufacturing systems. See YAG LASER.

Navsari

near-colorless, trade term used to describe diamonds that appear colorless in a face-up position, but which actually contain slight tints of yellow. See COLOR GRADING.

near-gem, (1) term used to describe a rough diamond whose color and clarity is such that it may be either polished or used in industry, depending on market conditions. In some manufacturing centers where labor costs are low, such rough can be economically fashioned for use in jewelry. (2) English translation of the Dutch proprietary name *Nier-Gem*. See NIER-GEM.

needle, fine, elongated inclusion rarely seen in diamonds, but common in sapphire and garnet. More correctly called an acicular inclusion.

negative crystal, cavity enclosed in a gemstone, the outline of which coincides with its possible crystal form. Rare in diamond.

neodymium-YAG Laser, see YAG LASER.

Nepal Diamond, originally a 79.50 ct. pear-shape diamond from India, reportedly colorless and flawless, believed to have come from the Golconda region. Owned by Nepalese royalty until the 1950s; purchased by Harry Winston in 1957 and repolished to 79.41 ct. Sold privately in Europe in 1961.

Nepal Pink Diamond, reported to be a 72 ct. old Indian cut diamond, described as rose pink. Current whereabouts unknown.

Netanya, diamond-manufacturing center specializing in small fancies, 40 kilometers (25 miles) north of Tel Aviv. Operations began in the 1950s; in 1992 there were some 192 factories employing an estimated 2,900 people.

neutron, uncharged atomic particle released during a fission reaction in a nuclear reactor. See IRRADIATED DIAMOND, REACTOR-TREATED DIAMOND.

Nevada diamond, misnomer for obsidian from Nevada, US. Also called Nevada black diamond.

New Almasi, Ltd., small diamond mining company operating near Mwadui, Tanzania, in conjunction with Williamson Diamonds. See WILLIAMSON DIAMOND MINE, WILLIAMSON DIAMONDS, LTD.

New Eland Mine, small diamond pipe mine near Boshof, Orange Free State, South Africa. Now closed; the tailings are being reworked by Trans Hex Group.

New Israel Club for Commerce in Diamonds, Ltd., one of three Israeli diamond bourses; member of the World Federation of Diamond Bourses. See BOURSE, WORLD FEDERATION OF DIAMOND BOURSES (WFDB).

New Rush, see KIMBERLEY MINE.

New South Wales, Australian state where alluvial diamonds have been found since the 1850s; until the discovery of the deposits in Western Australia, it was the country's principal diamond-producing region. Exploration efforts in New South Wales have increased in recent years.

New York, principal city in the state of New York, US, and center of the American diamond industry. The city's diamond manufacturers and dealers are concentrated around 47th Street in the borough of Manhattan. See MAIDEN LANE.

Niarchos Diamond, 128.25 ct. D-flawless pear-shape diamond, one of three large stones fashioned from a reportedly flawless and colorless 426.50 ct. rough found in the Premier Mine in 1954 and purchased by Harry Winston in 1956. (The others are a 27.62 ct. marquise and a 40 ct. emerald cut.) After cutting, Winston sold all three to Stavros S. Niarchos, Greek shipowner and industrialist. Repolished in 1987 to 128.21 ct.; it is also called the Ice Queen Diamond.

Niarchos Diamond (photo courtesy of Harry Winston, Inc.)

nick, small chip on a facet junction or girdle edge of a polished diamond, usually caused by a light blow; not to be confused with kerf.

nick

Niekerk, Schalk van, see VAN NIEKERK, SCHALK.

Niekerk's Hope, early alluvial diamond digging on the Vaal River, Cape Province, South Africa.

Nier-Gem, proprietary name for yttrium aluminum garnet (YAG). Marketed as a diamond simulant.

nitrogen, (N), trace element believed to be the cause of color in Type I yellow diamonds.

Nizam Diamond, partially fashioned diamond reported to weigh approximately 277 ct. in 1847. Models show it as a concave-based, elongated, domed stone covered with irregular, concave facets. Believed to have been found in the Kollur Mines of Golconda, India, around 1835. The diamond was once owned by the Nizams, the administrators and ruling family of Hyderabad. Also spelled Nizzam. Current whereabouts unknown.

nm, abbreviation for nanometer.

NMDC, see NATIONAL MINERAL DEVELOPMENT CORPORATION OF INDIA.

Nooitgedacht, alluvial diamond deposit near Barkly West, Cape Province, South Africa, once owned by De Beers Consolidated Mines. It has been worked by licensed diggers, and is now owned privately. See VENTER DIAMOND.

normal, imaginary line perpendicular to a surface at any point at which light strikes. Light behavior is often described relative to the normal. See ANGLE OF INCIDENCE, ANGLE OF REFLECTION, ANGLE OF REFRACTION, CRITICAL ANGLE, CRITICAL ANGLE CONE, TOTAL INTERNAL REFLECTION.

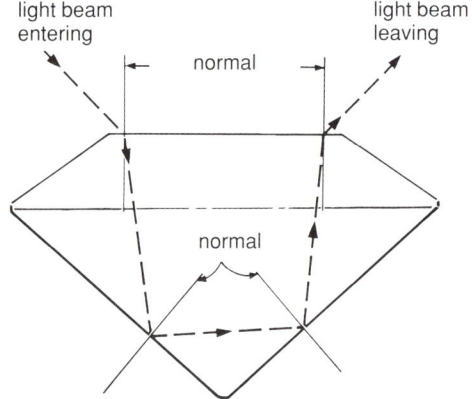

normal color range, range of diamond colors from colorless (D on the GIA color scale) and near colorless (H) down through light yellow and light brown (Z). Diamonds are generally considered less valuable as color becomes more noticeable, until the tone and saturation are deep enough to be called fancy color. To the untrained eye, little or no color is perceptible in small stones in the upper to middle part of this range. See BODYCOLOR, COLOR-GRADING.

north daylight, light source traditionally thought to be ideal for color grading diamonds; believed to vary little in intensity and color, to be relatively shadow-free, and to contain the least amount of ultraviolet. In the northern hemisphere, it is defined as the illumination from the northern sky between 10 o'clock and 12 noon on a moderately overcast morning during spring or fall; in the southern hemisphere, a similar standard is based on light from the southern sky. Most modern grading is done under controlled artificial light, although the Central Selling Organisation continues to color grade rough under natural light. Sometimes called north light. See COLOR GRADING, DIAMOND-LITE, FLUORESCENCE.

novelty cut

north light, see NORTH DAYLIGHT.

novelty cuts, cuts based on shapes such as stars, flowers, initials, and other representational motifs.

nuclear reactor, device which initiates and controls the splitting of atoms in radioactive materials such as uranium and plutonium. The neutrons and gamma rays produced by the process can be used to alter the color of diamonds. See IRRADIATED DIAMOND.

Nur-ul-Ain Diamond, oval drop-shape, brilliant-cut diamond estimated to weigh 60 ct. and described as rose pink, believed to have been fashioned (together with the Darya-i-Nur) from the Great Table Diamond in the early nineteenth century. In 1958 it was set with 323 smaller diamonds in a diadem created by Harry Winston for the Iranian Crown Jewels. The name means *Light of the Eye* in Persian.

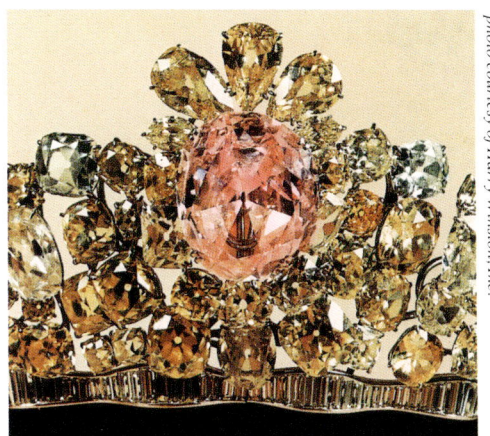

photo courtesy of Harry Winston, Inc.

Nur-ul-Ain Diamond

N. W. Ayer and Son, American advertising agency which has designed and placed generic product advertising for De Beers in the US since 1939. Soon after they were awarded the account, they introduced the slogan "Diamonds Are Forever". All US diamond marketing programs are developed and implemented by the firm; both the Diamond Information Center and the Diamond Promotion Service are located in Ayer's New York City office. See DIAMOND INFORMATION CENTER (DIC), DIAMOND PROMOTION SERVICE (DPS).

nyf, see NAIF.

O

Oaxacan diamond, misnomer for rock crystal quartz from Mexico. Also called Oacamer or Oaxacan quartz diamond.

objective lens, lens, or combination of lenses, in a compound microscope which produces an enlarged, inverted image of an object. The objective is usually the optical component closest to the subject. See OCULAR LENS.

Occidental diamond, misnomer for rock crystal quartz.

ocean mining, see OFF-SHORE MINING.

Ocean of Light Diamond, see DARYA-I-NUR DIAMOND.

octagon cut, eight-sided cut, usually a step cut, though it may be either a brilliant or mixed cut. The relative length of the sides, and the angles between them, may vary.

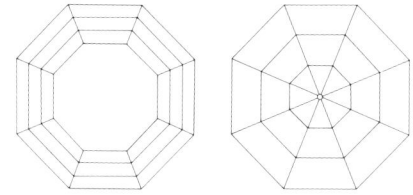

octagon cut

octagon work, process of placing the eight pavilion main facets and eight crown main facets on a diamond (the placement of the crown facets gives the table its octagonal shape). See BLOCKING, CROSS-WORKING.

octahedral, relating to the form or structure of an octahedron. See OCTAHEDRON.

octahedral cleavage, cleavage at right angles to any of the four octahedral directions in a diamond or other isometric crystal. See OCTAHEDRAL PLANE.

octahedral direction, imaginary line at right angles to an octahedral plane in either a rough or polished diamond. Cleavage can be effected at right angles to the octahedral direction.

octahedral face, one of the eight plane triangular surfaces which form an octahedral crystal. See CLEAVAGE PLANE.

octahedral plane, any plane parallel to one of the eight plane triangular surfaces which form an octahedral crystal. See OCTAHEDRAL DIRECTION.

octahedron, one of the seven basic forms of the isometric, or cubic, crystal system, with eight equilateral triangular faces, each of which intersects all three crystallographic axes at an equal distance from the center of the crystal. The octahedron is one of the most common forms assumed by diamond crystals. See HABIT.

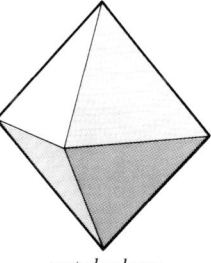

octahedron

ocular lens, the optical unit of a microscope through which the observer views the object under examination; the eyepiece. See OBJECTIVE LENS.

Oda, region in Ghana where alluvial diamond deposits are located.

off-center culet, culet which is not centered in relation to the girdle outline. When the variation is noticeable, it is considered a major symmetry feature. Also called an eccentric culet.

off-center table, table which is not centered in relation to the girdle outline; caused by polishing opposing crown facets at different angles or opposing bezel facets of different sizes. An off-center table may also be inclined in relation to the girdle plane. Also called an eccentric table.

off-color diamond, diamond with a tint of color, such as yellow or brown, which is apparent to the unaided eye.

official sample, range of rough diamonds representing the complete intake of the Central Selling Organisation, and against which official producer samples are prepared. Its purpose is to ensure that standards of assortment for both purchase and sale are consistent. See OFFICIAL SAMPLE.

off-shore mining, mining the sea-bed in waters from the high water line to the edge of the continental shelf. Various methods are used, ranging from diver-operated suction devices to underwater crawlers. Also called ocean or sea mining. See BEACH MINING; COLLINS, SAMUEL V.; DE BEERS MARINE (PTY.), LTD.

oilie, American term for a light yellow diamond which fluoresces blue in daylight. Also spelled oily. See FLUORESCENCE.

old carat, loosely defined unit of gemstone weight used prior to the standardization of the metric carat (200 mg) in the early twentieth century. Old carats ranged from 188.5 mg in Bologna, Italy, to 213.5 mg in Persia. See APPENDIX H.

old English cut, see SINGLE CUT.

old European cut, earliest known form of brilliant cut with a circular girdle. Characterized by a very small table, a heavy crown, and a great overall depth. Sometimes incorrectly equated with the old mine cut.

old mine cut, early form of brilliant cut with a nearly square or cushion-shape girdle outline, a

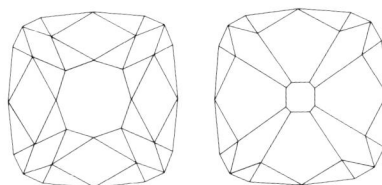

old mine cut

high crown, a small table, a deep pavilion, and a very large culet. Also called old miner, mine cut, Peruzzi cut, or triple cut brilliant.

old miner, see OLD MINE CUT.

old single cut, modified brilliant cut with an octagonal girdle outline, a table, eight bezel facets, eight pavilion facets, and (occasionally) a culet. Used primarily with small diamonds.

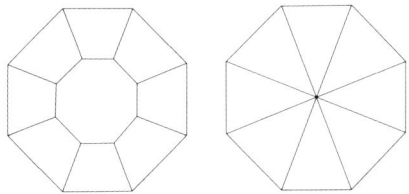

old single cut

one-grainer, see GRAINER.

on memo, see CONSIGNMENT.

opalescent, term used to describe a diamond which gives off iridescent reflections.

open bench mining, combination of open pit and underground mining, first used at the Premier Mine. A slot is excavated at the base of the open pit, leading to a collection area below in the underground works; the benches are then blasted loose; the ore drops through the slot, and is collected later. Also called bench mining or slot mining. See BENCH, BLOCK CAVING, CHAMBERING, PREMIER MINE.

open cast mining, excavation of mineral-bearing material at, or very close to, the earth's surface, followed by the replacement of overburden once the area being mined is exhausted. Open cast mining does not extend to great depths, but typically covers a large area; often applied in alluvial mining. See OPEN PIT MINING, UNDERGROUND MINING.

open culet, large culet, usually visible to the unaided eye through the table. See CLOSED CULET.

opening a diamond, polishing a window, to provide a clear view of the interior and locate inclusions prior to fashioning; performed only on large rough. See WINDOW.

Open Mine Museum, South African diamond museum which recreates the town of Kimberley as it was in the nineteenth century. Located adjacent to the site of the Kimberley Mine in Cape Province, South Africa; the museum's collection includes the Eureka Diamond and an unnamed 616 ct. rough yellow octahedron found at the Dutoitspan Mine in 1974. See KIMBERLEY, KIMBERLEY MINE.

open pit mining, mining process involving the excavation of mineral-bearing material by digging a pit. Once the pit becomes too deep to work economically, operations are usually transferred underground. See OPEN CAST MINING, UNDERGROUND MINING.

open pit mining

open setting, any mounting on which the stone's pavilion facets are open to the light. See A JOUR.

open table, large table, usually with a diameter of 65 percent or more. See CLOSED TABLE, SPREAD STONE, SWINDLED STONE, TABLE DIAMETER.

Oppenheimer, Sir Ernest (1880-1957), leading figure in the South African diamond industry; founder of the

Sir Ernest Oppenheimer

Anglo American Corporation and, from 1929 to 1957, Chairman of De Beers Consolidated Mines. Sir Ernest also served as Mayor of Kimberley, South Africa, and later (1924-1938) in the South African Parliament. Knighted by the British Crown in 1921 for his services during World War I, Oppenheimer ultimately became Chairman or Director of several major companies, primarily in mining, finance, and related industries.

Oppenheimer Diamond, 253.70 ct. octahedral diamond, described as light yellow; found at the Dutoitspan Mine in 1964. Purchased by Harry Winston and donated to the Smithsonian Institution in Washington, D.C., US, in memory of Sir Ernest Oppenheimer. Sometimes called the Dutoitspan Diamond.

Oppenheimer Diamond

Oppenheimer Syndicate, name sometimes used to differentiate between the original Diamond Syndicate in London and the new group created by Sir Ernest Oppenheimer in 1924. The Oppenheimer Syndicate devolved into the Diamond Corporation in 1930, and later into the Central Selling Organisation. See CENTRAL SELLING ORGANISATION (CSO), DIAMOND SYNDICATE.

optical density, degree to which a refractive material, such as diamond, slows the light entering it from the air. Differences in optical density result in differences in refractive index (RI).

optically dense, term describing any material which slows and bends light passing through it to a comparatively greater degree than in air. Optical density affects luster, scintillation, refractive index (RI), and brilliance. All gems are optically denser than air, but they vary in degree; diamond is optically very dense. See OPTICAL DENSITY, REFRACTIVE INDEX (RI).

optical properties, those characteristics of a gemstone which govern its interaction with light. Optical properties include color, refractive index, luster, reflection, dispersion, and refraction. See PHYSICAL PROPERTIES.

optical separator, device which separates diamonds from crushed blueground by registering the difference between their light-reflecting properties. See SEPARATION (2).

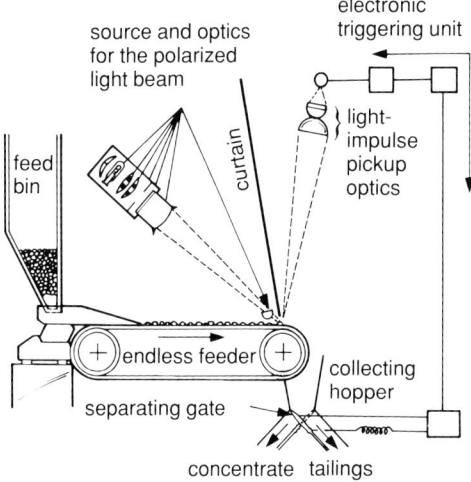

operating elements of the optical separator

orange diamond, fancy color diamond with a distinct orange hue. Orange diamonds may be red-orange to orangy yellow; the color saturation is often low.

Orange Free State, province in South Africa, once an independent republic. The Jagersfontein and Koffiefontein Mines, among others, are located there.

Orange River, large river forming part of the border between South Africa and Namibia. Many alluvial diamond deposits have been located along the Orange and the Vaal, its main tributary. As an ancient river, the Orange carried alluvial diamonds from the interior of the continent out into the Atlantic Ocean. See ALLUVIAL MINING, BEACH MINING, OFF-SHORE MINING.

Orange Tiffany Diamond, see TIFFANY DIAMOND.

Oranjemund, mining town on the coast of Namibia near the mouth of the Orange River, originally established by CDM. See NAMIBIA.

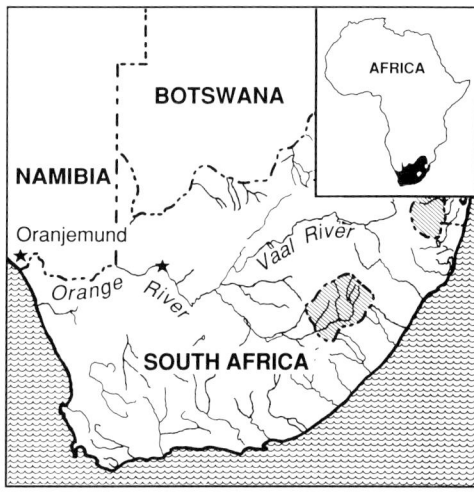

Orange River and Oranjemund

Orapa Mine, large kimberlite with a surface area of 106 hectares (262 acres) located on the edge of the Kalahari Desert, 240 kilometers (148 miles) from Francistown. Discovered in 1967, it was the first diamond mine to operate in Botswana; it is currently being mined as an open pit mine. A recovery plant and the town of Orapa are located nearby. See DEBSWANA DIA-

Orapa Mine

MOND COMPANY, JWANENG MINE, LETLHAKANE MINE.

Oregon diamond, misnomer for rock crystal quartz from Lakeview, Oregon, US.

O'Reilly, John, late nineteenth century itinerant trader entrusted by Schalk van Niekerk with taking the 21.25 ct. Eureka Diamond to Colesburg for examination in 1867. Because of his minor involvement, the Eureka is sometimes incorrectly referred to as the O'Reilly Diamond. See ATHERSTONE, WILLIAM GUYBON; EUREKA DIAMOND; VAN NIEKERK, SCHALK.

Oriental diamond, historical term once used to distinguish Indian from Brazilian diamonds.

origin of color report, report issued by a gem-testing laboratory, stating whether a diamond's color is natural in origin, or due to an enhancement process such as irradiation. See COATED DIAMOND, IRRADIATED DIAMOND.

origin (of diamond): diamonds have formed throughout the earth's history (possibly periodically) from carbon atoms in two rock types, peridotite and eclogite. Formation occurred at depths of 150-200 kilometers (93-124 miles) below the surface of the earth, at pressures of about 45-60 kilobars (650,000-870,000 pounds per square inch) and temperatures of 900°-1300°C. Dates of origin from 990 million to 3,300 million years have been established on specific diamond samples. See AGE (OF DIAMONDS), DIAMOND, DIATREME, EMPLACEMENT (OF DIAMOND), HYPABYSSAL ZONE, KIMBERLITE, LAMPROITE, XENOCRYST.

Orloff Diamond, 189.62 ct. Indian diamond, described as slightly bluish green, with a cut said to resemble "half a pigeon's egg." Its shape, facet arrangement, and the slight indentation on one side

Orloff Diamond

has led to the hypothesis that it may have been part of the Great Mogul Diamond, which disappeared after the Sack of Delhi in 1739. It was given to Catherine the Great of Russia (1729-1796) by her former lover, Count Grigori Orloff (1737-1808) and was set below the golden eagle in the Russian Imperial Scepter; it is now on display in the Russian Diamond Fund in Moscow. Also spelled Orlov, and sometimes called the Lasarev Diamond, or the Scepter Diamond.

Orpak Industries, Israeli manufacturer of robotic bruting machines. In conjunction with Daniel Legziel and Sons, the company has developed a fully-automated bruting system capable of uninterrupted, 24-hour operation. When announced in the early 1990s, it had a 60-stone capacity and was reported to be able to handle all forms of rough.

Ortlepp Diamond, small macle believed to be one of the first diamonds discovered in what was to become the Kimberley area. Found by Sarah Ortlepp in 1869, the diamond remained in her family for six generations, until it was placed on permanent loan to the Africana Museum in Johannesburg.

Ottoman Diamond, see TURKEY I DIAMOND.

out-of-round diamond, round brilliant-cut diamond which does not have a truly circular girdle outline. It may vary from slightly oval to squarish. See FINISH, MAJOR SYMMETRY, SYMMETRY.

out-of-round girdle, see OUT-OF-ROUND DIAMOND.

outside goods, diamonds which are not purchased directly by the Central Selling Organisation. Outside goods are traded in many diamond centers, particularly Antwerp.

oval brilliant cut, see OVAL CUT.

oval cut, (1) brilliant cut with an elliptical girdle outline; also called an oval brilliant cut. (2) obsolete barrel-shaped cut, circular in section and covered with triangular facets.

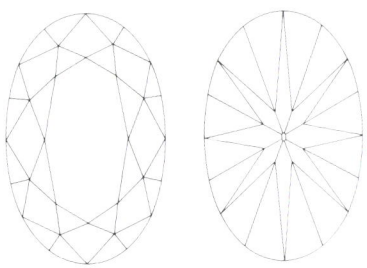

oval cut (1)

Oval Elegance, proprietary name for a 58-facet oval cut marketed by Lazare Kaplan. See OVAL CUT.

oval marquise, marquise with blunted rather than pointed ends. Used to obtain greater yield from the rough.

overblue, diamond which looks bluish in daylight, usually because of strong fluorescence. See OILIE, PREMIER DIAMOND.

overburden, sand, gravel, or rock which must be removed to reach underlying gem-bearing gravels.

overburden stripping, earth-moving operation whereby large quantities of overburden are removed to expose a primary source or an alluvial deposit underneath. The overburden, which is often very deep (some 46 meters—150 feet—at Jwaneng) is moved to areas which are not diamond-bearing, or which have already been worked out.

photo by James E. Shigley

overburden stripping

overgrowth, (1) thin, natural coating of calcium carbonate found on some rough diamonds, often preventing them from adhering to grease. (2) natural diamond coating on a rough diamond.

overhand shrinkage, underground mining technique where a vertical or near-vertical kimberlite dike is excavated from below by drilling and blasting the roof across its width. Some of the broken rock is removed immediately, but much of it (the shrinkage) is retained in the area

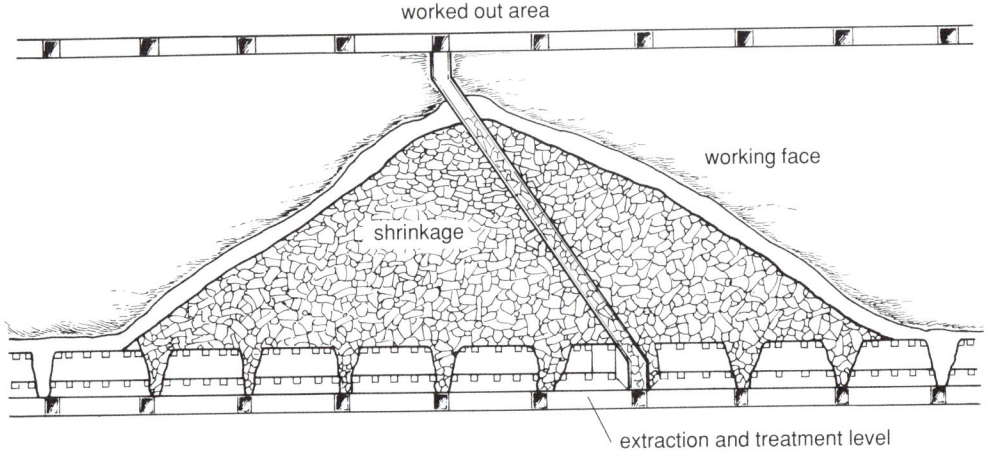

overhand shrinkage

below to provide access to the working face, and is drawn off only after all the drilling and blasting is completed and the working face has broken into the worked out area. See BELLSBANK MINE.

overmining, practice of mining only the higher grade deposits in a specific area.

overspread stone, see SWINDLED STONE.

oxidized crystal, diamond crystal having areas which contain iron oxide. In some alluvial diamonds, surface oxidation may be due to contact with the atmosphere, giving the crystal a false yellow, orange, or red color. In other diamonds, oxidation may occur along cracks and cleavages within the crystal. Also called oxidized diamond.

oxidized diamond, see OXIDIZED CRYSTAL.

oyster line, layer of fossilized oyster shells found in marine terraces along the coast of Namaqualand and Namibia which proved to mark the position of alluvial diamond deposits, and verified a theory first postulated by geologist Hans Merensky. See STATE ALLUVIAL DIGGINGS; MERENSKY, HANS.

P

P, abbreviation for *piqué*.

painted diamond, see COATED DIAMOND.

pampille cut, cut similar to, but usually more elongated than, the briolette; circular in cross section, with facets of different sizes and shapes arranged in rows and decreasing in number as they approach the points.

pan, shallow depression in the earth's surface, especially one containing a lake or pond.

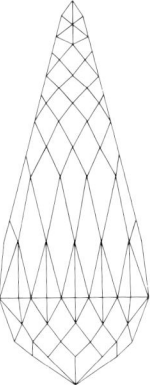

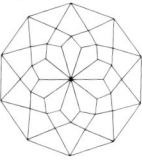

pampille cut

pane facet, see STAR FACET.

Panna, principal diamond-mining area in the state of Madhya Pradesh, India, where historic alluvial diamond diggings are located, together with three pipes, the Hinota, the Angore, and the Majhgawan. The Majhgawan, near the Ramkharia diggings along the Baghain River, is the only one being worked commercially today. See NATIONAL MINERAL DEVELOPMENT CORPORATION OF INDIA (NMDC), PANNA DIAMOND MINE.

Panna Diamond Mine, open pit mine working the Majhgawan pipe about 320 kilometers (200 miles) southeast of Agra, India. Operated by the National Mineral Development Corporation of India, the mine grade is thought to be low, but production is said to be primarily gem quality. See NATIONAL MINERAL DEVELOPMENT COMPANY OF INDIA (NMDC).

Panna Diamond-Mining Syndicate, company once licensed to mine diamonds in the Panna area of Madhya Pradesh, India. The company ceased operations when the mines were nationalized in 1957. See NATIONAL MINERAL DEVELOPMENT CORPORATION OF INDIA (NMDC).

Panna Group, historic group of alluvial diamond deposits between the Son and Sonar Rivers in India. The nearby Majhgawan Pipe is the only Indian mine in operation today.

Panna Group

panning, process of separating gems and other minerals from alluvial gravels by agitating the host material with water in a shallow pan. Less dense materials wash over the edge; heavier minerals, such as diamond, remain in the pan. Panning is a common prospecting technique, and is also used as a recovery method in small alluvial operations. It is also used when prospecting for precious metals. See BABY, JIG, RECOVERY, SEPARATION (2).

Papendorp, marine mining operation conducted within one of the concession areas on the coast of Namaqualand, South Africa. Diamonds are recovered by diver-manipulated suction pumps operated from small boats and from shore. See BEACH MINING, OFF-SHORE MINING.

paper marks, fine scratches or abraded facet junctions which occur when loose polished diamonds rub against each other in a diamond paper.

paperworn diamond, polished diamond with scratches or abraded facet junctions caused by contact with other loose diamonds in a diamond paper. See PAPER MARKS.

Paphian diamond, see PAPHOS DIAMOND.

Paphos diamond, misnomer for rock crystal quartz from Cyprus. Also called Paphros diamond or Paphian diamond.

Pará, minor diamond-producing state in Brazil.

paragon, (1) sixteenth century term for a diamond weighing 12 ct. or more. (2) obsolete term for a flawless diamond. See PARAGON DIAMOND.

Paragon Diamond, 137.82 ct., D-color, internally-flawless, modified shield-cut diamond fashioned from a 320 ct. rough found in Brazil. Purchased in Antwerp and set in a necklace by Graff Diamonds of London. Graded by GTL in 1989 and, to date, the largest, D-color, internally-flawless diamond GTL has graded. Paragon means *model of excellence.*

Paragon Diamond

parcel, see LOT.

parcel paper, see DIAMOND PAPER.

parcel price, see LOT PRICE.

Parsons, Charles Algernon (1854-1931), English engineer and inventor who in 1918 repeated Moissan's and Crookes' experiments in an unsuccessful attempt to produce synthetic diamond. See CROOKES, WILLIAM; MOISSAN, FERDINAND FREDERIC HENRI.

Parteal Mines, historic group of alluvial diamond deposits on the north bank of the Krishna River near its junction with the Munyero River, close to Golconda, India. Some were still being mined in 1850. Also spelled Partial and Parteel.

particle accelerator, see CYCLOTRON.

parure, matched set of jewelry, which usually includes a pair of earrings, necklace, brooch, bracelet, and ring; in the past, such sets also included aigrettes (a hair decoration), buckles, stomachers (a large, elaborate piece of jewelry worn on a bodice), and tiaras. French, meaning *ornament.*

Pasha of Egypt Diamond, originally a 40 ct. high-quality, old mine cut Indian diamond purchased by Ibrahim Pasha (1789-1848) of Egypt in 1848. Subsequent owners had it recut twice, first to 38.19 ct., then, in 1980, to a 36.22 ct. D-color, internally flawless, 16-sided brilliant cut. Thought to be privately owned in Italy.

paste, (1) glass imitation gemstone, usually made of flint glass or high-lead glass. (2) in a generic sense, any imitation gemstone.

Paul I Diamond, 13.35 ct. cushion-shape pink diamond, reportedly of high clarity, named for Paul I (1754-1801), son of Catherine the Great of Russia. Originally described as red, but the color may have been due to red foilbacking. Mounted on silver foil and set in a diadem, it is now on display in the Russian Diamond Fund in Moscow.

Pauline Trigère, proprietary name for synthetic strontium titanate. Marketed as a diamond simulant.

pavé setting, setting style in which many small gemstones are placed close together. The pavilions are recessed in holes, and held in place by metal beads worked up from the mounting itself, over the girdle edges.

pavé setting

pavilion, the portion of a polished diamond below the girdle; sometimes called the base. See PAVILION FACETS.

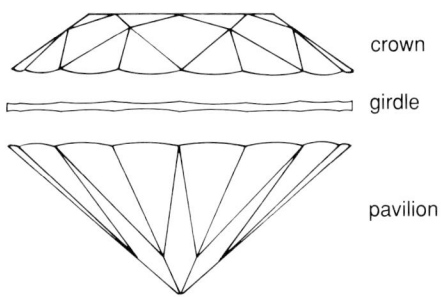

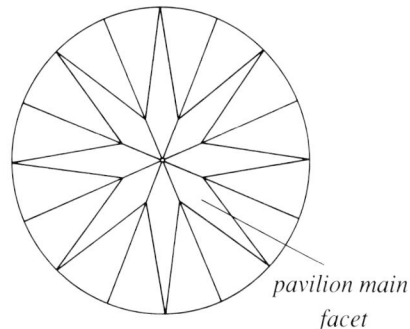

pavilion main facet

pavilion angle, angle between the girdle plane and the pavilion main facets. See CROWN ANGLE, FISHEYE, NAILHEAD, PAVILION DEPTH PERCENTAGE, PROPORTIONS, TOLKOWSKY THEORETICAL BRILLIANT CUT.

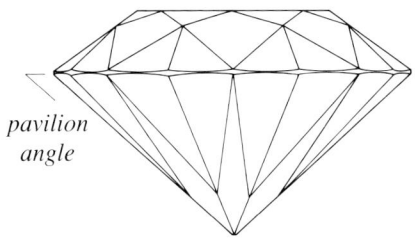

pavilion angle

pavilion bulge, bowing of the pavilion facets on a step cut as seen in profile. Excessive pavilion bulge adds weight, but it also produces light leakage and may make the stone difficult to set.

pavilion depth, see PAVILION DEPTH PERCENTAGE.

pavilion depth percentage, distance from the girdle plane to the culet, expressed as a percentage of the average girdle diameter on round brilliants, and as a percentage of the width on fancy shapes.

pavilion facets, facets on the pavilion of a diamond; often, the pavilion main facets.

pavilion main facets, large pavilion facets extending from the girdle to the culet on a brilliant-cut diamond. On round brilliants, sometimes called quoin or bottom-corner facets.

p.c., trade abbreviation for "per carat;" commonly used when expressing price. The price of a diamond is found by multiplying the price per carat by the weight.

Peace Diamond, (1) 56.20 ct. rough diamond found in Sakha (Yakutia), the Russian Federation, CIS, in 1962; named for the Mir Pipe (Mir means *peace*). Current whereabouts unknown. (2) 12.25 ct. cushion-shape, reportedly colorless diamond, sold by Sotheby's in 1938. Current whereabouts unknown. See MIR PIPE.

Peach-Blossom Diamond, 24.78 ct. pear-shape diamond, described as light pink, purchased by Louis XIV of France. Believed to have been among the jewels stolen from the Garde Mueble in 1792; it has been suggested that the Peach-Blossom Diamond and the Hortensia Diamond (which is on display in the Galérie d'Apollon at the Louvre in Paris) may be one and the same. See HORTENSIA DIAMOND.

Peacock Throne, large, canopied gold throne, 1.8 meters (six feet) high and 1.2 meters (four feet) wide, encrusted with diamonds, emeralds, rubies, and pearls; built in Delhi, India, between 1628 and 1635 for the Mogul emperor Shah Jahan (1592-1666) and taken to Persia after the Sack of Delhi in 1739. Jeweled peacocks are prominent above the canopy (hence the name) and the 116 ct. Akbar Shah is said to have been mounted in the eye of one of the peacocks. The throne was displayed at the Bank Melli Iran in Tehran during the reign of the last Shah. Some of the gems are said to have been stolen from it during the 1979 revolution. It was on display at the Central Bank of Iran in 1992. See IRANIAN CROWN JEWELS, SACK OF DELHI.

pear-shape brilliant cut, variation of the brilliant cut with a pear-shaped girdle outline and 56 to 58 facets. See PENDELOQUE.

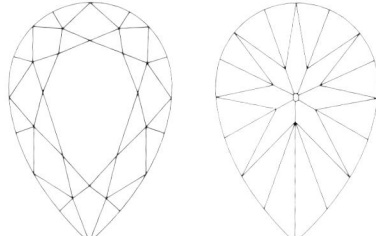

pear-shape brilliant cut

pear-shape rose cut, rose cut with a pear-shaped girdle outline, a flat, unfaceted base, a pointed, dome-shaped crown, and usually 24 triangular facets.

Pecos diamond, misnomer for rock crystal quartz from the Pecos River in Texas and New Mexico, US. Also called Pecos River diamond or Pecos Valley diamond.

pectolite, mineral which in its semi-translucent, white-to-gray form is sometimes found in kimberlite pipes.

Pelikaanstraat, historic center of the diamond industry in Antwerp, Belgium; named for *Het Pelikaentje*, a café which was located on the street. Diamond trade activity is now transacted in Hovenierstraat, Schupstraat, and Vestingstraat, all of which are located nearby.

PEMA, see COMPANHIA DE PESQUISAS MINERAS DE ANGOLA.

pendant-cut brilliant, see PENDELOQUE.

pendeloque, modified pear-shape brilliant cut in which the narrow end is longer and more pointed. Sometimes used synonymously with pear shape.

penetration twin, twin crystals which appear to penetrate one another but do not; diamonds sometimes occur as penetration twins.

Pennsylvania diamond, misnomer for pyrite.

pentagon cut, step cut with five sides of equal length (forming a regular pentagon).

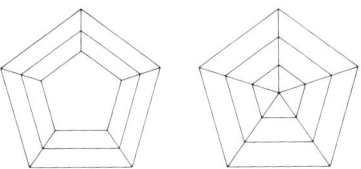

pentagon cut

Penthièvre Diamond, 10 ct. yellow oval brilliant-cut diamond, named for Louis-Jean Marie de Bourbon, Duc de Penthièvre (1725-1793). The diamond passed to his descendant Marie Amélie, consort of King Louis Phillipe (1773-1850); from her to her grandson, the Comte de Paris (1838-1894); and from him to the Duc d'Orleans, who sold it to the Duc d'Aumale. In 1886, the Duc d'Aumale bequeathed it, together with the Condé Diamond, to L'Institute de France. Set in a head band, it is now on display, with the Condé, at the Musée de Condé in Chantilly, France.

percussion mark, see BRUISE.

perfect, term sanctioned by the US Federal Trade Commission to designate a fashioned diamond which is flawless under 10x magnification and "not of inferior color or make."

perfection color, term sometimes applied to colorless diamonds. Also called gem color.

peridotite, one of two types of rock in which diamonds crystallize. See AGE (OF DIAMONDS), ECLOGITE, EMPLACEMENT (OF DIAMOND), KIMBERLITE, LAMPROITE.

Peruzzi cut, faceted diamond based on the octahedron but with rounded corners, alleged to have been developed in the seventeenth century by Vincenzio Peruzzi.

Peruzzi, Vincenzio (active ca. 1700), Venetian lapidary traditionally credited with improving the Mazarin cut and creating the brilliant cut. As with Lodewyk Van Bercken, the accreditation is questionable; the Peruzzi family were Florentine and there is no record of a Vincenzio. All diamonds with round outlines became known as brilliant-cut diamonds, but the first true 58-facet brilliant was unlikely to have been fashioned until much later. See PERUZZI CUT.

Petit Coeur Diamond, 25.22 ct. internally flawless, F-color, heart-shape diamond, one of three fashioned by Laurence Graff of London from a 278 ct. cleavage found in Guinea in 1982; later set in a necklace. See GRAND COEUR D'AFRIQUE DIAMOND.

phenomenal diamond, diamond which displays an unusual optical effect, such as fluorescence or phosphorescence. See CHAMELEON-TYPE DIAMOND, PREMIER DIAMOND, TRANSICHROMATIC.

Phianite, proprietary name for synthetic cubic zirconia. Marketed as a diamond simulant.

Philip II Diamond, diamond of approximately 48 ct., reportedly purchased by Philip II of Spain (1527-1598) in 1559. Current whereabouts unknown.

phosphorescence, continued emission of visible light by a material after the source of stimulating radiation (such as X-rays, cathode rays, ultraviolet light, or visible light) has been removed. Phosphorescent diamonds are unusual, although Type IIb diamonds phosphoresce to shortwave ultraviolet radiation. See CHAMELEON-TYPE DIAMOND, FLUORESCENCE, LUMINESCENCE, PHOTOLUMINESCENCE.

photoluminescence, emission of visible light by a material when exposed to visible light or ultraviolet radiation. Photoluminescent materials are called phosphorescent if luminescence continues after the light source is removed, fluorescent if luminescence is limited to the duration of their exposure. See EMISSION SPECTRUM, FLUORESCENCE, LUMINESCENCE, PREMIER DIAMOND, PHOSPHORESCENCE.

photometer, instrument which measures the strength of electromagnetic radiation in the ultraviolet to infra-red range. See SPECTROPHOTOMETER.

photomicrograph, photograph taken through a microscope. Photomicrographs are often taken of inclusions or surface blemishes on diamonds to record important or unusual characteristics.

Photostand, proprietary name for a cabinet equipped with corrected lighting instruments and a camera mount; used to photograph jewelry or gemstones, typically with an instant-film or 35mm camera. Manufactured by GIA Gem Instruments.

physical properties, characteristics of a gemstone other than its optical properties. Examples of physical properties include hardness, cleavage, fracture type, and specific gravity. See OPTICAL PROPERTIES.

picking table, simple recovery method using a flat or slightly inclined table on which diamond-bearing ore or gravel is spread, allowing diamonds to be seen and "picked out." Picking tables are often used in small alluvial operations. See RECOVERY, SEPARATION.

pick price, per-carat price paid for stones from a selection, or lot, when the purchaser is permitted to select, or pick, them individually. Typically a premium is added (over the lower lot price).

picotite, dark-brown, translucent to near-opaque chrome spinel (spinel containing chromium in place of aluminum); picotite is a constituent of South African kimberlites.

piggy-back diamond, assembled stone composed of a flat diamond set above, but not touching, a smaller diamond; the arrangement is concealed by a special mounting. See ASSEMBLED STONE.

Pigot Diamond, 48.63 ct. oval-cut diamond named for Baron George Pigot (1719-1777), British Colonial Governor of Madras, India, who is believed to have received it as a gift sometime around 1763. Because his heirs sold it by lottery in 1801, it is sometimes called the Lottery Diamond. Current whereabouts unknown.

pile, obsolete term for a nuclear reactor. See NUCLEAR REACTOR.

pile-treated diamond, obsolete term for diamonds treated in a nuclear reactor. See IRRADIATED DIAMOND.

pink diamond, fancy color diamond with a distinctly pink natural bodycolor, essentially a light, low-saturation red. Recent discoveries in Western Australia have increased the supply of pink diamonds.

pinpoint, small, rounded inclusion which at 10x magnification is visible, but not large enough to be distinguishable as an included crystal. Usually white; dark pinpoints are sometimes incorrectly called carbon spots or carbon pinpoints, but carbon does not occur as an inclusion in diamond.

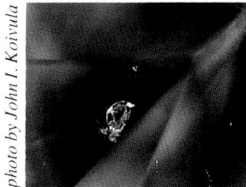

pinpoints, feather, and pink included crystal

photo by John I. Koivula

pipe, vertical, columnar mass of igneous rock which results from volcanic action. Pipes vary in size and shape. Kimberlite and lamproite pipes can be primary sources of diamond, but few have contained diamonds in economic quantities. Pipes typically form as tapered cones with four distinct sections: the surface crater; the gradually tapering diatreme below the crater; the hypabyssal zone which consists of sills and dikes; and the root. See APPENDIX G, DIKE, HYPABYSSAL ZONE, KIMBERLITE, LAMPROITE, ROOT, SILL.

pipeline, see DIAMOND PIPELINE.

pipe mine, mine established on a kimberlite or lamproite pipe from which ore is excavated for the eventual recovery of diamonds. See ALLUVIAL DEPOSIT, ELUVIAL DEPOSIT, FLUVIAL GRAVEL, PIPE MINING.

pipe mining, excavation of diamond-bearing ore from a kimberlite or lamproite pipe. Mining usually begins as an open pit operation on the surface and descends several hundred feet (a hundred meters); when this is no longer cost-effective, one of several underground mining methods may be used. See OPEN BENCH MINING, OPEN PIT MINING, UNDERGROUND MINING.

piqué, French, meaning *pricked*. (1) grade category in the CIBJO, IDC, and Scan. D.N. clarity-grading systems; corresponds to the Imperfect (I) range on the GIA clarity-grading scale. There are three grades in the category, abbreviated P_1, P_2, and P_3. Sometimes abbreviated P or PK. (2) especially in Europe, almost any clarity characteristic in a diamond visible to the unaided eye. See APPENDIX E, CIBJO INTERNATIONAL CLARITY/PURITY SCALE, GIA CLARITY-GRADING SCALE, IDC CLARITY-GRADING SCALE, SCAN. D.N. CLARITY SCALE.

Pirie Diamond, 1 ct. diamond, described as blue, bought in Paris in 1877 by Edwin W. Streeter. He once thought it to have been recut from the French Blue; this is now thought unlikely. Current whereabouts unknown. See FRENCH BLUE DIAMOND; STREETER, EDWIN W.

Pistoia diamond, misnomer for rock crystal quartz from Italy.

pit, (1) any very small opening on the surface of a polished diamond. (2) an etch pit or trigon on a rough diamond. (3) a large excavation dug for mining. See BRUISE, CAVITY, CHIP, NICK.

pit mining, see OPEN PIT MINING.

Pitt Diamond, see REGENT DIAMOND.

pitting, see PIT (2).

PK, abbreviation for piqué.

placer, alluvial deposit of heavy minerals such as diamonds, platinum, or gold concentrated on or near the surface of the earth by the effects of erosion and transportation by wind or water. See ALLUVIAL DEPOSIT.

planned leakage, see LEAKAGE, LIGHT RETURN.

plasma-enhanced chemical vapor deposition, see CHEMICAL VAPOR DEPOSITION (CVD).

Platberg, site of a Berlin Missionary Society station on the Vaal River, and possibly the location of one of South Africa's earliest diamond discoveries. An 1859 entry in the day book of the nearby Pniel Mission notes that a 5 ct. diamond was found near Platberg and purchased by a priest. If it was a diamond, its discovery would predate that of the larger Eureka (the first authenticated South African diamond) by seven years. Current whereabouts unknown. See CHARLEMONT DIAMOND, EUREKA DIAMOND, GORDON DIAMOND, HANGER DIAMOND, PNIEL.

plot, diagram of the facet arrangement of a particular polished gemstone on which symbols are used to indicate the size and sometimes shape of significant clarity characteristics, with additional written notations listing other details; used on grading reports and in appraisals. See PLOTTING SYMBOLS.

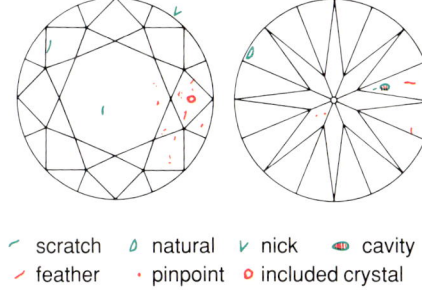

plot and plotting symbols

plotting, process of recording on a facet diagram the type, location, size, and sometimes shape, of all the significant clarity characteristics of a particular polished gemstone, using plotting symbols. See PLOT, PLOTTING SYMBOLS.

plotting symbols, system of conventional representations used in plotting (including lines, dots, icons, and letters; often in specific colors), representing various types of clarity characteristics. See PLOT, PLOTTING.

PMMC, see PRECIOUS MINERALS MARKETING CORPORATION.

Pniel, location of a major historical alluvial diamond deposit mined on the Vaal River northwest of Kimberley in South Africa; originally given to the Berlin Missionary Society by a Koranna tribal chief. Still a minor source of diamonds today. See PLATBERG.

pocket lens, see LOUPE.

pocket peddler, derogatory term once used to describe an individual diamond dealer who operated without a fixed business address.

Pocono diamond, misnomer for rock crystal quartz from Monroe County, Pennsylvania, US.

Pohl Diamond, 287 ct. alluvial diamond found by J.D. Pohl at Elandsfontein near Pretoria, South Africa, in 1934, shortly before the discovery of the Jonker Diamond; fashioned for Harry Winston by Lazare Kaplan. The rough, said to be of fine color but heavily included, yielded 15 polished diamonds, the largest of which, a 38.10 ct. D color, potentially flawless emerald cut, was sold in 1943 to Bernice Chrysler Garbish, daughter of the founder of Chrysler Motor Corporation; it was last sold in 1979. Current whereabouts unknown.

point, (1) unit of weight equal to one one-hundredth of a metric carat (0.01 ct). (2) the tip of a pear shape, marquise, heart shape, or other pointed fancy shape diamond. (3) very early cut with four facets that approximated the octahedral faces of the rough. Also called a point-cut diamond. See POINT CUT.

point cut, early diamond cut dating from the fourteenth century which resembled a four-sided pyramid. The intent was to smooth the octahedral faces to improve symmetry and luster; since octahedral faces cannot be polished easily, the polishing planes were worked at low angles to the faces.

Pointe de Bretagne Diamond, diamond of unknown weight and shape which reportedly belonged to the Dunois family of France. Francis I (1494-1547), who began the collection now known as the Crown Jewels of France, is said to have worn it in his cap. Current whereabouts unknown.

Pointe de Milan Diamond, point-cut diamond of unknown weight, believed to have been part of the dowry of Catherine de Medici (1519-1589) when she married Henry II (1519-1559) of France in 1533. She reportedly gave it to her daughter-in-law, Mary, Queen of Scots (1542-1587). Current whereabouts unknown.

pointer, term used to express (hundredths of a carat) the weight of a finished diamond that is less than one carat. Thus a diamond weighing 0.03 ct. can be called a "three-pointer," a 0.27 ct. stone a "27-pointer," etc.

pointing, point-to-point meeting of well-shaped facets. See FACET ALIGNMENT, SYMMETRY.

point naif, seventeenth century term for a diamond octahedron or other crystal shape on which the natural faces are easily distinguishable. See NAIF, NATURAL POINT.

polariscope, optical instrument used to determine whether a gemstone is singly or doubly refractive, and to detect anomalous double refraction (ADR) or strain. The gemstone is examined between two polarizing filters; one (the polarizer) is fixed, the other (the analyzer) rotates. See ANISOTROPIC, INTERNAL STRAIN, ISOTROPIC, REFRACTION.

Poli

Polar Star Diamond

Polar Star Diamond, 41.29 ct. cushion-shape diamond believed to be of Indian origin, and said to have belonged to Joseph Bonaparte (1768-1844), elder brother of Napoleon I. Purchased in the 1820s by the Russian Princess Tatiana Youssoupoff; last sold in 1980 to a Sri Lankan gem dealer. Also called the Youssoupoff Diamond.

Poli, area in Shandong Province, Peoples' Republic of China, in which several small diamond-bearing kimberlite dikes have been found north, northeast, and west of the town of Mengyin. See SHENGLI I MINE.

polish, the overall condition of the facet surfaces on a polished diamond. See BURN MARK, FINISH, POLISHING.

polished girdle, girdle which has been finished to a smooth surface. Not to be confused with faceted girdle. See FACETED GIRDLE.

polished goods, finished diamonds available for sale. See GOODS.

polisher, person who places and polishes facets on a diamond. Sometimes used in place of the more specific terms blocker, cross-worker, and brilliandeer.

polishing, process of placing facets on a rough diamond and providing their final finish. Sometimes used in a general sense, in place of the more specific terms blocking, cross-working, and brilliandeering.

polishing direction, direction in which diamond can be polished most easily, usually away from an octahedral face, toward a possible rhombic-dodecahedral face.

polishing dop, historic handmade tool consisting of a small retainer filled with a lead alloy which, when melted and cooled, held a diamond in place. The retainer was mounted on a bendable rod, thereby enabling polishers to change the position of the stone and thus the facet angles. Today dops are usually made of bronze or copper, with either a cup or a flat surface to which the diamond is affixed with cement. See BRUTING DOP, MECHANICAL DOP, PRESS POT, SAWING DOP, SEMI-AUTOMATIC DOP, SOLDER DOP.

polishing grain, see GRAIN.

polishing mark, see BURN MARK.

polishing wheel, see SCAIFE.

polish lines, tiny parallel grooves or ridges left on a diamond facet by the scaife during polishing. Polish lines run parallel to each other on any given facet, and do not cross facet junctions. See FINISH, GRAIN LINES, POLISH.

polycrystalline diamond, natural or synthetic diamond composed of many minute crystals. Because there is no common cleavage direction, it is very tough. Carbonado is a polycrystalline diamond.

polymorphism, ability of an element to assume different crystal structures under different geologic circumstances. When carbon crystallizes in the isometric (cubic) system, it forms diamond; when it crystallizes in the hexagonal system, it forms graphite. See DIMORPHISM.

polysynthetic twinning, (1) type of twinning in which the twinning planes are parallel, but reversed in respect to each other. It is thought to cause the laminated effect seen under magnification in some diamonds. (2) repeated twinning. See GRAIN LINES, TWIN CRYSTAL.

poor make, term used to describe a polished diamond with deficiencies in proportions, finish, or symmetry.

Popugayeva, Larissa A., Russian geologist credited with discovering the Zarnitza pipe, the first known kimberlite in the Sakha region of Siberia (now the Republic of Sakha [Yakutia], the Russian Federation, CIS), in 1954.

Porgès Diamond, 78.53 ct. emerald-cut diamond, described as champagne color, named for Jules Porgès, European diamond dealer and entrepreneur who formed the Compagnie Française des Mines de Diamant du Cap de Bonne Espérance (the French Company). Purchased by Harry Winston in 1962 and set in a yellow gold clip-pendant with rubies, emeralds, and 32 old-mine cuts, it was sold in the US in 1968. Current whereabouts unknown. See COMPAGNIE FRANCAISE DES MINES DE DIAMANT DU CAP DE BONNE ESPERANCE.

porknocker, derogatory term originally applied to Guianan gold and diamond prospectors; often used to describe illicit diamond diggers.

portable balance, any small balance which can be carried in a pocket or a briefcase, for weighing loose gems. Usually a mechanical balance with a fulcrum and a base, but sometimes hand-held. Portable electronic balances are available today. See CHAIN BALANCE, COUNTERWEIGHT BALANCE, DIAMOND BALANCE, ELECTRONIC BALANCE, MECHANICAL BALANCE, RIDER BALANCE, SINGLE-PAN BALANCE.

portable balance

Porter Rhodes Diamond, 153.50 ct. rough diamond octahedron, reportedly colorless, found in the Kimberley Mine in 1880; it helped dispel the myth that South African diamonds were inferior in color to those from India or Brazil. It was fashioned into a 73 ct. old mine cut and named for the claimholder, who became one of the first directors of De Beers Consolidated Mines (he was not related to Cecil Rhodes). Purchased by the second Duke of Westminster in 1926, as a wedding gift for his third wife, and later by the London jewelers Jerwood & Ward.

Porter Rhodes Diamond

It was repolished in Amsterdam to a 56.50 ct., D color, VVS₁, square emerald cut. Sold to the Maharaja of Indore in 1937, from whom it was acquired by Harry Winston in 1946, it was repolished to its present weight (54.99 ct.) before being sold to a client from Philadelphia. Winston later repurchased it and sold it to another client in Texas. In 1987, the Porter Rhodes was bought by Graff Diamonds of London at a Sotheby's New York auction.

portrait stone, see BEVEL CUT.

Portuguese cut, modification of the brilliant cut with five rows of facets on both the crown and pavilion. Sometimes applied to large diamonds.

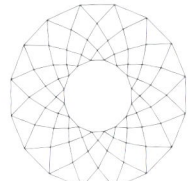 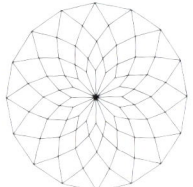

Portuguese cut

Portuguese Diamond, 127.02 ct. strongly fluorescent, emerald-cut diamond, reportedly flawless, believed to have been repolished from a 150 ct. cushion-shape diamond of uncertain origin. Purchased in 1951 by Harry Winston, from whom it was acquired by the Smithsonian Institution, Washington, D.C., in 1963.

Portuguese Diamond

Potemkin Diamond, see EUGENIE DIAMOND.

potentially flawless, term used to describe a diamond which, through repolishing to remove minor surface blemishes or shallow inclusions, can have its clarity grade raised to internally flawless (IF) or flawless (F).

pothole, hole in a riverbed, usually deeper than it is wide, formed by the abrasive action of churning, sand-laden water. Heavy minerals such as diamond tend to concentrate in potholes, creating exceptionally valuable alluvial deposits. See ALLUVIAL DEPOSIT, ALLUVIAL SORTING.

practical fine cut, brilliant cut based on the Tolkowsky theoretical brilliant cut, developed in Germany in 1949 by W.F. Eppler. It has a slightly larger table (56 percent), which produces a shallower crown (14.4 percent) and crown angle (33° 10'). It is frequently used in Europe for high quality diamonds. Also called the Eppler fine cut and the European fine cut. See SCANDINAVIAN STANDARD ROUND BRILLIANT; TOLKOWSKY, MARCEL.

Precious Minerals Marketing Corporation (PMMC), organization which replaced the Ghana Diamond Marketing Corporation in 1989, following changes in the legislation regulating the mining and sale of gold and diamonds in Ghana.

Precious Stones Act of 1927, law enacted to give the government of South Africa authority over all alluvial diamond deposits in the country, including the granting of claims and licenses. See PROCLAIMED AREA.

premier diamond, historic term for yellow diamonds which appear bluish in daylight due to strong blue fluorescence. Such diamonds are sometimes described as oily. See FLUOROCHROMATIC.

Premier Mine, large South African kimberlite mine in Cullinan, 40 kilometers (25 miles) east of Pretoria, South Africa. Discovered in 1903 and later operated by De Beers Consolidated Mines, the Premier was closed in 1932; it reopened as an underground mine in 1947. Diamonds are recovered by block caving and sub-level caving. The mine has been a source of several extraordinarily large, rare Type IIA diamonds, including the 3,106 ct. Cullinan Diamond (later presented to King Edward VII of Great Britain) and, it is believed, the 599 ct. Centenary Diamond. (Prior to 1903, the Wesselton Mine in Kimberley was known as the Premier.) See CENTENARY DIAMOND; CULLINAN DIAMOND; CULLINAN, THOMAS; PREMIER ROSE DIAMOND.

Premier Mine

Premier Rose Diamond, 137.02 ct. D-flawless pear-shape diamond, one of three fashioned from a 353.90 ct. rough found at the Premier Mine in South Africa in 1977. Named for diamond designer and cleaver Rose Mouw of the Mouw Diamond Works in Johannesburg, where it was polished by Dawie du Plessis. Also called the Big Rose; the others are the Little Rose, a 31.48 ct. D-flawless pear shape, and the 2.11 ct. D-flawless Baby Rose. Sold by the William Goldberg Diamond Corporation of New York in 1979.

Premier Rose Diamond

Premier (Transvaal) Diamond Mining Company, Ltd., a subsidiary of De Beers Consolidated Mines which operates the Premier Mine in South Africa.

premium, difference in price for rough or polished diamonds over and above an accepted list price, which fluctuates with general trading conditions. Factors affecting premiums on polished goods often include the provision of a diamond grading report from a recognized laboratory at the time of sale.

President Vargas Diamond, originally a 726.60 ct. rough diamond found in the San Antonio River, Minas Gerais, Brazil, in 1938; named in honor of then Brazilian President Getúlio Dornelles Vargas. Purchased by Harry Winston in 1939; 29 polished diamonds were fashioned from the rough. The largest, a 48.26 ct. emerald cut, was also known as the President Vargas, or the Vargas Diamond; it was sold to a private buyer in Texas, US, in 1944. Winston later repurchased and repolished the diamond to 44.17 ct. before selling it to an undisclosed client in 1961. Current whereabouts of all 29 stones are unknown.

press pot, metal pot into which a diamond is pressed before being inserted into a mechanical dop.

primary deposit, diamonds found in the host rock which carried them to the earth's surface. Kimberlites and lamproites are very occasionally primary deposits. See ALLUVIAL DEPOSIT, ELUVIAL DEPOSIT, FLUVIAL GRAVEL.

Princess cut, (1) popular square or rectangular modified brilliant cut; usually with 57 facets (21 crown facets, 32 pavilion facets, and four girdle facets), but occasionally a 144-facet rec-

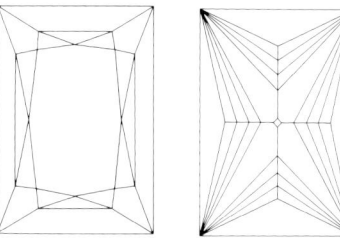

Princess cut

tangular or square brilliant. (2) early name for the profile cut. See PROFILE CUT.

prinz cut, small, polished, five-facet octahedron.

probe, see THERMAL INERTIA METER.

proclaimed area, land on which, under South African mining law, a duly constituted authority can issue prospecting and mining licenses. Similar legislation exists elsewhere. See DE-PROCLAIMED AREA, PRECIOUS STONES ACT OF 1927.

profile, side view of a gemstone.

Profile cut, cutting style which makes economical use of flat crystals; they are first sawn into plates, then fashioned with a series of V-shaped grooves on the bottom. The girdle outline may take a variety of shapes. The cut, described as "lively, but lacking in fire," was developed by Arpad Nagy of London in 1961. Originally called the Princess cut.

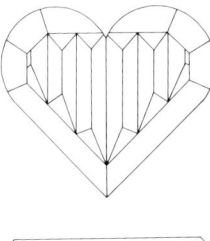

Profile cut

Progress Diamond, 80.66 ct. rough diamond found in the Mir pipe, Sakha (Yakutia), the Russian Federation, CIS; now in the Russian Diamond Fund in Moscow.

prong, narrow metal support, usually used in groups of four to six, to hold a gemstone in its mounting. Sometimes called claw. Sets of prongs which form a separate, pre-fabricated component are often called heads.

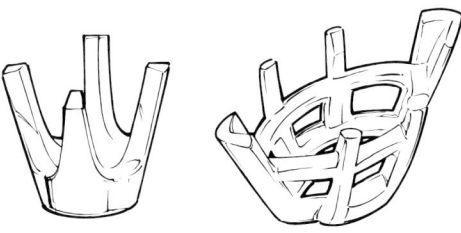

four- and six-prong settings

prong setting, see HEAD.

proportion grading, process in which the make of a polished diamond is evaluated through an analysis of its proportions. See FINISH, MAKE, PROPORTIONS.

proportions, relative dimensions and angles of a polished diamond and the relationships between them; these include table size, crown angle, crown height, girdle thickness, pavilion angle, pavilion depth, culet size, girdle outline, length-to-width ratio, and total depth. See FINISH, MAKE, MAJOR SYMMETRY.

ProportionScope, proprietary name for an instrument used to analyze the proportions of brilliant-cut diamonds weighing 0.18 to 8 ct. by projecting a silhouette of the stone onto a calibrated screen. Manufactured by GIA Gem Instruments. See DIAMOND PROPORTION ANALYZER.

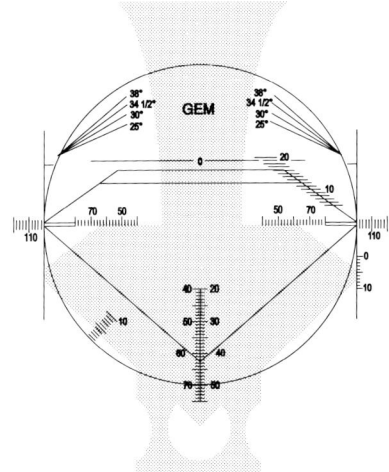

ProportionScope screen

prospecting, searching for mineral deposits.

prospector, person who searches for mineral deposits, usually with the intent to mine them or sell the rights.

protogenetic inclusion, inclusion which formed before the crystal in which it is contained. See EPIGENETIC INCLUSION, SYNGENETIC INCLUSION.

proton, positively charged atomic particle; one of the types of cyclotron-accelerated particles used to alter the color of diamonds. See CYCLOTRON-TREATED DIAMOND, IRRADIATED DIAMOND.

Province of the Cape of Good Hope, see CAPE PROVINCE.

Provincial Diamond Museum, major museum and tourist attraction in Antwerp, Belgium, founded in 1972; its extensive displays illuminate many aspects of diamonds and the role that Bruges, Antwerp, and the Kempen have played in the development of the diamond industry.

Pudong, industrial district in Shanghai, People's Republic of China, in which construction of a diamond manufacturing and trading facility is scheduled for completion in 1995.

Puerto Rico, island at the northeastern end of the Caribbean Sea, a commonwealth of the United States and an important diamond-manufacturing center.

pulsator, see JIG.

Punch Jones Diamond, 34.46 ct. diamond crystal, described as greenish gray, found near Peterstown, West Virginia, US, in 1928. Named after the discoverer's son, William P. "Punch" Jones, it is on permanent display in the Smithsonian Institution, Washington, D.C.

Punch Jones Diamond

photo courtesy of Sotheby's

pure, see CLEAN.

purest water, archaic term for top-color transparent diamonds. See WATER.

purity, see CLARITY.

purple diamond, fancy color diamond with a distinctly purple natural bodycolor, relatively rare.

pyrope garnet, mineral in the garnet group; chemical composition, $Mg_3Al_2(SiO_4)_3$. It has a refractive index (RI) of 1.714 to 1.742 and above, a specific gravity (SG) of 3.78, a hardness (Mohs scale) of 7 to 7.5, and a vitreous luster. It is considered an indicator mineral for kimberlite, and also occurs as an inclusion in diamond.

Quadrillion Cut, proprietary name for a rectangular brilliant cut with 49 facets (21 crown facets, 24 pavilion facets, and four girdle facets); developed by Ambar Diamonds of Israel in 1981.

quality, (1) the relative excellence of a diamond's color, clarity, and cut or make in relation to a predetermined set of standards. (2) in Europe, a synonym for clarity, often used when sorting and grading rough diamonds.

Quality Analysis Report (QAR), see DIAMOND GRADING REPORT.

quarter, quarter carat (0.25 ct.) diamond.

quartz, doubly refractive mineral with refractive indices of 1.544-1.553, birefringence of 0.009, specific gravity of 2.65, dispersion of 0.013, and hardness (Mohs scale) of 7. Chemical composition, SiO_2; in its colorless form, it is sometimes used as a diamond simulant. See RHINESTONE.

Quartz diamond, misnomer for rock crystal quartz from Yugoslavia.

Quasuma diamond, see ARABIAN DIAMOND.

Quarzo diamond, misnomer for rock crystal quartz from Isère, France.

Quebec diamond, misnomer for rock crystal quartz from Cape Diamond, Quebec, Canada.

Queen Elizabeth Pink Diamond, see WILLIAMSON PINK DIAMOND.

Queen of Belgium Diamond, see REINE DES BELGES DIAMOND, LA.

Queen of Holland Diamond, originally a 136.25 ct. cushion-shape diamond fashioned in Amsterdam in 1904. Named for Queen Wilhelmina (1880-1962) and sold to the Maharajah of Nanangar, India, in 1930. Acquired by the William Goldberg Diamond Corporation of New York, US, it was repolished in 1978 to 135.92 ct. and graded as D-color, internally flawless. Now privately owned.

Quisumah diamond, see ARABIAN DIAMOND.

quoin facets, first nine facets blocked on a round brilliant-cut diamond after it has been bruted. The table and four other facets (which become the bezel facets) are placed on the crown. The other four (the pavilion main facets) are placed on the pavilion. The angle and placement of quoin facets help determine the shape and symmetry of the finished diamond. See BLOCKER, BLOCKING.

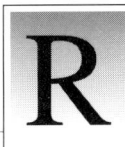

Radiant Cut, proprietary name for a cushion- or square-shape brilliant cut with 70 facets. Developed by Henry Grossbard in 1977; redesigned in 1978.

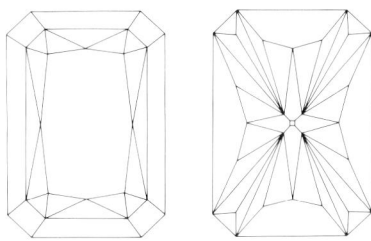

Radiant Cut

radium, radioactive element, found in minute quantities as a decay product in uranium ore; has been used to treat diamonds. It emits alpha particles and gamma rays, and eventually decays into lead. See RADIUM-TREATED DIAMOND.

radium-treated diamond, diamond the color of which has been changed (usually to green) by exposure to radium bromide, although other radioactive compounds, such as americium oxide, may be used instead. Color penetration is very shallow and can be removed by repolishing. Not commonly practiced; radium-treated diamonds remain radioactive. Good trade practice dictates that irradiation of any kind be disclosed to a potential buyer. See AMERICIUM-241, AUTORADIOGRAPH, IRRADIATED DIAMOND.

radius-dressing diamond tool, diamond dressing tool set with a single diamond, the cutting edge of which has been fashioned to a specific radius.

Railway diamond, misnomer for rock crystal quartz from India.

Rainbow Diamond, proprietary name for synthetic rutile. Marketed as a diamond simulant.

Rainbow Gem, proprietary name for synthetic rutile. Marketed as a diamond simulant.

Rainbow Magic Diamond, proprietary name for synthetic rutile. Marketed as a diamond simulant.

Rajah of Matan Diamond, see MATAN DIAMOND.

Raj Red Diamond, 2.33 ct. reportedly brownish orange-red diamond, believed to have come from India. Current whereabouts unknown.

Ramat Gan, Israel's leading diamond-manufacturing and trading center; in 1992, there were some 299 factories active, employing nearly 4,000 people. Located on the outskirts of Tel Aviv, the area's diamond industry developed during the late 1960s and early 1970s. It operates within three interconnected buildings (the Noam, the Maccabi, and the Shimson); a fourth is under construction.

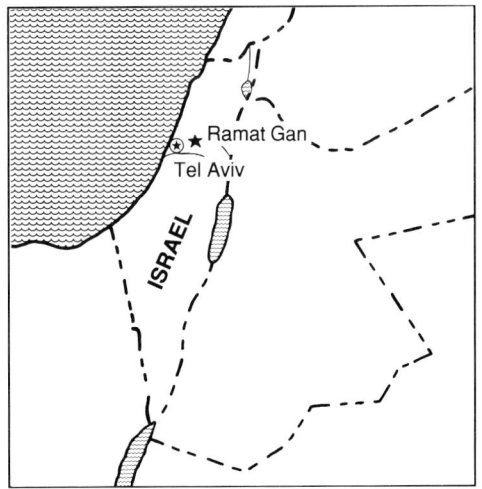

Ramat Gan

Ramkharia, alluvial deposit along the Baghin River 47 kilometers (29 miles) from Majhgawan, in India. See MAJHGAWAN, PANNA, PANNA DIAMOND MINE.

rare white, (1) term, together with the qualifier rare white +, on the CIBJO and IDC color-grading scales for near-colorless diamonds; rare white + is equivalent to F, and rare white to G, on the GIA color-grading scale. (2) alternative term in the Scan. D.N. color system for the equivalent traditional grade top wesselton. See APPENDIX D, CIBJO INTERNATIONAL COLOR-GRADING SCALE, GIA COLOR-GRADING SCALE, IDC INTERNATIONAL COLOR-GRADING SCALE, SCAN. D.N. COLOR SCALE.

rarest white, alternative descriptive term in the Scan. D.N. color-grading system for the traditional top grade river.

rati, unit of gemstone weight equivalent to 0.91 ct., used in India. Named for the red seed of a plant in the licorice family which was the original standard of weight in that country. Also spelled ratti or rutee. See CAROB SEED.

ratio method, technique used to estimate the table percentage of a diamond while looking down on the crown with the culet and table centered; the distance between the girdle edge and the table edge can be compared to the distance between the table edge and the culet as seen through the table. A ratio of 1:1 indicates a table percentage around 54 percent; 1:1¼, a 60 percent table; and 1:1½, a 65 percent table. See BOWING METHOD.

ratti, see RATI.

Raulconda Diamond, 103 ct. diamond recorded as having been seen by Tavernier at the Raulconda Mine in India in the seventeenth century; current whereabouts unknown.

Rayner Diamond Gauge, proprietary name for an instrument, calibrated in millimeters, used to measure diamonds.

Rayner Diamond Refractometer, proprietary name for a refractometer with a diamond hemicylinder; measures the refractive indices of gemstones up to 2.10.

Rayner Diamond Tester, proprietary name for a thermal inertia meter. See THERMAL INERTIA METER.

reactor, atomic, see NUCLEAR REACTOR.

reactor-treated diamond, diamond the color of which has been altered to green by treatment in a nuclear reactor; annealing can then change the green to orange-yellow to brown. Color penetrates the entire diamond, which remains radioactive for some time. Good trade practice dictates disclosing the nature of such treatment to a potential buyer. See CYCLOTRON-TREATED DIAMOND, DISCLOSURE, IRRADIATED DIAMOND.

reclaimed diamonds, industrial diamonds which have been recovered from used tools and reprocessed.

recovery, general term for any of several methods used to separate diamonds from diamond-bearing ores and alluvial concentrates. See BABY, ELECTROMAGNETIC SEPARATION, ELECTROSTATIC SEPARATION, GREASE BELT, GREASE TABLE, HEAVY-MEDIA SEPARATION, HYDROCYCLONE SEPARATION, JIG, LONG TOM, OPTICAL SEPARATOR, PANNING, PICKING TABLE, RECOVERY PLANT, ROTARY WASHING PAN, SCRUBBER, SEPARATION, STATIC CONE, TROMMEL.

recovery plant, processing plant where diamonds are recovered from ore, or from alluvial concentrates.

recut, see RECUTTING.

recutting, refashioning a polished diamond to improve its clarity or proportions, repair damage, or modernize an old cut. Often called repolishing when the work is minor.

recut weight, weight of a diamond after recutting. Recut weight can often be estimated with considerable accuracy before the work is done.

Red Cross Diamond, originally a 375 ct. reportedly yellow rough diamond, found at the De Beers Mine in 1900. Polished in Amsterdam into a 205.07 ct. square cut; because of the pavilion faceting arrangement, a Maltese cross is visible through the table. Presented as a

Red Cross Diamond

photo courtesy of CSO

gift from the London Diamond Syndicate to the British Red Cross Society and the Order of St. John of Jerusalem in 1918 to raise funds after World War I. Last sold at auction in 1977; current whereabouts unknown.

red diamond, fancy color diamond with a distinctly red natural bodycolor. Red is one of the rarer fancy colors in diamonds.

Red Diamond, 5.05 ct. reportedly flawless, red emerald-cut diamond, fashioned in Amsterdam from a 35 ct. rough found in 1927 at Lichtenburg, South Africa. Last sold in 1970. See HALPHEN DIAMOND, HANCOCK RED DIAMOND, RAJ RED DIAMOND.

reflection, bouncing back of light when it strikes a polished surface. Approximately 17 percent of the light striking the external surface of a polished diamond vertically is reflected back into the air; the greater part enters the stone. Light striking an internal surface of a polished diamond at an angle greater than the critical angle (24°26') is reflected back into the diamond (total internal reflection). See ANGLE OF REFLECTION, BRILLIANCE, LEAKAGE, REFRACTION.

reflectivity meter, device used to measure the approximate refractive index of a polished gemstone by measuring the infra-red light reflected from its surface; can be used on gemstones with refractive indices (RIs) above the 1.81 upper limit of standard refractometers, although the results are not always accurate or repeatable. Flatness and cleanliness of the surface, polish, refractive index, internal reflections, and high dispersion may affect the accuracy of readings. Reflectivity meters do not measure birefringence. See BIREFRINGENCE.

reflector, inclusion in a diamond which, due to its location, is reflected in such a way that its image appears in more than one facet.

reflector

refraction, bending and slowing of light as it passes at an oblique angle from a medium of one optical density (such as air) into a medium of greater optical density (such as diamond). The strength of refraction depends on the angle at which the light passes between the two, and the degree to which the second medium reduces its speed. See ANGLE OF REFRACTION, ANISOTROPIC, ANOMALOUS DOUBLE REFRACTION (ADR), ISOTROPIC, REFRACTIVE INDEX (RI).

refractive index (RI), measure of the extent to which light is bent as it enters or leaves a gemstone at an angle other than perpendicular to the surface; it is expressed as the ratio of the speed of light in air to its speed in the gemstone. All other factors being equal, the higher a stone's RI, the greater its brilliance. Diamond's RI is 2.417. See ANGLE OF REFRACTION, CRITICAL ANGLE, OPTICAL DENSITY, REFRACTION, REFRACTOMETER.

refractometer, instrument used to measure a gemstone's refractive index (RI). Standard refractometers with glass hemicylinders can test gemstones with RIs below 1.81; hemicylinders of spinel, synthetic cubic zirconia, or diamond raise this limit. See CONTACT LIQUID, RAYNER DIAMOND REFRACTOMETER.

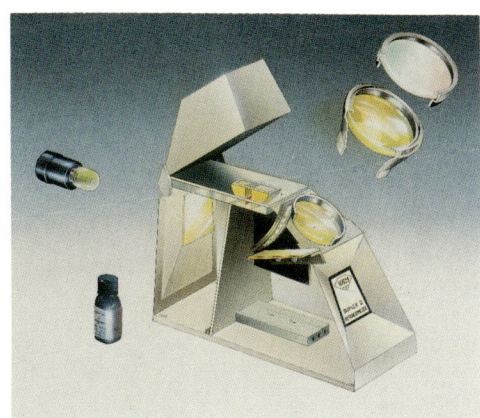

refractometer

Regalaire, proprietary name for yttrium aluminum garnet (YAG). Marketed as a diamond simulant.

Regale of France Diamond, diamond alleged to be "as large as a bird's egg." According to legend, King Louis IX of France exchanged the diamond for a lead image of St. Thomas à Becket at the saint's shrine in Canterbury, England. Such exchanges are a common motif in medieval hagiography; there is no evidence the story is true.

Regent Diamond, 410 ct. rough diamond reportedly found at the Parteal Mines in India in 1701. Bought by Thomas Pitt, a merchant and President of Fort Madras, it was fashioned into a 140.50 ct. cushion-shape brilliant in England and named after its first owner; it became known as the Regent when it was sold to Philippe II (1674-1723), Duke of Orleans, then Regent for the future Louis XV, in 1717. Stolen in the robbery of the Garde Mueble in 1792, it was recovered and set in the sword worn by Napoleon I at his coronation in 1802. Now on display in the Galérie d'Apollon at the Louvre Museum in Paris.

Regent Diamond

Registered Jeweler, title awarded by the American Gem Society to retail jewelers who complete specified courses and examinations.

Registered Supplier, title awarded by the American Gem Society to individuals who are affiliated with member wholesale firms, and who complete specified courses and examinations.

regular, sorting term for a well-formed octahedron.

Reine des Belges Diamond, La, a 50 ct. cushion-shape diamond owned by Queen Marie Henrietta of Belgium, wife of King Leopold II (1835-1909). She had received it as a gift from her mother, the wife of the Archduke Joseph, Palatine of Hungary. Later refashioned into a 40 ct. emerald cut, it is believed still to be in the possession of the Belgian Royal Family. Also known as La Reine Diamond.

Reitz Diamond, 650.80 ct. irregular octahedron found in the Jagersfontein Mine in 1895. Named for Francis William Reitz, then president of the Orange Free State, in which the mine is located. The rough yielded two major diamonds: a 13.34 ct. pear shape which was sold to Dom Carlos I of Portugal in 1896 (its subsequent history is unknown) and a 245.35 ct. cushion cut, which was ultimately named the Jubilee in celebration of the 60-year anniversary of the coronation of Britain's Queen Victoria. In 1937, the Jubilee was sold to Paul-Louis Weiller, founder of Air France; it was exhibited in Washington, D.C., US, and Geneva, Switzerland in 1960, and later was on display in the De Beers Diamond Pavilion in Johannesburg, South Africa.

Jubilee Diamond, fashioned from the Reitz rough

rejection, (1) rough diamonds of poor quality from which only a low polished yield can be expected; includes small, misshapen, broken, poor color, and low clarity rough diamonds. (2) diamond with more inclusions than a spotted stone. See SPOTTED STONE.

rejection chip, small, misshapen diamond crystal or a broken piece of poor quality rough diamond; once applied only to better quality industrial stones, now used for cuttable or inexpensive gem quality diamonds. See CHIP.

relief, distinctness with which an object (such as an inclusion) stands out against its background (such as the host gemstone). In diamond grading, high-relief inclusions have a greater effect on the clarity grade than low-relief inclusions of similar size and in similar positions.

Rembrandt Diamond, 42 ct. polished diamond, reported to be black and fashioned from a 125 ct. rough to celebrate four centuries of diamond manufacturing in Amsterdam. Named for Dutch painter Rembrandt van Rijn (1606-1669). Current whereabouts unknown.

repeated twinning, see POLYSYNTHETIC TWINNING.

Replique, proprietary name for yttrium aluminum garnet (YAG). Marketed as a diamond simulant.

repolishing, refashioning a polished diamond to correct minor faults in its clarity or proportions. See RECUTTING.

reserve mining area, known location of an alluvial diamond deposit which has been prospected but not yet mined; often the target of illicit diamond diggers. See ILLICIT DIAMOND MINING.

restricted alluvial digging, South African alluvial diamond deposit where mining is permitted under license. The number of individuals allowed to work the deposit is also specified. See PRECIOUS STONES ACT OF 1927, PROCLAIMED AREA.

Retail Jewelers of America (RJA), see JEWELERS OF AMERICA (JA).

Rhine diamond, misnomer for colorless beryl or rock crystal quartz. See RHINESTONE.

rhinestone, originally a colorless quartz pebble from the Rhine River Valley; now loosely applied to foilbacked and colorless lead-glass imitations of diamond.

Rhodes, Cecil John (1853-1902), British colonial entrepreneur and statesman, founder and first chairman of De Beers Consolidated Mines and one of the first to see the need for a single-channel system for marketing diamonds. Rhodes also served in the Parliament of the Cape Colony from 1881 until his death; he became Prime Minister in 1890, but was forced to resign in 1896. He is buried in the Matopos Hills in Zimbabwe, originally called Rhodesia in his honor, and is memorialized by the Rhodes Scholarships at Oxford University, which were funded in his will.

Cecil John Rhodes

Rhodesia, see ZIMBABWE.

rhombic-dodecahedron, see DODECAHEDRON.

rhomboid cut, four-sided, parallelogram-shaped step cut.

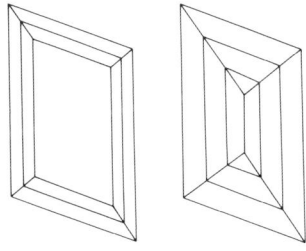

rhomboid cut

RI, see REFRACTIVE INDEX.

rib line, see FACET JUNCTION.

Richelieu Diamond, 19 ct. heart-shape, rose-cut diamond, reportedly of fine quality, bequeathed to the French Crown by Armand-Jean du Plessis, Cardinal Richelieu (1585-1642), Chief Minister of France under Louis XIII. During the reign of Louis XIV, the diamond was set in an earring; it was stolen in the robbery of the Garde Meuble in Paris in 1792 and its current whereabouts are unknown.

rider balance, mechanical balance with counterweights which are moved along a beam until they and the gemstone being weighed are in equilibrium. See CHAIN BALANCE, COUNTERWEIGHT

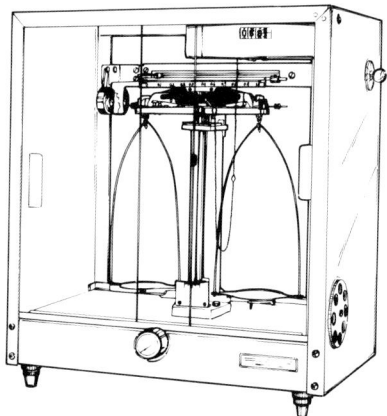

jeweler's balance using a combination of rider weight, chain, and counterweights

BALANCE, DIAMOND BALANCE, ELECTRONIC BALANCE, MECHANICAL BALANCE, PORTABLE BALANCE, SINGLE-PAN BALANCE.

Rietfontein South, diamond treatment plant operated by Alexcor 30 kilometers (18 miles) south of Alexander Bay on the Atlantic coast of South Africa. Opened in April 1992, the plant, which contains primary and secondary crushing units and screening and scrubbing circuits, is said to be capable of processing 300 tons of alluvial material per hour. See ALEXCOR, STATE ALLUVIAL DEPOSIT.

river, (1) archaic term for a transparent, colorless diamond. (2) traditional term for the top color grade (for stones over 0.47 ct.) on the Scan. D.N. color scale, equivalent to GIA color grades D and E. See APPENDIX D, GIA COLOR-GRADING SCALE, SCAN. D.N. COLOR SCALE.

river diggings, alluvial diamond-mining operations which take place in ancient watercourses and in running streams and rivers; historically called wet diggings. See ALLUVIAL DEPOSIT, DRY DIGGINGS.

River of Light Diamond, see DARYA-I-NUR DIAMOND.

River Styx Diamond, black diamond crystal found in the Bultfontein Mine and fashioned into a 28.50 ct. brilliant and a 7 ct. marquise. Current whereabouts unknown.

RJA, Retail Jewelers of America, Inc. See JEWELERS OF AMERICA.

Roberts-Victor Mine, small diamond mine consisting of a pipe and two fissures near Boshof, Orange Free State, South Africa; diamonds are recovered by sub-level caving. Noted for well-formed octahedra with a very light blue bodycolor. Also known as the Rovic Mine.

Robodiam, proprietary name for a line of automated faceting and bruting machines manufactured and marketed by Hakodiam of Belgium. The company's Faceted Rondist Machine, introduced in 1990, is said to have a grain-seeking capability and can handle between 4 and 200 facets on rounds (0.15 ct. and larger) and on a wide range of fancy-shape sawn stones or makeables. The product line also includes bruting and stone-centering systems.

rock crystal quartz, transparent, colorless, single-crystal quartz which is sometimes used as a diamond simulant. There are several hundred misnomers for this stone.

Rockeater mv, one of the first marine diamond-prospecting vessels equipped with undersea pumps to recover diamonds in off-shore deposits. Owned by Marine Diamond Corporation (MDC), it was shipwrecked, like others in the MDC fleet, a victim of the dangerous Namibian coastline. See COLLINS, SAMUEL V.; OFFSHORE MINING.

rocker, see CRADLE.

Rockwell indentation hardness test, hardness test used for metals; a cone-shaped diamond is pressed into the metal being tested to a standard depth, while its relative resistance is measured.

Rojtman Diamond, 107.60 ct. cushion-shape diamond, said to be yellow; purchased by Harry Winston in 1957 and repolished to 107.46 ct. Mounted in a clip-pendant combination and sold in the US in 1963; it is named for its owner.

rondelle, (1) flat, disk-shaped cutting style with faceted edges, often employed for gemstones used as spacers on strung beads. (2) disk-shaped cutting tool with a variable number of teeth around its edge. Also spelled roundelle, rondel.

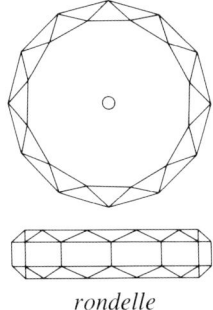
rondelle

rondisting, Dutch, the final shaping of the girdle once the initial eight facets have been blocked and cross-worked. Called final girdling in English. See BRUTING.

Ronit, proprietary name for a line of computerized bruting machines manufactured and marketed by Electronit Diamond Machines of Israel.

root, the bottom of an ore deposit, such as a kimberlite or lamproite pipe.

Rosario Oeste, regionally important alluvial diamond deposit in Mato Grosso, Brazil.

rose, see ROSE CUT.

rose cut, historic cut characterized by a flat base, a circular girdle outline, a pointed, dome-shaped crown, and a varying number of triangular facets. Thought to have originated in India, and to have been introduced into Europe by Venetian polishers in the fifteenth century; it is sometimes called a rosette cut or rosie. Now obsolete. See BRILLIANT CUT, DOUBLE ROSE CUT, SINGLE CUT.

rose recoupée, see DOUBLE-DUTCH ROSE CUT.

rosette, see ROSE CUT.

rosie, see ROSE CUT.

Roskomdragmet, the Committee on Precious Metals and Gemstones of the Russian Federation. It administers the Russian Diamond Fund and the state depository, Gokhran, for which it also purchases diamonds to maintain the strategic stockpile. See ALMAZJUVELIREXPORT, ALMAZY ROSSII-SAKHA, GOKHRAN, KRISTALL, RUSSIAN DIAMOND FUND, YAKUTALMAZ.

Rossini Jewel, proprietary name for synthetic strontium titanate. Marketed as a diamond simulant.

rotary washing pan, mechanical device used to separate diamonds from alluvial concentrates

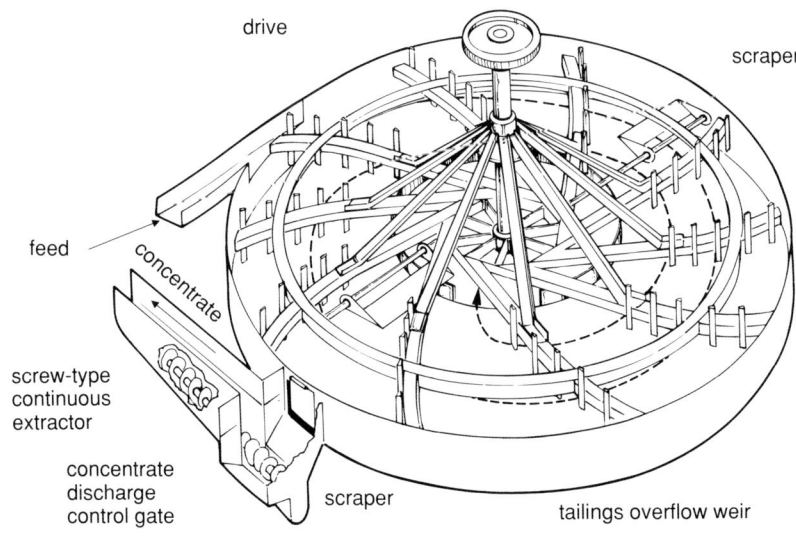
rotary washing pan

or crushed or weathered ore. The ore is introduced into a large circular pan, with water and fine clay particles which form a heavy medium, or "puddle." The lighter material is floated off over a central weir; heavy material, including diamonds, sinks to the bed and is raked to the side for collection by rotating scrapers. See HEAVY-MEDIA SEPARATION, HYDROCYCLONE SEPARATION, RECOVERY, SEPARATION (2), STATIC CONE.

rough, see ROUGH DIAMOND.

rough diamond, diamond of either cuttable or industrial quality, as it is recovered from the earth, prior to undergoing any manufacturing process.

rough diamonds

rough girdle, irregular, pitted, or granular girdle surface, often severely bearded; caused by being rounded up or bruted too quickly. See BRUTING, POLISHED GIRDLE.

roughs, small unpolished diamonds, often set in inexpensive bunch rings. See BUNCH RING.

round bort, see BALLAS.

rough girdle

round brilliant, see STANDARD ROUND BRILLIANT.

Roundiam, proprietary name for a line of automated faceting and bruting machines manufactured and marketed by B. Varticovschi of Israel. The company's Roundiam Multi-Facet, introduced in 1990, was capable of cutting from 16 to 110 facets, with programmable sequencing. The Roundiam-B is an automated rondisting and bruting machine.

rounding up, see BRUTING.

Rovensky Diamond Necklace, diamond-and-platinum necklace set with 213.10 ct. of diamonds, including a reportedly colorless, flawless 46.50 ct. pear shape. Named for its owner, Mae C. Rovensky, wife of industrialist John E. Rovensky, it was last sold in 1957. Current whereabouts unknown.

Rovic Mine, see ROBERTS-VICTOR MINE.

Royal Asscher Diamond Company, Amsterdam diamond-manufacturing firm founded in 1936 by brothers Abraham and Joseph Asscher to succeed their father's I.J. Asscher Company. Originally called the Asscher Diamond Company; the title Royal was bestowed on the firm in 1980 by Queen Juliana of the Netherlands.

Royal Cuts, line of four trademarked fancy cuts developed by the Israeli firm of Raphaeli-Stschik to make the most of flat or misshapen rough. Co-designed by Gershon Stschik and Chumi Raphaeli, they are significantly wider at the top than traditional fancy shapes or round cuts and look 50 percent larger than traditional fancies of the same carat weight. See BARONESS CUT, DUCHESS CUT, EMPRESS CUT, GRACE CUT.

Rudd, Charles (1844-1916), longtime business partner and close friend of Cecil Rhodes. Rudd was associated with Rhodes in all his business endeavors, including the formation of De Beers Consolidated Mines; he was instrumental in obtaining the Rhodes/Rudd concession, which led to the formation of Rhodesia as a British colony.

run of mine, term for a sample of cleaned but unsorted rough diamonds taken directly from a mine or alluvial deposit, and on which valuations are based.

Russalmaz, the external polished diamond sales division of Almazjuvelirexport; among others, it has offices in Belgium, Canada, Germany, Singapore, and Switzerland. See ALMAZJUVELIREXPORT, GLAVALMAZZOLOTO, KOMDRAGMET, KRISTALL.

Russalmazzoloto, former Federal Directorate for Diamonds and Diamond Manufacturing of the Russian Federation. Established in late 1991, the organization replaced Glavalmazzoloto. In October, 1992, certain aspects of its work, such as rough diamond mining and marketing, were assumed by Almazy Rossii-Sakha. See ALMAZY ROSSII-SAKHA, GLAVALMAZZOLOTO.

Russia, historic name for the Czarist state predating the USSR and corresponding roughly to the Russian Soviet Federative Socialist Republic and the present Russian Federation of the Commonwealth of Independent States. Minor alluvial diamond deposits were found in the northern Ural Mountains of Russia in 1829. See COMMONWEALTH OF INDEPENDENT STATES (CIS).

Russian Diamond Fund, one of the world's greatest collections of gems and jewelry. Housed in the Kremlin in Moscow, it includes many of the historical jewels acquired by Russian rulers prior to 1917, and some of the exceptional stones discovered since, primarily in the Republic of Sakha (Yakutia) in Siberia. Also called the Russian Treasury of Diamonds and Precious Stones. See ROSKOMDRAGMET.

Russian Federation, independent state in the CIS, formerly the Russian Soviet Federative Socialist Republic (RSFSR, the largest constituent republic within the former Soviet Union or USSR). The Russian Federation now comprises some 20 republics (of which Sakha, which contains the principal diamond-mining region in the Federation, is one) and 70 regions. Significant kimberlites have also been located near Arkhangelsk, South of the Kola Peninsula. See ALMAZY ROSSII-SAKHA, COMMONWEALTH OF INDEPENDENT STATES (CIS), RUSSIA, SAKHA, YAKUTALMAZ.

Russian Portrait Diamond, see RUSSIAN TABLE PORTRAIT DIAMOND.

Russian Table Portrait Diamond, approximately 25 ct. flat, irregular pear-shape diamond. It is set in an old Indian gold-and-enamel bracelet and is now in the Russian Diamond Fund in Moscow. Also called the Russian Portrait Diamond.

Russian Treasury of Diamonds and Precious Stones, see RUSSIAN DIAMOND FUND.

Russia-Sakha Diamonds, see ALMAZY ROSSII-SAKHA.

Rutania, proprietary name for synthetic rutile. Marketed as a diamond simulant.

rutee, see RATI.

rutile, synthetic, see SYNTHETIC RUTILE.

S

Sack of Delhi, (1) turning point in the history of the Indian subcontinent when armies led by the Mogul Babur, "The Lion of the North," overran troops defending Ibrahim Lodi, the Sultan of Delhi, at the battle of Panupat in 1526. The spoils of Babur's victory included many jewels, most notably the Koh-i-Nur Diamond, held for safe-keeping in the Fort of Agra. (2) historic event triggered when the Persian general Nadir Shah routed the Indian army at Karnal (in 1738) and entered the city of Delhi, ending over two hundred years of Mogul rule in India. When rioting broke out in the following year, an estimated 150,000 people were killed and the city was looted. The Koh-i-Nur, the Florentine, the Shah, and the Darya-i-Nur Diamonds and such objets d'art as the Peacock Throne were seized and transported to Persia (now Iran). See DARYA-I-NUR DIAMOND, FLORENTINE DIAMOND, IRANIAN CROWN JEWELS, IRANIANS, KOH-I-NUR DIAMOND, PEACOCK THRONE, SHAH DIAMOND.

Saint-Maime diamond, misnomer for rock crystal quartz from France.

Sakha, Turkic name for an autonomous republic, known as Yakutia in Russian, the principal diamond-bearing region in the Russian Federation, CIS, and one of the world's largest producers of gem quality and industrial diamonds. Major discoveries were made in the Sakha region of Siberia (then a part of the Russian Soviet Federative Socialist Republic of the former USSR) in the early 1950s. The Mir, Udachnaya, Aikhal, International, and Jubilee are among its most important diamond mines. A 1992 agreement between the Russian Supreme Soviet and the Government of the Republic of Sakha granted Sakha control of 20 percent of the diamonds mined in its territory. Sakha's Siberian climate is the coldest in the inhabited world; temperatures in January average -43.5°C (-46°F) and only 19°C (66°F) in July; the permafrost is up to 305 meters (1,000 feet) deep. See AIKHAL PIPE; ALMAZY ROSSII-SAKHA; MALAYA BOTUOBOYA RIVER; MIR PIPE; MIRNYI; RUSSIAN FEDERATION; SAKHA KOMDRAGMET; SIBERIA; SOBOLEV, VLADIMIR S.; SYTIKANSK PIPE; UDACHNAYA PIPE; VILYIUY RIVER; YAKUTALMAZ.

Sakha Komdragmet, the Diamond Fund of Sakha.

Salt, Frederick B., see MAREK, JAN IVO.

Samada Mine, kimberlite pipe mined near Virginia, Orange Free State, South Africa. Diamonds were being recovered by open pit methods in 1992. Also known as the Kaalvallei Mine.

Sambalpur Group, historic group of alluvial diggings on the Mahanadi River in Godwara, India; believed once to have been the richest of the ancient Indian deposits.

Sambalpur Group

Sancy Diamond, 55 ct. pear-shape, double rose cut, Type II diamond with triangular and pentagonal facets. Believed to be of Indian origin, it was allegedly one of three diamonds taken from the body of Charles the Bold by Swiss mercenaries following an attack on Nancy, France, in 1477. It later came into the possession of the French Minister, Nicolas Harlay de Sancy (1546-1627), and was pledged to raise money for both Henri III (Valois) and Henri IV (Bourbon), before being sold to England's James I in 1604. It again served as collateral in 1644, to help finance the Royalist cause in the English Civil War; when the loan was not repaid, the diamond was forfeited to the Duke of Epernon. Purchased by Cardinal Jules Mazarin (1602-1661) and, upon his death, bequeathed to the French Crown, together with the Mirror of Portugal and Mazarin Diamonds. Unlike the other gems, it is not thought to have been stolen in the robbery of the Garde Mueble in 1792, having supposedly been pledged earlier to a Spanish Marquess by French revolutionaries for a million francs. Purchased by the Russian Prince Nicholas Demidoff (1773-1829) in 1828 and sold to William Waldorf Astor (1848-1919) in 1892. Purchased by the Banque de France and the Musées de France in 1978, it is now displayed in the Galérie d'Apollon at the Louvre in Paris. See CHARLES THE BOLD, LITTLE SANCY DIAMOND, MAZARIN DIAMONDS, REGENT DIAMOND.

Sancy Diamond

photo courtesy of CSO

sand, trade term for minute rough gem diamonds which can pass through a 1.78 millimeter (0.07-inch) sieve. See DIAMOND SIEVE.

San Pedro de las Bocas, area of alluvial diamond deposits near the confluence of the Paragua and Caroní Rivers in Venezuela.

sapphire, corundum, a natural gemstone which, in its colorless synthetic form, is often used as a diamond simulant. It is doubly refractive, with refractive indices of 1.762-1.770, a specific gravity of 4.00, dispersion of 0.018, and a hardness (Mohs scale) of 9. Luster is vitreous to subadamantine.

Sapphirized Titania, proprietary name for synthetic rutile. Marketed as a diamond simulant.

Saratoga diamond, misnomer for rock crystal quartz from New York, US. Sometimes marketed as a diamond simulant.

SAREMCI, see SOCIETE DE RECHERCHES ET D'EXPLOITATIONS MINIERES EN COTE D'IVOIRE.

saturation, the strength, purity, or intensity of a color; when color is present, saturation ranges from neutral gray to pure, vivid hues. With hue and tone, saturation is one of the three dimensions of color. See BODYCOLOR, COLOR GRADE, COLOR GRADING.

Savoy Diamond, 54 ct. table-cut diamond which Tavernier reported was in the Crown Jewels of the House of Savoy in the mid-seventeenth century. Current whereabouts unknown.

saw, see DIAMOND SAW.

sawable, (1) classification for rough diamonds, often octahedra or dodecahedra, which will yield more weight as two stones if they are sawn before being polished. (2) (plural) classification given to parcels of small rough diamonds which need to be sawn prior to polishing. See MAKEABLE.

sawing, process used to divide a diamond into two smaller pieces with a mechanized disc

sawing

coated with oil and diamond abrasive. Sawing follows directions at right angles to cleavage planes. See DIAMOND SAW.

sawing dop, brass retainer mounted on a short shaft in which a diamond is held with a mixture of plaster of Paris and glue during the sawing process. See HOLLOW DOP.

sawing grain, see GRAIN.

sawing rate, imprecise way of describing the length of time required to saw through a diamond crystal; it depends on a number of variables, including the size and structure of the crystal, the different hardnesses encountered within it, and the sawing methods employed. See DIRECTIONAL HARDNESS, GRAIN.

Saxon diamond, misnomer for colorless topaz. Also called Saxony diamond.

Saxon Diamonds, historic group of diamonds including the Dresden Green, Dresden White, and Dresden Yellow; at one time there were supposedly some 7,000 carats of gemstones in the collection, which was begun by Augustus the Strong, Duke of Saxony, at the end of the seventeenth century. Now on display in the Green Vaults in Dresden, Germany.

Saxon White Diamond, see DRESDEN WHITE DIAMOND.

scaife, flat, cast-iron wheel, 31 to 46 centimeters (12 to 18 inches) in diameter, used to grind and polish facets on diamonds. Driven by a vertical shaft at speeds ranging from 2,500 to 5,000 rpm and traditionally charged with diamond powder mixed with a liquid compound or binding agent; modern scaifes are often impregnated with diamond powder by their manufacturers. Grinding and polishing are done on different sections of the wheel. Diamond-charged scaifes are also used for polishing colored stones and for a variety of industrial processes. Also spelled skeif or skaif. See BLOCKING, CROSSWORKING, BRILLIANDEERING.

scale, see BALANCE.

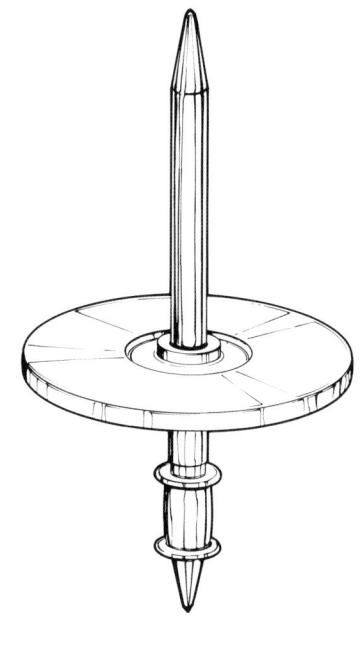

scaife

Scandinavian Diamond Nomenclature (Scan. D.N.) and Grading Standards, set of guidelines and standards for diamond clarity grading, color grading and nomenclature, cut grading and description, and certification; introduced in 1970 and now used in Denmark, Finland, Norway, and Sweden. See CIBJO RULES OF APPLICATION FOR THE DIAMOND TRADE, IDC RULES FOR GRADING POLISHED DIAMONDS, SCAN. D.N. CLARITY SCALE, SCAN. D.N. COLOR SCALE, SCAN. D.N. SCALE FOR THE QUALITY OF CUT.

Scandinavian standard round brilliant, set of proportions for the round brilliant, proposed in 1970 by Herbert Tillander and members of the Scan. D.N. Committee as a standard for adoption in Europe. These proportions are: table diameter, 57.5 percent; crown angle, 34°30'; crown height, 14.6 percent; pavilion angle, 40°45'; pavilion depth, 43.1 percent; and crown height to pavilion depth ratio, 1:2.95. See SCANDINAVIAN DIAMOND NOMENCLATURE (SCAN. D.N.) AND GRADING STANDARDS.

Scan. D.N., see SCANDINAVIAN DIAMOND NOMENCLATURE AND GRADING STANDARDS.

Scan. D.N. clarity scale, range of diamond clarity grades running from flawless (F) and internally flawless (IF), through two grades each of very, very slightly included (VVS), very slightly included (VSI), and slightly included (SI), and three grades of *piqué*. See APPENDIX E, CIBJO INTERNATIONAL CLARITY/PURITY SCALE, CLARITY, CLARITY GRADING, CLARITY-GRADING SCALE, CLARITY-GRADING SYSTEM, GIA CLARITY-GRADING SCALE, IDC CLARITY-GRADING SCALE, SCANDINAVIAN DIAMOND NOMENCLATURE (SCAN. D.N.) AND GRADING STANDARDS.

Scan. D.N. color scale, range of color grades used for colorless to light yellow, light brown, or light gray diamonds. The traditional terms used as Scan. D.N. color grades are: River, Top Wesselton, Wesselton, Top Crystal, Crystal, Top Cape, Cape, Light Yellow, and Yellow. Scan. D.N. also allows use of two sets of alternate descriptive terms and recommends the parenthetical addition of the appropriate GIA letter grade, *e.g.,* River (D) or River (E). See APPENDIX D, CIBJO INTERNATIONAL COLOR-GRADING SCALE, COLOR GRADING, COLOR-GRADING SCALE, COLOR-GRADING SYSTEM, GIA COLOR-GRADING SCALE, IDC INTERNATIONAL COLOR-GRADING SCALE, SCANDINAVIAN DIAMOND NOMENCLATURE (SCAN. D.N.) AND GRADING STANDARDS.

Scan. D.N. scale for the quality of cut, range of grades for describing the make of a polished diamond. The four grades—very good, good, medium, and poor—are divided into 10 subgrades. (The IDC Rules allow for use of the same four terms to describe proportions and finish separately.) See AGS CUT-GRADING SYSTEM, CUT, CUT GRADING, FINISH, FINISH GRADING, MAKE, PROPORTIONS, PROPORTION GRADING, SCANDINAVIAN DIAMOND NOMENCLATURE (SCAN. D.N.) AND GRADING STANDARDS.

Scepter Diamond, see ORLOFF DIAMOND.

Schaumberg diamond, misnomer for rock crystal quartz from Schaumberg, Germany. Sometimes used as a diamond simulant.

Schüller Mine, see LENA MINE.

Schumacher Diamonds, American diamond manufacturer based in North Dakota; developer of a computer-operated, visually centered bruting system.

Schweizer Reneke, town in Transvaal Province, South Africa, where authorized diggers sell their production to licensed buyers.

scintillation, flashes of light reflected from a polished diamond, seen when either the diamond, the light source, or the observer moves. Besides diamond's inherent optical properties, scintillation depends on the number and size of the facets, the precision of the facet angles, and the quality of the polish. Sometimes called sparkle. See BRILLIANCE, DISPERSION.

sclerometer, instrument for measuring scratch hardness in which a sharp diamond point is drawn across a polished surface on the test material; weight is added incrementally until a scratch is produced. The final weight is compared with that required to produce a similar scratch on standard minerals. On the sclerometer scale, diamond has a value of 140,000; sapphire 1,000; and talc 1.13. See ABRASION TEST, ATOMIC BONDING, BRINELL HARDNESS TEST, DIRECTIONAL HARDNESS, HARDNESS POINTS, INDENTATION TEST, KNOOP INDENTATION TEST, MOHS SCALE, SCLEROMETER, SCRATCH HARDNESS, TOUGHNESS, VICKERS HARDNESS TEST.

scraper, (1) winch-driven, multi-ton horseshoe-shaped piece of equipment used in underground mining to recover loose ore in block caving. (2) self-propelled or tractor-hauled excavating machine used to remove overburden on the surface. See SCRAPER DRIFT.

scraper drift, concrete-lined drift extending across a kimberlite pipe, with inclined openings at intervals in its sides through which ore released by block caving can enter. A large scraper is dragged back and forth through the drift, pulling loose ore from the openings and dragging it to a collection area. See DRIFT, SCRAPER.

photo by Robert E. Kane

scratch

scratch, narrow, shallow, rough-edged abrasion on the surface of a diamond; under magnification, it appears as a faint white line. Caused by contact with other diamonds. See ABRASION, PAPERWORN DIAMOND.

scratch hardness, resistance of a material to scratching, judged by the ease with which a material of a known hardness scratches it. See HARDNESS, HARDNESS POINTS, MOHS SCALE, SCLEROMETER, SCRATCH.

screw micrometer, see MICROMETER.

scribbling ring, ring set with a diamond octahedron, the point of which was used to write affectionate messages and initials on glass. Popular between the sixteenth and nineteenth centuries.

scrubber, recovery apparatus consisting of a large rotating drum into which ore and water are fed; used on broken kimberlite in mines where the clay content is high. See JIG, ROTARY WASHING PAN, SEPARATION (2), TROMMEL.

sea mining, see BEACH MINING, OFF-SHORE MINING.

Sea of Light Diamond, see DARYA-I-NUR DIAMOND.

secondary diamond deposit, see ALLUVIAL DEPOSIT.

second bye, historic color-grading term for rough diamonds slightly tinged with yellow; now obsolete. See BYE, LIGHT OFF-COLOR.

sedimentary rock, rock formed over time from earth, sand, and gravel deposited by water, wind, or ice. See IGNEOUS ROCK.

seed crystal, (1) minute crystal around which a natural crystal may grow. (2) small synthetic or natural crystal used in several synthesis processes to stimulate the growth of a synthetic gem. See CZOCHRALSKI PULLING METHOD.

see-through effect, visibility of any distinct image, such as a line of print, viewed through a transparent, faceted gemstone placed face-down on top of it. Occurs in materials with a low RI and a relatively large critical angle; it is unusual in diamonds, except when they have been poorly fashioned. Several diamond simulants show the see-through effect.

see-through effect

selective absorption, process by which a material absorbs some wavelengths of light while it transmits others. The wavelengths which are absorbed and the degree of absorption depend on the chemical composition and crystal structure of the material; transmitted wavelengths contribute to a material's perceived bodycolor. Absorbed wavelengths may show as dark lines or bands in a spectroscope or as peaks in a spectrophotometer. See ELECTROMAGNETIC SPECTRUM, LIGHT ABSORPTION.

semi-automatic dop, mechanical gemstone holder attached to a tang which allows the polisher to change a diamond's position without removing it from the dop, thus keeping polishing angles constant. Used mostly for small diamonds. Different semi-automatic dops are used for crowns, pavilions, and brilliandeering. Also called an automatic dop. See AUTOMATIC POLISHING MACHINE, DOP, MECHANICAL DOP, SOLDER DOP.

semi-conductor, crystalline material which conducts electricity with an efficiency capacity

semi-mount, jewelry mounting, pre-set with small diamonds, to which one or more large stones may be added.

semi-navette, fancy cut shaped like half a marquise. Often recut from a broken marquise.

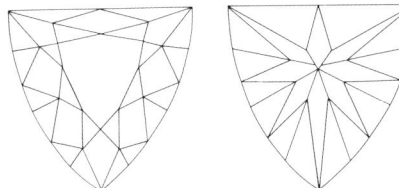

semi-navette

senaille, small diamond fashioned with a flat base and irregular triangular facets. Similar to a rose cut.

Sendelingsdrift, alluvial diamond deposit on the south bank of the Orange River in Namaqualand, South Africa. Diamonds are found in gravels in a prehistoric river channel and are recovered by overburden stripping, mechanical mining, and hand sweeping.

separation, (1) process of distinguishing specific species and varieties of minerals from one another, and natural materials from synthetics. (2) process of isolating and removing specific minerals (such as diamond) from ore; a variety of methods is used. See BABY, ELECTROMAGNETIC SEPARATION, ELECTROSTATIC SEPARATION, GREASE BELT, GREASE TABLE, HEAVY-MEDIA SEPARATION, HYDROCYCLONE SEPARATION, JIG, LONG TOM, OPTICAL SEPARATOR, PANNING, PICKING TABLE, RECOVERY, ROTARY WASHING PAN, SCRUBBER, STATIC CONE, TROMMEL.

separation plane, interface where the parts of an assembled stone meet. See ASSEMBLED STONE, DOUBLET, TRIPLET.

serie, term for polished diamonds which range from 0.19 ct. to 1.49 ct. in size. See MELEE, SIZES.

set, manufacturer's term for either a group comprising two star facets and the four adjacent upper-girdle facets, or a group comprising four lower-girdle facets on a brilliant-cut diamond. Originated through the use of a lead dop; with the diamond held in solder, polishers could only see one such "set" of facets at a time. See FACE.

setter, (1) originally the person who set the rough or prepared diamond into a dop for sawing, bruting, and polishing. Today, the term commonly refers to one who sets the stones in sawing dops, but it may also be used to describe the technician who positions diamonds in automated polishing machines. (2) person who sets diamonds or other gems in jewelry. Also called a mounter.

setting, (1) part of the mounting in which a polished diamond is set. (2) act of placing a polished diamond in a mount. (3) act of setting a diamond into a dop for sawing, bruting, or polishing. See HEAD, SETTER.

SG, see SPECIFIC GRAVITY.

SG liquids, see HEAVY LIQUIDS.

shadow pattern method, visual test to distinguish brilliant-cut diamonds from such simulants as strontium titanate, CZ, GGG, and YAG. The stone to be tested is placed table-down in an immersion cell partly filled with methylene iodide and illuminated by direct light; a brilliant cut produces a distinct shadow pattern for each material which is reflected in the liquid. Very small diamonds do not produce readable patterns.

Shah Diamond, 88.70 ct. bar-shape, light yellow, partially polished diamond of Indian origin which bears the engraved names of three of its previous owners and appropriate dates according to the Islamic calendar. The first two are "Burhan-Nizam-Shah-II, 1000" (ruler of the Indian province of Ahmadnagar, 1591) and "Son of Jahangir Shah, Jahan Shah, 1051" (1641). (Jahan [1592-1666] completed the Peacock Throne and had the Taj Mahal constructed.) The diamond then passed to his son, Aurangzeb (1618-1707); Tavernier described it after his visit to the Emperor's court in 1665. It is believed to have been seized in the Sack of Delhi in 1739. The third inscription reads "Kadjar Fath Ali Shah" (1797-1834), Shah of Persia in 1824. In 1829, the diamond was given to Czar Nicholas I of Russia (1796-1855) by the Persian government to prevent further warfare between the two countries. Now in the Russian Diamond Fund in Moscow. See SACK OF DELHI.

Shahidan Mines, diamond-mining company which once operated in the Panna district in the state of Mahdya Pradesh, India. Now defunct.

Shah Jahan Table Cut Diamond, 56.71 ct. octagonal, reportedly light pink, table-cut diamond with two drillholes. Depicted in a portrait of Shah Jahan (1592-1666), it is probably one of the "Three Tables" described by Tavernier. Believed to have been taken to Persia after the sack of Delhi in 1739, it is thought to have been given to Empress Elizabeth of Russia two years later. Last offered for sale in 1985 in Geneva by a seller who stated that the diamond had been in his family since 1893. See SACK OF DELHI.

Shah Jahan Table Cut Diamond

photo courtesy of CSO

Shah of Persia Diamond, 99.52 ct. yellow, cushion-shape diamond which was brought to the US in 1923 by Russian General V. Starosselky. It was claimed to have been recut from the 137.27 ct. Florentine Diamond. The Shah of Persia Diamond was acquired from a Los Angeles gem dealer in 1957 by Harry Winston. Sold privately in 1965. See SACK OF DELHI.

shallow crown angle, crown angle of less than 32°. Shallow crown angles often reduce a diamond's dispersion and make it more susceptible to chipping at the girdle. See CROWN HEIGHT, PAVILION DEPTH PERCENTAGE.

shallow cut, see SHALLOW DIAMOND.

shallow diamond, diamond with a total depth of less than 58-60 percent, causing increased light leakage and loss of brilliance. See CROWN HEIGHT, DISPERSION, PAVILION DEPTH PERCENTAGE, REFRACTION.

shallow pavilion, pavilion depth considerably less than 40 percent, causing increased light leakage and loss of brilliance. Among other faults, shallow pavilions can cause internal reflections of the girdle which are sometimes visible through the table; often called fisheyes. See PAVILION ANGLE, TABLE REFLECTION.

shape, (1) face-up girdle outline of a polished diamond or other gem, such as round brilliant, pear, marquise, heart, oval, or square. (2) sorting term for rough diamonds in which two of the octahedral axes are longer than the third. (3) to brute a rough diamond before polishing. See BRUTING, OCTAHEDRON.

sharp, (1) small diamond with a sharp edge, cemented in a dop and used to kerf another diamond in preparation for cleaving. (2) small diamond, which may take various shapes, used to brute diamonds or round up a girdle in the final stages of polishing.

Shearwater Bay mv, mining vessel owned by De Beers Marine, equipped with small-scale recovery equipment and used for deep-water sampling in exploration operations off the Atlantic coast of southern Africa.

shellac, organic resinous substance used in the preparation of varnishes and cements; often used as an adhesive to retain diamonds during bruting, sawing, or cleaving.

Shengli 1 Mine, kimberlite reportedly being mined at Mengyin, Shandong Province, People's Republic of China; said to be smaller than the Wafangdian Mine and believed to be a small producer. The discovery of one large yellow stone of 119 ct. has been announced. See CHINA, PEOPLE'S REPUBLIC OF (PRC); WAFANGDIAN MINE.

Shepherd Stone Diamond, see AKBAR SHAH DIAMOND.

shield cut, many-sided step or brilliant cut resembling a shield in outline. The lengths and angles of the sides vary. See GUINEA STAR.

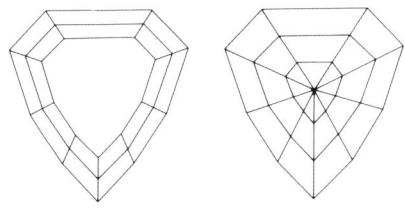

shield cut

Shipley, Robert M. (1887-1978), founder of the Gemological Institute of America (GIA) in 1931 and the American Gem Society (AGS) in 1934; originator of GIA's first gemological courses; Fellow of the British Gemmological Association (FGA); author of *Famous Diamonds of the World* (1939), and editor of *The Dictionary of Gems & Gemology* (1945) and *The Jeweler's Pocket Reference Book* (1947).

Robert M. Shipley

shock conversion, synthesis process which combines high heat with high-pressure-generating shock waves; used to convert graphite into synthetic industrial diamond and/or lonsdaleite. See LONSDALEITE.

shot ballas, see BALLAS.

shot bort, see BALLAS.

shoulders, curved edges of the girdle outline between the head and the belly on an oval or pear-shape diamond. See BELLY, HEAD.

SI, abbreviation for slightly included.

SIBEKA, see SOCIETE D'ENTREPRISE ET D'INVESTISSEMENTS S.A.

Siberia, region within the former Union of Soviet Socialist Republics, extending from the Ural Mountains to the Pacific Ocean; the area where most Russian diamond mining takes place. See AIKHAL PIPE; MALAYA BOTUOBOYA RIVER; MIR PIPE; MIRNYI; SAKHA; SYTIKANSK PIPE; SOBOLEV, VLADIMIR S.; UDACHNAYA PIPE; VILYIUY RIVER.

Siberian Diamond, see STALINGRAD DIAMOND.

Sierra Leone, country on the Atlantic coast of West Africa, where diamonds were first discovered in 1930; production began in 1934. Alluvial deposits are concentrated along rivers and valleys in the center of the country, and some kimberlitic occurrences have been located. Sierra Leone has produced many well-formed octahedra and some exceptionally large diamonds. Mining was nationalized in 1970; the deposits are now largely depleted. See STAR OF SIERRA LEONE DIAMOND.

Sierra Leone Selection Trust, Ltd. (SLST), once the principal diamond-mining company in Sierra Leone. Replaced by the National Diamond Mining Company of Sierra Leone (DIMINCO), which is now defunct.

sieve, see DIAMOND SIEVE.

sight, one of ten sales scheduled each year at which the Central Selling Organisation offers rough diamonds to selected clients (who are, accordingly, called sightholders). Sights are held in London, England; Lucerne, Switzerland; and Kimberley, South Africa. The term is also loosely applied to the parcels of rough diamonds offered for sale, to the boxes in which they are contained, and to various other aspects of the event. See ALLOCATION, CENTRAL SELLING ORGANISATION (CSO), SIGHTHOLDER.

sightholder, diamond dealer or manufacturer invited by the Central Selling Organisation to buy rough diamonds at a sight. The number of sightholders may vary according to economic conditions; in 1992 there were reported to be about 150. See ALLOCATION, CENTRAL SELLING ORGANISATION (CSO), SIGHT.

Sights Committee, panel of CSO personnel responsible for determining the amount of rough diamonds to be sold at the upcoming sight and, where possible, matching available supplies with specific requests entered earlier by DTC brokers on behalf of individual sightholders. See ALLOCATION, BROKER, SIGHTHOLDER.

sill, tabular igneous intrusion paralleling the planar structure of the surrounding rock.

silver cape, historic grading term for a near colorless to faint yellow diamond. Small diamonds in this grade usually show no color when mounted, but large stones appear faint yellow to the trained eye. Obsolete. See CAPE.

simili diamond, misnomer for rock crystal quartz or glass.

simulant, see DIAMOND SIMULANT, SIMULATED STONE.

simulated stone, any substance which imitates a natural gemstone in appearance. See DIAMOND SIMULANT.

single cut, cutting style with a circular girdle, a table, eight crown facets, eight pavilion facets, and (very rarely) a culet. Used mostly on diamonds weighing less than 0.05 ct. Originally known as the Mazarin cut; sometimes called an eight cut, or eight-by-eight.

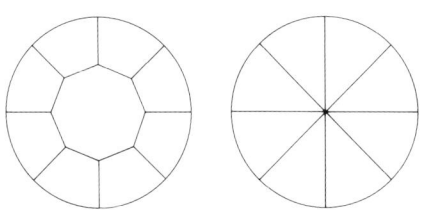

single cut

single-layer diamond dressing tool, diamond dressing tool which contains several diamonds on the tool face. See DIAMOND DRESSING TOOL.

single-pan balance, mechanical balance with one pan and a set of counterweights housed inside the instrument; a counter shows the total weight. See CHAIN BALANCE, COUNTERWEIGHT BALANCE, DIAMOND BALANCE, ELECTRONIC BALANCE, MECHANICAL BALANCE, PORTABLE BALANCE, RIDER BALANCE.

singly refractive, see ISOTROPIC.

Sitykansk, see SYTIKANSK PIPE.

six-facet rose cut, rose cut with a circular girdle outline; a flat, unfaceted base; a pointed, dome-shaped crown; and six large facets.

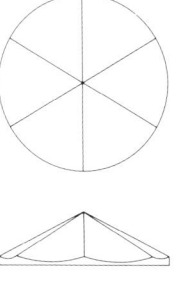

six-facet rose cut

sixth, trade term for a sixth of a carat, approximately 0.15 ct.

sizes, name given to polished diamonds weighing more than 1.50 ct. See MELEE, SERIE.

skaif, see SCAIFE.

skeif, see SCAIFE.

skew facets, see GIRDLE FACETS.

skill facets, see GIRDLE FACETS.

skin, surface of a rough diamond, a small part of which is sometimes left on polished diamonds to indicate that maximum weight has been retained from the rough. See NATURAL.

skiver, term used by diamond setters to describe a long, narrow, shallow chip on a diamond; caused by the incorrect use of setting tools.

skull melting, process used to produce synthetic cubic zirconia, in which zirconia powder and a chemical stabilizer are melted together in a crucible, or "skull." See SYNTHETIC CUBIC ZIRCONIA.

slaves' diamond, misnomer for colorless topaz. Sometimes marketed as a diamond simulant.

slightly imperfect, see SLIGHTLY INCLUDED (SI).

slightly included (SI), grade on the GIA clarity-grading scale for diamonds with inclusions and surface blemishes which are usually invisible to the unaided eye, but which can be seen easily or very easily under 10x magnification; inclusions are often centrally located and noticed immediately. In larger sizes and in some fancies, they can sometimes be seen without magnification. There are two grades in this category, abbreviated SI_1 and SI_2. The CIBJO, IDC, and Scan. D.N. clarity scales each have a corresponding SI category. See APPENDIX E.

slightly tinted white, (1) term on the CIBJO and IDC color-grading scales for near colorless diamonds. Comparable to the GIA color grades I to J. (2) in the Scan. D.N. color-grading system, an alternative descriptive term for the traditional grades top crystal and crystal. See APPENDIX D.

slightly yellowish, in the Scan. D.N. color-grading system, an alternative descriptive term for the traditional grade cape.

slot mining, see OPEN BENCH MINING.

small, (1) polished diamond, smaller than mêlée (0.15 ct.). (2) rough diamond less than 0.75 ct. in weight.

Smoke Creek, area of numerous alluvial deposits in Western Australia's Kimberley region. Discovered in 1979 by the Ashton Joint Venture, the find led to the discovery of the AK1 pipe. The Smoke Creek and Limestone Creek deposits were mined between 1983 and 1985; operations recommenced in 1989. See ARGYLE DIAMOND MINES, WESTERN AUSTRALIA.

Smolensk, city 420 kilometers (260 miles) southeast of Moscow, in the Russian Federation, CIS; site of a major diamond manufacturing plant administered by Kristall. See KRISTALL.

Sobolev, Vladimir S. (1908-1982), Russian geologist who first suggested correctly that diamonds might be found in central Siberia. His hypothesis was based on geological similarities between Siberia and the Kaapvaal craton in southern Africa.

Sociedade Portuguesa de Empreendimentos (SPE), company formed in 1987 by former shareholders of DIAMANG to aid the failing Angolan diamond industry. The group was formed to prospect for diamonds, train technicians, and value rough diamonds for official export. See COMPANHIA DE DIAMANTES DE ANGOLA (DIAMANG).

Sociedade Portuguesa de Lapidação de Diamantes (DIALAP), Portuguese company founded in 1957 to polish a portion of the rough diamonds mined in Angola. Now specializes in brilliant and fancy cuts above one carat.

Société d'Entreprise et d'Investissements S.A. (SIBEKA), off-shoot of a Belgian diamond mining company formed in 1919 as the Société Minière du Bécéka to mine diamonds in the Belgian Congo (now Zaire). Through the Société Minière de Bakwanga (MIBA), it has an interest in the mining of kimberlite and alluvial deposits at Mbuji-Mayi. Today the company is involved in prospecting and mining on an international scale; manufacturing, processing, and marketing synthetic diamonds; and manufacturing superabrasive tools. SIBEKA has prospected for diamonds in the US, Canada, Brazil, People's Republic of China, and Central African Republic. Mining operations continue in Brazil and Zaire.

Société de Recherches et d'Exploitation Diamantifères (SOREDIA), subsidiary of Compagnie Minière de L'Oubangui Oriental (CMOO), once one of the principal diamond-

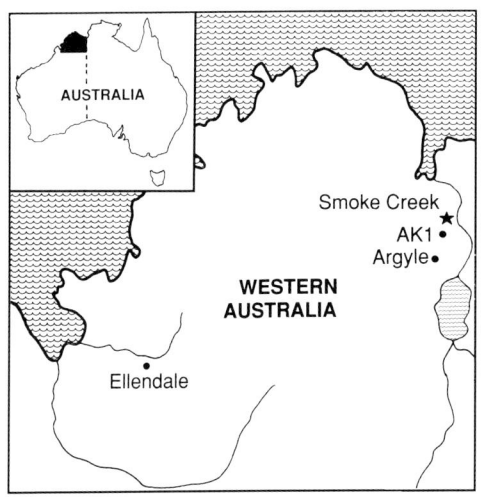

Smoke Creek

mining companies in the Central African Republic. Nationalized in 1969.

Société de Recherches et d'Exploitations Minières en Côte d'Ivoire (SAREMCI), formerly the major diamond-mining company working the Tortiya alluvial deposits in central Côte d'Ivoire (Ivory Coast). Operations ceased in 1975.

Société Diamantifère de la Côte d'Ivoire (SODIAMCI), small diamond-mining company which once operated alluvial diamond deposits in the Séguéla district in the Côte d'Ivoire.

Société Forestière et Minière du Congo (FORMINIÈRE), once one of the principal diamond-mining companies in Zaire. Established in 1906, it was granted a 99-year concession on mineral, timber, and agricultural resources in what was then the Belgian Congo by King Leopold II of Belgium (1835-1909). FORMINIÈRE discovered the Tshikapa alluvial deposits in 1912 and the Bakwanga sites in 1918. It controlled all legal mining in the country until 1960. Today the mine at Mbuji-Mayi is operated by MIBA. See MBUJI-MAYI, SOCIETE MINIERE DE BAKWANGA (MIBA).

Société Guinéene de Recherches et d'Exploitations Minières (SOGUINEX), French subsidiary of Consolidated African Selection Trust (CAST). Formed in 1932 to mine four alluvial deposits along the Baoule River in Guinea, the company recorded its first production in 1934. It later located several other deposits and some small kimberlite pipes; these were severely depleted by illicit diggers in the 1950s. Nationalized in 1961.

Société Minière de Bakwanga (MIBA), state diamond mining company which mines primary and eluvial deposits at the Miba mine in Mbuji-Mayi, Zaire. See MBUJI-MAYI.

Société Minière de Beyla, diamond company which, together with SOGUINEX, operated concessions in the Kankan district of eastern Guinea, producing mainly industrial diamonds for sale exclusively in France; production ended in 1960.

Société Minière de Carnot, one of several diamond-mining companies in the Central African Republic; nationalized in 1969.

Société Minière de la Lueta, diamond-mining company in Zaire, a member of the Entre-Kasai-Luebo Group.

Société Minière du Bécéka, see COMPAGNIE DU BAS-CONGO-KATANGA (BCK), SOCIETE D'ENTREPRISE ET D'INVESTISSEMENTS S.A. (SIBEKA).

Société Minière du Kasai, diamond-mining company in Zaire, a member of the Entre-Kasai-Luebo Group.

Société Minière du Luebo, diamond-mining company in Zaire, a member of the Entre-Kasai-Luebo Group.

Société Minière du Zamza, small diamond-mining company in the Central African Republic, nationalized in 1969.

SODIAMCI, see SOCIETE DIAMANTIFERE DE LA COTE D'IVOIRE.

sodium-vapor lamp, monochromatic light source used with optical instruments such as refractometers; it usually provides sharper readings than a white-light source. The RIs of most gemstones are usually taken with a sodium-vapor lamp.

SOGUINEX, see SOCIETE GUINEENE DE RECHERCHES ET D'EXPLOITATIONS MINIERES.

solder dop, traditional acorn-shaped brass dop which, filled with a mixture of lead and tin solder, holds a diamond in place during polishing. A short copper shaft attaches the dop to the tang; bending the shaft determines the facet angles. Since only a small part of the diamond is exposed, a skilled worker is needed to set the stone properly and, because heat generated by polishing can soften the solder, it is sometimes necessary to stop and reset it. Because of their lead content, solder dops also generate dangerous fumes; they have been largely replaced by mechanical dops, but are still used occasionally to polish large diamonds. Often called a lead or polishing dop. See SET, SETTER.

solitaire, a single diamond set in a ring.

Somerset, proprietary name for yttrium aluminum garnet (YAG). Marketed as a diamond simulant.

Sonoma diamond, misnomer for rock crystal quartz from Sonoma County, California, US.

SOREDIA, see SOCIETE DE RECHERCHES ET D'EXPLOITATION DIAMANTIFERES.

Sorel, Agnès (1422-1450), mistress of Charles VII of France and the first woman to publicly disobey sumptuary laws limiting the wearing of diamonds to royalty. Charles commissioned a number of pieces to satisfy Sorel's enthusiasm for diamonds; his patronage contributed in making the jeweler's trade a distinguished craft.

Sorella, proprietary name for synthetic strontium titanate. Marketed as a diamond simulant.

sorter, skilled worker who separates rough gem or polished diamonds into groups according to weight, shape, clarity, and color. See GRADER.

sort house, mine facility where rough diamonds are hand-sorted and separated from other minerals such as ilmenite, garnet, and zircon. (These minerals possess certain properties similar to diamond and not all of them are extracted during the treatment and recovery process.)

sorting, process of separating rough gem or polished diamonds into groups according to weight, shape, clarity, and color. See GRADING.

South Africa, Republic of, country located at the southernmost tip of the African continent and a major source of diamonds since their discovery near the Orange River at Hopetown, Cape Colony (later Province), in 1866. Today, the country's largest producers are the inland kimberlite pipes of the Finsch, Kimberley, Koffietein, Premier, and Venetia Mines, all of which are operated by De Beers Consolidated Mines. Important alluvial deposits are located in Namaqualand on the Atlantic coast, south of the Orange River. They extend south from Alexander Bay to De Punt, approximately 193 kilometers (120 miles) north of Capetown; offshore marine concessions are also operated along this coastline. Diamonds are polished in Capetown, Johannesburg, and elsewhere.

Southern Fissures Mine, narrow, almost vertical kimberlite fissure near Boshof, South Africa. Diamonds were recovered by overhand shrinkage, but mining operations have been temporarily suspended. See OVERHAND SHRINKAGE.

South-West Africa, see NAMIBIA.

Sovêr Mine, narrow, almost vertical kimberlite fissure near Barkly West, South Africa. Diamonds are recovered by overhand shrinkage. See OVERHAND SHRINKAGE.

Soviet Union, see COMMONWEALTH OF INDEPENDENT STATES, RUSSIAN FEDERATION.

sparkle, see SCINTILLATION.

Sparklite, proprietary name for heat-treated colorless zircon; marketed as a diamond simulant.

Spaulding Diamond, see STEWART DIAMOND.

SPE, see SOCIEDADE PORTUGUESA DE EMPREENDIMENTOS.

special, Central Selling Organisation term for a rough diamond over 10.80 ct. Such diamonds are not included in regular CSO sight boxes; their sale is negotiated separately on a final yield basis with manufacturers who specialize in fashioning larger diamonds. Also used adjectivally, *e.g.,* a special stone.

specific gravity (SG), ratio of the weight of a material to that of an equal volume of water at $4°C$ ($39.2°F$). Diamond has a specific gravity of 3.52 ($\pm$.01). See HEAVY LIQUIDS, HYDROSTATIC WEIGHING METHOD.

specific gravity liquids, see HEAVY LIQUIDS.

spectrometer, optical instrument designed to measure wavelengths of light rays which compose the spectra of transparent materials, and their RIs. See ABSORPTION SPECTRUM, ELECTROMAGNETIC SPECTRUM, SELECTIVE ABSORPTION.

spectrophotofluorometer, instrument used to determine those wavelengths of light which excite fluorescence in a material; it also analyzes the wavelengths which make up its fluorescent emission spectrum. See ABSORPTION SPECTRUM, ELECTROMAGNETIC SPECTRUM, EMISSION SPECTRUM, SPECTROSCOPE, SPECTRUM.

spectrophotometer, instrument which measures the amounts of ultraviolet, visible, and/or infra-red radiation transmitted (or absorbed) by a given material. Results can be shown on a meter, or, on a recording spectrophotometer, in graph form. See ABSORPTION SPECTRUM, ELECTROMAGNETIC SPECTRUM, 595 NM LINE, SELECTIVE ABSORPTION, SPECTROSCOPE, SPECTRUM.

spectroscope, optical instrument which produces a visible spectrum by passing white light through a prism or diffraction grating. When a transparent material, such as a gemstone, is placed between the light source and the spectroscope, the material absorbs some of the incident light; the resulting absorption spectrum can then be examined. Absorption spectra help identify some gemstones and detect certain forms of enhancement. See LIGHT ABSORPTION, 595 NM LINE, SELECTIVE ABSORPTION, SPECTROMETER, SPECTROPHOTOMETER, SPECTRUM.

spectrum, common ellipsis for white light spectrum, the bands of colors representing the various wavelengths which compose white light. Seen when white light is passed through a prism, they appear as a range, running from red (the longest wavelengths) to violet (the shortest). Also called the visible light spectrum. See ABSORPTION SPECTRUM, DIFFRACTION GRATING, ELECTROMAGNETIC SPECTRUM, SELECTIVE ABSORPTION, EMISSION SPECTRUM, SPECTROSCOPE.

Spectrum Collection, collection of 41 reportedly natural fancy color diamonds, ranging in weight from 0.20 ct. to 6.87 ct. Assembled by A.V. Gumuchian in New York City, and displayed at the American Museum of Natural History from 1976 to 1985.

speculative stone, rough diamond the quality, color, shape, or coating of which, or the combination of these factors, makes it difficult to predict the final yield.

Spencer Bay mv, mining vessel owned by De Beers Marine and equipped with a small-scale recovery system; used in sampling and exploration operations off the Atlantic coast of southern Africa.

Sperrgebiet, German, meaning *restricted area*; name given to a large strip of land along the Atlantic coast of Namibia after diamonds were discovered in 1908. The country was a German colony at that time. Now mined by CDM.

spherical aberration, failure of a lens to bring all points in the same plane into focus at once, producing a distorted image. It can be corrected by combining lenses with different focal lengths. See APLANATIC LENS, CHROMATIC ABERRATION, REFRACTION.

spherical bort, see BALLAS.

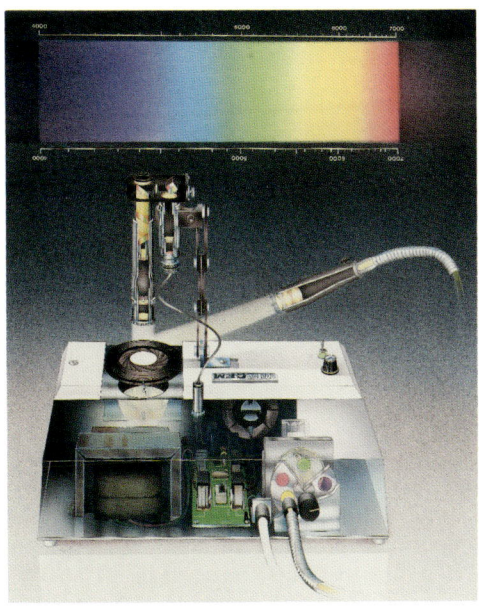

spectroscope

spinel, natural gemstone, the colorless synthetic version of which is commonly used as a diamond simulant. It is singly refractive, with a refractive index of 1.718, a dispersion of 0.020, a specific gravity of 3.60, and a hardness (Mohs) of 8; its luster is vitreous to subadamantine. See SYNTHETIC SPINEL.

spiral cut, brilliant cut with a spiral arrangement of facets on either the crown or pavilion.

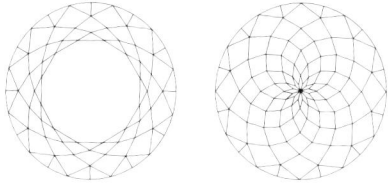

spiral cut

Spirit of Hope Diamond, see STAR OF PERSIA DIAMOND.

split-brilliant cut, modification of the standard round brilliant with 20 crown facets, 20 pavilion facets, a table, and a culet.

split grade, in the GIA color-grading system, a color grade which falls midway between two grades (*e.g.,* G-H or K-L). Split grades are no longer issued on GTL Diamond Grading Reports, but are sometimes used in retail jewelry appraisals, especially for mounted goods where grading cannot be as precise as it is with loose goods. See APPRAISAL, DIAMOND GRADING REPORT, GIA CLARITY-GRADING SCALE, GIA COLOR-GRADING SCALE, MASTER DIAMONDS.

splittable, term for a rough diamond from which no major polished stone can be fashioned, but from which valuable fragments can be obtained by lasering, sawing, or cleaving, thus making it economic to manufacture.

splitter, person who splits a rough diamond along a cleavage plane after it has been kerfed by a laser. Not to be confused with a cleaver, who hand-kerfs the diamond with a sharp before cleaving it, and sometimes plans the design of the polished stone. See CLEAVER, CLEAVING, LASER KERFING.

splitting, division of a rough diamond along a cleavage plane after it has been kerfed by a laser. Not to be confused with cleaving. See CLEAVING, LASER CUTTING, SPLITTER.

Spoonmaker's Diamond, see KASIKCI DIAMOND.

spotted goods, see SPOTTED STONE.

spotted stone, rough sorting term for a diamond crystal containing inclusions visible to the unaided eye.

spread stone, diamond with a thin crown and a table larger than 60 percent. Spread stones are sometimes called fisheyes. See SWINDLED STONE, TABLE DIAMETER.

square antique cut, historic, squarish brilliant cut with rounded corners. Sometimes called an old mine cut.

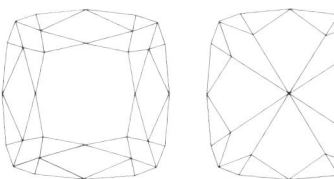

square antique cut

square cut, step-cut or brilliant-cut diamond with a square girdle outline: four equal sides enclosing equal angles, and sharp corners.

square emerald cut, emerald cut with four equal sides.

Sri Lanka, formerly Ceylon, an island nation in the Indian Ocean off the southeast tip of the Indian subcontinent, which in recent years has developed a diamond manufacturing industry.

stability, degree to which a gem material resists alteration by heat, light, or chemicals.

Stalingrad Diamond, 166 ct. rough diamond found near Mirnyi in 1968, in what is now Sakha (Yakutia), the Russian Federation, CIS. Now in the Russian Diamond Fund in Moscow. Also called the Siberian Diamond.

STAMICO, see STATE MINING COMPANY OF TANZANIA.

standard brilliant, see STANDARD ROUND BRILLIANT.

standard color range, see NORMAL COLOR RANGE.

standard comparison set, see MASTER DIAMONDS.

standard cut, see BRILLIANT CUT.

standard round, see STANDARD ROUND BRILLIANT.

standard round brilliant, round brilliant cut, the shape of which was originally based on the octahedron. It has 57 or 58 facets: a table, 8 bezel facets, 8 star facets, and 16 upper-girdle facets on the crown; and 8 pavilion main facets, and 16 lower-girdle facets; it may or may not have a culet on the pavilion.

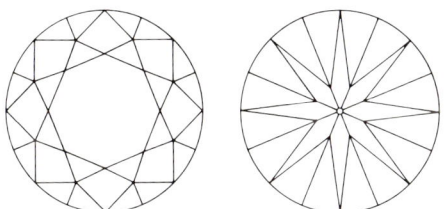

standard round brilliant

standard stones, see MASTER DIAMONDS.

star cut, (1) brilliant-cut diamond with pavilion facets which form a star pattern when seen through the table. (2) star-shaped brilliant cut.

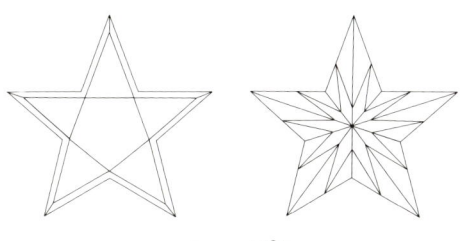

star cut (2)

star facet, one of the eight triangular facets which form the sides of the table on a brilliant-cut diamond.

Starilian, proprietary name for synthetic strontium titanate. Marketed as a diamond simulant.

Star Mine, narrow, vertical kimberlite fissure in Theunissen, South Africa.

Star of Abdul Aziz, 59 ct. D-flawless pear-shape diamond, named for the King of Saudi Arabia and last sold in 1988. Current whereabouts unknown.

Star of David diamond, (1) rough diamond containing a 180° interpenetration twin which creates the outline of a Star of David on the crystal. (2) rough diamond, reportedly shaped like a Star of David, found in Transvaal Province, South Africa, in 1955. Current whereabouts unknown.

Star of David diamonds (1)

Star of Denmark Diamond, reportedly fancy yellow 34.29 ct. diamond, fashioned from a 105 ct. rough found at the Kimberley Mine, South Africa, in 1885. Once owned by Queen Kapiolani of Hawaii, and sometimes called the Kapiolani Diamond. Now privately owned.

Star of Dresden Diamond, see ENGLISH DRESDEN DIAMOND.

Star of Egypt Diamond, 105.19 ct. octagonal step-cut diamond, reportedly colorless, recut from a 106.75 ct. (old carats) diamond. Originally acquired as a 250 ct. oval by the Khedive of Egypt around 1850, it was sold in 1880 when the Khedive went into exile. The new owner had the diamond recut into a 105.51 ct. emerald cut and exhibited it in Amsterdam. The diamond reappeared shortly before World War II and was described as being white in color and "an exceptional gem of extraordinary fire." Purchased by London jewelers Wilson & Gill, it was later sold to Egypt's King Farouk but vanished after his abdication in 1952. Current whereabouts unknown.

Star of Este Diamond, 26.16 ct. Indian diamond, said to be of "perfect form and quality," once owned by the Este Family, rulers of the province of Modena, Italy, between the thirteenth and eighteenth centuries. A diamond of similar description was reportedly purchased by King Farouk of Egypt in 1951. Current whereabouts unknown.

Star of Independence Diamond, 204.10 ct. rough diamond purchased by Harry Winston in 1975 and fashioned into a D-flawless 75.52 ct. pear shape. Named in honor of the American Bicentennial; sold to a Middle Eastern buyer in 1976.

Star of Minas Diamond, see STAR OF THE SOUTH DIAMOND.

Star of Murfreesboro Diamond, 35.25 ct. rough diamond, described as blue, discovered in 1964; the second largest diamond yet found at the Crater of Diamonds State Park, Arkansas, US. Current whereabouts unknown. See UNCLE SAM DIAMOND.

Star of Persia Diamond, 88 ct. light yellow round brilliant diamond; mounted in a brooch with 107 baguettes and sold by Harry Winston in 1965 to a Middle Eastern buyer. Also called the Good Hope Diamond, the Spirit of Hope Diamond, and the Turkestan Diamond.

Star of Sarawak Diamond, 70 ct. diamond from the island of Borneo; purchased by the Rajah of Sarawak in the late 1870s and later displayed in London. Current whereabouts unknown.

Star of Sierra Leone Diamond, 968.90 ct. rectangular cleavage found near Kono, Sierra Leone, in 1972. The largest alluvial (and third largest gem quality) diamond ever found, it was originally purchased by Harry Winston and fashioned into 11 stones. It was later decided that the largest of these, a 143.20 ct. emerald cut, should be recut, because it contained an inclusion. This produced an additional seven diamonds, one of which was a D-flawless emerald cut of 32.52 ct. All but the latter were set in the "Star of Sierra Leone" brooch. Altogether, 13 of the 17 diamonds fashioned from the Star of Sierra Leone Diamond were flawless; all of them were sold in 1975. Only the 32.52 ct. diamond has reappeared; set in a ring, it was auctioned at Sotheby's New York in 1988; the whereabouts of the others are unknown.

Star of Sierra Leone brooch

emerald cut fashioned from the Star of Sierra Leone Diamond

Star of South Africa Diamond, 47.69 ct. pear shape modified brilliant-cut diamond fashioned from an 83.50 ct. (old carats) rough found by a shepherd named Swartboy near the Orange River in 1869; news of its discovery caused a

Star of South Africa Diamond

rush to what would become the alluvial diggings on the Vaal and Orange Rivers and the discovery of kimberlite pipes in the Kimberley area. Fashioned in Amsterdam, it was sold to the wife of the first Earl of Dudley. Sold at auction by Christie's in Geneva to an unnamed buyer in 1974.

Star of Spalding Diamond, see STEWART DIAMOND.

Star of Süleyman, 93.86 ct. oval diamond fashioned from a 149 ct. rough; named for Süleyman the Magnificent (1495-1566), Sultan of the Ottoman Empire. Last sold in 1957. Current whereabouts unknown. Also spelled Suleiman, Suleman, Suliman.

Star of the East Diamond, 94.80 ct. D-color, pear-shape diamond reported by some sources to be of Indian origin and once owned by Sultan Abdul-Hamid II of the Ottoman Empire (now Turkey). Evalyn Walsh McLean bought it from Cartier in Paris in 1908; she often wore it together with the Hope Diamond. Harry Winston bought both diamonds from her estate in 1949. The Star of the East was sent to King Farouk of Egypt in 1951, but was never paid for; it took Winston several years to retrieve it. Sold in 1969; the new buyer later requested that it be mounted in a pendant on a V-shaped diamond necklace with two flawless matching pear-shape diamonds attached. The Star of the East was displayed at the Metropolitan Museum of Art, New York, US, in 1982 at a reception marking the fiftieth anniversary of Harry Winston. The firm repurchased the diamond in 1992.

Star of the East Diamond

Star of the South Diamond, (1) 261.24 ct. rough diamond found near Bagagem, Minas Gerais, Brazil in 1853. (The town was later named Estrêla do Sul after the diamond.) Fashioned into a 128.80 ct. oval brilliant cut by the firm of Coster in Amsterdam, the diamond was purchased by a syndicate of French diamond dealers and named "Star of the South." It was then shown at the London Exhibition of 1862 and the Paris Exhibition of 1867. Later purchased by Mulhar Rao, Gaekwar of Baroda, the diamond was inherited by his son who, in 1934, stated that both the Star of the South and the English Dresden were mounted in a necklace among his family's jewels. Believed to be privately owned in India. Also called Estrêla do Sul Diamond and Star of Minas Diamond. (2) 14.37 ct. D-color, kite-shaped diamond, first fashioned in India, but repolished from 15.28 ct. by Harry Winston in 1950. Once owned by Evalyn Walsh McLean, it was last sold in 1981.

Star of Yakutia Diamond, 232 ct. diamond said to have been found near Mirnyi, in what is now the Republic of Sakha (Yakutia), the Russian Federation, CIS, in 1973. Its discovery was reported just three months after that of the Fifty Years of Aeroflot Diamond, which also weighs 232 ct., suggesting that the latter may have been renamed the Star of Yakutia. Said to be the largest Russian diamond found to date, it is now in the Russian Diamond Fund in Moscow.

Star Tania, proprietary name for synthetic rutile. Marketed as a diamond simulant.

State Alluvial Diggings, important alluvial diamond deposits discovered at Alexander Bay, south of the Orange River in Namaqualand, Cape Province, South Africa, in 1926. Operated by the South African government and leased to small mining companies from 1927 to 1989; they are now mined by Alexcor (formerly Alexander Bay Development Corporation). Also called the Namaqualand State Diggings. See ALEXCOR, RIETFONTEIN SOUTH.

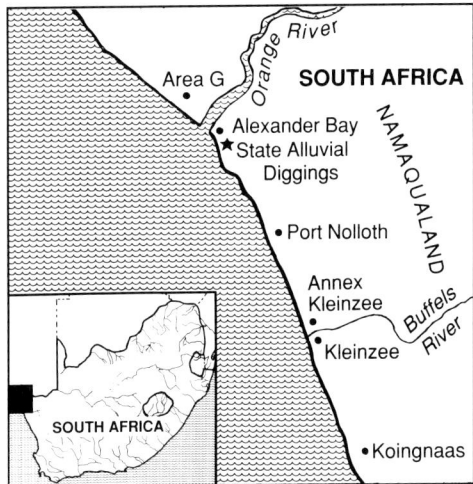

State Alluvial Diggings

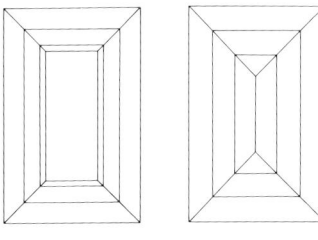

step cut

State Mining Company of Tanzania (STAMICO), state-operated company formed to manage all diamond and mineral mining operations in Tanzania following nationalization in 1971. Production levels throughout Tanzania have declined steadily throughout the 1970s and 1980s, but exploration has increased; over 300 new kimberlites have been found, primarily in the eastern Tanzanian craton. See TANZANIA; WILLIAMSON DIAMONDS, LTD.; WILLIAMSON DIAMOND MINE.

static cone, separating apparatus used in diamond recovery plants, consisting of a large funnel-shaped container filled with water, crushed ore, and ferrosilicon (a finely grained, corrosion-resistant metal powder). Waste floats to the top; diamonds sink to the bottom. See HEAVY-MEDIA SEPARATION, HYDROCYCLONE SEPARATION, RECOVERY, SEPARATION (2).

St. Claude, historic diamond-manufacturing town in the Jura region of France supplying the Swiss watch industry; now of minor importance.

step cut, cutting style in which long, narrow, four-sided facets are arranged in rows parallel to the girdle on both the crown and pavilion. There are usually three rows, although this may vary. Emerald cuts and baguettes are examples of step-cut designs.

step-cut bead, spherical bead covered with four-sided facets. Rarely used with diamonds.

step-cut briolette, cutting style closely related to the briolette, circular in cross section and entirely covered with four-sided facets except at the ends, where the facets are triangular.

Stephanie Diamond, 67.55 ct. round brilliant-cut diamond purchased by Harry Winston in 1957 and set in a clip. Now owned privately in Saudi Arabia.

Sterns Diamond, SEE STERNS STAR DIAMOND.

Sterns Star Diamond, 85.93 ct. fancy yellow, round brilliant-cut diamond, reportedly flawless, obtained from a 223.60 ct. octahedron found at the Dutoitspan Mine in 1972. Two other diamonds were fashioned from the rough, a 21.04 ct. emerald cut and a 6.08 ct. marquise. Purchased by Sterns, a retail jewelry company in South Africa, it has since been sold in New York.

Stewart Diamond, 296 ct. rough diamond, reportedly yellow, found at the historic Waldeck's Plant on the Vaal River, South Africa, in 1872 by two prospectors, Robert Spalding and Antonie Williams. Fashioned into a 123 ct. brilliant cut, it was named for the merchant who purchased it. Sometimes called the Star of Spalding Diamond, it is privately owned.

stewartite, rare type of bort which occurs in lumps with a cinder-like structure and dull sheen; it is magnetic, due to magnetite impurities. Named for James Stewart, former manager of the Kimberley Treatment Plant. See BALLAS, CARBONADO, CRUSHING BORT, FRAMESITE.

Stolberg diamond, misnomer for rock crystal quartz from Stolberg near Aachen, Germany. Also called Stollberger diamond.

stone, (1) rough sorting term for a well-formed diamond octahedron. (2) diamond industry term for any polished diamond or other gemstone.

stone paper, see DIAMOND PAPER.

Stoppani gauge, measuring device designed to calculate the dimensions of a mounted diamond. Tables and formulas then enable the user to calculate an estimated weight of the diamond with reasonable accuracy. Modern versions include a programmed calculator with digital readout.

strain, internal irregularity caused by inclusions or structural anomalies in a gemstone; present to varying degrees in most rough diamonds, and a determinant of the way the stone may be manufactured. A polariscope is used to judge the intensity of the strain, which ranges from "very light" to "very heavy"; the amount of strain present determines whether the diamond can be lasered or sawn. A rough diamond containing heavy strain may be considered a rejection. Sometimes called stress. See POLARISCOPE, REJECTION.

strain birefringence, see ANOMOLOUS DOUBLE REFRACTION (ADR).

strain double refraction, see ANOMALOUS DOUBLE REFRACTION (ADR).

Straits stone, derogatory term for a poor quality diamond fashioned in Matapura, Kalimantan, on the island of Borneo.

Strass diamond, misnomer for glass, especially glass with a high lead content; sometimes used as a diamond simulant. Named for Georges Strass, an eighteenth century French jeweler, and sometimes spelled Stras. See LEAD GLASS.

strass glass, see LEAD GLASS.

Streeter, Edwin W., (active ca. 1880) famous London jeweler and author of *Great Diamonds of the World* (1882) and *Precious Stones and Gems* (1888).

stress, see STRAIN.

strip mining, method of diamond mining in which shallow overburden is removed in relatively narrow strips (12-15 meters, 40-50 feet) and placed in an adjacent strip which has been previously mined. See OPEN CAST MINING.

Strongite, proprietary name for colorless synthetic sapphire. Marketed as a diamond simulant.

strontium titanate, man-made, transparent, essentially colorless crystalline material sometimes used as a diamond simulant. It is singly refractive, with a refractive index (RI) of 2.409, a specific gravity of 5.13, a hardness (Mohs) of 5 to 6, and a dispersion of 0.190; its chemical composition is $SrTiO_3$. Marketed under various proprietary names.

Strykloof Mine, marine deposit being mined in the Admiralty strip along the coast of Namaqualand, South Africa. Diamonds are recovered by diver-manipulated suction devices operated from small boats and from shore.

subadamantine luster, surface appearance brighter than vitreous luster, but not as bright as adamantine. Characteristic of well-polished garnets and zircons.

sub-level caving, underground mining method in which ore drilled and blasted loose at one level is dropped through a slot to a level below, there to be collected and transported to the surface. See BLOCK CAVING, OPEN BENCH MINING, OPEN PIT MINING.

substitute, see DIAMOND SIMULANT.

suction dredger, large-diameter flexible suction device used in marine mining operations to suck diamond-bearing gravel from the sea-bed. Sometimes fitted with powerful seawater jets

suction dredger

to break up overburden on the bottom prior to dredging. See OFF-SHORE MINING.

sulfur diamond, misnomer for pyrite.

sulfuric acid, H_2SO_4, colorless, highly corrosive acid often used to remove polishing residue from diamonds; also used in the manufacture of chemicals, fertilizers, and explosives. Also spelled sulphuric. See ACID CLEANING.

Sultan Abdul-Hamid II Diamond, a 70.54 ct. fancy yellow diamond sold in 1983, together with the Emperor Maximilian Diamond and the Idol's Eye, in one of the biggest single transactions in the history of diamond sales. Current whereabouts unknown.

Sultan of Morocco Diamond, 35.27 ct. square cushion-shape diamond, reportedly bluish gray, said to have been owned by the Youssoupoff family since 1840. Purchased by Cartier's of New York from Prince Felix Youssoupoff in 1922, it was last sold privately in America in 1972. See POLAR STAR DIAMOND.

Sumelpur Mines, ancient diamond deposits on the Koel River near Sumelpur, India.

Sumitomo synthetic diamond, intense yellow, gem quality synthetic Type Ib diamond, first produced by Sumitomo Electric Company in 1985. Sumitomo synthetics fluoresce chalky greenish yellow or yellow when exposed to shortwave ultraviolet radiation and show un-

Sumitomo synthetic diamonds

usual graining, veining, and color zoning; they do not show the Cape lines typical of natural Type Ia yellow diamonds. Used primarily as heat sinks in the electronics industry. See THERMAL CONDUCTIVITY.

Sunflower Cut, registered name of one of the five "Flower" cuts created in 1988 by CSO consultant Gabi Tolkowsky. The cut increases the yield from low color crystals with good depth and volume, and can be fashioned into a variety of shapes. Emerald cuts, squares, and tapers have 53 facets; the marquise has 69, and the pear or heart shape can have 49 or 55, depending on the number placed on the crown. See DAHLIA CUT, FIRE-ROSE CUT, FLOWER CUTS, MARIGOLD CUT, ZINNIA CUT.

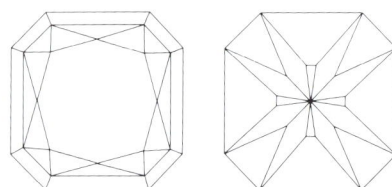

Sunflower Cut

supplier, (1) individual or company specializing in the wholesale distribution of rough or polished diamonds, other gems, or manufactured jewelry. (2) wholesaler or jobber who functions as a retail jeweler's immediate source of loose or mounted goods and manufactured jewelry. See BROKER, DEALER, MANUFACTURER.

Surat, India's largest diamond-manufacturing center, located 260 kilometers (162 miles) north of Bombay. In 1992, the city's several thousand factories employed approximately 150,000 workers specializing in a complete range of small goods; most diamonds are manufactured by traditional methods, but modern technology, including semi-automatic polishing machines and laser kerfing systems, was being introduced in 1992.

surface graining, grain lines on the surface of a finished diamond, usually due to different crystallographic orientations.

surface graining

surface markings, see GROWTH MARKINGS.

Swartboy, shepherd who found an 83.50 ct. (old carats) diamond (later cut into the Star of South Africa Diamond), near the Orange River in 1869; he was paid 500 sheep, 10 head of cattle, and a horse for his discovery. Also spelled Swaartboy, Swartbooi, Zwartbooi, Zwartboy.

swindled stone, trade term for a polished diamond which has been fashioned to maximize the weight or yield from the rough, with little regard for its make or proportions. Often adversely affects brilliance and dispersion. See MAKE, YIELD.

swindling, trade term for fashioning a diamond to maximize the weight or yield from the rough, with little regard for its make or proportions. Often adversely affects brilliance and dispersion. See MAKE, YIELD.

Swine Creek diamond, misnomer for rock crystal quartz from Ashtabula County, Ohio, US.

Swiss cut, (1) brilliant cut with 16 crown facets, 16 pavilion facets, and a table; also called a "16/16." (2) any diamond with 24 facets and a table on the crown.

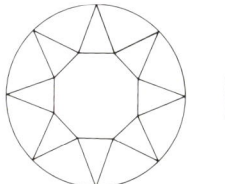 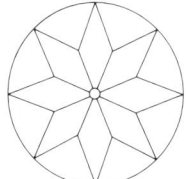

Swiss cut (1)

symmetry, grading term for the exactness of shape and placement of facets. Faults affecting symmetry include off-center culets and tables, poor facet alignment, misshapen facets, out-of-round girdles, and wavy girdles. See CUT, EXTRA FACETS, FINISH.

syngenetic inclusion, inclusion which formed inside the host crystal at the same time as the host (*e.g.,* olivine and garnet in diamond). See EPIGENETIC INCLUSION, PROTOGENETIC INCLUSION.

synthetic, man-made material which has the same chemical, physical, and optical properties as its natural counterpart.

synthetic cubic zirconia (CZ), transparent, colorless, man-made material marketed as a diamond simulant under a number of proprietary names. It is singly refractive, with an R.I. of 2.15 and an S.G. of 5.80; its dispersion is 0.060; and its hardness 8.25 to 8.5 (Mohs scale). Yellow CZ is used to imitate fancy intense yellow diamonds, but CZ does not show the 415 nm absorption line seen in fancy diamonds (although it may show lines in the 453 nm and 478 nm areas).

synthetic diamond, man-made diamond, produced either by subjecting carbon-bearing material such as graphite to high temperature and pressure or by the chemical vapor deposition method. The Swedish company Allmana Svenska Elektriska Aktiebolaget (ASEA) is believed to have achieved the first repeatable synthesis of diamond in 1953, but their results were not published at the time; General Electric Company announced a successful synthesis of diamonds in 1954, followed by De Beers in 1959. Colors range from black to dark green, light green, red, yellow, blue, and colorless (Type IIa diamonds). Millions of carats of industrial-quality synthetic diamond are now manufactured annually using high pressure techniques; gem quality synthetic diamonds have been produced experimentally by De Beers Diamond Research Laboratories, General Electric Company, and facilities in the CIS, and commercially by Sumitomo Electric Company. See CHEMICAL VAPOR DEPOSITION (CVD), DE BEERS SYNTHETIC DIAMOND, GENERAL ELECTRIC COMPANY (GE), SEED CRYSTAL, SUMITOMO SYNTHETIC DIAMOND, THIN FILM DIAMOND COATING.

synthetic diamond grit, abrasive powder made of minute synthetic diamonds. See NATURAL GRIT.

synthetic rutile, man-made transparent rutile, sometimes used as a diamond simulant. It is doubly refractive, with refractive indices of 2.616-2.903, a birefringence of .287, a specific gravity of 4.26, a dispersion of 0.330, and a hardness (Mohs) of 6 to 6½; its chemical composition is TiO_2. Colors include light yellow, brownish red, and greenish blue to bluish green. Produced since 1948; marketed under a number of proprietary names.

synthetic sapphire, man-made corundum (sapphire) sometimes used in its colorless form as a diamond simulant. It is doubly refractive, with refractive indices of 1.762 to 1.770, a birefringence of .008 to .010, a specific gravity of 4.00, a dispersion of .018, and a hardness (Mohs) of 9; its luster is vitreous to subadamantine.

synthetic spinel, man-made spinel often used in its colorless form as a diamond simulant. It is singly refractive with a refractive index (RI) of 1.728, a dispersion of 0.02, a specific gravity of 3.60, and a hardness (Mohs) of 8; its luster is vitreous to subadamantine.

synthetic strontium titanate, see STRONTIUM TITANATE.

Sytikanskaya, see SYTIKANSK PIPE.

Sytikansk Pipe, kimberlite discovered in 1956 approximately 30 kilometers (18 miles) from Aikhal in what is now Sakha (Yakutia), the Russian Federation, CIS; mining started in the 1980s. Although the grade is low, the pipe is reported to have produced a number of diamonds over 20 ct. Also spelled Sitykansk.

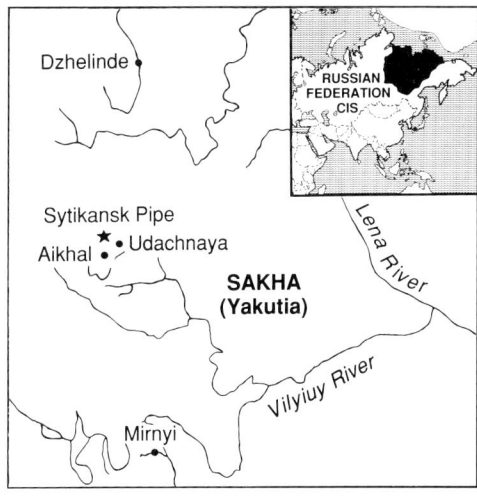

Sytikansk Pipe

T

table, large facet in the center of the crown of a polished diamond. See TABLE DIAMETER, TABLE PERCENTAGE.

table cut, (1) simple polishing style believed to be the earliest symmetrical form produced by fashioning rough octahedral diamonds. Opposing points were ground to form a large culet and a larger table; the faces were polished slightly off the octahedral plane. (2) variation of the bevel cut with a large table.

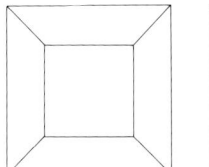 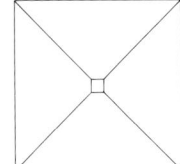

table cut

table diameter, on a round brilliant-cut diamond, the distance, usually expressed in millimeters, between any two opposing corners of the table. On fancy cuts, the distance between table corners measured across the width of the diamond. On an emerald cut, the width of the table measured across its narrowest direction. See TABLE GAUGE, TABLE PERCENTAGE.

Table Diamond, large diamond, reportedly high in quality, purchased by Francis I of France (1494-1547) in 1532. Current whereabouts unknown.

table dop, (1) flat-headed brass bruting dop in which the table of the diamond is affixed. (2) dop which holds a diamond in place while its table is being polished.

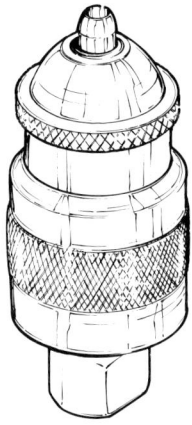

table dop (2)

table-down, position of a polished gemstone when its culet is pointing up; opposite of face-up. In the GIA color-grading system, diamonds in the normal color range are usually color graded table-down, fancy colors face-up. It is the easiest position from which to pick up a polished diamond with tweezers.

table gauge, measuring device made of transparent acetate with a printed scale calibrated in tenths of a millimeter; used under magnification to measure the table of a diamond.

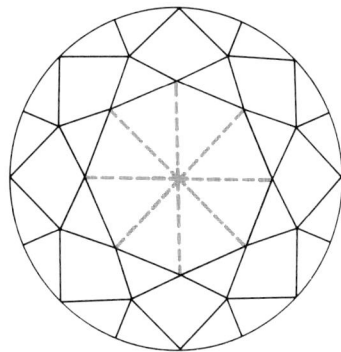

table diameter

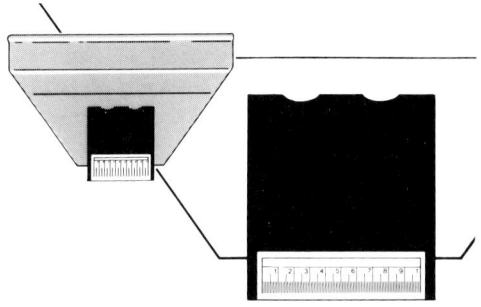

table gauge

table measurement, dimension of a diamond's table diameter, as measured directly, normally using a table gauge, and expressed in millimeters to the nearest 0.1 mm. See TABLE DIAMETER, TABLE GAUGE, TABLE PERCENTAGE.

table percentage, for round brilliant cuts, the size of the table expressed as a percentage of the average girdle diameter; obtained by dividing the largest table diameter by the average girdle diameter. On fancy cuts, the size of the table expressed as a percentage of the narrowest girdle diameter or width; determined by dividing the width of the table by the width of the girdle. See AVERAGE GIRDLE DIAMETER, PROPORTIONS.

table reflection, reflection of the table facet seen in the pavilion facets of a round brilliant-cut diamond. The apparent size of the table reflection depends on the pavilion angle, which also determines the pavilion depth; thus the apparent difference in size between the table and its reflection can be used to estimate pavilion depth percentage.

table size, see TABLE DIAMETER.

tablet cut, cut in which both the crown and the pavilion of the diamond are bordered by broad, parallel facets; there may be other minor facets present. See DARYA-I-NUR DIAMOND.

Taj-e-Mah Diamond, 115.06 ct. irregular Mogul cut diamond from India (probably Golconda), reportedly colorless and high in quality. Considered a sister stone to the Darya-i-Nur Diamond, it was taken by the Persians during the Sack of Delhi in 1739 and is now among the Crown Jewels of Iran. Taj-e-Mah means *Crown* (or *Crest*) *of the Moon*. See IRANIAN CROWN JEWELS, SACK OF DELHI.

Taj Mahal Diamond, see TAYLOR HEART DIAMOND.

Tancheng, area in Shandong Province, People's Republic of China, the site of alluvial deposits believed to have derived from kimberlites near the town of Mengyin. Mining has been attempted in Xiaobuling, Chengiabu, and Huamatun. See CHINA, PEOPLE'S REPUBLIC OF (PRC).

Tancheng

tandem diamond dressing tool, dressing tool in which diamonds are set one below the other in the matrix of the tool. See DIAMOND DRESSING TOOL.

Tanex, Ltd., company which, under the terms of a 1992 agreement with the Tanzanian government, prospects and mines for diamonds in that country. Tanex is a wholly-owned subsidiary of Willcroft Company of Bermuda which, in turn, is a subsidiary of De Beers Centenary AG.

tang, device which holds a polishing dop; weights are often placed on the tang to increase the pressure bearing on the scaife. Sometimes spelled tong.

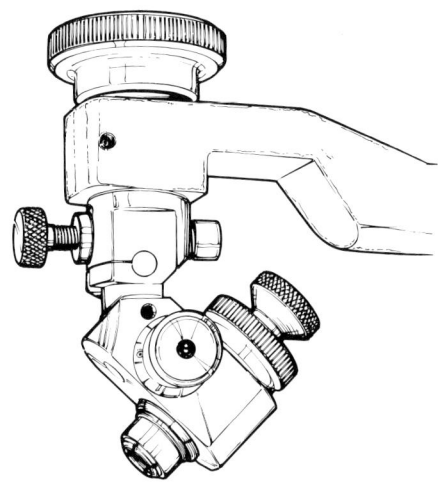

tang

Tanganyika, see TANZANIA.

Tania-59, proprietary name for synthetic rutile. Marketed as a diamond simulant.

Tanzania, East African country, formerly Tanganyika, which was a minor source of alluvial diamonds until 1940, when Canadian geologist Dr. John T. Williamson discovered the pipe now known as the Williamson Diamond Mine at Mwadui, 145 kilometers (90 miles) south of Lake Victoria. The Williamson was a strong producer for over 30 years, but current output is very small. The nearby New Almasi operation and the Kahama pipes are producing, but production levels have dropped since the state nationalized all mining operations under STAMICO in 1971. Exploration efforts have increased; in 1992, the government entered into a joint exploration and mining agreement with a De Beers affiliate to prospect in the Mwanza, Shinyanga, and Tabora regions; over 300 kimberlites have been found, 44 of which have yielded diamonds. See KAHAMA PIPES; NEW ALMASI, LTD.; STATE MINING COMPANY OF TANZANIA (STAMICO); WILLIAMSON DIAMONDS, LTD.; WILLIAMSON DIAMOND MINE; WILLIAMSON, JOHN T.

taper, small, thinly-tapered fancy-shape diamond. See TAPERED BAGUETTE.

tapered baguette, modification of the rectangular baguette in which one end is narrower than the other.

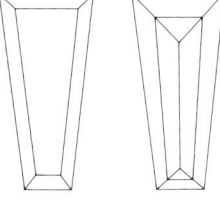

tapered baguette

tapered pentacut, modification of the pentagon cut, produced by varying the lengths and angles of its sides.

Tapillion Cut, proprietary name for a tapered baguette with a brilliant-cut pavilion, marketed by World Fancies.

Tasmanian diamond, misnomer for colorless topaz from Australia.

Tavernier, Jean-Baptiste (1605-1689), French traveler, gem dealer, author, and jeweler who became known as "the father of the modern diamond trade." During his six journeys to India and the Middle East, Tavernier saw some outstanding gem collections, which he described in *Les Six Voyages de Jean-Baptiste Tavernier*, published in 1676. Many of the stones he acquired on these trips were sold to Louis XIV of France.

Tavernier A Diamond, 51 ct. oval brilliant-cut diamond, one of several bought by Tavernier in India and sold to Louis XIV of France in 1669. Stolen from the Garde Meuble during the robbery of the French Crown Jewels in 1792 and never recovered.

Tavernier B Diamond, 32 ct. rough diamond acquired by Tavernier in India and sold to Louis XIV of France in 1669. Current whereabouts unknown.

Tavernier Blue Diamond, 112.5 ct. (old carats) Mogul cut diamond, reported to be blue, purchased by Tavernier in India about 1642 and sold to Louis XIV of France in 1669. Believed to have been recut into the 67.5 ct. (old carats) heart-shape French Blue Diamond in 1673. Stolen from the Garde Meuble in 1792; it is thought the diamond may have been recut twice before reappearing in London in 1830 as the 45.52 ct. cushion shape we know today as the

Hope Diamond. Also known as the Blue Diamond of the Crown. See HOPE DIAMOND.

Tavernier C Diamond, 31 ct. brilliant-cut diamond sold by Tavernier to Louis XIV of France in 1669. Stolen from the Garde Meuble in 1792 and never recovered.

Tavernier Pear Diamond, a 54.75 ct. pear-shape diamond brilliant reportedly seen by Tavernier in India in 1658. Some historians believe the stone was taken by the Persians during the Sack of Delhi in 1739. Current whereabouts unknown. See SACK OF DELHI.

Taylor-Burton Diamond, internally flawless 69.42 ct. F-G color, pear-shape diamond fashioned by Harry Winston from a 240.80 ct. cleavage found at the Premier Mine in 1966. Purchased by actor Richard Burton for his wife, screen actress Elizabeth Taylor, in 1969; repolished to 68.09 ct. in 1979, and last sold in 1980. See CLEAVAGE.

photo courtesy of Harry Winston, Inc.

Taylor-Burton Diamond

Taylor Heart Diamond, flat, heart-shape diamond of unknown weight, with the name of Mumtaz Mahal, wife of Shah Jahan, engraved on it. Given to screen actress Elizabeth Taylor by her husband, actor Richard Burton, on her 40th birthday in 1972. Originally called the Taj Mahal Diamond (Shah Jahan built the Taj Mahal as a tomb for Mumtaz Mahal). Current whereabouts unknown.

Tel Aviv, second largest city in Israel and the country's third largest diamond-manufacturing center; 78 factories employed 1,650 people in 1992. A focal point for the Israeli diamond trade since the 1930s, Tel Aviv is adjacent to Ramat Gan, the nation's major diamond-manufacturing and trading center.

templet facet, one of the first four bezel facets polished after the table is placed on a brilliant-cut diamond.

tenacity, see TOUGHNESS.

Tennant Diamond, 112 ct. yellow rough diamond given to London mineralogist James Tennant in 1873 by one of his students. Later fashioned into a reportedly flawless 68 ct. stone. Current whereabouts unknown.

tension crack, irregular fracture around an inclusion, the result of stress.

tension crack

Tereschenko Diamond, 42.92 ct. Type IIb, fancy blue, pear-shape diamond, probably of Indian origin, first owned by the Tereschenko family of Russia; sold in 1916, prior to the Russian Revolution. Last sold by Christie's (Geneva) in 1984 to a Saudi Arabian dealer. The final bid, $4.6 million, was at the time the highest price ever paid for a diamond at auction.

tetrahedron, one of the seven basic forms in the cubic (isometric) crystal system; it has four triangular-shaped faces.

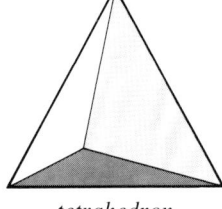

tetrahedron

tetrahexahedron, one of the seven basic forms in the cubic (isometric) crystal system. It resembles a cube on which each face is replaced by four faces shaped like isosceles triangles.

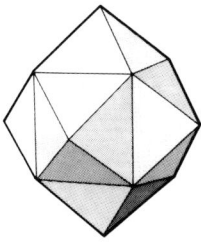

tetrahexahedron

Thailand, country occupying the western half of the Indochinese peninsula and the northern two-thirds of the Malay peninsula in Southeast Asia; a diamond manufacturing center since the late 1970s. Traditionally a source of and manufacturing center for colored stones such as rubies and sapphires. Thailand's diamond industry has expanded rapidly since 1980; low costs, a highly skilled labor force, strong government support, and joint efforts by foreign investors and Thai partners have fueled its growth. In 1992, the country had 34 factories employing approximately 8,000 workers. Gemopolis, a large complex of manufacturers, trading offices, a loose stone bourse, Customs office, hotels, and workers' quarters opened in January, 1993. See GEMOPOLIS.

thermal conductivity, relative ability of a material to transfer heat. Diamond's thermal conductivity is the highest of any material, which is why diamonds feel cool to the touch, and why synthetic diamonds are used as heat sinks in industrial applications. See DE BEERS SYNTHETIC DIAMOND, SUMITOMO SYNTHETIC DIAMOND, TYPE IIA DIAMOND.

thermal inertia, property which determines how quickly a material's surface temperature changes when subjected to a specific amount of heat for a known period of time. Diamond's thermal inertia is higher than that of any simulant.

thermal inertia meter, instrument used to separate natural and synthetic diamonds from diamond simulants by measuring the rate at which the surface temperature changes when subjected to a specific amount of heat for a known period of time. It consists of two temperature-sensitive switches called thermistors; when the instrument touches the stone, the first thermistor heats it while the second measures the rate at which heat is conducted away from the heat source. Diamond dissipates heat much faster than its simulants. Also called a diamond probe or thermal tester. See THERMAL CONDUCTIVITY.

thermal tester, see THERMAL INERTIA METER.

thermochromatic, having the property of changing color when heated.

thermoluminescence, emission of visible light by a material when heated. Some diamonds thermoluminesce blue when heated to about 200°C (392°F).

thermophosphorescence, continued emission of visible light by a material which has been heated, after the heat source has been removed.

thick crown, crown height noticeably greater than 16.2 percent of the average girdle diameter; usually seen in older cuts. See OLD EUROPEAN CUT, OLD MINE CUT.

thick girdle, girdle which is obvious to the unaided eye, typically at least twice as thick as a medium girdle and thicker than is needed to prevent chipping. The extra thickness simply adds weight to the finished stone.

thin crown, crown height noticeably less than 16.2 percent of the average girdle diameter; commonly seen in spread stones.

thin film diamond coating, thin coating of synthetic diamond applied to a surface, usually by chemical vapor deposition, to improve its resistance to abrasion or its thermal conductivity. See CHEMICAL VAPOR DISPOSITION (CVD).

third, third of a carat (0.30-0.35 ct.).

thread-grinder diamond dressing tool, tool set with a single diamond, either rough or shaped, used to dress thread-grinder wheels. See DIAMOND DRESSING TOOL.

three-facet rose cut, obsolete cutting style with a circular girdle outline, a flat, unfaceted base, and a pointed crown with three large facets.

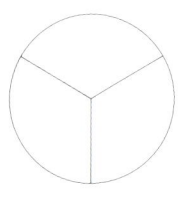

three-point diamond, diamond with a table fashioned nearly parallel to a possible octahedral face.

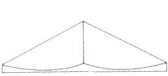

three-facet rose cut

Three Tables, group of three table-cut diamonds, ranging from 48 ct. to 52 ct. (old carats), seen in India by Tavernier in 1665 and believed to have been taken by the Persians during the Sack of Delhi in 1739. Current whereabouts unknown. See SACK OF DELHI; SHAH JAHAN TABLE-CUT DIAMOND; TAVERNIER, JEAN-BAPTISTE.

Throne Diamond, 90 ct. diamond reported by Tavernier as being one of the principal ornaments in the Peacock Throne. Current whereabouts unknown. See PEACOCK THRONE; SACK OF DELHI; TAVERNIER, JEAN-BAPTISTE.

Tiffany Diamond, 287.42 ct. rough diamond octahedron, reportedly fancy yellow, thought to have been found in claims belonging to the French Company in the Kimberley Mine, South Africa, around 1878. Fashioned in Paris into a 128.51 ct. square antique modified brilliant cut, with 90 facets: 41 on the crown and 49 on the pavilion. Purchased by Tiffany and Co. in New York in 1879. See COMPAGNIE FRANCAISE DES MINES DE DIAMANT DU CAP DE BONNE ESPERANCE.

Tiffany Diamond
photo courtesy of Tiffany & Co.

Tiffany head, high, four- or six-prong head with V-shaped openings between the prongs; introduced in 1886 by Charles L. Tiffany for setting solitaires. Also called a Tiffany setting or Tiffany mount.

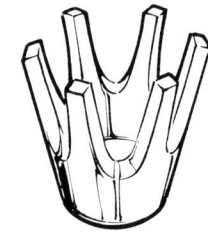

Tiffany head

Tiffany mount, see TIFFANY HEAD.

Tiffany setting, see TIFFANY HEAD.

tilted table, table which is not parallel to the girdle plane.

tinted diamond, (1) diamond which shows very light or light traces of color, usually yellow, although it may be brown or gray. (2) coated diamond.

tinted white, (1) term on the CIBJO and IDC color-grading scales for faint yellow diamonds, equivalent to grades K to L on the GIA color-grading scale. (2) alternative term in the Scan. D.N. color-grading system for the top cape grade, equivalent to K-L on the GIA color-grading scale. See APPENDIX D.

Tiros I Diamond, 354 ct. rough brown crystal found near Tiros, Minas Gerais, Brazil in 1938. Current whereabouts unknown.

Tiros II Diamond, 198 ct. rough crystal, described as rose-colored, found near Tiros, Minas Gerais, Brazil in 1936. Current whereabouts unknown.

Tiros III Diamond, 182 ct. rough crystal, described as colorless, found near Tiros, Minas Gerais, Brazil in 1936. Current whereabouts unknown.

Tiros IV Diamond, 173 ct. rough crystal, described as brown, found near Tiros, Minas

Gerais, Brazil in 1938. Current whereabouts unknown.

Tiros Lilac Diamond, 12.25 ct. rough crystal, described as lilac-colored, found near Tiros, Minas Gerais, Brazil in 1938. Current whereabouts unknown.

Tiru Gem, proprietary name for synthetic rutile. Marketed as a diamond simulant.

Titangem, proprietary name for synthetic rutile. Marketed as a diamond simulant.

Titania, proprietary name for synthetic rutile. Marketed as a diamond simulant.

Titania Brilliant, proprietary name for synthetic rutile. Marketed as a diamond simulant.

Titania Midnight Stone, proprietary name for synthetic rutile. Marketed as a diamond simulant.

Titanium, (1) chemical element (Ti). (2) proprietary name for synthetic rutile. Marketed as a diamond simulant.

Titan Oval Diamond, 51.31 ct. E-flawless oval diamond, fashioned in 1979 from a 98 ct. rough from South Africa. Current whereabouts unknown.

Titanstone, proprietary name for synthetic rutile. Marketed as a diamond simulant.

Toegepaste Laser Technologie, Belgian-based manufacturer of automated laser cutting machines for the diamond industry.

Toktogul Diamond, 37.56 ct. rough diamond found at Mirnyi, in what is now Sakha (Yakutia), the Russian Federation, CIS, around 1955; now in the Russian Diamond Fund in Moscow.

Tolansky, Samuel (1907-1973), British scientist, Professor of Physics at the University of London, Fellow of the Royal Society, and authority on the structure of diamond; inventor of a refined optical technique capable of measuring differences in height as small as 0.5 nanometer on a diamond's surface. Author of *The Microstructure of Diamond Surfaces, The History and Use of Diamond*, and *The Strategic Diamond*.

Tolfa diamond, misnomer for rock crystal quartz from Italy.

Tolkowsky, Marcel (1899-1991), author of *Diamond Design* (1919) which proposed a set of recommended proportions designed to produce the greatest brilliance consistent with high dispersion on round brilliant-cut diamonds. His results were similar to the proportions developed empirically by Henry D. Morse. See AMERICAN BRILLIANT CUT; MORSE, HENRY D.; TOLKOWSKY THEORETICAL BRILLIANT CUT.

Tolkowsky theoretical brilliant cut, round brilliant cut based on the theoretical work of Marcel Tolkowsky, calling for a 53 percent table; 60-61 percent total depth, which usually includes a girdle thickness of 0.7 percent to 1.7 percent; 16.2 percent crown height; and 43.1 percent pavilion depth. The crown angle is 34°30' and the pavilion angle is 40°45'. Also called the ideal cut. See AMERICAN BRILLIANT CUT; MORSE, HENRY D.; TOLKOWSKY, MARCEL.

tone, degree of darkness or lightness of a color; the extent to which it approaches white (colorless) or black; together with hue and saturation, tone is one of the three dimensions of color. See HUE, SATURATION.

tong, see TANG.

toolstone diamonds, industrial diamonds of a shape and quality suitable for cutting and forming a variety of metals.

topaz, gemstone which, when colorless, is sometimes used as a diamond simulant. It has refractive indices of 1.609-1.617, birefringence 0.008, specific gravity 3.53, dispersion 0.014, and hardness (Mohs scale) 8; its luster is vitreous.

top-break facets, see GIRDLE FACETS.

top cape, (1) historic term for yellowish diamonds which when mounted show a faint yellow color even to the untrained eye; sometimes called light cape. (2) term on the Scan. D.N. color scale for diamonds (over 0.47 ct.) in this color range; equivalent to K-L on the GIA color-grading scale. See APPENDIX D.

top-corner facets, see QUOIN FACETS.

top crystal, historic term for near-colorless to faint yellow diamonds. (2) term on the Scan. D.N. color scale for near-colorless diamonds (over 0.47 ct.); equivalent to GIA color grade I. See APPENDIX D.

top-half facets, see GIRDLE FACETS.

top light brown, obsolete term for near-colorless diamonds, around J on the GIA color-grading scale.

top main facet, see BEZEL FACET.

topping, manufacturing term sometimes used to describe the division of a rough diamond weighing more than one carat into two unequal parts.

top silver cape, historic term for faint yellow diamonds at the top of the cape series. Small mounted diamonds in this range face up colorless; large stones show some color to the trained eye.

top Wesselton, (1) historic term for near-colorless diamonds; in small sizes they face up colorless; the color of larger stones is noticeable only to the trained eye. The name comes from the Wesselton Mine in South Africa. (2) term on the Scan. D.N. color scale for diamonds in this range, comparable to F-G on the GIA color-grading scale. See APPENDIX D.

total depth, see TOTAL DEPTH PERCENTAGE.

total depth percentage, the depth from table to culet, expressed as a percentage of the average girdle diameter in round brilliant cuts, and in fancies as a percentage of the girdle width. Most diamonds today have a depth between 53 and 63 percent. See PROPORTIONS.

total height, see TOTAL DEPTH PERCENTAGE.

total internal reflection, reflection of light when it strikes the internal "surface" or gem/air interface inside an optically dense material (such as diamond) at an angle greater than its critical angle. See CRITICAL ANGLE.

total weight, combined weight of all the diamonds set in a given piece of jewelry.

toughness, resistance to breaking, chipping, or cracking; also called tenacity. See DURABILITY, HARDNESS.

trace element, element found in a mineral in extremely small quantities, and not part of its basic chemical composition. Trace elements sometimes present in diamonds include aluminum, barium, calcium, chromium, copper, magnesium, iron, nitrogen, silicon, silver, sodium, lead, strontium, titanium, and boron, among others. Trace elements can change a diamond's physical properties, including its color. See CHEMICAL COMPOSITION, TYPE IA DIAMOND, TYPE IB DIAMOND, TYPE IIA DIAMOND, TYPE IIB DIAMOND.

trade term, jargon or descriptive idiom used primarily within an industry, but sometimes by the general public as well. Such terms are not necessarily technically correct.

transichromatic, descriptive term applied to diamonds that change color temporarily under certain conditions (*e.g.,* going from darkness into light or under exposure to X-rays). See CHAMELEON-TYPE DIAMOND, DOUBLE-COLOR DIAMOND, FLUOROCHROMATIC, THERMOCHROMATIC.

transmission of light, passage of light through a material. See LIGHT ABSORPTION, SELECTIVE ABSORPTION.

transparency, degree to which a material transmits light without appreciable scattering, so that objects beyond it are entirely visible.

Transvaal, province in northeastern South Africa in which several kimberlite pipes and alluvial diamond deposits occur. The Premier and Venetia Mines are located in the Transvaal.

Transvaal Blue Diamond, 25 ct. blue pear-shape diamond fashioned from a rough found in the Premier Mine, the Transvaal Province, South Africa. Current whereabouts unknown.

Transvaal Diamond, 67.89 pear-shape diamond, reportedly champagne-colored, fashioned from a 240 ct. rough found in the Transvaal Province, South Africa. Originally fashioned into a 75 ct. diamond with 116 facets, it was repolished to improve its proportions. Donated to the Smithsonian Institution in Washington D.C. in 1977, where it is now on display. Also called the Victoria-Transvaal Diamond.

trap brilliant cut, step-cut diamond with a circular girdle outline.

trap cut, see STEP CUT.

trapeze cut, four-sided step cut with two parallel sides of unequal length.

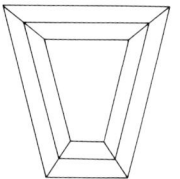 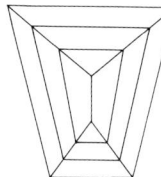

trapeze cut

Trapeze Diamond, proprietary name for a 48-facet tapered or straight baguette with a brilliant cut pavilion, marketed by the Trapeze Diamond Corporation.

trapezohedron, one of the seven basic forms in the isometric, or cubic, crystal system; it has 24 faces and resembles an octahedron on which each face has been replaced by three four-sided faces. Also called tetragonal trisoctahedron and isositetrahedron.

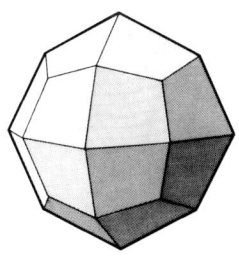

trapezohedron

Treasure Trove Diamonds, Ltd., small diamond-mining company which once operated the Doornkloof and Sovêr Mines, near Barkly West, Cape Province, South Africa. Now defunct.

treated diamond, diamond the appearance of which has been altered by any unnatural, post-recovery process such as irradiation (color) or fracture filling (clarity). See ENHANCEMENT, IRRADIATED DIAMOND.

treatment, see ENHANCEMENT, FILLED DIAMOND, IRRADIATION, TREATMENT PLANT.

treatment plant, facility in which diamond-bearing ore or alluvial concentrates are treated by crushing, washing, screening, and processing to recover the final product. Usually called a treatment and recovery plant.

Trenton diamond, misnomer for rock crystal quartz from Herkimer County, New York, US.

Triamond, proprietary name for yttrium aluminum garnet (YAG). Marketed as a diamond simulant.

triangle cut, three-sided step cut.

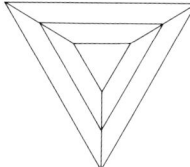 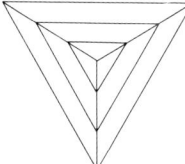

triangle cut

triangular brilliant cut, three-sided modified brilliant cut with curved sides, rounded corners, and (usually) 44 facets, including a faceted girdle. Popular in the 1970s. Usually fashioned from shallow rough and sold in matched pairs. Also called trilliant, trillion cut, or triangular modified brilliant cut.

triangular modified brilliant cut, see TRIANGULAR BRILLIANT CUT.

Triângulo Mineiro, see MINING TRIANGLE.

triboluminescence, emission of light by a material when it is rubbed. Some diamonds are triboluminescent.

Trielle Cut, trademarked name for a triangular brilliant designed by the Trillion Diamond

Company, a subsidiary of LF Industries, New York, US. Developed by Leon Finker in the 1930s; patented by LF Industries in the 1970s. Originally called the Trillion Cut, but that name was released for general use in 1991.

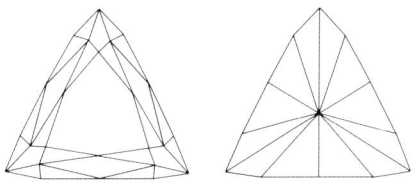

Trielle Cut

trigon, triangular indented growth mark found on the octahedral faces of a rough diamond and sometimes seen on naturals; it is usually, but not always, oriented opposite to the crystal face on which it appears. Behind every trigon is an inclusion which is often difficult to see even under 10x magnification. See ETCH PIT.

trilliant, name used by the Royal Asscher Diamond Company of Amsterdam since 1970 for a triangular brilliant cut with curved sides and a high crown.

trillion cut, see TRIELLE CUT.

triolette cut, modified shield-shape cut developed by Marvin Samuels for the Premier Gem Corporation of New York, US. See INCOMPARABLE DIAMOND.

triple-cut brilliant, full-cut brilliant developed in the seventeenth century with star, bezel, pavilion main, and upper and lower girdle facets. Sometimes used to describe old mine cuts.

triplet, assembled stone having three parts bonded together with a thin layer of cement.

triplet lens, see TRIPLET LOUPE.

triplet loupe, compound magnifying device corrected for both spherical and chromatic aberration. Most jeweler's loupes are triplets. See DOUBLET LOUPE, LOUPE.

Tri-sakti Diamond, 166.85 ct. rough diamond found in 1965 near Banjarmasin, Kalimantan, on the island of Borneo. Fashioned by the Asscher Diamond Company of Amsterdam into a 50.53 ct. emerald cut, reportedly flawless and described as blue-white, and sold privately in Europe on behalf of the Indonesian government. *Tri-sakti* means *Three Principles*, a reference to the motto of the Indonesian Republic (nationalism, religion, and unity).

trisoctahedron, 24-sided diamond crystal in which each octahedral face appears to have been subdivided into three protruding faces; common in gem diamonds.

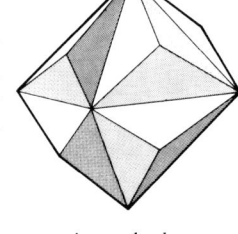

trisoctahedron

trommel, device used to separate diamond-bearing gravels in the early days of South African mining. Gravel was put in a rotating, perforated cylindrical drum; fine material such as diamonds dropped through a series of variously sized holes, while other material passed along the cylinder and out the end. See BABY, RECOVERY, SCRUBBER, SEPARATION (2).

true canary, historic term for a fancy color intense yellow diamond, usually Type Ib, which shows no fluorescent or visible light absorption spectrum at normal temperature, and which sometimes fluoresces orange under longwave ultraviolet radiation. The term is used to distinguish such stones from yellow diamonds with a cape spectrum.

truer, see DIAMOND PRESSING TOOL.

Tshikapa, town at the junction of the Tshikapa and Kasai Rivers in western Zaire; an important rough diamond trading center in an area of alluvial diamond mining covering approximately 20,000 square kilometers (7,700 square miles).

turbo scaife, alloyed scaife which is harder than conventional cast iron scaifes; used to polish macles or naats. See SCAIFE.

Turkestan Diamond, see STAR OF PERSIA DIAMOND.

Turkey I Diamond, 140 to 147 ct. diamond reported to have been of fine quality and part of the Turkish Regalia in 1882. Also called the Ottoman Diamond. Current whereabouts unknown.

Turkey II Diamond, see KASIKCI DIAMOND.

Tuscan Diamond, see FLORENTINE DIAMOND.

Tweepad, alluvial deposit in the Buffels Marine Complex operated by the Namaqualand Mines Division of CDM; located on the Atlantic coast of South Africa.

Twentieth-century cut, modified brilliant cut with 80 facets, similar to the Jubilee cut, in which the table has been replaced by extending the eight star facets.

Twenty-fifth Party Congress Diamond, 67 ct. diamond found in the Mir Pipe at Mirnyi in 1976, in what is now Sakha (Yakutia), the Russian Federation, CIS. Current whereabouts unknown.

Twenty-third Communist Party Congress Pipe, small kimberlite located 15 kilometers (9 miles) east of Mir in Sakha (Yakutia), the Russian Federation, CIS. It reportedly produces large numbers of slightly greenish diamonds.

twin crystal, crystal distorted at the atomic level early in its growth as a result of changes in the orientation of atoms; as atoms continue to attach themselves to the re-oriented segment, another crystal begins to form, intergrown with the first. Twin crystals can be made up of two or more such intergrown crystals holding planes of atoms in common. See CONTACT TWIN, CRYSTAL STRUCTURE, GRAIN LINES, INTERPENETRATION TWIN, MACLE, POLYSYNTHETIC TWINNING.

twinning, see TWIN CRYSTAL.

twinning line, see GRAIN LINES.

twinning plane, plane of atoms shared by twinned crystals at the location where the growth orientation changes. See CONTACT TWIN, CRYSTAL STRUCTURE, GRAIN LINES, INTERPENETRATION TWIN, MACLE, POLYSYNTHETIC TWINNING.

twinning wisp, see GRAIN LINES.

twisted stone, diamond with grain layers which are not on parallel planes, or one with partial twinning.

twisting, fast blocking technique in which the diamond is turned to position the softest polishing direction against the polishing wheel.

two-grainer, see GRAINER.

two-point, diamond on which the table has been polished parallel to a dodecahedral plane.

Type Ia diamond, diamond containing clusters or aggregates of nitrogen atoms as impurities in the crystal lattice; such diamonds show a dark line at 415 nm in the spectroscope, and are electrical nonconductors. Most yellowish diamonds are Type Ia. Sometimes subdivided into Type IaA, Type IaB, and Type IaAB, according to the forms of nitrogen aggregates present. These subdivisions can be distinguished by differences in infra-red absorption spectra.

Type Ib diamond, diamond containing mostly single, isolated nitrogen atoms dispersed throughout the crystal lattice. Only a small percentage of natural diamonds colored by nitrogen are Type Ib; they are often fancy yellow diamonds with a more saturated color than Type Ia diamonds. All synthetic yellow diamonds containing nitrogen are Type Ib. See CANARY DIAMOND, DE BEERS SYNTHETIC DIAMOND, SUMITOMO SYNTHETIC DIAMOND, SYNTHETIC DIAMOND, TRUE CANARY.

Type IIa diamond, rare type of diamond with an exceptionally pure chemical composition: almost all carbon, with negligible amounts of nitrogen or boron. Such diamonds are often very large; usually colorless, though sometimes pink, brown, or blue-green; and inert to shortwave ultraviolet radiation. Type IIa diamonds do not conduct electricity, but are very efficient conductors of heat; they are used as heat sinks in the electronics industry. See THERMAL CONDUCTIVITY, TYPE IB DIAMOND.

Type IIb diamond, very rare type of diamond in which boron substitutes for some carbon atoms. They are electrical semi-conductors, and so extremely sensitive to temperature changes that they can be used to measure fluctuations of temperature within 0.002°C; they phosphoresce to shortwave ultraviolet. Most natural blue diamonds are Type IIb. See AUDIO CONDUCTION DETECTOR, CONDUCTOMETER, HOPE DIAMOND.

Type III diamond, see LONSDALEITE.

Tyrone diamond, misnomer for rock crystal quartz from Ireland.

U

Udachnaya, town about 80 kilometers (50 miles) from Aikhal in the Republic of Sakha (Yakutia), the Russian Federation, CIS, near the Udachnaya Pipe. Also called Polyarnyi.

Udachnaya Pipe, largest active diamond mine in the Republic of Sakha (Yakutia), the Russian Federation, CIS. Discovered in 1955, the open pit mine is 400 kilometers (250 miles) north of Mirnyi, 25 kilometers (15 miles) south of the Arctic Circle, and 45 kilometers (30 miles) from the town of Udachnaya. Udachnaya means *success*. See AIKHAL PIPE.

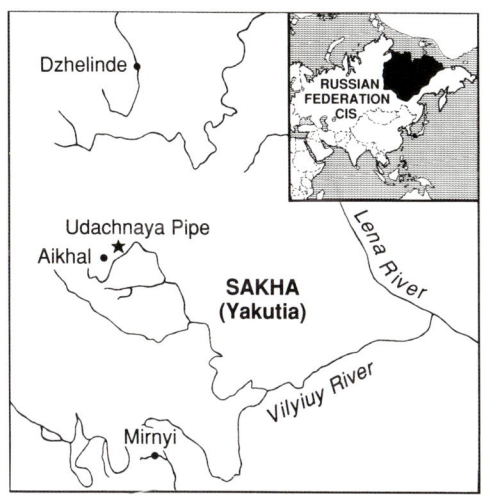

Udachnaya Pipe

Ultra High Pressure Units, Ltd., division of De Beers Diamond Research Laboratory formed in 1960 to produce synthetic diamonds for commercial applications. See DE BEERS SYNTHETIC DIAMOND, DIAMOND RESEARCH LABORATORY (DRL), SUMITOMO SYNTHETIC DIAMOND, SYNTHETIC DIAMOND.

ultraviolet, portion of the electromagnetic spectrum with wavelengths shorter than the violet end of the visible light spectrum. Ultraviolet radiation is invisible to the human eye but it excites visible fluorescence in some diamonds, often blue, but sometimes orange, yellow, greenish yellow, or green. See JAGER, PREMIER DIAMOND, ULTRAVIOLET FLUORESCENCE.

ultraviolet fluorescence, visible fluorescence produced in a gemstone when exposed to ultraviolet radiation. It occurs in some diamonds: it is usually blue, but may be orange, yellow, greenish yellow, or green. Some diamonds fluoresce to longwave ultraviolet; others react to shortwave ultraviolet. See JAGER, PREMIER DIAMOND.

ultraviolet lamp, artificial source of ultraviolet radiation used to test for fluorescence in gemstones. Longwave lamps emit wavelengths centered around 365.4 nanometers, shortwave lamps around 253.7; both have dark filters to screen out visible light produced incidentally by the lamps.

umbrella effect, pattern created by a concentration of color around the culet of some cyclotron-treated diamonds. Internal reflections in a round brilliant-cut diamond cause the affected area to resemble an open umbrella when seen

umbrella effect

through the table. Also called cloverleaf effect. See IRRADIATED DIAMOND.

Uncle Sam Diamond, 40.23 ct., very light brown rough diamond, found at the Crater of Diamonds State Park in Murfreesboro, Arkansas, US, in 1942. The largest gem-quality diamond found in North America, it was fashioned into a 12.42 ct. VVS_2 emerald cut. Current whereabouts unknown. See CRATER OF DIAMONDS STATE PARK.

Uncle Sam Diamond

underground mining, process of removing minerals from the earth by sinking a vertical shaft, or excavating horizontal or inclined tunnels into, across, and around an orebody, and bringing the ore and its associated minerals to the surface. See BEACH MINING, OFF-SHORE MINING, OPEN BENCH MINING, OPEN PIT MINING.

uneven color, see COLOR ZONING.

Union of Soviet Socialist Republics (USSR), see COMMONWEALTH OF INDEPENDENT STATES.

unit cell, smallest cluster of atoms which incorporates both the characteristic chemical composition and the basic crystal structure of a given material.

United States of America (US), large country in the North American continent and a minor source of diamonds. Although diamonds have occasionally been found in other states, the lamproite pipe deposit in Murfreesboro, Arkansas, is the only primary source known to have produced diamonds of any size. The city of New York is an important diamond trading center. See APPENDIX B, CRATER OF DIAMONDS STATE PARK, FORTY-SEVENTH STREET (47TH), MURFREESBORO, PUNCH JONES DIAMOND, UNCLE SAM DIAMOND.

Unnamed Brown Diamond, 545.67 ct. dark brown, Fire Rose cushion-cut diamond, fashioned from a 755.50 ct. rough found at South Africa's Premier Mine in 1986. The diamond was employed to test the advanced cutting technology devised by CSO consultant Gabi Tolkowsky and a select team in Johannesburg before work began on the Centenary Diamond. Polished by master diamond cutter Dawie du Plessis, the diamond has 148 facets: 55 above the girdle; 69 below the girdle; and 24 on the girdle. The largest polished diamond in the world in 1992. Owned by De Beers Consolidated Mines. See CENTENARY DIAMOND, CULLINAN I, FIRE ROSE CUT.

unplanned leakage, see LEAKAGE, LIGHT RETURN.

unpolished culet, culet which has not been completely polished; it may look frosted under 10x magnification.

unripe diamond, archaic misnomer for rock crystal quartz or colorless zircon.

Unzue Heart Diamond, 30.82 ct. heart-shape diamond, described as dark fancy blue, which was falsely rumored to have belonged to French Empress Eugénie (1826-1920). Actually purchased in 1910 by Cartier's shortly after it was cut, and sold to an Argentine client for whom it was renamed the Unzue Heart Diamond. Last sold in 1964 by Harry Winston to Marjorie Merriweather Post, who later donated the diamond to the Smithsonian Institution in Washington, D.C., US, where it is on display. Sometimes called the Unzue Blue or Eugénie Blue Diamond.

Unzue Heart Diamond

photo courtesy of Smithsonian

upper-break facets, see GIRDLE FACETS.

upper-girdle facets, see GIRDLE FACETS.

Upper Guinea, see GUINEA.

Ural Mountains, see RUSSIAN FEDERATION, CIS.

USSR, see COMMONWEALTH OF INDEPENDENT STATES.

USSR Diamond Fund, see RUSSIAN DIAMOND FUND.

Uubvley, historic name for an important alluvial mining area along the Namibian coast between Oranjemund and Lüderitz; also known as Area U. Operated by CDM. See AFFENRUCKEN, GEMSBOK, KERBEHUK, MARINE AREAS, MITTAG.

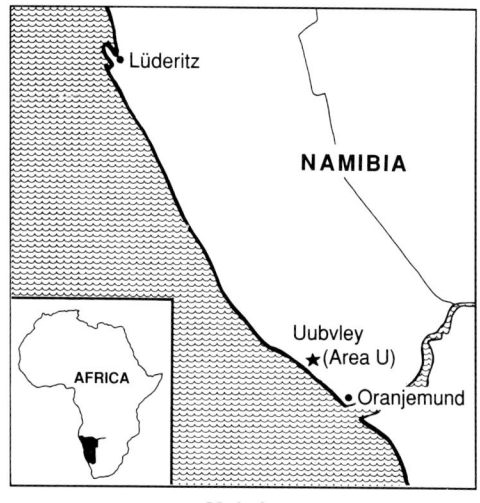

Uubvley

Vaal River, major South African river and, prehistorically, a watercourse presumed to have been an important agent in transporting diamonds away from eroding kimberlites and relocating them in secondary alluvial deposits. The existing river and its prehistoric channels have been the site of numerous diamond diggings, including many around Barkly West, since 1869. See BARKLY WEST, ORANGE RIVER, RIVER DIGGINGS, WALDECK'S PLANT.

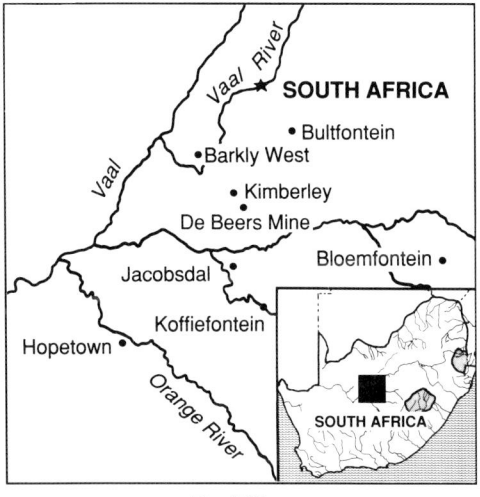

Vaal River

Vainer Briolette Diamond, 116.60 ct. fancy light yellow briolette-cut diamond, fashioned with 192 facets from a 202.85 ct. octahedron by M. Vainer, London, in 1985. It is the largest briolette ever fashioned, and was at the time the largest rough to have been polished in London for more than 30 years. Sold to the Sultan of Brunei.

Valentina Tereshkova Diamond, 61.66 ct. rough diamond found at the Mir Mine in what is now the Republic of Sakha (Yakutia), the Russian Federation, CIS. Named for the first woman cosmonaut. Now in the Russian Diamond Fund in Moscow.

Valery Bykovsky Diamond, large rough diamond of unknown weight, said to be in the Russian Diamond Fund in Moscow.

Vallum diamond, see VELLUM DIAMOND.

van Bercken, Lodewyk, mid-fifteenth century diamond polisher in Bruges, traditionally credited with the invention of the polishing wheel and the use of diamond powder for polishing diamonds (but this is known to have predated his era). He is sometimes said, on dubious authority, to have fashioned the Sancy Diamond. There is a statue of van Bercken close to the Meir, Antwerp's main shopping area, and another in the Beurs voor Diamanthandel, one of the city's diamond bourses. Also spelled Lodewijk van Berghem or van Berkem. See BEURS VOOR DIAMANTHANDEL N.V.; BRUGES; PERUZZI, VINCENZIO; SANCY DIAMOND.

van Berghem, Lodewyk, see VAN BERCKEN, LODEWYK.

Van de Graaff generator, obsolete type of atomic particle accelerator, once used to irradiate diamonds, changing their color to blue. See IRRADIATED BLUE DIAMOND, IRRADIATED DIAMOND, TYPE IIB DIAMOND.

van Niekerk, Schalk, South African farmer who in 1866 came into possession of the 21.25 ct. rough diamond which was to be known as the Eureka, and later, in 1869, the 83.5 ct. rough diamond which was ultimately named the Star of South Africa. The publicity which ensued from this second discovery started the great South African diamond rush. See EUREKA DIAMOND; JACOBS, ERASMUS; STAR OF SOUTH AFRICA DIAMOND; SWARTBOY.

vapor deposition, see CHEMICAL VAPOR DEPOSITION (CVD).

Vargas Diamond, see PRESIDENT VARGAS DIAMOND.

Vega Gem, proprietary name for colorless synthetic sapphire. Marketed as a diamond simulant.

Vellum diamond, misnomer for rock crystal quartz cut in Vellum, India. Also spelled Vallum.

Venetia Mine, large open-pit mine working two kimberlite pipes, KI and KII, discovered in 1980 near Messina in northern Transvaal Province, South Africa; operated by De Beers Consolidated Mines. Limited production began in 1990; full production, at an estimated 5.9 million carats a year, is anticipated in 1993. The mine is named for the farm on which it is located.

Venetia Mine

Venezuela, country on the northern coast of South America and a regionally important source of diamonds since their discovery in 1901; serious prospecting began in 1912. Alluvial deposits have been found in the Guiana Highlands, near the Brazilian border.

Venice, northern Italian city where diamond cutting in Europe is said to have begun in the early 1300s. By the seventeenth century, its central Mediterranean location and trade routes from India made Venice the world's most important diamond manufacturing and trading center. See PERUZZI, VINCENZIO.

Venter Diamond, 511.25 ct. octahedron found in 1951 at the Nooitgedacht diggings near Barkly West, Cape Province, South Africa. Later sold and fashioned into 20 diamonds. See NOOITGEDACHT.

Vereniging Beurs voor den Diamanthandel, Amsterdam diamond bourse; member of the World Federation of Diamond Bourses (WFDB). See BOURSE, WORLD FEDERATION OF DIAMOND BOURSES (WFDB).

Verilux, see DIAMONDLUX.

Vermaet, Willem, one of Europe's earliest known diamond cutters, who fled to Amsterdam from Antwerp in 1586 to escape religious persecution.

vertical crater retreat, method of underground mining introduced at the De Beers Mine in 1988 as an alternative to sub-level caving. Large holes were drilled down 70 meters (230 feet) to create a collection area, and the pipe was successively crater-blasted toward the upper level, allowing ore to drop into the collection area to be hauled away.

very light yellow, see DARK CAPE.

very slightly imperfect, see VERY SLIGHTLY INCLUDED.

very slightly included, GIA diamond clarity grade category describing diamonds containing minor inclusions and blemishes that can be seen under 10x magnification, but which are not visible to the unaided eye. There are two grades in this category, abbreviated VS_1 and VS_2. The CIBJO, IDC, and Scan. D.N. clarity scales each have a corresponding VS category. See APPENDIX E.

very, very slightly imperfect, see VERY, VERY SLIGHTLY INCLUDED.

very, very slightly included, GIA diamond clarity grade category describing diamonds containing minute inclusions and blemishes which are very difficult to see under 10x magnification. There are two grades in this category, abbreviated VVS_1 and VVS_2. The CIBJO, IDC, and Scan. D.N. clarity scales each have a corresponding VVS category. See APPENDIX E.

Vespa Gem, proprietary name for colorless synthetic sapphire. Marketed as a diamond simulant.

vezel, see FEZEL.

Vickers hardness test, indentation test using a pyramid-shaped diamond to test the hardness of minerals (other than diamond) by making and measuring an indentation under controlled conditions. It is the most accurate test for very hard materials; indentations are so small they must be measured under a microscope. See BRINELL HARDNESS TEST, DIRECTIONAL HARDNESS, HARDNESS, HARDNESS POINTS, INDENTATION TEST, KNOOP INDENTATION HARDNESS TEST, MOHS SCALE, SCLEROMETER, SCRATCH HARDNESS.

Victoria Diamond, 457.50 ct. (old carats) rough diamond found in South Africa, possibly at one of the Kimberley mines, in 1884. Fashioned in Amsterdam in 1887 into a 184.50 ct. oval brilliant, which was purchased by the Nizam of Hyderabad in 1891, and a 20 ct. round brilliant. Variously called the Jacob Diamond, the Imperial Diamond, the Victoria I, the Victoria Imperial Diamond, or the Great White Diamond. Current whereabouts of the smaller stone unknown.

Victoria Imperial Diamond, see VICTORIA DIAMOND.

Victoria Transvaal Diamond, see TRANSVAAL DIAMOND.

Vidisco, Israeli manufacturer of computerized centering machines for the diamond manufacturing industry.

Vilyiuy River, one of the rivers that drain the diamond-bearing region of the Republic of

Vilyiuy River

Sakha (Yakutia), the Russian Federation, CIS. Dredging of alluvial deposits began in 1957, 32 kilometers (20 miles) downstream from the Mir Pipe; operations at the town of Mirnyi were halted in 1980 and resumed in 1990.

violet diamond, fancy color diamond with a distinctly violet natural bodycolor, relatively rare.

visible light spectrum, see SPECTRUM.

vitreous luster, glass-like appearance of a gemstone's surface, usually seen in gem materials with refractive indices lower than that of diamond, such as diamond simulants. See ADAMANTINE LUSTER, LUSTER.

Voorspoed, kimberlite mine in the district of Kroonstad, Orange Free State, South Africa. Owned by De Beers Consolidated Mines, it has been closed since before the First World War.

Voskhod-2 Diamond, large rough diamond reported to be in the Russian Diamond Fund in Moscow.

VS, see VERY SLIGHTLY INCLUDED.

VVS, see VERY, VERY, SLIGHTLY INCLUDED.

Wafangdian Mine, mine located near Fu Xian, in Liaoning Province, People's Republic of China, where diamonds are recovered from a kimberlite pipe and from alluvial deposits. Production expanded in 1990 and a new heavy media treatment plant has been commissioned.

Wagner, Percy Albert, author of *The Diamond Fields of Southern Africa* (Johannesburg, 1914), an authoritative and comprehensive work on the geology, mineralogy, and mining of diamonds there.

Waldeck's Plant, historic site of alluvial diamond deposits near Kimberley on the Vaal River, Cape Province, South Africa.

Walderite, proprietary name for colorless synthetic sapphire. Marketed as a diamond simulant.

Walska Briolette Diamond, 95 ct. diamond which once belonged to Ganna Walska, opera star of the 1930s and '40s. Sold at auction in 1971; later acquired by Van Cleef & Arpels of New York. Current whereabouts unknown.

Walska Heart Diamond, 21 ct. heart-shape diamond which once belonged to opera star Ganna Walska. Sold at auction in 1971; current whereabouts unknown.

washing pan, SEE ROTARY WASHING PAN.

Washington Diamond, 89.23 ct. D-color, pear-shape diamond, one of two (the other is 42.98 ct.) that Harry Winston had fashioned in 1976 from a 342 ct. South African rough. Named for American President George Washington. Last sold in 1977; current whereabouts unknown.

water, historic term once used in Europe to describe either the color or transparency of a diamond. The term was typically qualified as first water, second water, etc.

waterworn, term describing a rough diamond or other gemstone which has been smoothed, rounded, or given a frosted surface appearance by tumbling with gravels and other waterborne materials in a stream, river, or ocean. Sometimes called riverworn. See ABRASION, ALLUVIAL SORTING.

wavy girdle, girdle that does not remain parallel to a single plane.

weathering floor, large, flat area graded, steamrolled, and enclosed by high fences, once used in separating diamonds from kimberlite. Diamond-bearing blueground, which is relatively hard, was spread out and allowed to break down through exposure to the elements; the process was often expedited by steamrollers. Modern recovery equipment has made the process obsolete. Also called floor. See HARDEBANK, LUMPS, YELLOWGROUND.

well, dark-looking center caused by excessive light leakage in a diamond cut with a deep pavilion. See NAILHEAD, DEEP PAVILION.

well made, term describing a well-proportioned diamond with a good finish.

Wellington diamond, proprietary name for synthetic strontium titanate. Marketed as a diamond simulant.

Welsh diamond, misnomer for rock crystal quartz from Wales, Great Britain.

Weskus Mine, marine deposit in the Admiralty strip off the coast of Namaqualand, South Africa; diamonds are recovered by mechanical excavation and shore-based, diver-manipulated suction pumps.

Wesselton, (1) historic color-grading term for near-colorless diamonds. Small diamonds face up colorless; in larger stones, color is noticeable only to a trained observer. Named for the Wesselton Mine in South Africa, traditionally considered a source of high color diamonds. (2) term used on the Scan. D.N. color scale for diamonds (over 0.47 ct.) in the near-colorless range, equivalent to the GIA color grade H. See APPENDIX D.

Wesselton Mine, important kimberlite pipe mine, discovered in 1890 near Kimberley, South Africa. Originally called the Premier Mine in honor of Cecil Rhodes; renamed the Wesselton for Petrus Wessel, owner of the Benaaudheidsfontein farm on which the pipe was located, when the pipe now known as the Premier Mine was discovered near Pretoria in 1902. Operated by De Beers Consolidated Mines; diamonds are recovered by block caving and sub-level caving.

Wesselton Mine

Wesselton Simulated Diamond, proprietary name for synthetic spinel. Marketed as a diamond simulant.

West End Diamond Mine, small diamond mine near Postmasburg, Cape Province, South Africa.

Western Australia, Australian state which occupies the western third of the continent and contains the country's most important diamond deposits. Alluvial deposits were discovered along Limestone Creek and Smoke Creek near Lake Argyle in the Kimberley mountain region in 1976; diamond-bearing pipes were found at Ellendale in 1978, and the AK1 pipe (now called Argyle) was discovered in 1979. See ARGYLE DIAMOND MINE, ASHTON EXPLORATION JOINT VENTURE, AUSTRALIA.

Westminster Tiara, see GROSVENOR, HUGH R.

wet diggings, see RIVER DIGGINGS.

Wetenschappelijk en Technisch Onderzoekcentrum voor Diamant (WTOCD) (Scientific and Technical Research Center for Diamonds), research facility located in Lier, Belgium, associated with the Hoge Raad voor Diamant of Antwerp and partially funded by the Belgian government to develop new technology in support of the Belgian diamond industry. Certain WTOCD projects are marketed by Comdiam n.v. See COMDIAM, HOGE RAAD VOOR DIAMANT VZW (HRD).

wheel mark, see BURN MARK.

whistle cut, four-sided step cut with one tapered end, which resembles a whistle.

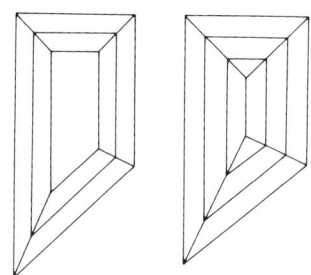

whistle cut

white, (1) term on the CIBJO and IDC color-grading scales for near-colorless diamonds, equivalent to the GIA color grade H. (2) alternative term on the Scan. D.N. color scale for the equivalent traditional color grade Wesselton. See APPENDIX D.

white diamond, term generally used to describe colorless to near-colorless transparent diamonds. See COLOR GRADE, COLOR GRADING, COLOR-GRADING SCALE, FACE UP WELL.

white light, light containing a balanced mixture of all wavelengths in the visible portion of the electromagnetic spectrum. See ELECTROMAGNETIC SPECTRUM, SPECTRUM.

White Saxon Diamond, see DRESDEN WHITE DIAMOND.

white-stone diamond, misnomer for a colorless diamond simulant composed of any of a variety of materials.

White Tavernier Table Diamond, see GREAT TABLE DIAMOND.

whole stone, diamond which cannot be sawn due to its shape or structure. Whole stones are polished without preliminary sawing or cleaving and produce only one finished diamond. See MAKEABLE, SAWABLE.

Wichita diamond, misnomer for rock crystal quartz from Lawton, Oklahoma, US.

Wicklow diamond, misnomer for rock crystal quartz from Wicklow, Ireland.

William II of Holland Diamond, 10 ct. pear-shape diamond engraved with an intaglio portrait of William II of Holland dating from the mid-sixteenth century; on display at the Chicago Museum of Natural History.

Williams, Alpheus F. (1875-1953), son of Gardner Williams; mining engineer and one-time general manager of De Beers Consolidated Mines; author of *The Genesis of the Diamond* (London, 1932) and *Some Dreams Come True* (Cape Town, 1948). See WILLIAMS, GARDNER.

Williams, Gardner (1842-1922), mining engineer, first general manager of De Beers Consolidated Mines, and author of *The Diamond Mines of South Africa* (London, 1902). See WILLIAMS, ALPHEUS F.

Williamson, John T. (1907-1957), Canadian geologist, once employed (1935-38) by the Tanganyika Diamond and Gold Development Company; in 1940, Dr. Williamson discovered what became known as the Williamson Diamond Mine, near Mwadui, Tanganyika (now Tanzania); owner of Williamson Diamonds until his death. See NEW ALMASI, LTD.; STATE MINING COMPANY OF TANZANIA (STAMICO); WILLIAMSON DIAMOND MINE; WILLIAMSON DIAMONDS, LTD.

John T. Williamson

Williamson Diamond Mine, diamond-bearing kimberlite with the largest surface area (146 hectares/361 acres) of any known diamond mine. Discovered in 1940 by Canadian geologist Dr. John T. Williamson, it is located near Mwadui, Tanzania, about 145 kilometers (90 miles) south of Lake Victoria. Geological analysis indicates that the force of the volcanic eruption drove the kimberlite and other rocks to the surface into a large, circular crater; gravels, diamonds, and debris filled the crater and spilled over its walls into what is now known as the Almasi Valley. After Williamson's death in 1957, the mine was bought as a joint venture by the government-owned State Mining Company of Tanzania and Willcroft Diamonds, a subsid-

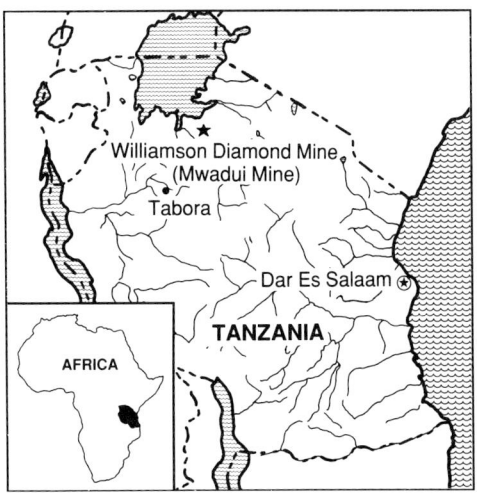

Williamson Diamond Mine

iary of De Beers Centenary AG. Over a 30-year period, the mine produced a high percentage of gem quality stones, including the Williamson Pink Diamond; current production is very small. Also known as the Mwadui Mine. See NEW ALMASI, LTD.; STATE MINING COMPANY OF TANZANIA (STAMICO); WILLIAMSON DIAMOND MINE; WILLIAMSON DIAMONDS, LTD.; WILLIAMSON, JOHN T.; WILLIAMSON PINK DIAMOND.

Williamson Diamonds, Ltd., mining company established in Tanzania in 1940 by Dr. John T. Williamson to mine the kimberlite at Mwadui. The mine is now owned jointly by Willcroft Diamonds, a subsidiary of De Beers Centenary AG, and the State Mining Company of Tanzania. See NEW ALMASI, LTD.; STATE MINING COMPANY OF TANZANIA (STAMICO); WILLIAMSON DIAMOND MINE; WILLIAMSON, JOHN T.

Williamson Pink Diamond

Williamson Pink Diamond, 54 ct. light pink rough diamond found at the Williamson Diamond Mine in Tanzania in 1947. Presented to England's Princess Elizabeth (later Elizabeth II) as a wedding gift, it was fashioned into a flawless 23.60 ct. round brilliant in 1948. One of the largest polished diamonds of this color, it is mounted in the center of a brooch representing an alpine rose, surrounded by five colorless diamonds as petals.

Wimbledon Mine, small kimberlite mine near Kimberley, Cape Province, South Africa.

window, (1) facet polished on a coated or rough-surfaced diamond to permit the designer to see into the interior and determine the color, clarity, and structure of the rough crystal before deciding how it will be fashioned. (2) see-through effect which is the result of too-shallow pavilion angles; usually occurs in step cuts. See LEAKAGE, SEE-THROUGH EFFECT.

window cut, modification of the hexagon cut which resembles a rectangle with two beveled corners. See HEXAGON CUT.

wing, area between the belly and point of a marquise, pear-shape, or heart-shape diamond.

Winston, Harry (1896-1978), New York diamantaire and retailer. Under his direction his firm, Harry Winston, Inc., bought and resold such notable diamonds as the Idol's Eye, the Arcots, the Nepal, the Briolette of India, the Star of the East, the Indore Pears, and the Eugénie Blue. Winston was also involved in the design and fashioning of the Jonker, Vargas, Niarchos, Lesotho, Taylor-Burton, Winston, Star of Sierra Leone, and Star of Independence Diamonds, among others. He donated the Dutoitspan and Hope Diamonds to the Smithsonian Institution in Washington, D.C., US.

Harry Winston

Winston Diamond, 62.05 ct. pear-shape diamond, reportedly flawless and colorless, fashioned for Harry Winston in 1953 from a 154.50 ct. rough found in the Jagersfontein Mine in 1952. The diamond was sold to the King of Saudi Arabia in 1959. Returned to Winston the following year, it was recut to 61.80 ct. and resold in 1963, along with the 59.46 ct. Louis XIV Diamond. The two stones were auctioned in Switzerland in 1981.

Winston Heart-Shape Diamond, 40.97 ct. heart-shape diamond re-fashioned in 1980 from a 59.25 ct. emerald cut. (The latter was originally obtained from a 206 ct. rough.) Last sold in Europe in 1980.

Winston Pink Diamond, 22.84 ct. pink marquise diamond, reportedly flawless, sold first by Harry Winston in 1975; last sold in 1987.

wire-drawing dies, see DIAMOND WIRE-DRAWING DIE.

wisp, see FEATHER.

Wittelsbach Diamond, 35.50 ct. blue diamond from India, which King Philip IV of Spain gave to his 15-year-old daughter Margareta Teresa when she married Emperor Leopold I of Austria in 1664. In 1720, it was bequeathed to Archduchess Maria Amalia, who married Crown Prince Charles Albert of Bavaria; Wittelsbach was his family name. When the country became a republic in 1931, the Wittelsbach and other items from the Bavarian Crown Jewels were sold at auction. It disappeared briefly, re-surfaced in Belgium in 1962, and was sold to a private collector in 1964.

Wodehouse, John (1826-1902), first Earl of Kimberley, Under-Secretary of State for Foreign Affairs and later Secretary of State for the Colonies at the time of the discovery of diamonds in South Africa; both the South African city of Kimberley and the Kimberley mountain range in Western Australia were named for him.

Wodehouse, Philip (1811-1887), British governor of the Cape Colony at the time of the discovery of diamonds in South Africa, and the original purchaser of the Eureka Diamond.

Wolmaransstad, trading center for licensed diggers and diamond dealers in the Transvaal Province, South Africa.

World Diamond Congress, biennial event organized by the World Federation of Diamond Bourses and the International Diamond Manufacturers' Association and held in different diamond centers. Representatives of member associations hold separate meetings and attend a final joint session. Since 1947, the Congress has been held in Austria, Belgium, England, France, Israel, Italy, the Netherlands, Singapore, and the United States; the Silver Jubilee World Diamond Congress was held in London in 1991, the 1993 event in Antwerp. See INTERNATIONAL DIAMOND MANUFACTURERS' ASSOCIATION (IDMA), WORLD FEDERATION OF DIAMOND BOURSES (WFDB).

World Federation of Diamond Bourses (WFDB), leading international collective of some 20 diamond bourses, clubs, and exchanges. Founded in 1907 as the Federation Mondiale Internationale, it became the WFDB after World War II. The Federation works to maintain stable market conditions by formulating and enforcing trading regulations and ethical standards, improving communications between members, and acting as an arbitrator in the settlement of international disputes. See INTERNATIONAL DIAMOND MANUFACTURERS' ASSOCIATION (IDMA), WORLD DIAMOND CONGRESS.

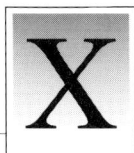

xenocryst, crystal or crystal fragment found in, but not formed by or related to, magmas such as kimberlite or lamproite. Diamond is a xenocryst.

xenolith, geological term for rocks which are foreign to the matrix in which they are found. Eclogite and peridotite xenoliths, the predominant diamond-bearing xenoliths, are often located in kimberlite and lamproite pipes.

Xiyu, area in Shandong Province, People's Republic of China, in which a small group of diamond-bearing kimberlite pipes and dikes has been found, approximately 14 kilometers (9 miles) north of the town of Mengyin.

X-ray, electromagnetic radiation with very short wavelengths (between 0.01 and 10.0 nanometers), used in various diamond testing procedures. Diamonds are transparent to X-rays; they usually fluoresce during exposure.

X-ray diffraction analysis (XRD), method of identifying materials by passing X-rays through them and analyzing photographic images of their diffracted patterns. Different materials have distinctive diffraction patterns.

X-ray fluorescence, emission of visible light by a diamond or other gem material during exposure to X-rays. Diamonds usually fluoresce blue, although other colors are sometimes seen. Because most diamonds fluoresce under X-rays, X-ray fluorescence is sometimes used to separate diamonds from other materials in the recovery process. See X-RAY SEPARATOR.

X-ray luminescence, see X-RAY FLUORESCENCE.

X-ray separator, mechanism used to separate diamonds from concentrates using X-rays and a pneumatic ejector. See ELECTROMAGNETIC SEPARATION, ELECTROSTATIC SEPARATION, OPTICAL SEPARATOR, RECOVERY, SEPARATION.

X-ray topography, technique used to map a diamond's crystal structure by measuring the distance between atoms. X-ray topography can reveal specific lattice characteristics and defects (growth stratifications, twinning, etc.) of individual diamonds; when recorded, such characteristics constitute a unique and easily identifiable "fingerprint." See LONSDALE, KATHLEEN.

X-ray transparency, ability of a material to transmit the short wavelengths of X-rays. Gem diamond is highly transparent to X-rays.

Y

YAG, see YTTRIUM ALUMINUM GARNET.

YAG laser, laser system employed in cutting diamonds which uses a neodymium-doped yttrium aluminum garnet (Nd-YAG) crystal. The output from a YAG laser has a wavelength in the near-infra-red band of the spectrum, is invisible to the eye, and can cause serious eye damage. See LASER.

Yakutalmaz, division of Almazy Rossii-Sakha which is responsible for the mining of diamonds within the Republic of Sakha. See ALMAZY ROSSII-SAKHA, SAKHA.

Yakutia, see SAKHA.

Yehuda treatment, clarity enhancement method which uses a glass-like material to fill, and thus reduce the visibility of, surface-reaching inclusions in diamonds. Can usually be detected by a flash effect seen with magnification and darkfield illumination; the filling can be damaged or removed during certain jewelry repair operations. See FILLED DIAMOND, KOSS TREATMENT.

yellow, alternative Scan. D.N. color scale term for diamonds (over 0.47 ct.) at the low end of the light yellow range, equivalent to GIA color grades S-Z.

yellow diamond, see CANARY DIAMOND, CAPE, CHAMPAGNE DIAMOND, COLOR GRADE, CRYSTAL, DARK CAPE, FANCY COLOR DIAMOND, LIGHT YELLOW.

yellowground, kimberlite which has been broken down and oxidized by weathering. See BLUEGROUND, DIATREME, HARDEBANK, KIMBERLITE.

yellowish, alternative term on the Scan. D.N. color scale for the traditional grade light yellow; equivalent to O through R on the GIA color-grading scale. See LIGHT YELLOW.

Yengema, town near Sierra Leone's alluvial diamond diggings.

yield, (1) total weight of a polished diamond after manufacturing, usually expressed as a percentage of the weight of the rough. See MAKE. (2) term for the number of carats per 100 metric tons of ore removed from a mine. See LOAD.

Yincheng, area in Hubei Province, People's Republic of China, in which alluvial diamond occurrences have been recorded along the Dafushui, Xiaofushui, and Junshui rivers, and at Huangjiachong, north of the town of Yangcheng. None of the deposits are considered capable of supporting mining operations.

Youssoupoff Diamond, see POLAR STAR DIAMOND.

yttrium aluminum garnet (YAG), man-made material once commonly used as a diamond simulant. It is singly refractive, with a refractive index of 1.833, a specific gravity of 4.55, dis-

Yehuda treatment: before (top) and after (bottom) the fractures have been filled

photos by John I. Koivula

persion of .028, and a hardness (Mohs scale) of 8.25; its luster is vitreous. Although YAG is designated as a garnet and duplicates garnet's crystal structure, its chemical composition, $Y_3Al_5O_{12}$, does not correspond to that of any natural garnet.

Yuan River, river in Hunan Province, People's Republic of China, where alluvial diamond deposits have been found. They have been worked by local farmers; attempts at mechanical dredging were underway in 1992. Diamonds from the Yuan are thought to be 80 percent gem quality; the largest rough diamond discovered to date is 43.29 ct.

Yubileiny Diamond, 32.56 ct. rough diamond found near Mirnyi, Yakutia (now Sakha, the Russian Federation, CIS) in 1956. Current whereabouts unknown.

Zaba Gem, trade name for synthetic rutile. Marketed as a diamond simulant.

Zabeltitzter diamond, misnomer for rock crystal quartz from Poland.

Zaire, Republic of, country in west central Africa, formerly the Belgian Congo, and one of the world's largest producers of industrial diamonds since 1907. Western Kasai, the major mining region, is the site of kimberlite, eluvial, and alluvial deposits, the most important of which are at Mbuji-Mayi, where the Miba Mine is located. The Kasai and Tshikapa Rivers are important secondary sources; kimberlites are also mined near Katanga (now Shaba). See MIBA, MBUJI-MAYI, TSHIKAPA.

Zairebrit Exploration, prospecting company which began diamond exploration efforts in southeastern Zaire in 1972.

Zale Light of Peace Diamond, see LIGHT OF PEACE DIAMOND.

Zarnitza, first diamond-bearing kimberlite pipe found on the central Siberian plateau in what is now Sakha (Yakutia), the Russian Federation, CIS. Discovered in 1954 by Larissa Popugayeva, the large pipe (nearly 20 surface hectares; 50 acres) was not mined for a number of years, due to the relatively low grade. The chance of finding very large diamonds eventually led to a decision to begin operations, but production levels are said to be low. Zarnitza means *summer lightning*.

Zenithite, trade name for strontium titanate. Marketed as a diamond simulant.

Zimbabwe, country in south central Africa, formerly Rhodesia, where diamond-bearing kimberlites have been located close to the Limpopo River. See RHODES, CECIL JOHN.

Zinnia Cut, registered name for one of five "Flower Cuts" developed by CSO consultant Gabi Tolkowsky. A round with a faceted girdle, it combines brilliant and step-cut design to increase brilliance, scintillation, and color consistency in lower color rough, and provides greater yield from irregularly shaped crystals. See DAHLIA CUT, FIRE ROSE CUT, FLOWER CUTS, MARIGOLD CUT, SUNFLOWER CUT.

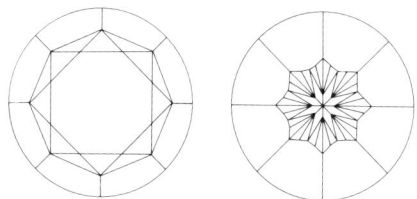

Zinnia Cut

zircon, brilliant, dispersive gemstone, used in its colorless form as a diamond simulant. (It is often heat-treated to render it colorless.) Zircon is doubly refractive, with a specific gravity of 4.7, refractive indices of 1.92 to 1.98, birefringence of .000-.059, dispersion of 0.038, and a hardness (Mohs scale) of 7.5; its luster is subadamantine. Sometimes called the "war bride's diamond" because of its popularity during the 1940s, when natural diamonds were scarce in many parts of the world.

zirconia, cubic, see SYNTHETIC CUBIC ZIRCONIA.

Zlata Prata Diamond, 38.72 ct. rough diamond found in what is now Sakha (Yakutia), the Russian Federation, CIS; now in the Russian Diamond Fund. Zlata Prata means *Golden Prague*.

Z master diamond, diamond in a GIA-graded master set that separates fancy color yellow diamonds from the colorless to light yellow range. See COLOR GRADING, COLOR-GRADING SCALE, FANCY COLOR DIAMOND, GIA COLOR-GRADING SCALE, MASTER DIAMONDS.

APPENDICES

Appendix A

Other Notable Diamonds

Name	Carats	Color	Shape	Origin	Disposition
Abadia do Duorados	104	brown	rough	Brazil; 1938	
Abadia do Duorados Lilac	63	pink	rough	Brazil; 1936	
Abadia do Duorados Rose	33	pink	rough	Brazil	
Abaeté	238	pink	rough	Brazil; 1926	
Abaeté Brilliant	144		rough	Brazil; 1791	
Abaeté Rose	118	pink	rough	Brazil; 1929	
Abbas Mirza	130		table	India; 1832	
Antique Cushion	57	yellow	cushion		Sold, 1972.
Arc	381		rough	South Africa; 1921	
A. Steyn	141.25		rough	South Africa; 1912	
Austrian Yellow Brilliant			oval	unknown; (ca. 1600)	
Barkly Breakwater	109.25		rough	South Africa; 1905	
Berglen	416.25		rough	South Africa; 1924	
Bob Craig	100		rough	South Africa; 1917	
Bob Grove	337		rough	South Africa; 1908	
Brady	330		rough	South Africa; 1902	
Brazilia	176.20	light blue	rough	Brazil; 1944	Cut in Rio de Janeiro.

Note: This table lists a sampling of the many notable diamonds on record. It generally includes only rough stones over 100 ct. or polished stones over 50 ct.; the exceptions are fancy colors or very fine colors, as well as stones with interesting provenance or disposition. Color descriptions are given only when reasonably reliable.

APPENDIX A, CONT.

NAME	CARATS	COLOR	SHAPE	ORIGIN	DISPOSITION
Broderick	412.50		rough	South Africa; 1928	
Burgess	220		rough	South Africa	
Carbonado Casco do Burro	2,000	bort	rough	Brazil	
Carbonado do Sergio	3,167	bort	rough	Brazil; 1905	
Carbonado Pontesinha	267.53	bort	rough	Brazil; first reported 1938	
Carbonado Xique-Xique	931.60	bort	rough	Brazil; 1905	
Carmo do Paranaiba	245	brown	rough	Brazil; 1937	
Carns	107		macle	South Africa; 1891	
Cedro do Abaeté	194	pink	rough	Brazil; 1967	
Changlin	158.79	yellow	rough	China; 1977	
Christopher Black	58.10	black	cushion		Sold by Harry Winston, 1969.
Cinnamon Century	32.16	brown	pear shape		
Cross of Asia	106.26	yellow			Fashioned so a Maltese cross shows through the table.
Crown of Charlemagne	42.50	blue	round brilliant		Recut to 37.05 ct. for Harry Winston, 1949.
Cruzeiro Ou Vitoria	261		rough	Brazil; 1942	Fashioned into six stones.
Dan Campbell	192.50		rough	South Africa; 1916	
Darcy Vargas	460	brown	rough	Brazil; 1939	
Diário de Minas Gerais	375.10		rough	Brazil; 1941	Fashioned into several stones.
Du Toit I	250	yellow	rough	South Africa; 1871	
Du Toit II	127	yellow	rough	South Africa; 1871	
Emperor Justinian	25			ca. 548	(Probably apocryphal.)

NAME	CARATS	COLOR	SHAPE	ORIGIN	DISPOSITION
Fineberg-Jones	206	"high quality"	rough	South Africa; 1911	
Flaming Star	21.90	"good color" fluoresces intense orange to LW UV	pear	South Africa	Purchased by Baumgold Brothers, New York, 1967.
Gaby Delys	28.25	yellow	heart		
Goiás	600		rough	Brazil; 1906	Allegedly shattered with a hammer.
Golconde Doré	130	yellow	emerald		Stolen, 1980.
Golden Dawn	133	white	rough	South Africa; 1913	Fashioned into a 61.50 ct. brilliant; sold to Aga Khan, 1926.
Golden Maharaja	65.60	yellow-brown	pear		Sold in New York, 1991.
Gordon Orr	62	"very fine"	rough	India; 1883	Cut into a 24.85 ct. brilliant.
Great Harry			lozenge		Owned by James I of England, 1605.
Grima	55.91	"high quality"	pear		Sold in England, 1972.
Harlequin	22		pear		Originally owned by Duke Karl Alexander (1733-1773); set in a 97-stone diamond necklace on display at the Württemberg Landesmuseum, Stuttgart, Germany.
Harry Young	269.50	yellow	rough	South Africa; 1913	
Heart	35	colorless	heart	India; 1600s	Said by Tavernier to have belonged to Mogul Emperor Aurangzeb.
Heart of Antwerp	38.40		heart		Exhibited in Antwerp in 1979 during the 75th Anniversary of the Antwerp Diamond Bourse.
Howeson	24	blue			
Independencia	106.82		rough	Brazil; 1941	

APPENDIX A, CONT.

NAME	CARATS	COLOR	SHAPE	ORIGIN	DISPOSITION
Jalmeida	109.50	yellow	rough	Brazil; 1942	
João Neto de Campos	201		rough	Brazil; 1947	
Julius Pam	246		rough	South Africa; 1889	Fashioned into 123 ct.
June Briolette	48.42	"light greenish yellow"	briolette		Set in a wreath-shaped pin.
Juscelino Kubitschek	174		rough	Brazil; 1954	
La Favorite	50.28	"fine quality"			
Leopold	10		brilliant		Given to Queen Astrid of Belgium by her husband, King Leopold III (1901-1983); now owned privately.
Lesotho B	527		rough	Lesotho; 1965	
Lesotho C	383	brown	rough	Lesotho; 1969	Fashioned into 10 stones, the largest a 24 ct. marquise.
Lisa Blue	37.21	blue	round brilliant		Recut to 37.05 ct. for Harry Winston, 1961; sold in Europe, 1967.
Litkie	205		rough	South Africa; 1891	
Mahomet IV	24			Turkey; ca. 1600s	(May be apocryphal.)
(Merriweather Post—See Rovensky, below)					
Minas Gerais	172.50	white	rough	Brazil; 1937	Fashioned into an 80 ct. brilliant.
Mouawad Lilac Pink	24.44	pink			Purchased by jeweler Robert Mouawad, 1976.
Mouawad Splendour	101.84	D	pear mixed		Purchased by jeweler Robert Mouawad, 1990.
Mouawad White	48.28	D	marquise		Purchased by jeweler Robert Mouawad, 1990.

NAME	CARATS	COLOR	SHAPE	ORIGIN	DISPOSITION
Myrle McFarlin	49.40	fancy yellow	emerald		Sold to McFarlin in 1956; stolen, 1968.
Napoleon	34		brilliant		Reportedly owned by Napoleon, mounted in the hilt of his sword; possibly apocryphal.
Nawanagar	148		brilliant	Russia	Owned by the Maharanee Gulabkumberba of Nawanagar.
Nooitgedacht	325	yellow	rough	South Africa; 1953	
North Star	32.41	blue	pear	South Africa	
Nova Estrella do Sul	140	"greenish"	rough	Brazil; 1937	
Nur-ud-Deen		pink			Set in a cross owned by Prince Alexander Tzary; sold, London, 1898.
Orchid	9.93	pink	emerald		Fashioned from a 30.45 ct. rough by Lazare Kaplan in 1935; sold, 1965.
Orpin-Palmer	117.50	"dull white"		South Africa; 1902	
Otto Borgstrom	121.50	yellow	octahedron	South Africa; 1907	
Pam	112-115		rough	South Africa; (1891)	Fashioned into a 56.60 ct. brilliant.
Patos	324	brown	rough	Brazil; 1937	
Patrocinio	120.36		rough	Brazil; 1851	
Pink Mouawad	21.06	pink	cushion		Purchased by jeweler Robert Mouawad; 1989.
Pope Paul III					Given to Pope Paul III by Holy Roman Emperor Charles V, 1536.
Premier	86.40		emerald		Set in a pendant clip with 157 brilliants and sold by Harry Winston, 1958.

APPENDIX A, CONT.

NAME	CARATS	COLOR	SHAPE	ORIGIN	DISPOSITION
Presidente Dutra	409		rough	Brazil; 1949	Fashioned into 36 stones.
Prince Edward of York	60.25	"high quality"	pear	Africa; late 1800s	
Princess Mathilde	16.25		hexagon		Owned by Princess Mathilde, cousin to Napoleon III, and later by Sultan Abdul-Hamid II of Turkey. Sold in Paris, 1933.
Princie	34.64	pink	cushion		Set in a pendant surrounded by colorless brilliants, on a necklace of baguettes by Van Cleef & Arpels.
Queen Frederica	2	"colorless"	table		Engraved with a portrait of Queen Louisa Wilhelmina of the Netherlands.
Queen of Albania	49.03		pear	South Africa	Reportedly belonged to Queen Geraldine of Albania, 1940s.
(Regent of Portugal)	215		round brilliant	Brazil; 1775	(Thought to be a topaz.)
Riccia	15	pink			Owned by Prince de la Riccia.
River Styx		black	rough	South Africa	Fashioned into a 28.50 ct. brilliant and a 7 ct. marquise.
Rosa de Abaeté	80.30		rough	Brazil; 1935	
Rose d'Angleterre					Bequeathed to Anne of Austria by Cardinal Mazarin, 1661.
Rovensky	31.40	D	cushion		Purchased by Harry Winston in 1957 and recut to 31.20 ct.; renamed the Merriweather Post Diamond.
Russian Table	68				Said by Streeter to have been among the Russian Crown Jewels, 1882.
Samantha Smith		"high quality"		Russia	Russian Diamond Fund.

NAME	CARATS	COLOR	SHAPE	ORIGIN	DISPOSITION
Sea of Glory	66				Originally believed to be among the Iranian Crown Jewels; missing, 1966.
Searcy	27.21	"light yellow"	hexoctahedron	Arkansas, US; 1925	Owned by Tiffany's, New York.
Segima	70				Reportedly owned by the Sultan of Matan, 19th century.
Shakespeare Marquise	50.62	D	marquise		One of two stones fashioned from a 154 ct. rough, 1970.
Shepherd	18.30	fancy yellow	cushion		Smithsonian Institution.
Slijper	7.25		rough		(Contains an included octahedron.)
Southern Cross	118	pink		Brazil; 1929	
Star of Bombay	47.39	fancy yellow	cushion		
Star of Diamonds	107.50	"high quality"		South Africa; 1870s	May be the Rojtman Diamond.
Star of Minas	179.38		rough	Brazil; 1910 or 1911	Also called the Estrêla do Minas or Estrêla do Sul.
Star of the Sky	40.68	blue	pear	India	Purchased by Harry Winston and set with a 39.28 ct. light blue marquise in a pendant; sold in Europe, 1958.
Stephanie	67.55		round brilliant		Purchased by Harry Winston in 1957 and set in a clip; owned privately in the Middle East.
Stonewin	78.54		emerald		Fashioned from a 232 ct. rough purchased by Harry Winston in 1958; sold, 1962.
Tablet Stone	25.52		pear		Originally set in a Gothic gold bracelet; then set in the Russian Grand Imperial Crown; now in the Russian Diamond Fund.

APPENDIX A, CONT.

NAME	CARATS	COLOR	SHAPE	ORIGIN	DISPOSITION
Tigereye	178.50		rough	South Africa; 1913	Fashioned into a 61.50 ct. brilliant.
Turkey I	140 to 147				Reported to have been part of the Turkish Regalia, 1882.
Van Zyl	229.25			South Africa; 1913	
Venter	511.25	yellow	rough	South Africa; 1951	Fashioned into 32 stones in Johannesburg.
Vitória	328.34			Brazil; 1943	Purchased by Harry Winston and fashioned into 44 stones.
Webster Kopje	125			South Africa; 1907	
Windsorton	140		rough	South Africa; 1961	
Woyie River	770	"colorless"	rough	Sierra Leone; 1945	Fashioned into 30 stones, 1953.

Appendix B

American Diamonds

Name	Carats	Color	Rough Shape	Origin	Disposition
Amarillo Starlight	16.37			Arkansas; 1975	
Arkansas	17	yellow	octahedron	Arkansas	Smithsonian Institution, Washington, D.C.
Birmingham	4.25	"slightly yellowish"	octahedron	Alabama; 1900	Stolen from the American Museum of Natural History, New York, 1965.
Burlington	2.11	colorless		Wisconsin; 1893	
Chief of Carlisle	13.50		octahedron	Arkansas; 1966	
Clinch River	3			Tennessee; 1889	
Cotton Belt	11.92			Arkansas; 1963	
Dewey	23.75	"poor quality"	octahedron	Virginia; 1884	Originally called the Or-i-Noor; recut to 11.15 ct. by Henry D. Morse.
Doubledipity	32.99	"medium yellowish brown"	aggregate of seven intergrown cubes	California; 1987	
Dowagiac	10.87		rounded hexoctahedron	Michigan; 1895	
Dysortville	4.33	"fine quality"		North Carolina; 1870s	Stolen from the American Museum of Natural History, New York, 1964.

Note: Because diamonds found in the United States are rare, this table lists nearly all those on record.

APPENDIX B, CONT.

NAME	CARATS	COLOR	ROUGH SHAPE	ORIGIN	DISPOSITION
Eagle	15.37	"light yellow"	rounded dodecahedron	Wisconsin; 1867	Bought by Tiffany's; sold to J.P. Morgan, who donated it to the American Museum of Natural History, New York; stolen, 1964.
Eisenhower	3.11			Arkansas; 1957	Mounted in a pendant.
Enigma	17.83	opaque "brown"		California; 1987	
Flat Creek	1.81	"good"		Tennessee	
French Coral	7.25	yellow		California	
Garry Moore	6.43	"intense yellow"	modified trisoctahedron	Arkansas; 1960	
Jeopardy	3.90	yellow-brown	aggregate	California; 1987	
Lee	4.50		distorted octahedron	Alabama; 1900	Stolen from the American Museum of Natural History, New York, 1964.
Lewis and Clark	14	"slightly yellow"		Montana; 1990	
Maxwell	3	"greenish"		Indiana; 1863	
Milford	6	"high color"		Ohio; 1879	
Morrow	4.50	"yellowish"		Georgia; 1887	
Mounce	18.20	light brown		Louisana; 1969	Fashioned into three stones: a 3.47 ct. oval; a 2.75 ct. heart; and a 2.27 ct. marquise.
Oregon	3.87	"grayish green"	distorted octahedron	Wisconsin; 1893	Stolen from the American Museum of Natural History, New York, 1964.
Plymouth	2.65	colorless		California; 1934	
Saukville	6.57			Wisconsin; 1881	

NAME	CARATS	COLOR	ROUGH SHAPE	ORIGIN	DISPOSITION
Searcy	27.21	"light yellow"	hexoctahedron	Arkansas; 1925	Owned by Tiffany's, New York.
Serendipity	14.33	"pale grayish olive green"	aggregate of seven intergrown cubes	California; 1987	
Stanley	4.87	"greenish yellow"		Indiana; 1900	Fashioned into two stones, 1.12 ct. and 1.06 ct.
Star of Arkansas	15.33	"fine quality"		Arkansas; 1955	Fashioned into an 8.27 ct. marquise.
Theresa	21.25	(zoned)		Wisconsin; 1886	Fashioned into several stones.
Young	1.66	light green		Indiana; 1898	Smithsonian Institution, Washington, D.C.

APPENDIX C

THE IRANIANS

A collection of 23 large diamonds formerly among the Crown Jewels of Iran. Current whereabouts uncertain.

No.	Ct. Wt.	Shape	Color
1	152.16	rectangular old brilliant	silver cape
2	135.45	old cushion-shape brilliant	cape
3	123.93	old cushion-shape brilliant	silver cape
4	121.90	multi-faceted octahedron	cape
5	114.28	old cushion-shape brilliant	silver cape
6	86.61	rounded, triangular brilliant	cape
7	86.28	irregular Mogul cut	silver cape
8	78.96	old cushion-shape brilliant	cape
9	75.29	old cushion-shape brilliant	cape
10	75.00	pendeloque	silver cape
11	75.00	pendeloque	silver cape
12	72.84	irregular pear shape	champagne
13	65.65	rectangular old brilliant	cape
14	60.00	cushion-shape brilliant	yellow
15	57.85	round brilliant	silver cape
16	57.15	cushion-shape brilliant	silver cape
17	56.19	cushion-shape brilliant	silver cape
18	55.67	cushion-shape brilliant	cape
19	54.58	irregular oval Mogul cut	colorless
20	54.35	old cushion-shape brilliant	peach
21	53.50	old cushion-shape brilliant	silver cape
22	51.90	oval Mogul cut	colorless
23	38.18	multi-faceted trapezoid cut	colorless

Note: The stones numbered 19, 20, 22, and 23 are thought to be from India; the rest are from South Africa. Number 23 is thought to be the Hornby Diamond described by Edwin Streeter in 1882. Most of the color descriptions use historical color terms from the South African mines.

APPENDIX D

COLOR-GRADING SCALES

	GIA	CIBJO/IDC[1]	Scan. D.N.[2]	AGS	GIA
(colorless)	D	Exceptional White+	River	0	D
	E	Exceptional White		1	E
	F	Rare White+	Top Wesselton	2	F
(near colorless)	G	Rare White		3	G
	H	White	Wesselton	4	H
	I	Slightly Tinted White	Top Crystal	5	I
	J		Crystal		J
(faint yellow)	K	Tinted White	Top Cape	6	K
	L				L
	M	Tinted Color	Cape	7	M
	N				N
(very light yellow)	O				O
	P			8	P
	Q				Q
	R				R
	S			9	S
	T				T
	U				U
(light yellow)	V				V
	W			10	W
	X				X
	Y				Y
	Z				Z

1. CIBJO Rules (1991) permit combining the Exceptional White and Rare White divisions into one level each for stones under 0.47 ct.

2. Traditional terms; Scan. D.N. (1979) also allows use of two alternate sets of descriptive terms.

Appendix E

Clarity-Grading Scales

GIA	CIBJO/IDC[1]	Scan. D.N.[1]	AGS
FL	LC	FL	0
IF		IF	1
VVS_1	VVS_1	VVS_1	
VVS_2	VVS_2	VVS_2	2
VS_1	VS_1	VS_1	3
VS_2	VS_2	VS_2	4
SI_1	SI_1	SI_1	5
SI_2	SI_2	SI_2	6
I_1	P_1	P_1	7, 8
I_2	P_2	P_2	8, 9
I_3	P_3	P_3	9, 10

KEY

FL	flawless	LC	loupe clean
IF	internally flawless		
VVS	very, very slightly included (very, very small inclusions)		
VS	very slightly included (very small inclusions)		
SI	slightly included (small inclusions)		
I	included	P	*piqué*

1. CIBJO Rules (1991) permit combining of VVS, VS, and SI divisions into one level each for stones under 0.47 ct. Scan. D.N. (1979) advises the same simplification, and the substitution of LC for both FL and IF, for stones under 0.47 ct.

Appendix F

Proprietary Names of Man-Made Simulants

SYNTHETIC CUBIC ZIRCONIA:
CZ
Diamond-Z
Diamonique II
Djevalit
Phyanite

GADOLINIUM GALLIUM GARNET:
GGG
Galliant
Triple G

SYTHETIC SAPPHIRE:
Crown Jewels
Diamondite
Diamondette
Diamonflame
Gemette
Walderite

SYNTHETIC SPINEL:
Alumag
Lestergem
Magalux
Strongite
Wesselton Simulated Diamond

YITTRIUM ALUMINUM GARNET (YAG):
Amatite
Alexite
Dia-Bud
Diamite
Diamogem
Diamonair
Diamone
Diamonique
Diamonte
Di'Yag
Linde Simulated Diamonds
Nier-Gem
Regalaire
Replique
Somerset
Triamond

STRONTIUM TITANATE:
Bal de Feu
Brilliante
Continental Jewels
Diagem
Diamontina
Dynagem
Fabulite
Kenneth Lane Jewel
Lustigem
Marvelite
Rossini Jewel
Sorella
Pauline Trigere
Wellington
Zenithite

SYNTHETIC RUTILE:
Astryl
Diamothyst
Gava Gem
Jarra Gem
Johannes Gem
Kenyagem
Kima Gem
Kimberlite Gem
Lusterlite
Miridis
Rainbow Diamond
Rainbow Gem
Rainbow Magic Diamond
Rutile
Saphirized Titania
Star-Tania
Tania-59
Tirum Gem
Titangem
Titania
Titania Brilliante
Titania Midnight Stone
Titanium
Titanium Rutile
Titanstone
Zaba Gem

Appendix G

AGES OF DIAMOND DEPOSITS

Premier Mine—1,200 million years

West African kimberlites—1,100 million years

Brazilian conglomerates—1,000 million years

Indian conglomerates—500 million years

Mir Pipe—450 million years

Roberts Victor—106 million years

Kimberley area—100 million years

Dutoitspan—87 million years

Tanzanian kimberlites—50 million years

Southwestern Africa coast alluvial deposits—recent

Appendix H

Local Weights of Old Carats Before Standardization of the Metric Carat

Alexandria	191.7 mg
Amsterdam	205.1
Antwerp	205.3
Arabia	194.4
Austria-Hungary	206.1
Berlin	205.5
Bologna	188.5
Brazil	192.2
Constantinople	205.5
East Indies	196.9-205.5
Florence	196.5
France	205-205.5
Frankfurt	205.8
Hamburg	205.8
Lisbon	205.8
London	205.3-205.5
Madras	205.5
Persia	213.5
Russia	205.1
Spain	199.9
Turin	213.5
Venice	207.0
Vienna	206.1